FLASH OF EDEN

BY

PAUL FERRARA

Foreword by Digby Diehl

authorHOUSE®

AuthorHouse™
1663 Liberty Drive, Suite 200
Bloomington, IN 47403
www.authorhouse.com
Phone: 1-800-839-8640

First published by AuthorHouse 11/20/2007

ISBN: 978-1-4343-4071-9 (e)
ISBN: 978-1-4343-4070-2 (sc)

Library of Congress Control Number: 2007907591

Printed in the United States of America
Bloomington, Indiana

This book is printed on acid-free paper.

FOREWORD

By Digby Diehl

The last phrase in this amazing autobiography is: "The right place at the right time." That old bromide has never described anything more accurately than this book. Paul was born in 1939 – a great year for movies and everything else – in Los Angeles. He grew up a typical California kid with an awareness of the cultural excitement that was building in the fifties and exploded in the sixties. Paul exploded on the scene right along with the zeitgeist.

He got to the Theater Arts Department at UCLA in 1963, a year before I did, and we both instinctively knew it was the place to be. Although we hung out at the Gypsy Wagon scene, where each of us pontificated about our views on Fellini, Truffaut, Godard or Antonioni, he gravitated toward the editing rooms of the Film School, then headed by the legendary Colin Young. Drawn by the charisma and energy of young actors such as Tim McIntire and Paul Winfield, I spent my hours on or around the stages. Both of us, I recall, loved professor Hugh Gray, whose insightful History of Film course opened a lot of young minds to the potential of the medium.

It was at UCLA, of course, that Paul met Jim Morrison and Ray Manzarek. He developed a close relationship with both of them that has lasted past Jim's short life and continues with Ray today. I knew Jim and Ray casually as fellow students but as they became famous, I was held at arm's length because I became known as an early rock n' roll critic and journalist. Paul, on the other hand, had and has an intimate relationship with the Doors that is detailed in this book for the first time. He worked with them in many roles, traveled with them, and enjoyed those dizzying "Light My Fire" years of success with them.

For both personal and professional reasons, I found Paul's descriptions of his experiences with the Doors riveting. There's plenty of sex, drugs, and rock n' roll here, and it will undoubtedly bring many readers to this book. But as I read on, I became equally fascinated with the rich story of Paul's own life as an artist, flower child, filmmaker, husband and father – always a Whole Earth kind of guy.

Another old bromide is: "If you can remember the sixties, you didn't really live through them." Paul proves that one wrong. He remembers everything about the sixties, the seventies, the eighties, the nineties and – well, he has impressive recall of an impressive life. In many ways, through all of the people he has met and all the places he has been, he is a prototypical Child of the Century.

By the time Jim Morrison died in Paris on July 3, 1971, Paul had discovered a wonderful escape from the urban angst of Los Angeles on a mountaintop rancho near Santa Fe in New Mexico. He eventually ends up working again in showbiz with trips to various cinematic locations where he worked hard and rubbed elbows with famous folk. For example, he tells of traveling to the swamps near New Orleans as key grip for Jim Jarmusch on Down by Law in 1986; he worked lots of CBS TV shows, including Remington Steele and Hill Street Blues; in 1987, he worked on a documentary in St. Louis about Chuck Berry's sixtieth birthday, with Keith Richards, Linda Ronstadt and Eric Clapton; and working on Barfly, he hung out with Charles Bukowski, Mickey Rourke, and Faye Dunaway. In a nonchalant way, he mentions that he hired Harrison Ford to work for him before Ford was an actor.

That's why this is such an enjoyable book. You don't know who you are going to meet on the next page. You have no idea what adventure Paul is heading into next. Maybe that's it: he writes about his life as though it is a series of adventures. Through the wives, the girlfriends, the drugs, and the decades, he seems to be much the same guy we met at the Gypsy Wagon at UCLA – and life just keeps coming at him like a freight train.

I never asked Paul about the title of his book, although any good Doors fan could tell you that it comes from "Waiting for the Sun" on the Morrison Hotel album. In his lyrics, Jim implies that the first intimations of the rising sun are a "flash of Eden." After reading this autobiography, I think that Paul uses the same phrase to suggest that each life is an amazing fast track experience, and despite the complexity, the intensity, or even the length of time we have on earth, for each of us, it is just the briefest "flash of Eden."

DIGBY DIEHL
Pasadena, California
September 30, 2007

Contents

IN THE HOUSE OF LOVE

When "Light My Fire" broke on national radio, The Doors had been an L.A. band that played in San Francisco and New York on occasion. When the song started to climb in the national charts, the tours began. I was lucky enough to have been there at the time as the band's only staff photographer. I was just finishing up the concert book and poster that would be sold at concerts. I began shooting 16mm film of the group wherever I could. This was not an easy assignment. Most people shy from the eye of the camera. It's a process of wearing them down by being there so much that they get used to you. I had melted into the group's psyche and was filming at ease.

The early tours took us to places like Ohio where the kids in the audience still had short hair and were wearing suits. I was in the audience a lot, shooting Jim on stage. Jim and I had a close relationship. The other three Doors had wives and girlfriends and left right after the shows for their hotel rooms or whatever. I was single, and Jim acted as if he was even though he had a steady girlfriend. I developed a scheme to line up the pretty willing young girls for after-show partying. I usually gave out the hotel name and address, including our room numbers.

On one particular night in Ohio, Jim and I were in rooms next to one another. By the time we packed up after the concert and hit a few bars, the hallway in front of our rooms was filled with young girls. They were lined up along the velvet-crested wallpaper. It was an older hotel with steam heat and dark wood paneling. I don't think you can ever get used to something like that! So many beautiful girls. I had done my job well. It wasn't like in the

1

movie "Almost Famous" where there were tons of band members and roadies, etc. Here there were only girls, Jim and I. They swarmed around us as we approached our rooms. Jim made it into his room with a very pretty girl and shut the door. I turned around to a line of girls. This was the Soft Parade.

We had a busy night ahead of us. We opened the door joining our two rooms and had a dialogue going. If they couldn't have Jim, they wanted me. They didn't even know who I was. They thought I was a band member. The first girl into my room asked if I was the bass player. I said yes. She took her clothes off. She was a corn-fed blonde around 18 or 19 years old. Long and lean, just how I liked them. Her skin was pale, her breasts were young and fresh. How they learned to fuck like porn stars was beyond me. She talked about Jim as she straddled me, bucking like a cowgirl. She wanted to do Jim next. I promised her I would make that happen. I knew neither Jim nor I wanted sloppy seconds, but I still promised. She didn't want to leave and there were still several girls waiting in the hallway. I heard Jim's door slam. His girl had left and he had grabbed another. I helped my girl to dress and showed her to the door. Another girl stepped in and the scene started all over again.

I don't know if anything can prepare you for an experience like this. We were young and full of energy, thank god, and did the best we could. We were making it up as we went along. An older attractive woman approached me in my doorway. She had the hand of a younger girl who she introduced as her daughter. They were both blonde and blue-eyed. The mother was dressed a little like a hippie; the daughter was a carbon copy. They wanted to meet Jim. They wanted to touch the greatness. I told them to wait right there. I went to the door joining our rooms and entered slowly. Jim had his current girl pinned against the headboard and was slamming her as hard as he could. I whispered in his ear about the mother and daughter team standing outside in the hall. He took a double take at me and smiled. "Yeah," he motioned. He hadn't missed a stroke. His current girl looked up at me with a giant grin on her face. She was fucking Jim Morrison, what more could she ask for? I brought the mother and daughter into my room. When Jim finished with the cheerleader he was fucking, he showed her out, promising to see her again. He was building a sexual fan base one at a time and I was going to help him all I could. He came into my room and met the mother-daughter team.

The three of them went into his room. I can only imagine what happened because he didn't tell me about it, and my imagination will have to do.

Before the concerts there was a ritual of drug use and drinking alcohol that took Jim to a fever pitch. He performed with reckless abandon and that was what the audience ate up. They came to see him freak out or leap off the stage into the audience or whatever. They expected it. He tried to outdo himself night after night. In the beginning it was all good and he did it before every show. He took acid a lot and followed it with Jack Daniels whiskey and beer. He was unpredictable. It was what drove everybody crazy, most of all, his band members. His wildness on stage was understandable knowing what concoctions he was ingesting before the show. The shows were sometimes uneven depending on Jim's condition. Sometimes he was brilliant and other times he was too drunk and only mumbled into the mike.

Usually by the time we got back to the hotel after the shows we were screaming with residual excitement, Jim especially. It wasn't easy to come down from the type of high he was experiencing. The sex helped. Eventually we exhausted ourselves and fell asleep for a few hours until the wake-up call that road manager Bill Siddons had left for us dialed through on our room phones. We had to scramble to catch the next plane to Kansas or wherever and repeat the whole thing again that night. It became a blur where we were. The sleep deprivation, drugs and alcohol put us in a twilight zone. All musicians who have been on the road have talked about it. You lose track of time and space. The only thing that snaps you back to reality is the concert and the screaming fans.

The limos would deliver us to the backstage area where we'd file out and into the auditorium. I tried to grab as many camera shots of this as I could. The audience was shouting for Jim. Most of the time we walked to the dressing room as the opening act was finishing and had a moment to collect our thoughts. When the door opened and the promoter told us The Doors were on, I scrambled to be first, shooting as they filed by me and onto the stage. John would start with the drumbeats that opened the set, and the group was off and into the only reality they knew, their music. Jim encouraged kids to come up on the stage and join him. This caused trouble because the promoters had hired people to stop them from doing just that. There were frequent confrontations that became more and more violent as things progressed. There were mini-riots and people were getting roughed up.

The press was eating this up and each article they wrote caused bigger crowds to come and experience this phenomenon.

Was Jim in control or out of control? When he was sober in the mornings he talked about Marshall McLuhan's articles on mass communications and the existential nature of theatre, things like that. He seemed to know what he was doing. He had a plan, but by the time the actual show went on all that theory was out the window and he was a predator. High on whatever and practicing a form of shamanism, Jim created illusion and made his audience join him in a trance-like place, seeking them out and whipping them into a frenzy. The music was so good that, combined with Jim's sinister plot to hypnotize his audience with his crazy game and his delicate poetry, the crowd was destined to go wild.

When I first met Jim at UCLA in the Film Department, he was rather ordinary looking. Like so many of us, he was changing with the times. We all let our hair get long. The influences of the Beatles and the Stones gave us a sense of an alternative way to dress. The hippie generation was born. Music worshipers. Drug experimenters. Jim was no exception. His long hair framed his pretty face. He looked like a child. His body had little muscle. He was not a masculine threat, not alpha in any way. I think that was some of his appeal. He was soft, confident, shy offstage and a charmer.

Ray describes Jim's poetry so well in his book Light My Fire: "His words always a place of magic. A refuge from the howling, madness of the night. I knew we were human and strong and good and divine when I read his words. I knew we could all face the terror. Of our ability to rise upward, out of the mud, into that great golden orb of energy that warms and protects us." He was truly a poet. The combination of his words and the music was to die for. His lyrics had a sophistication that no other rocker had. His beauty, that childlike smile, his mischievous nature, those songs: this was going to be big. Women were throwing themselves at him. He was like a Pied Piper. The girls were following us onto the planes and to the next gig. What is it about women, that most of the time they protect their pussy like it is sacred and other times they use it like a weapon? They know how weak men are and can accomplish the most amazing feats using their sexuality. Jim encouraged some of the best and even paid for their flights.

Once there was a girl who traveled with us for a couple of days. We later found out she was under age. Her father was a politician. There was a momentary problem when the father thought she had been kidnapped. She talked to him on the phone and assured him she hadn't been kidnapped and promised to return on the next flight. Some girls look older with just a little makeup and clothes. They lie about their age all their life until they actually <u>are</u> old! Oh well, there were plenty more where she came from. She left and the sexual crusade continued, night after night. There was sex in the limo, on the rooftop, in the hot tub you name it. We were taking care of business. All this took place with the band members and their wives and girlfriends in close proximity. Sometimes they knew what was happening and other times they had no idea.

In those days the tours were short, maybe a week or ten days, not like today's bands that go out for a year. Believe me, after ten days of this excitement it seemed like a year. We dragged ourselves to the airplane for the return flight and mostly slept through it. At LAX we were usually met by our girlfriends and friends. It was a sigh of relief to be back. Jim would be greeted by Pam and they would embrace. I would drop off my exposed film, return the equipment I had rented, and head up to my house on Woodrow Wilson and my own bed.

Two days later Jim would be back at the office where there was a waiting list of ladies phone numbers. He had semi-celebs wanting to fuck him, and some became his on again-off again girlfriends. It is no wonder that toward the end of his career he hid behind a beard. I'm sure he had burnt out. Girls told stories of his rough sex, unfulfilled sex, and nothing-in-return kinds of stories. What did they expect? He couldn't love them all. He could have sex with them but he had little love left. It was hard to come down, and my sleep was filled with dreams and memories from past and present.

CHILDHOOD

My mother and father were both first generation Italian-American. The story goes they met at a streetcar stop on Vermont Avenue in Los Angeles. My mother and father attended the local dances and had met before, but that meeting on Vermont Avenue is when they made their first date. They became a couple. Ballroom dancing was a favorite pastime for both of them, and they were asked by mutual dancing friends to be witnesses to their wedding. The four of them drove to Yuma, Arizona. As they witnessed their friends' wedding, my father spontaneously asked my mother "Why don't we get married?" My mother was approaching 30 years old and had recently broken up with her boyfriend. She said yes. He was a polite, clean, well-mannered man and time was ticking for the both of them. They were married on June 20, 1937.

"The Wizard of Oz," "Gone With The Wind" and "Wuthering Heights" were all released in 1939. It was a good year for films. Louis Armstrong recorded "Jeepers Creepers" and President Franklin D. Roosevelt made the first speech on T.V. The World's Fair was in New York and the BBC announced that W.W. II had begun. Gandhi started the first of many fasts, protesting autocratic rule in India. John Steinbeck's book "The Grapes of Wrath" came out followed by Hemingway's novel "The Snows of Kilimanjaro." "Over the Rainbow" sung by Judy Garland was on the radio. There were two huge earthquakes that year, one in Chile that killed 30,000 and one in Turkey that killed 100,000 people.

At 2:55 p.m. on November 16, 1939 Catherine, my mother, gave birth to me in the California Hospital on South Hope Street in Los Angeles. Years later, I found myself working on a movie on location in the same hospital where I was born. The scene was a woman delivering a baby boy. I remember feeling very strange: deja vu or something. I don't remember much of my childhood, but certain events still haunt me today through photos I've seen and stories I've been told.

My sister was born four years later. Marietta was delivered by Caesarean and it took my mother awhile to recover. It was strange no longer being the center of attention. The story goes that one day my mother walked into the kitchen and found me strangling my sister in her highchair. It's hard to be replaced by someone who receives all the attention you used to get. It pretty much stayed that way until I moved out of my parents' house 17 years later. I never tried to kill her again, but sometimes I wanted to.

My mother, Edna Catherine, was a beautiful woman with the looks of a movie star. I mean, really! My father, Frank Paul, was handsome in a rugged Italian way. His occupation was as a men's clothing salesman and he always dressed as sharp as he could. I've seen photos of them ballroom dancing during their early days together. My father won several trophies with other dance partners before he met my mother. Those trophies were displayed in every home we ever had.

As a small child I remember my father being responsible for music in our home: big band stuff, Sinatra, and other contemporary music. Italian opera was played quite often. Caruso was very popular. We had a large stereo console that was used a lot. Before television, people listened to radio. We would all huddle around the speakers and listen to the "Green Hornet" and other mysteries. Jack Benny was a favorite and could always make us laugh. We had a large front room that you stepped down into. Its large arched front window had a stain glass section at the top, a coat of arms.

My father's father came from a small town in Sicily named Corleone, famous for the Mafioso. In "The Godfather" Al Pacino goes there to hide out. He meets and marries a girl who is blown up in their car in front of his eyes. In the movie, the town was named after Pacino's father, Don Corleone as played by Marlon Brando. My father was Italian through and through but he wasn't a Mafia type guy. He was actually very reserved and not at all like the stereotyped Sicilian.

I was very lucky to grow up in the Vermont Knolls. It was a beautiful place in those days. The houses were mostly Spanish with arches and stucco and tile roofs. My father always had roses and other plants that crowded the little patio entrance. We had a nice lawn in the front and we played there a lot. I remember eating what looked like white candy that was on the grass. It was dog poop. Ooops. As a child, I remember one of my pastimes was to float sticks and paper along the gutter. When conditions were perfect, there was a good flow of water. I would run along keeping track of my small vessel for as long as I could before it disappeared out of sight.

At some point I began taking care of our front yard. Little by little I added a couple other neighbors' yards and bingo, I was in business. Before the lawn biz I used to earn a little cash shining my father's shoes. I always liked earning money. My own cash! Some years later, my father introduced me to Shorty, the man that operated the paper stand on Vermont near where he worked. I started to sell papers after school in front of Thrifty's and made a couple of bucks a day. I did that for a year or so, but my father caught Shorty cheating me on my pay, and that was the end of that! But I remember going into Thrifty's and buying snacks with my own money.

My father worked in a clothing store not far from my paper stand: Miller's Store For Men. I would take the store its papers and see my dad. Years later he would begin his own business in a small store about a block from Miller's called Frank's. It didn't sit well with his boss and they never spoke again. I ended up working there during my high school days.

One day about six years after my birth, my mother took me by the hand and walked me to Raymond Avenue Grammar School. It had the nickname of The City Farmers. Its playground faced Normandie Avenue. Along the fence near Normandie was a half-acre plot of earth that had taken the shape of a small farm, complete with chickens and rabbits. I loved that space; it smelled so good. Once they passed out little chicks for the kids to take home and raise.

We lived on 81st Street at #1224 and our house had a nice back yard. I built a small cage for my chicks and raised them until they were a couple of years old. They had no rooster and did not lay a lot of eggs. My mother came from Italian farmer stock and suggested we eat them. I freaked out violently and petitioned for their freedom. Finally, a year later and after much badgering from my parents, I agreed that my mother could trade them off at the local butcher shop. She promised she was going to trade them for different chickens. She came home with two packages of chicken and we ate chicken for dinner that night.

Years later she told me that we had actually eaten my pets. She used to tell the story of how her mother, who died in my bedroom, used to kill chickens by grabbing their necks and swinging them around in a circle breaking their necks. It was how life used to be before they invented grocery stores and butcher shops, she said. It makes any one disconnect for a moment and try to understand where their food comes from! That probably was the lesson that little school was trying to teach us, no matter how upsetting it was.

It was a very free time, being a small kid in the forties. I did not completely understand the war thing and the earthquakes. I was very occupied with the world immediately surrounding me. I used to walk home with one of my neighbors, M. C. and we used to cut through the Pepperdine College campus. One day they were excavating alongside a large pipe. The trench was open and we started playing down in the hole. I forget the exact way it happened, but M.C. ended up with her pants down, resting on her stomach and face down on the large pipe. I examined her quite well, thank you. I still remember how she smelled. We repeated this ritual for maybe a month or two, until they covered up the pipe with dirt.

In that same backyard on 81st Street where I raised the chickens, was a giant old peach tree. Some years there were bumper crops. I used to pick and load them on a small wagon and sell them up and down the block. They were very sweet and large, and I sold all I had. All my neighbors were ready for them by the time I got there. Some years later my father decided to cement over the back yard and make an enclosed patio. Bye, bye, peach tree.

It turned out kind of nice with a barbecue and stuff, and later it came in handy for parties. C's parents lived around the block. They were also Italian-Americans and they were friends of my parents. They were the first ones in our neighborhood to get a T.V. Of course, it was a black and white console, the newest thing going. We used to walk around the corner on certain nights to see the Milton Berle show at their house. Later everyone started watching wrestling. I remember Baron Leone; he was very popular with the Italians: very theatrical, with long flowing blonde hair. I think he wore a cape into the ring.

I started to branch out and met some kids from the neighborhood who became lifelong friends. The first acquaintance I made was Don Talbot, and we started walking to school together every day. We shared many after-school hours together, and we experienced many childhood firsts together. Eventually we ended up together in the Embassy, a high school social club. We met Benny Brewer who also became a good friend in high school and a fellow member in Embassy. He lived along our path to school, and we would pick him up in the morning and walk together.

Across from Raymond Avenue School on Western was a small mom and pop store that sold sodas and candy, among other things. You could buy candy for a penny then and sodas were only a nickel. It was a favorite place to visit. Bubble gum was big then; with each piece you got a baseball card or something that could be collected or traded.

In kindergarten, my favorite time of day was after recess when we all laid down on platforms and took a nap. Later I became very interested in sports: dodge ball, kickball and tetherball were my favorites. In the summertime everybody hung out on the playground of the school and played caroms or kickball or baseball. It was the center of the universe. Hopalong Cassidy, a T.V. cowboy star, once paid a visit to our school. I remember his horse and I remember his gun. He had Indians with him; it was so exotic.

I joined the Cub Scouts and went to meetings in the school auditorium. I had the uniform and badges and stuff. It was fun belonging to something. We had a purpose. Our small group, or den, would have adventures all over the city along with the current den mother. We met once a week, ate cookies, and made stuff out of paper and wood, etc. We had to learn certain lore passed on by the leaders and were tested on it. Natural wisdom, and respect for parents and getting along.

Once there was a great trip to the San Diego Zoo. There I was, standing in front of the gorilla cage in my little Cub Scout uniform. I had a cap, scarf and badges, and I felt like military or something. Anyway, this giant gorilla charged the wire separating us, leapt up grabbing the fence, and spat on me. For a moment we were face to face, and I jumped back and cried like hell. For years after that I had dreams of a gorilla walking, sort of pacing, on the roof of the house on 81st Street. I could hear the footsteps! I never understood why he taunted me so much. Why not just swing down and crash through my window and get it over with? He never did. That was the beginning of many sleepless nights that have plagued me right up to current times. Although the gorilla is no longer on the roof, there are many other formidable monsters to deal with.

The neighbors on the east side of our house had a large Doberman Pinscher who terrorized me and the other kids that played in our yard by pressing up against the screen on his window and barking like crazy when you least expected it: the element of surprise. Once he got loose and terrorized the entire neighborhood. He finally ended up attacking his owner; he grabbed the woman who was feeding him by the throat. That was the end of him.

Our garage at that house had doors, which swung open and had small squares of window across the top. We didn't have a car for a long time and the garage was mine. I used to drag large cardboard boxes home, refrigerator and stove containers from an appliance store on Vermont. I arranged them into a sort of a condominium-type structure inside the garage. We played in there a lot, my sister and I and anyone else that came over. I remember collecting papers and discarded mail from peoples' trash. They became our important papers; we used to arrange them and exchange them and pretend to know about their importance.

My small circle of friends, including my sister, started to collect playing cards and trade them vigorously among ourselves. Some of us had hundreds of them. There were pictures of horses rearing up and paintings from the masters and all kinds of interesting artwork. It was a lot of fun.

A boy down the street named Warren and I used to get into trouble a lot. Once we snuck into a neighbor's backyard and discovered a hole in the ground. It looked like it tunneled out to the street. We took lots of paint cans from the garage and one by one emptied their contents into the hole, running back and forth to the front of the house, checking on the progress of the paint. By the time anyone realized what was happening, we had made quite a mess. Our mothers had to clean it up.

One day when I was returning from school, there was a lot of commotion in front of my house. An ambulance was there and they were loading my mom into the back on a stretcher. Someone told me I was in a lot of trouble. A week earlier I had found a garter snake in the yard and captured it in a jar. I was taking care of it in the laundry room, but one morning it disappeared. I didn't think much of it until that day. The snake had crawled into the drainpipe on the sink where my mother did the laundry. When she filled the sink with water, the snake came up for air. She had reached into the soapy water and grabbed the snake. When she discovered what was in her hand, she had a mild heart attack. My bad.

One time I stuck my arm into the wringers on the washing machine and it sucked me in up to my little shoulder. Thank god my mother was standing close to me. She flew across the room and hit the release on the rollers. The machine opened up just as my neck was approaching.

I think it was my idea to take piano lessons. Or, maybe it wasn't my idea, I am not sure. But before I could change my mind, there was a piano in the front room and I had a piano teacher coming to the house. Mr. Harrington was a tall mean bastard, and he spoiled the whole experience for me. The piano was in front of a large bay window that looked out onto the street, and I could see my friends playing and riding their bikes. It was totally hard to concentrate, but I learned the basics. There was a recital that my father took time off from his job to attend. I made so many mistakes that everyone was laughing at me. I kept trying to get it right. I finally finished and the people applauded, probably just glad to be rid of me. I stopped playing after that. My sister took it up and was quite good at it. I think I took up the ukulele.

Don and I met a guy our same age named Richard Ballew. He lived a little further from us and attended a different school, and we became inseparable. We all had bikes and took a lot of pride in their appearance. We started roaming the neighborhood looking for stuff to do.

One of our favorite pastimes was terrorizing the local pool hall. In the alley behind it was an entrance that always stayed open, probably for air or something because everyone smoked in those days, especially in a pool hall. We could smell the tobacco and alcohol as it found its way along the air passing through the door. We could see silhouetted figures moving in slow motion as they found their shots around the table. It was always quiet.

We would gather up some empty soda cans, ride our bikes in single file and throw them into the open doorway. The sound was loud as the cans ricocheted off the concrete steps and into the room. We could hear the men screaming as we peddled like hell down the alley, turned a quick right and disappeared into the neighborhood. We did that a lot, always waiting until things cooled down to strike again.

Paul Ferrara

MY SISTER, MARIETTA,
AT THE PIANO

One day we found a building on the corner of Manchester and Vermont with an open entrance that led to its second story rooftop. We visited the local grocery store dumpster and found some rotting fruit, and then went to the roof to wait. The buses were our targets, maybe because they were so large. We would wait for the bus to take off with its new passengers and then let go with the fruit onto its top as it moved past us underneath. I don't know why we never got caught.

We used to hang around the campus of Pepperdine College. It was only three blocks from my house. We found a door to one of the science labs left open on a Saturday. We could see the jars of preserved animals and fetuses from outside. We went in and started to examine the jars and opened a few. We dumped them into the sink and were examining the various specimens, when someone dropped a jar and it shattered on the floor. Someone passing by must have heard it. Security guards found us, and our parents had to come to the University's security office and get us. They read us the riot act and we left with our moms.

Every summer we all got buzzes, a short sort of G.I. haircut. Every kid shopped at J.C. Penney's and had the same clothing. I mean the boys anyway all had white tee shirts, Levi's and black Keds high top tennis shoes. In the winter everybody wore a heavy Pendleton shirt over his tee shirt, and that was pretty much it.

Don Talbot's dad was a musical instrument salesman. Don had a trumpet and took lessons. He was a very handsome blonde boy, the same exact age as me. His dad had two very cool cars. One was a mint green '52 Chrysler Imperial. It smelled like new and probably was. The other was a strange looking '46 Nash fastback. I rode in those cars a lot, as his mother would drive us to various functions. Once I shut the door of the Chrysler on my finger on the way home from school, and couldn't speak for several minutes. It was discovered when the car stopped to let me out. I was so embarrassed I held it in. Later I think I cried as my finger turned black and swelled up.

There was never a car in my family. My father claimed his eyes were not good enough to drive. I think it deferred him from the military draft. In 1953 my mother finally stepped up and got her license and a car: a '53 Mercury hardtop convertible with white and pink leather tuck and roll upholstery. It had a matching exterior color of salmon pink. It was very cool.

Richard, Don and I rode our bikes everywhere we could. It was our first taste of freedom. I'm not sure we handled our freedom very well; it was a new thing. We were testing our surroundings like the pool hall ritual, those poor old guys. We discovered the Manchester Park Swimming Pool and that took our minds off the marauding nature of our existence. At the pool we met people that further expanded our sphere of friends. Some of our new friends were not exactly positive influences on us. Some kids had older siblings that would transfer knowledge and habits down like smoking cigarettes and stealing candy and stuff. Not all of it was good for us, but it was necessary. We had a local ice cream parlor we liked to go to. One day I discovered a fly in my sundae. I complained and the young woman brought me a fresh sundae and apologized. Wow that was cool. Every time there was a new worker at the ice cream parlor we tried the same act out. I brought a fly and toward the finish of my sundae placed the fly in the ice cream and again complained. It worked for some time until they figured out what I was pulling.

Richard Ballew's older brother showed us how to polish and detail our bicycles. We spent many hours fussing over our bikes. By this time they had morphed into custom machines, each one with a cool candy apple paint job with riser handlebars and chopped fenders. Richard's older brother had custom cars and was our introduction to cars. We saw him polishing his Mercury and keeping it perfect. He used to take us on short rides that made us feel so grown up.

Tommy Crossen owned the television and radio store. Tommy and his wife Mary were good friends of my parents. My father had met him on Vermont Avenue. Tommy was a handsome man and was constantly portrayed in the ads for his store in the newspapers. He was well known in the neighborhood.

I grew up a Catholic and attended St. Michael's on Manchester Avenue. Tommy and Mary were Irish Catholic and we attended the same church. On my first communion I was riding home in the back of Tommy Crossen's Lincoln; he had been my godfather in the ceremonies and he gave me a gift of ten bucks in an envelope. It flew out the window as I admired it. We did not go back, for some reason. Oh well.

My mother swears that both Tommy and his wife Mary died some years later of a sex-related disease. I guess Tommy used to play around a lot. Las

Vegas was his favorite destination; he even took my dad once. My father was very secretive about the circumstances of that trip.

Every summer the Crossen family went to Newport Beach for vacation and rented a small cottage on the water's edge. We eventually followed their lead and rented a cottage near theirs. Those were good times, exploring the Back Bay in a small rowboat, fishing and swimming. There was a dredging machine toward the Back Bay area that had mountains of shells piled up next to it. We explored every day in that small boat.

After I made my communion I started on classes for my confirmation. On Saturdays a couple of times a month I had to attend catechism. It is basically Bible study with extra strict thrown in. A preparation for a ritual called Confirmation, a passage into Catholic manhood. I was not too interested and I used to ditch the class as much as I could. There was a small custom car shop two blocks away; it had hot rods and all kinds of cool stuff. I spent much of the time there when I was supposed to be studying the Bible.

It's a drastic difference between grammar school and Junior High. It was a lot further away and we could take the bus. Talbot's mom took us on rainy days. The rest of the time we walked or took the bus. As we soon learned, we could stick out our thumbs out and hitchhike. It was safe then and we did it quite often. A new kid moved into a house on our path, we made friends and stopped by to pick him up on our journey to school. His father wasn't there, maybe he didn't have one, but his mother was a rocker. We were always invited into the kitchen where she was smoking and listening to Elvis, Fats Domino or Jerry Lee. It was the first time I heard "Rock around the Clock" by Bill Haley and the Comets. It was another life-changing moment. We all started smoking cigarettes not long after the beginning of our Junior High school experience.

Girls! There were after school dancing sessions in one of the recreation rooms that provided us with close contact with the opposite sex. What was sex, anyway? My mother and father had taken us to movies forever. We would walk once a week to the local theatre. I saw a lot of movies and knew about romance and girls, but I had never really smelled one except maybe for M.C. at Pepperdine. Now we were dancing close and it was enough to arouse anyone.

Cars really took on an importance. Older guys in cars picked up their girlfriends after school. They were probably in the 9th grade. They had the girls, all right. Had to have a car! After-school also would mean smoking and sometimes watching a fight. Somehow the word would spread that so-and-so 'got into it' in the cafeteria and were meeting after school to fight. There was such a thing as a choose-off: that was when a guy would walk up to another guy and challenge him to a fight. There were times when the fights lasted 5 minutes or longer. That's a long time for a fight and toward the end the guys were usually on the ground wrestling. Sometimes there were fifty kids gathered around as the fight moved from behind a storefront into the alley and ending on some grass. The cops didn't show up very often and that allowed the scene to play out till the end. The next day it was the main topic of conversation.

Chuck Berry was singing, "Roll Over Beethoven" and we got introduced to the YMCA. There was an established club called the Bobcats at the Y. It was pretty much where all our older friends were. All of us joined. There would be Bible study for about 30 minutes and then we would go to the enclosed yard and play basketball or whatever sport was in season. The Bobcats were members of a sports league that had games at night, or sometimes on Saturdays. We played football, basketball and baseball. We traveled all over our area; South Central L.A., playing other YMCA teams from different neighborhoods. Again, we were branching out. We had a good team anchored by Dave VanHorbeck, George Bradbury and a guy I didn't know much about named Mophet. They were focused on sports ahead of the rest of us. We learned as much as we could from them; they were our inspiration. We won our share of championships.

An alley is a small street that runs between the backs of opposing houses, common in South Central L.A. One day Don, Richard and I were on our bikes and we cut down an alley close to Richard's house. There was an open garage with some car parts and stuff and a young man in his mid-20's standing over the parts. Chuck Carlson was a handsome man. His blonde hair was longer than anyone's at the time. He had recently returned from Korea where he was an airplane mechanic. I think he was suffering from some experience he had in the war because he never liked to talk about Korea. He was the first hot rodder we met. He was installing a 1950's Oldsmobile overhead engine into the body of a Model T Ford. We stopped and watched him for a long time and when he couldn't avoid us any longer, we became friends. We helped him whenever we could but mostly we were his rooting section.

I stayed friends with him for years. He helped me with my first car, a 1940 Ford coupe. A friend and I had installed a new engine in it and we couldn't make it start. Chuck came to our rescue. He hooked the coupe up to another car and we towed it while in gear. This caused the engine to turn over and over until finally the gas worked its way through the line into the carb and down into the block, where a small jolt of electricity from the spark plug ignited it. It exploded, sending the piston crashing toward the crank and thus turning the transmission, then the drive shaft, and finally the rear end and the tires. Whew, did you follow that? During this experience, Chuck decided to pour some gas directly into the carb. It burst into a flame that burned Chuck's hand pretty bad. We drove to the doctor and they dressed his wound. He didn't complain and the car started running good after that. I learned respect for gas that day.

One summer the Y had a summer camp experience at a place near Mammoth Mountain. Our parents signed some papers, paid some money, loaded us up into a large 5-ton stake bed truck early in the morning and off we went ... the first time to leave the concrete behind, the first time away from our parents. The trip took several hours we mostly slept and sang. Fishing, hiking and swimming ... what more could you ask for? We all slept four to a tent. There were giant bonfires every night. The leaders would play the guitar and we sang "99 Bottles of Beer on the Wall." At the end of the fire each night, one of the leaders would tell a story. One night the story dealt with werewolves killing people in the forest, and he said it was a "true story." We kind of believed him. I thought about that story for a long time. I'm sure it was meant to keep us from wandering off in the dark forest we were sleeping in.

Everybody had turns cooking, and we all learned to make pancakes. Once we found a six-pack of beer in the creek behind our camp and drank it all. This made the shadows from the campfire dance even harder on the trees near our tent. It was definitely spooky in the woods at night. We were part of a revolving group of Y.M.C.A. tenants from different parts of the state. The camp was ours for two weeks. We did this for enough years that I got the idea of life outside my small city existence. We learned to catch fish, clean them and cook them for supper. We took organized hikes through the Devils Postpile area. There were gushing rivers everywhere. Our camp was at the base of the Mammoth Mountains, an area famous for the ski resort that was at the top. There is snow on the peaks late into June with plenty of runoff. We visited the June Lakes as well as the hatchery where we all got to catch a few fish. There were a lot of fish in the stream behind the hatchery and for a charge you could fish. Near the end of the two weeks we had some of our fish frozen and took them home. My mother was overjoyed and cooked them immediately for dinner. I was very proud.

Once I was lying in the tall grass alongside the stream trying to unsnag my hook. I stood up and noticed something black on my stomach. It was a deer tick. They had to burn it with a match before it could be removed from my skin. Ticks bite you and start digging their head into your skin. They won't let go unless you heat their bodies up. The lessons from experiences like summer camp are very important.

We learned about a vacant lot where kids had built ramps and jumps for bicycles. It was near Imperial and Western and a long bicycle ride, but the ride was worth it. We could ride our bikes down a steep hill picking up a lot of speed so when we hit the bottom we were flying and you then hit a small berm that acted as a launching pad. We would fly off the top of it and hopefully land safely on the other side. Many cuts and bruises. This was the beginning of what they now call motocross or BMX bike racing. The forks on the front wheels were damaged from bad landings, so I constantly had to buy new forks. We learned to work on our bikes ourselves. When we couldn't handle the job we took the bike to Vermont. There was a cool guy that had a shop and he was very generous with his time and friendship. He would show us tricks so that we might try the job ourselves next time.

I had three separate newspaper delivery routes, each for a different paper. I threw the papers on the porch of my customers every day. One time when I was sick, my mother did my route for me. I never figured out exactly how she did it, but she did.

The years between the late forties and early fifties were very interesting and tumultuous, to say the least. The Korean War was a huge deal; it makes Iraq pale in comparison. There were 54,246 Americans killed and another 100,000 wounded. It was brutal and the threat of nuclear catastrophe hung in the air. We had to do atomic bomb drills in school, where we would duck under our desks, much the same drill as for an earthquake. The total body count of the Korean War was around a million dead with another million wounded. That's huge. The guys who came back, like our friend Chuck

Carlson, had seen a lot of death and it made them numb, bitter, pissed off and generally anti-social. Every war creates casualties. The overall effect spreads out into the society and effects grandparents, loved ones, children, and especially the ones that lived it, the soldiers.

In 1953 "The Wild One" starring Marlon Brando was released. Boy, did that film stir the pot! It was banned in England for fourteen years. In America the fear was that it would cause its audience to copycat its story and cause delinquency and riots. Black leather pants and motorcycles were "in." A rebellion was underway, and it peaked with the James Dean film "Rebel Without a Cause." Family life was changed forever. We finally started to question certain values our parents were trying to pass along to us. Marlon Brando's character says it best in the movie "The Wild One" when one of the background girl dancers asks him, "Hey, Johnny, what are you rebelling against?" While tapping out a jazzy beat on the top of the jukebox, he replies, "What've you got?" The teenage members of society picked up on the bitter sentiment. We were mad and we didn't know whom we were mad at. "Rebel Without a Cause" was a film about frustration. We had become frustrated and it manifested itself in our lifestyle. We all got leather jackets and identified with our movie heroes.

Years later my mother would repeat over and over, "What happened to you, you were such a sweet little boy?" Well, that's what happened to Chuck Carlson, Marlon Brando and the rest of us. Since I started writing this story, Marlon has died. His was an illustrious life and he lived it to the max. He leaves a legacy of films, many depicting the brooding nature of the times we were born into.

We became cool. We picked up on the soundtrack of "The Wild One." It was created by Shorty Rogers and was jazzy and cool. This was our introduction to the world of jazz music. It became an obsession and we tracked down everything Shorty Rogers had done; that led to other musicians like George Shearing and Stan Kenton. We had all their albums and started to follow the progressive jazz movement of the times. It took us to Hermosa Beach and the Lighthouse Café, legendary home of Stan Getz and many other west coast jazz musicians. We were way too young to get in, but we could stand outside by the Dutch door and listen as long as we wanted. We frequented that club a lot as we got older.

About this time we graduated to racing bikes that had gears you could shift. We had to travel to a place near downtown Hollywood to buy them. They were faster and we could travel farther. We rode as far as the beach several times; they were all day excursions. I purchased a new 10-speed with money earned working for my father's business, and parked it outside while I ran in to pick up my pay. When I went back out, my bike was gone. It was a big lesson. Don't trust anyone.

In 1955 Shorty Rogers arranged the music for Elmer Bernstein's score for "The Man with the Golden Arm." The film starred Frank Sinatra as a jazz musician trying to kick heroin. There it is, a disaffected generation that turns to jazz and heroin, the beginning of the Beatniks and the Beat Generation. Enter Kerouac and the existential group that soon followed. Drugs became a topic of discussion. Wine did suffice as we wondered where the drugs were. Wine did take you out there, where poetry and Venice Beach coffeehouses were. Bongos and dark glasses were in. We became hip.

My parents added a second story to the house on 81ˢᵗ Street. My parents had a new bedroom upstairs, as did my sister. I inherited the large downstairs bedroom, so I finally got my own room. My parents' old bedroom in the rear of the house was converted into a den complete with a huge flagstone fireplace. The closet was converted into a walk-in bar, always stocked with the essential alcohols. It became a cool place to sample booze. My friends and I would sample the stuff and replace the missing alcohol with water. We did that for years and nobody ever said anything. That's where we watched television and where the family gathered every night.

In the winter we had fires. When I was little, I was told not to come near the Christmas tree with a match. Of course, that was the first thing I did. They were right. Once, after Christmas was over, I tried to burn the dried-up little spruce that had been decorated with Christmas ornaments the week before. I cut it up and stuffed it into the fireplace. Well, anyone that has ever seen a Christmas tree burn knows that they really burn fast and hot. This one was no different; it started burning like hell and I almost burned the house down again. Fortune had it that my mother was near enough to grab the tree and rush it out the door. What is it with fire? Even grown people can't stop playing with it.

My mother always had a commercial sewing machine in the house. She made good money sewing garments for a lady named Mrs. Hagus. The machine was originally in the washroom at the rear of the house, the same washroom where the snake incident took place. As a small child I would sit on the linoleum floor of that room as she sewed away the day. I remember studying the underneath of that machine. It had a lot of moving parts and was fun to watch. My mother even knew how to fix the belts and keep it running. Some of my interest for the mechanical stuff probably came from these early memories.

Eventually when I could handle a pair of scissors, I turned the collars and cuffs and anything that needed to be turned inside out. You sew something in the reverse, so as you finish sewing it you must reverse it so as not to see the sewing. There was always work for me. My mother always had money because of her enterprise in the laundry room. When the second story was added to the house, the machine was moved upstairs to a room that had been designed to be the sewing room. The windows faced south and it was a bright warm place. That little room later became my temporary bedroom when my grandmother got sick and had to move into my bedroom on the first floor.

My mother's mom had become quite ill with diabetes. She needed a lot of care and my mother wanted to take care of her. She was moved in the back of a large truck, complete with a hospital-style bed, into my bedroom. I moved upstairs into the sewing room. It was small but we made it do. The sewing machine went back downstairs. My mother had two brothers, Earl and Fonsie, and a sister named Edith. Edith had been living with my grandmother in grandmother's house. Edith had a heart condition and when it became worse, Grandmother came to live with us. Her sons and daughters came to visit at least once a week. They would come at night and stay for several hours.

I was into models then and made little balsa wood hot rods from kits. I talked Earl into teaching me to drive. It took a lot of nerve for him to let me learn in his beautiful black 1948 Pontiac. It was usually at night that we drove through the neighborhood, and he taught me how to work the clutch. For those of you who learned in a car with an automatic transmission, you might not understand the bucking and bumping that goes on when a clutch is not used properly. I will always be grateful for those lessons; may he rest in peace.

Edith had two kids: Sonny was away in the Army; her daughter Jackie was much older than me and had a boyfriend named Pat that she eventually married. While Jackie visited with her grandmother in my bedroom, Pat showed me how to make model airplanes. We worked on the kitchen table. We had basic kits that consisted of rough pieces of balsa wood that he carved into the coolest little army fighter planes, complete with paint jobs and decals. We eventually started building larger models including ships complete with sails and rigging. May he also rest in peace.

My mother's family was very earthy and the men were into construction. Strong builds, they wore tee shirts and work pants. My father was very gentile. He didn't have much to do with my mother's brothers, but they sure treated me good. I think I grew up more like them than my father. I take after my mom a lot, the same looks and earthy attitude: Mother's boy. I didn't get much love from my father. My mom says that he didn't get any from his dad and he didn't know any different. However he was a good father, always providing wonderful surroundings for our family.

My mother had a string of childhood illnesses that left her in a weakened condition. She was not a completely healthy person and started to show signs of illness. My father noticed her weight loss and shortly after, my grandmother was moved to a nursing home. About a week after she arrived there, her condition worsened. She told my mother she wanted to be in her own house and she was taken back there. One day while my mother was visiting her, Earl and Edith were having a loud argument in the kitchen. My grandmother asked my mother what all the noise was; my mother told her they were fighting. My mom says she sighed and turned onto her side and died.

At the funeral I was made to kiss my grandmother goodbye. Someone lifted me up. I freaked out at the sight of the pale corpse of my grandmother. I struggled but lowered down to her face and my lips touched her cheek. It was cold and the smells were strange. I have never forgotten that moment. The story goes that Edith borrowed some money against my dead grandmother's house. She couldn't make the payments, the bank took the house, and Edith went to live with her daughter Jackie.

Around this time I had my first flying dream. It was a dream that would reoccur through out the rest of my life. Usually I was being chased by someone, neighborhood kids or grownups or anyone. As I was trying to get away I ran faster and faster until there was lift-off. It was a gentle kind of flying. It became quiet and I could see the people back on the ground as they looked up at me. The wind on my face was cool and refreshing. There was only one problem and that was all the wires from the telephone and electric service everywhere. I managed to avoid them somehow. I always awoke feeling refreshed and the dream stayed with me throughout the day. I have read that flying dreams are not that uncommon and usually indicate some form of escapism.

Elvis was first played on the radio in 1954 and the Russians tested a nuclear weapon. I learned to drive and was about to graduate from Jr. High School. Marlon Brando comes out with "On the Waterfront." The sex stuff was heating up with some necking and real excitement. "From Here to Eternity," the film with Frank Sinatra, was a good romantic education. Burt Lancaster and Deborah Kerr rolling around in the surf was enough to make most of us wet.

Some years before this Don Talbot and I were camping in a friend's back yard and he taught us how to masturbate. Suddenly you were your own best friend. Whenever that mysterious urge began to show itself, you kind of knew what to do with it

George Washington High School was where I would be going; it was the big time. Jr. High was just a trial for me, an introduction to the big picture. Washington High was twice the distance Horace Mann was, but in the opposite direction. We used the bus to travel south on Normandie to 108th Street and then walked a block to enter the schoolyard. It was a large campus, about a full city block. Its full-sized football field had a track that encircled it. The bleachers were along one side of it, and underneath them was a good place to smoke and hang out.

I was medium height and very thin, perfect for running but not a lot else. I eventually got into cross-country running. Everybody wanted to play football; they had all the chicks. The football games were the highlight of the semester. Teams from all over South Central competed for the championship of the area. We used to get our asses whipped by all the black schools to the east: Jefferson, Manuel Arts and Fremont, among others. Our mostly white student body was fighting the Goliath, the faster, the meaner and often larger opponent. It was even scary just to attend those games. There were fights that broke out near those events and you could get hurt. Sometimes a girl was beat up and that really pissed everybody off. The next game with that school would usually end up in some sort of revenge violence.

There was an inner area to the campus that everyone called the quad. Its lawn was surrounded by walkways, and it was where all the socializing took place. Don Talbot, Rich Ballew and I ended up in the quad looking at all the girls and new guys that we had never seen before. Kids from all the surrounding Junior Highs came to Washington High. It was the center of our universe for several years. Even after we graduated, we were coming back for younger girlfriends, parties, etc.

The older kids had cars and they cruised around the block after school showing off their cars. Some had customized their rides and others had their parent's car. Others just cruised looking to pick up their girlfriends in whatever they could get to drive. We were already cool, listening to jazz and belonging to the Bobcats. Almost all the guys in the Bobcats ended up in Washington High. Some had older brothers and it sort of smoothed the way for us. We were among the first to be asked to join a social club. They handed out invitations. There were three major boys clubs: The Embassy, The Keys and The Yoeman.

In Jr. High it was discovered that I had a small talent for singing. I had good pitch and a soprano range, and was asked to join the choir. I accepted: again, a lot of girls. Besides, there was something cool about singing.

Some of my early friends at Washington were Dick Ensch and Mike Brunneto. They both played the guitar and sang Kingston Trio songs. I started to sing with them and got into folk music because of it. Peter, Paul and Mary. "Puff the Magic Dragon" and "Blowin' In the Wind." It was my first introduction to Bob Dylan's music, but of course I didn't know it at the time. They also snow skied and introduced me to that. As soon as we could we piled into a V.W. and set off to Mammoth Mountain again, this time in the winter. A guitar was always along and Warnnie Noack, another Embassy member, had now joined us. He had a good voice and we tried to sing harmonies. The Four Freshmen were popular, their harmonies turned on a whole generation. It eventually turned into Boyz II Men, but that is getting too far ahead.

Dick's older brother, Mike, led the folk music thing. Mike was ahead of his time, or at least, the first person we knew that surfed. One day Mike went surfing and never came back. He had gone to Mexico with some friends and disappeared. Several days later he was discovered about a hundred miles south on the beach. Mike was our first friend to die, but certainly was not to be the last.

We had heard all kinds of stories about what high school was going to be like. Hazing was mentioned, which meant making a person feel small by abusing him physically and mentally. It's a ritual that is repeated in many organizations. I think it's to test the person, to see what they are made of and how they react. It can really piss some people off. Others are sent running home to their mothers, but some glide through the experience unaffected. It's like being calm under fire. It's an indication of how you're going to react when the shit really hits the fan. It's a gauge of sorts as to your "cool." Well, some of that happened.

So, girls! … There was a complement of three girls clubs at Washington: the Sub Debs, the Coeds and the Delta Y. All the cool girls ended up in these clubs. The main functions of these clubs were to raise money and to throw parties and more parties and functions for the sole purpose of getting the girls together with the boys. That's why they called them social clubs.

Somewhere around my 14th or 15th year I was allowed to purchase a car although the legal age for a license at that time was 16. My mom was cool about a lot of things. She let me smoke in her presence. She treated me like a grownup. I found a 1940 Deluxe Ford coupe; it was exactly like a guy's from school. The owner didn't live far from me and advertised it in the local paper. I bought it with money I had been saving, around two hundred bucks, and drove it home. The prior owner had used it primarily to carry his golf equipment. For the longest time I found golf balls stuck in the most unlikely places. I didn't have a license, so I parked it in the garage where the cardboard box condo had been. I proceeded to explore it with a fine toothcomb. I couldn't drive the car yet, so I started to customize it the best I could. I stripped away all the stuff I didn't need: sun visor, mud flaps, and curb feelers were removed. The chrome on the car was a little pitted and discolored. I removed all of it and had it re-plated. I put a '30 Ford floor shift in to replace the column shift it came with. It just looked cooler!

In those days the radios were what they were. The best you could do was replace some of the plastic and chrome pieces to make it look as good as possible. It was strong enough to get the local stations, and there was plenty of cool music on some stations in those days. Chuck Berry was a favorite with "Roll Over Beethoven" and "Sweet Little Sixteen." I used to sit in that car in the garage and imagine myself cruising along with the rest of the people listening to the radio. Sometimes after I had fixed something on the car, I would test-drive it down the driveway toward the street in the front of the house. One of the first times I did this, the brakes failed and I shot across the street in front of the house and hit the neighbor's car that was parked there. Not much damage, and I was told not to do that anymore. Insurance matters.

An older kid from the other side of Vermont became a car buddy of mine. Van Bushman went to another school, was a little bit older and had a reputation about his cars and his ability to work on them. He worked at the Chrysler dealer on Western and delivered parts to all the body shops and auto repair places in our neighborhood and sometimes beyond. I eventually ended up working there myself.

One of the places we delivered to was Pickering Sheet Metal. It was located at 108th and Avalon in a predominately black section of town, referred to as Watts. They ordered a lot of the rear wheel fender trims made of chrome, which they used on the catering trucks they manufactured. The foreman was a cool bodybuilder that everyone called Pic. He was the owner's brother and pretty much ran the factory. I asked him one day about a job and he said sure. I started the next week and was working there when the Watts riots broke out in the 60's. The police pulled someone over for something on 115th and Avalon. They roughed the driver and his mother up, much as they do today. Rodney King comes to mind. A crowd formed and the incident was witnessed by everyone. It developed into a riot that practically destroyed the city. Watts was on fire and random violence spread into the other neighborhoods. The 77th Street Police Station was the main responder. It was open season on blacks and a lot of vigilante stuff was going on. It lasted for three or four days. Pickering was shut down when the rioters climbed the fences and tried to enter the factory. We were pelted with rocks and bottles as we tried to leave on the third day. Nobody went back to work for at least a week after that.

On August 11, 1965 the Watts riots were headlines. National headlines. It started next to my work place and had progressed into a national incident. Who knew! There were many different points of view at the time. Ebony, a black magazine, expressed the sentiment that the L.A. Police had caused the entire incident. The injustice that the community had suffered, the bigotry

28

and the prejudice, had caused the riots. The incident on 115th and Avalon just sparked it into a rebellion.

There were other rebellions in the sixties but this one was set apart in history by its magnitude and surprise. Life Magazine took the position that no matter what injustice had occurred in the past, they condemned the people's reaction to it. It lasted for 7 days and was a vivid lesson in the polarization of race relationships at that time. The blacks not only burned every commercial building in sight, but they looted them first. There were pictures of people leaving buildings carrying all sorts of appliances, clothing and stuff. The National Guard was called out to take back the city. There were pictures on the nightly T.V. of National Guardsmen manning a machine gun post on a corner, buildings on fire. Buildings were burning and firemen were trying to put out the blazes. The people who originally witnessed the brutal arrest of Marquette Fry and the unnecessary assault of his mother and brother sure did start something.

Everyone knows that the police are robots and are stigmatized by fear. I have seen it firsthand. It seems to be either people, like the ones who become cops, are attracted to the job of roughing up people, or the job itself creates monsters out of ordinary people. I personally believe that some people just like to hurt people and the fear just accelerates it. Sometimes it's good to see someone fight back but I might add, it can be somewhat dangerous. Back to the story.

HIGH SCHOOL

One day I was standing in the quad at Washington High School and was handed an envelope. I had received an invitation to attend the get-together introduction parties for the various social clubs I already mentioned. I chose the Embassy because I knew people in that club. Babe was a friend from Jr. high school and his brother Dale was a member of Embassy. We were so punked, our mothers had to take us to the member's house where the tryouts were held, and drop us in front.

Inside, the members were beaming at the prospect of new flesh: cool kids who were going to grow up and make them proud by getting the chicks, fighting the battles and generally making them look good just to be with us. And that is probably what we were thinking, as well. There were maybe 30 new guys there that night. The members gave us an introduction to the club and somewhat spelled out the ratting thing, a form of hazing. The info about the hazing had gotten to us before that party, although I don't think we took it as seriously as we should have. About a week later the three boys clubs announced their picks. Babe and I were accepted into the Embassy. Richard Ballew and Don Talbot followed the next semester, and eventually all four of us were members.

We didn't know it then but our fate was sealed. A chain reaction had begun that would continue indefinitely. I met people who have remained my friends and dear to me until today. Some have died but most are just scattered in the wind. Through all the marriages and divorces and special circumstances, those early relationships have stuck. We became family. All the stories you hear about the gangs today are true. The gang becomes the family, more important than your real parents. It fills a need for camaraderie. We were strong as a group and sensed a feeling of power. There was a lineage of cool people that you were related to. The association fed off this feeling. The feeling fed off the association. Like that!

The first meeting took place at Warren Balfour's house. Our mothers dropped us off. We were herded into the garage. The lights were turned off. We sat in darkness. We waited for the general meeting to take place. When they were through, the garage door was opened. They stared at us like we were dinner. Holy shit, two days ago these guys pretended to like us. We were given gunnysacks to wear. They terrorized us no end. I remember being blindfolded and led one by one into a room. I was placed on a small box about two feet high and told to drop my pants. There was a 10 lb. weight tied to a short string. Someone tied the other end to my penis. The blindfold was put back in place. The weight was put in my hand and I was told to drop it upon command. While I was holding it, someone I didn't see cut the string with snips. "Shit," I thought, "this will tear my little pecker off." Imagine there are thirty guys all watching your dick and your reactions. Someone said drop it. I did. We all did. We were committed. That's what the members wanted to see. If someone showed cowardice or fear, they ran the risk of being dropped from the rat class. Some guys did drop out, but a core group of die-hards stuck it out. Most of hazing is designed to humiliate and scare. It's under that pressure that you reveal your stuff, what you're made of.

There was a concoction brewed weekly that we were forced to drink. Usually Bob Bowlus was the chemist. He was a sadistic fucker. The brew consisted of nasty things, probably not fit for human consumption. We called it buzzard puke. We gagged and threw up a lot. Once Bowlus made me chew a cigar and eat some of it. I got so ill that still to this day the smell of a cigar makes me want to throw up. I found out later I had nicotine poisoning.

The girls clubs were pledging at the same time. After the meetings on Wednesday nights, we sometimes hooked up with the girls who were pledging and had their meetings the same night. It made it all worthwhile. It was the light at the end of the tunnel. From the beginning of these encounters with the girls clubs, the kids paired up. To this day some remain married.

An easy weekly meeting was a little degradation like mowing the lawn and washing all the members' cars. That was a lot of cars. We were never to be in the presence of a member outside the meeting: not in public, not at the drive-in, not at school, that kind of thing. Sometimes a member would take you on a special mission by yourself to clean his yard or do something he didn't want to do. Their attitude during the one on one determined whether you liked or disliked them, and it signified who liked you. Inside a club of thirty guys it breaks down further into smaller cliques, but when it came to the big stuff, the club came together like an army.

Warren Balfour played the trumpet, Bill Plummer played bass, and they both belonged to a band. They were both cool guys and treated me with compassion during my rat days. Warren ended up with a big jazz band and toured. Last I heard, he was teaching music at Long Beach State. Bill went off and joined the drug world. He got better on the bass for his experience and made a few albums. He eventually married a black lady and the last I heard he was doing a music thing in Idyllwild. We showed up at as many of their gigs as we could. They played at our proms and parties for a long time. Music played a big part at the club functions. June Christie and the Four Freshmen were staples. They sang sexy, slow tempo songs that talked of love. We all know girls like love. The slow tempo made for some close contact and romantic lighting was in.

Making out was the thing to do. It meant heavy kissing and touching and boners and hot little girls that wanted us to feel them. Their bodies had a lot of soft place to touch. Real sex did happen, but it was far and few between. Later on after couples broke up and no longer were current, you heard the dirt: who fucked who and what it was like. But all was quiet during the romance.

EMBASSY S' 57

40 FORD

59
BONNIVILLE

At the same time I was pledging for the Embassy, I joined a car club that Van Bushman belonged to, the T Timers. It was a national group with small clubs scattered all over the country. We had meetings, jackets and events that took place around drag racing and custom car shows. Van and I went to drag races every Sunday at Long Beach, Pomona or San Gabriel. Each of those cities had professional courses and the events were sanctioned by NHRA, the National Hot Rod Association. Trophies were handed out. Howard Stubbins, a member of my pledge group and a fellow member of Embassy, and his dad had built a 1938 Chevy Coupe. It was sea foam green and perfect in appearance. It had a 270 GMC engine installed and turned in the low 90's at the ¼-mile drag races. The miles per hour were important, but the elapsed time that it took to cover the quarter mile was what determined the winner of a race. We saw Howard and his dad from time to time at the track; it must have been cool to have your dad in on the car thing with you. The totally altered dragsters of the day only completed the course at speeds of around 135 to 160 mph. Their elapsed time was in the 6-second range. Van Bushman's '49 Ford with a Chrysler engine was fast; it went off at around the mid nine's or so. He won some Sundays.

I had replaced the original engine in my '40 Ford coupe with a Dodge Red Ram engine and was ready to try at the track, it turned in the high 80's. It wasn't as fast as some but it sure was beautiful. I had white tuck and roll upholstery installed. The car was dark forest green, and later I had beautiful flames painted on the front. Gary Grimes, also from my pledge class, was the first to have his car striped by Von Dutch. We all went with Gary to Hollywood and watched while Von Dutch did it. He had an electric skateboard and some other strange toys, if I remember correctly. We were so hip. Gary's '47 Chevy coupe was painted a cool beige. Von Dutch added some black and green pinstripes. Gary had his mufflers customized. They were pretty short glass packs. They came from a header system that was built to break his 6-cylinder engine into two exhaust lines. The glass pack mufflers started to rap as the car reached the peak in each gear. It sounded like a drum. It was a beautiful sound. Everyone tried to achieve a sound from the exhaust system. That sound is still popular today.

By the time I got into Embassy, my car was pretty much finished. It had a lowered front end that gave it a feeling of a rake, the term for a car dropped in the front. I used to drive the '40 Ford coupe around and around the school, showing it off, cruising like everyone else. We were getting all our ideas from car magazines that were introduced in the 50's. Custom Car and others led the way for artists like Chuck Barris to begin franchises for body shops all over the place. It was a phenomenon all over the country. People were arranging their cars into all sorts of statements. The '49 Mercury from the James Dean movie "Rebel Without a Cause" was an example of where it all came from. The movie "Back to the Future" took it into the realm of time travel. This whole part of our life, the cars, started with Chuck Carlson in the alley behind Dick Ballew's house.

Chuck eventually lost his job at LAX and drifted into the surfing lifestyle that was emerging at the time. The last time I saw him, he was living on top of the small store at 22nd Street by the Strand in Hermosa Beach. All of the cool people from Washington High School went to 22nd Street in Hermosa; we ruled that little beach. At the same time we were partying there, the surfing thing began to happen. Ensch and some of my friends were early surfers. I even tried it once in awhile, but to me it was too much work for that small time you got to ride the wave. I stayed on the beach with the girls and the wine.

About two weeks before our pledging was through we were asked to meet at Centinela Park near Slauson Avenue instead of at someone's house. This turned into a terrible, dirty experience. At the end of a night of pushing and shoving, we were forced to apply Tabasco sauce to our genitals. It's hot on your lips and in your stomach. Don't try it on your balls! The pain was intense and lasted for hours. The members eventually left us there in the dark. I remember finding some soft cool mud and applying it to myself. It helped a little bit. I thought I would be sterile or something. Years later I had a beautiful son, so I guess it was just the skin that was affected but believe me, it was something you're never going to forget.

The pledging thing was almost over. A lot of the guys already had girlfriends and some had cars. Jerry Brooks, another pledge brother, had a '39 Plymouth 4-door and we rode around in that a lot. He was a ladies man and there were always plenty of girls in that car. A lot of making out and feeling up went on in the back seat of that car. We used to pull into the ever-popular drive-in theaters that were scattered around our neighborhood and kind of watch the movie. Whoever had a car with a trunk usually stopped before the ticket booth, crammed a couple of people in, and slipped through the ticket booth undetected. Most of the time we were there we were making out with girls and drinking with our friends who used to pull their cars along side us. We lived in those cars. A lot of babies were made in the back seats of those cars! If you stayed for the late movie, the crowds thinned out and sometimes the fog settled in. You were alone in the car with your girl. Blouses came off, zippers unzipped and sex in the drive-in took place. Drive-in theatre was the thing. We lived for the experience. Sometimes the movie was good but most the time it was just the backdrop to our partying.

It was only about three months in reality, but it seemed like three years. We pledged in the summer and our pledging lasted until the school year in the fall. We were humiliated, beaten, fed food and other things. We never really figured out what all that shit was and I still don't want to know. The last night of hazing consisted of being blindfolded and taken to the sand dunes of Playa Del Rey. We were stripped of our clothes and gunnysacks were placed over our heads. You could still see through the small openings enough to know who was next to you. We were marched up the dune and given approximately three hundred swats with large wooden paddles that the guys had built in wood shop. Our asses all bled; we couldn't sit for days. We begged, but they just kept on swinging We were next to the waste treatment center, the one with the three tall towers next to the beach. There were lights on the towers to keep the planes from LAX from hitting them when they took off. In those days the planes didn't take off as regularly as they do now, but it was often enough to drown out some of our screams. Somehow we made it through that experience.

We started off the next semester as members of the prestigious Embassy. We had sweaters with Embassy written on them. We had survived. Wow, what a sense of accomplishment. The rest of the student body looked at you differently. There were 10 guys in our Rat class, and today I still am in contact with some of them. Our class consisted of Gus Bailey, Butch Ellis, Dick Ensch, Gary Grimes, Ed Hutton, Babe Hill, Warren Noack, Howard Stubbins, John Waid, and me. One of the responsibilities of being in a club was solidarity. There was a message passed around one day during school that someone had been harassed in Inglewood and there was to be a fight at the local hamburger stand after school. Everyone from all three boys clubs met there after school. Sure enough, the strangers pulled their cars in one by one. There must have been twenty guys. That was O.K., we had at least twenty guys, Larry Thomas was there and more were on the way. The fight broke out and it was chaos with so many guys swinging and wrestling. Out of the corner of my eye I saw a bat come out and the guy swung it into a dude's head. His eye fell out and was hanging on his cheek. Holy shit, this fighting was for real. As I stared at the eye, a fist hit me across the side of my head. I turned to see that my best friend Babe had hit me by mistake. He said "sorry" and turned to another guy and started pounding away. The fight lasted for maybe fifteen minutes. The cops finally came and everybody scattered. It felt like we won, and those guys from Inglewood didn't come around anymore.

A lot of the guys met girls during those high school days who belonged to the various girls clubs, married them, and are with them still today. Talbot is still with Margie, a member of the Sub-Debs. At last report, Howard Stubbins was running a fire station in Redondo Beach and building Harleys for sale, still married to Janet Stumph (who I dated until they met.) Babe met his wife Diane during this time. It turned out that she was in an abusive home and one day Babe and I drove my car over to her parents' house and got her. I don't think she ever went back. She moved into the back bedroom with Babe at his parents' home. They later married and had two beautiful daughters, Autumn and Kelly. Diane became a dancer at the Whiskey A Go Go and near the end of their marriage got into LSD and flipped out. She left the girls and Babe to fend for themselves, ran off with a biker gang and had 'Bitch' tattooed on her chest. We didn't see her for years; she surfaced again later suffering from brain damage. Poor baby.

I met my first real girlfriend at this time. Her name was Bonnie Goeman and she lived close to me so I was at her parents' house a lot. She was smarter than me, a few years younger and beautiful, your typical idea of a blue-eyed blonde. She was slender with a very feminine body for her age. We did homework together on her kitchen table. I picked her up for school in the mornings in the Ford coupe. We had a lot of fun in that car. We parked in the dark near her house any chance we could. We both learned how to make out and took it to the edge of sex. She learned how to satisfy me without compromising her virginity, if you know what I mean. Use your imagination. Eventually we progressed to some serious stuff. Once we were alone and in her bedroom after school. Her parents and her sister were not home. Our clothes were off and we were close to penetration when the front door opened and we freaked. I grabbed my clothes and flew out the bedroom window into the backyard. We were together for a few years and she was my date for graduation prom. We were drifting along together. Her parents planned a trip to Hawaii one summer and she met someone else, or at least that's what she said. She broke my heart with a letter she sent from her vacation. Things weren't the same after that. I started to not seek attachments.

I was out of high school and my hormones were raging. Gus Bailey had an older sister and her steady boyfriend passed on the information about Vera to Gus. Vera was a prostitute. Gus made the arrangements over the phone and a small group of us went to see her one night. We sat in her small front room as one by one we went to her bedroom for our first lesson at all-out sex. She was young and sexy and black. The room was dark with candles and some cheap material hung over the window. She was the first lady to show me what she wanted and how to do it. It was Sex 101. As I was about to climax she stuck her finger in my ass. I don't remember what happened next. All I remember was thinking I had cum for the first time. We visited Vera a few more times. I felt an addiction for sex coming on. On our third time there, we were all sitting in the front room waiting our turn when the front door opened and two plain- clothes vice cops came in. They asked us what we're doing there and we gave some lame excuses. They took all our driver licenses and threatened to call our parents. We pleaded. They finally let us go with a warning and we got the hell out of there. I called Vera a week later and learned the two cops were there to get laid. They were just playing with us.

Larry Thomas pledged the next semester with Richard Ballew and became a good friend of mine. We dated sisters for a while. He had been a child protégé Judo champion and was so good that the fights he got in never lasted more than a few seconds. A guy would throw a punch at Larry; Larry would side step it and grab the guy's arm and throw him to the ground so fast, the dude would just get up and walk away in amazement. He came to many of our rescues. Thank you, Larry. Later I got him a job at Pickering Sheet Metal where I was working. I had good hands just like my mother, and Pickering was where I learned to work with my hands. I got quite good at laying out patterns on sheet metal and cutting them out, forming the metal into various shapes and actually installing the pieces onto trucks that were being custom-built to sell snacks at construction sites. You have seen catering trucks: shiny stainless steel that is waffled with creases that look like diamonds. Larry died in Hawaii. He and his wife Sandy had been in a terrible car accident and while he was in the hospital, he was given some medication that caused him to have a stroke. He was in a wheelchair and his health had worsened. He suffered a heart attack in his sleep that killed him.

I had raced, polished, and refined my '40 Ford Deluxe to the max. I was moving on from hot rods to custom stuff. I started seeing the new Chevy's and Fords that my friends were getting. The girls gravitated toward the newer cars as well. The T Timers had a booth at the L.A. County Fairgrounds in Pomona. My coupe had been picked to be on display; I was so proud. Along came this Japanese dude who offered me several thousands of dollars for it. It wasn't near what I had put into it, but it seemed like a reasonable offer and I accepted. That had been my first car. I loved that car, more than I loved Bonnie Goeman. Both experiences seemed to move me forward. I bought a wreck car that I drove to work and saved my money.

I had three thousand dollars in the bank. Chevy and Pontiac ruled in 1959. General Motors was on top with the Corvette and hot V-8 engines that were winning all the races. My mother accompanied me to the local Pontiac dealer on Vermont and I bought a brand new Pontiac Bonneville for cash. It was white with sea foam green tuck and roll leather interior. I had it lowered and added Appleton spotlights. It was beautiful, and plenty of girls thought so, also.

I cruised that car up and down Manchester every night, visiting the drive-in restaurants that were springing up everywhere. You could sit in your car and order food that they placed on a tray that attached to your window. The local radio stations were jammed with good music. You could eat, socialize and listen to the radio at the same time and your car was very visible under the lights. We liked to show off our cars. I think people still like to show off their cars. I remember cruising to South Gate sometimes to visit other car people and drive-ins. We discovered a new restaurant that was mostly take-out; it was the first McDonald's. It was big and garish for those days with plenty of plastic and neon. They advertised the amount of hamburgers they had sold on a sign outside: a couple of hundred thousand, which seemed like a lot at that time.

Something I am not proud of happened on a regular basis during my high school days. The new Oldsmobile Fiestas, Dodge Lancers, and a few others that were coming out had very fancy hubcaps that everyone wanted to put on their cars. We started stealing them and putting them on our cars, and it actually progressed into a small cottage industry. We would cruise around at night. If we spotted an Olds with Fiesta hubcaps, we pulled over. Three or four guys would jump out with screwdrivers, pop them and be back in our car and gone in 15 seconds. Some guys including myself had a trunk full of stolen hubcaps. I hate to admit it but on occasion I sold a set of hubcaps. We even progressed into stealing the spare tires out of some Chryslers that had unlocked trunks. When you see custom cars with fancy hubcaps, think about where they are from. Nobody I knew could afford brand new parts from Oldsmobile. No one I knew ever got caught; it was a wonder. We had some close calls but never an arrest.

One night a group of us guys from Embassy went out to dinner. I don't remember what the occasion was. At the end of a huge meal complete with drinks and dessert, somehow we forgot to pay and walked out. In the car someone asked who had paid; no one had paid. Wow, that was easy! We decided to try that again. We went into the Copper Kettle and ordered big steak meals with all the trimmings. The food came in waves. We were all full and ordered elaborate deserts. Someone asked the waitress where the restroom was. We said thank you and she left the table. Two people got up and went to the restroom. One person went to the phone booth, pretended to make a call and then slipped out the back door. The two guys left at the table took their cues from the activity in the room to get up and walk casually out the door. The table was empty, but we always tried to leave a tip for the waitress. Once outside we all quickly made our way to the car that was about a half a block up the side street in the dark. We called it Eat it and Beat it. It was a joke that we made into an artistic statement: it was our caper. If pulled off right it was such a joy, and we laughed about the experience for weeks. Years later we talked about it and hoped the sweet waitresses didn't have to pay for our dinners. We didn't think that was possible. Surely the restaurant had insurance for that kind of thing.

Another place we liked to eat was in Manhattan Beach called La Paz. It was a Mexican restaurant and they served us pitchers of beer in the back patio. There was an open fire pit for comfort with glass to shield you from the night. You could see the Manhattan Pier from the patio.

One night in the middle of winter after way to many beers someone decided to jump off the end of the pier. It was 2 o'clock in the morning and pitch black outside. Babe led the charge as usual and Ron Ellis followed. We were in disbelief as we followed them out to the end of the pier. They took off their clothes and jumped into the dark surf below. The pier is very high, maybe fifty or sixty feet off the surface of the water. The fall alone could kill someone not to mention the rip current that could drag you off shore. The water is about 20 feet deep. They waited until a large swell was forming and jumped. The swell carried them toward the shore and then broke into foam over their heads. The white water cleared and they were still there. We followed along on the pier above them as the next swell carried them closer to the shore. They finally dragged themselves up onto the sand. They put their clothes back on and we went back to the La Paz, the fire and more beer.

Ron says they did it again on different nights maybe four or five more times. He still lives in Manhattan Beach and says both of his sons, and countless others have done the jump. It is of course against the law. That jump has taken on a mythical like reputation. Ah, youth.

The six social clubs at Washington High collectively saved money all year and in the summers joined ranks at either Crestline near Big Bear or a favorite place near Seal Beach, called Venetian Square, to rent cabins and party. The parties lasted the better part of two weeks. It was so much fun; the girls were away from their parents and went a little wild. There was a lot of romance with plenty of sticky fingers and whatever else you could get. I don't think our parents ever really knew what we were doing.

A few years after I graduated and was still attending these functions, I was driving the new 1959 Pontiac Bonneville. Larry had a new '59 Chevy Impala and had arrived at the party in Crestline before me. I arrived late and as I approached the cabin where all my friends were, my Bonneville hit some dirt on the road and started sliding. I took advantage of this to burn some rubber, showing off as usual. I slid sideways and ran my car into Larry's. It was ugly; my whole rear fender had been smashed. Larry's car had considerable damage also. He was very kind and didn't get mad. My insurance paid for his car. I had mine repaired but the car never felt the same after that and I started thinking of selling it.

I was driving to work at Pickering in Watts when I saw an accident take place right in front of me. A car smacked into a dog. The car tried to avoid the dog but hit him anyway, and the dog went flying through the air and landed in front of my car. The car that hit the dog sped off and there I was. The dog was struggling to get to its feet, but clearly its hindquarters were smashed. I decided to try to help the dog get out of the street to where he could die peacefully. It was a small pit bull terrier, and I approached with some caution. I grabbed him by the back of the neck with one hand and lifted his shattered body with the other. Everything was going well until I turned to carry the dog to the curb. An approaching car started skidding toward me. I freaked out and let go of the dog's neck for a moment. He turned and bit me on the hand; his jaw was locked on my thumb. I finally got to the curb and freed my hand, which was bleeding profusely. I wrapped a rag around my hand and got out of there.

When I arrived at work and told my foreman what happened, he sent me to the hospital. While I was checking in with the nurse at the reception, I noticed a beautiful girl not in uniform in the office sitting at a typewriter; she smiled and I smiled back. I got my hand sewed up and was in the process of leaving when the head nurse handed me a piece of paper with a phone number on it. She said it was from the pretty girl at the typewriter, and she wanted to talk to me. I smiled at the pretty girl and left, and later that night I called her. She was great to talk to. Her name was Alana and she was from Tahiti. She was working at the hospital in Watts during summer but would return to junior college in the fall. We talked all week long, every night, and we made a movie date for Friday night.

She lived in Long Beach, and we drove to the local drive-in theatre. She was beautiful, dark hair, slender and with large breasts. It was happening so fast. We were making out. She unzipped my pants and gave me the most incredible blowjob I had ever had. I was in love. We went together for the better part of a year. Her ex-boyfriend followed us from time to time but we never confronted one another. I understood why he was unhappy with her leaving him. I would pick her up at her house and before we left the street she lived on, her head was in my lap. I once asked her how she learned to do that. She replied that in the South Pacific they train you right. Maybe I should go to the South Pacific.

Miles Davis burst onto the scene with his "Kind of Blue" album. We listened to it over and over. Coltrane and Thelonius Monk also arrived in '59 but they were too far out for us. We were not sophisticated enough yet; it was very deep music.

John Waid, one of my best friends, had an older brother named Kenny. Kenny was a short, clean-cut looking kid, as was John. They came from a neighborhood further north, more toward the USC area, and had a lot of Spanish friends in the 39th Street gang. We heard a lot of stories about their friends in that gang and their exploits. John could call on help in special circumstances. Kenny was a fighter. He was probably meant to be a boxer; he just liked to fight. John took after his brother but wasn't as aggressive, but he was always ready to stand up and slug it out with some asshole. Years later, someone tried to rob Kenny as he was leaving a club in Hollywood late at night. I am sure he put up a fight. Someone hit him in the head with a gun butt. He was okay for a few days but then he died in his sleep from the injury.

John and I were pretty close. The cha-cha was in and was soon followed by the twist. We both liked to cha-cha and we frequented clubs and dances that featured Latin bands. John ended up marrying Rachel, a Spanish girl and a sister of one of the guys in the 39th Street gang. This cemented him to that gang which lasted until his divorce. John could do impersonations of famous people that could crack you up. It was clear he had a talent for showbiz.

John took me toward the ethnic side of life even further than the one I had been raised in. Once John and I traveled downtown to the Shrine Auditorium to see Ray Charles. He did about an hour of everybody's favorites including "I Got a Woman" and then he introduced someone who was a rising star and had a new record out. It was Stevie Wonder, or Little Stevie Wonder, as he was known then. He was only 12 or 13 at the time. He played "Waterboy" and "Fingertips." Johnny and I were the only white dudes there. We had cheap seats in the balcony but we got a real hit off that night.

Some time after we graduated high school, John Waid started studying acting and doing small parts in the local theatres. John and I traveled north to the Monterey Jazz Festival. That was a long way to go for music but in those days life was a blast and who cared. John remembers Horace Silver as his favorite performer. We tried to sleep at Ford Ord where John had done his basic training but it didn't work out, and we ended up sleeping in our car.

I was called a wop more times than I care to remember. In those days the term 'wop' was tossed around in a cute way, mostly by friends. I wasn't sure what people meant. I was very proud to be of Italian ancestry even though I wasn't sure why. I later found out that my heritage was both good and bad; I guess all races have skeletons in their closets. It was usually the English people that were the most verbal about race. They, of all people, should be ashamed of themselves. They have mistreated whole nations of people in the name of the Queen and the subsequent filling of her purse with the bounty from such endeavors. The French were right up there with the Brits. They have so much karma to live through. I am afraid the USA followed in their footsteps and took it to a new level with slavery.

It was the early sixties. Max Pavasik, a friend from Washington High, left in a bus headed for Mississippi. He was a political activist, the only one I knew and way ahead of the rest of us. He was going to the south to march in the Freedom movement. Martin Luther King was leading the way. Black people were tired of being discriminated against. It was the beginning of something that is still taking place today. A lot of people got hurt and many went to jail. Max made it back to the neighborhood and is famous in my mind.

Butch Ellis had a younger brother, Ron. He came into Embassy with Richard Ballew. Ron had a shitty home life and he and Butch were the first to get an apartment after high school. I became the third roommate and I tried living outside my parent's house; I must have been 17 or 18. Ron worked for a swimming pool contractor; he used to come home covered in cement dust. He was making really good money and bought a silver '58 Corvette. We ate a lot of canned lasagna and drank a lot of booze. We had parties all the time and the girls came and went like the weather. Once I went to Ron's parents' house for Thanksgiving dinner. His father was drunk as usual. He ended up throwing the turkey that his mother had prepared through the television set screen. I got a real good picture of why Butch and Ron had moved out.

Larry Thomas and I were both working at Pickering Sheet metal building catering trucks. One day a customer was picking up some trucks to drive back to Florida, and he offered Larry and I jobs in Florida. We didn't think much of the offer. Where was Florida? We were both working a lot and decided to take a vacation to Trinidad to check out the steel drum sound that came from there. We had fallen in love with the music; it was so exotic and mellow. I sold my '59 Pontiac to some car lot in Culver City and bought a 1935 De Soto from a friend of Van Bushman's, and we prepared to drive it to Florida and catch a plane to Trinidad. I have 8mm footage of Larry and I driving off from his parents' house beginning the journey. I don't know what Kerouac and those guys did, but we styled our trip from the beginning to be a bohemian adventure. I mean, come on … a 1935 De Soto 4-door sedan with no first gear or reverse as the transportation: we were just asking for excitement!

It was after the Cuban missile crisis of October 1962 and little did we know that planes were no longer flying anywhere near Cuba. Cuba was in our direct path heading to Trinidad, but we were not thinking of stuff like that when we took off. We were cruising along in the De Soto at night just across the border of Arizona. It was raining like hell and the windshield wipers didn't work when we hit a flash flood. The rain was running off the desert landscape so fast it had formed rivers of mud that were flowing across the highway. With no warning we hit the river of water and mud like a wall and the car came to a sudden stop. The engine sputtered but somehow we managed to get across the water that was gushing in through the doors and came to a rest on the other side. We did have a flashlight. The engine had been drenched with water and it had gotten into the carburetor. We crawled into the back and slept the night away. In the morning I removed the gas lines and did the best I could under the circumstances to remove the water from the engine. Between my efforts and help from the sun, we got it dried out and went on our way.

The bearings in the radiator fan started making noise just outside Deming, New Mexico. That old car hadn't seen use like this for years! We were pushing her and she seemed up to it. It was the same car that you see in old Hollywood movies, usually a taxicab in New York. It had spoke wheels, believe it or not, and the spare was mounted on the trunk. The fan vibrated on the used-up bearings, flew off and penetrated the radiator. We were broken down again. Now what? Someone towed us to a small gas station where they allowed me some space and a few tools so I could take the radiator out. If you have ever driven through the desert, you probably noticed that there are plenty of radiator shops along the highway, even in those days. It's hot and that's usually where the cars have trouble, in the cooling system. The guy there said he could fix the radiator. Unbelievable, but he did and it held water.

Next, we needed a new water pump. The guy at the radiator shop pointed to a parts house down the street and said we could try to find one there. The place had wooden floors, a wooden counter and some old desert rats that were playing cards and smoking near a window that was so dirty you couldn't see through it. We told the guy behind the counter what we needed. He thought for a moment and motioned us to follow him to way in the back of the building where there were some tall shelves. He climbed up a ladder and there, covered in an inch of desert dust, was our water pump. Again, unbelievable! In the old 8mm footage of the incident, Larry operated the camera as I clowned around, pretending to shovel parts out of the engine compartment. We got the car back together and continued our journey. We had already done the hard part, and the rest was clear sailing.

At a coffee house near the border where we crossed into Texas, we met some guys that were students at a college near there. They highly recommended we visit Juarez, Mexico. It was on our way, just across the border from Del Rio, Texas. Once we crossed the border into Mexico, we were to head east to Boys Town: prostitutes and booze. We headed south for Del Rio. Our De Soto sedan looked good as we headed down the dirt road that led out of Juarez and toward Boys Town. We had no trouble finding it. There were potholes the size of swimming pools and police carrying shotguns walking down the middle of the street. Boys Town was about one block long with buildings on either side. Each building was a bar and whorehouse combined. There must have been a thousand college age guys walking from one bar to the next in a steady stream. Larry and I went in the first one we came to. The drinks were cheap. We were under age in the U.S. but not here. Drink we did! One girl in particular caught our eye. She was a deaf mute and very pretty: slim and not too slutty looking. Her name was Mumbles. We did her as well as a few others. It was only two dollars and we each spent the better part of 10 dollars.

Later as we pulled into Miami, Larry was having trouble pissing. We went to the local clinic and he learned he had gonorrhea. I was luckier and didn't get any disease. We had to spend time in a hotel while he got well. We stayed at the old Fountainblue on the beach for several days. Larry met a girl by the pool that was with her mother, and he had an affair the best he could while recovering from the clap.

39 DESOTO

PAUL AND LARRY THOMAS

Paul Ferrara

ME AND MY MOTHER

PRODUCTION STILL 'THE RAINMAKER'

We were broke and hadn't even bought our tickets to Trinidad. We looked up the guy who had offered us jobs at Pickering. We were in luck, as he had two trucks that had been in wrecks. He had sent for the parts to fix them but didn't quite know who to ask to do the repairs. We worked for a couple of weeks and repaired the trucks. We had to be careful as we lay under the trucks in the dirt because there were scorpions everywhere. He was very happy and we were welcomed to stay and work for him. We took the money and went to buy our tickets.

There were no flights going near Cuba, like I mentioned. We were shot down. We were told the Bahamas had steel drums. That sounded like the best way to save our adventure, so we left our car at the catering place that we had worked for and took off. Now, Larry and I had never been anywhere outside of California. This was big! It was my first plane ride, and I think it was Larry's first, also. We landed and made our way to the one hotel on the island. It was built in the '40s and was a grand old hotel. We had to buy our drinking water. It was delivered to our room. It made you appreciate the states; we take water for granted. The cars had right hand steering and driving was on the left side of road, the exact opposite of what we were used to. We got the hang of it and rented a small convertible sports car. We drove around, circling the island looking for adventure.

We saw a lady down by the water trying to install a sail on a small sailboat. We pulled over and decided to check it out. She was older, maybe forty or so, but still attractive. She accepted our help. We got the sail up and she offered to pay us, but we declined. She asked us if we had ever sailed before. We lied and told her, of course we had. We became her crew for her daily cruises that took us to various different islands one by one. There are hundreds of islands there. It was beautiful; the water was crystal clear and a turquoise blue. Her name was Peggy. She fed us and treated us like family. I have a few moments on film.

Once we came home from a day of sailing and she invited us to dinner at a friend's house. We carried her duffle bags and walked up the dock, across the highway and into the jungle. There was a large old colonial house complete with pillars on the front. Inside we met someone she introduced as the Governor of the island. We sat at a long table with several other guests. From the duffle bag that was not far from the table we heard a loud croak, and a huge frog crawled out of the opening and leapt through the air, landing on the table and upsetting some food. It was one of those moments that stuck in my memory, both funny and a little frightening at the same time. The pomp of the occasion turned into a laughing good time. Now that I look back, I think Peggy was gay: she had short hair and sometimes a woman companion. One by one we checked out every nightclub on the island, night after night. We even ventured into shantytowns that we were advised not to visit. If Larry wasn't afraid, neither was I. The lure of steel drums and rum led us on.

Our stay in the Bahamas came to an end and we flew back to Miami. We were broke. On the way back home we decided to drive up the center of Florida instead of back through the Okeefenokee Swamp we had crossed coming in. We stopped at a small lunch stand for a burger. There was this large brown-eyed girl that waited on us and was interested in our journey. She said she wished she could get away from there. She motioned to her dad behind the counter and asked if she could leave with us. We looked at each other. So many girls, so little time. She waved goodbye from the diner as we pulled away and headed north to the Carolinas. I never forgot her, and I imagined all sorts of stories about her dad and her and her feelings of being trapped.

We were crossing Mississippi and looking a little ragged, and got pulled over for being odd and out of place. They examined our car and us and finally let us go. We were now dead broke and eating peanut butter and mayonnaise sandwiches. We had to send for some money and waited until it arrived at the Western Union. The money provided the gas and peanut butter to limp back across the USA toward L.A.

We pulled north out of Flagstaff in Arizona and visited the Grand Canyon. The De Soto was hanging in there, and we had arranged the back seat into a living area complete with sleeping space. We were eaten by mosquitoes all through the south and were thankful to be in the high desert. It felt good to be in the crisp air of Arizona looking out across the most amazing sight I had ever seen.

We finally got to Needles, the first little town in California you come to after leaving Arizona. It was hot, maybe 110 degrees. There is a long climbing section of Route 66 that heads west out of Needles. It's a steady three thousand foot climb, maybe five miles long and very demanding on the cooling system of cars. There were cars pulled over all along the side with their hoods up and hot steam shooting into the air from their engine compartments. We headed for L.A. and sailed by all the stranded motorists; we were happy to be in the De Soto with its new cooling.

When we got home I sold the De Soto to Butch Ellis for fifty bucks and a bicycle. I needed another car. Strangely enough, a friend of Van Bushman's was selling his '35 De Soto. What was it with these De Sotos? He was a mechanic at a Chrysler dealer and it had been his pet car for years. He had put a brand new Chrysler V-8 in it and it was fast. I bought it and we raced everyone in town. It came with a sign that had a handle you waved out the window. It read: WE WON. The beauty of it was that it looked completely stock. We would pull next to a new Chevy and egg the driver into a race. Chevy's were fast in those days; they had the best engine going. We would take off from a signal and as I shifted to second gear, leap ahead of the guy. The race was over so fast. That's when someone in the back seat would wave the sign: WE WON. We both would pull up to the next red light and stop. The drivers usually said something like, "What the hell is under that hood?" They wanted to know why they had been beaten so badly.

I decided to enroll in El Camino Jr. College. Dick Ensch was going there and I had wasted enough time; two years had passed since my graduation from high school. I enrolled in the pre-med program, which meant plenty of science and math. I had to take an elective sport requirement and I first chose archery: simple enough, can't get hurt and again, plenty of girls. The coach was Hengstellar, and he also taught wrestling and boxing. I can't remember why, but I ended up in both the boxing class and then his wrestling class. I must have liked him or was just ready for some punishment. He was a demanding sort of guy and would make us run around the track for hours at a time. People that weren't up to it used to puke. I had come from cross-country and I managed the running ok, but the wrestling was tough. I have never experienced anything as kick-ass in my life as wrestling and boxing also, for that matter. The two-minute rounds seemed to last a lifetime. Whether it was boxing or wrestling, the amount of energy spent was huge.

I met Dave Pritchard in one of Hengstellar's classes. He was in the acting department. I thought he was a pretty boy, except he had been working with weights for years and was as strong and buff as they come. He studied the German language and was very studious, a good example for me. John Waid got a part in a play in a small community theatre, and I accompanied him to one of his rehearsals. The director said that the small part of the window washer that enters the scene causing a commotion had to be cast, to better understand the timing of the scene. As I sat in the dark audience watching the rehearsal, he asked me if I would mind doing the part to help with the timing. John encouraged me and I said ok. My part required me to enter from the rear of the set and begin washing the exterior of the set's window. I had been cast and I continued the part right through the production. I even took a bow at the end of the play each night. There was a strange, exciting feeling that rushed through me as the play progressed up to the curtain call. The lights blind you a little and you're standing there while hundreds of people applaud. Shit, this is what has been missing! Some approval. I was hooked. I changed my major the first chance I could and joined Dave Pritchard in the theatre department. My dad was mad; he wanted me to be a doctor and asked if I was going to be a fag like the rest of the actors in the world. Once he got over the shock, he was the first to attend my various theatrical endeavors.

A man named Dr. Howard Banks ran the Theatre Department at El Camino. He billed himself as the Shakespeare authority in our area. We built a complete replica of the Globe Theatre in Stratford, England where Shakespeare had performed his plays. It was quite accurate and the school plays received a lot of attention. I did everything from work on costumes to small parts. Painting the sets, lighting, and daily drama exercises were the curriculum. I started getting confident about acting. I got my first good small part in Richard the Third. Victor Nastasia was also in the Theatre Department and we became friends. He got me a job at Andy's Pizza and taught me my first guitar scale.

Dave Pritchard from wrestling and I became close friends. My parents had moved to Ladera Heights, which was in the opposite direction and further away from El Camino. I accepted Pritchard's offer to become roommates. We found a cool red cabin-like house in Hermosa Beach two blocks from the ocean with three bedrooms. We found a third guy to go in with us. I met Russ Heatherington at El Camino and we had mutual friends, but Dave and Russ did not get along and eventually Dave had to kick his ass and evict him.

The Theatre Department was a close-knit group of people and there were parties all the time. Jeannie Appel was a beautiful blonde from Palos Verdes. She looked a little French and had beautiful breasts for her size. A lot of guys wanted her. We dated for a while and Pritchard dated her best friend. The four of us used to end up at the red cabin in Hermosa a lot.

Larry Thomas was working a temporary job downtown in the garment district. He knew people downtown because he went there everyday to teach Judo. The story goes that he was pushing a rack of garments down the street, took a break and stepped into a bar for a beer. He was sitting next to a man who started up a conversation. Larry was very good looking and had a great personality. The man told Larry that he needed help with this great idea to buy garments in Europe and sell them to the chain stores like Sears or Penney's or Robinson's. Larry went to Europe and bought some hot items. When he came back, they landed a deal with a major chain. The next thing I heard was that Larry was driving a Ferrari. They hit the jackpot! He was riding high for a long while and ended up with two Ferraris. He got into cocaine. He called me one Christmas when I was at the ranch. He was being nostalgic and wanted to know if I was happy ... I told him I was.

I needed money. I went back to Pickering Sheet Metal and asked if they would let me work part-time. Al the owner was the best boss I ever had. Not only did he let me name my own hours, but he also invited me to his house for dinner so I could become acquainted with his daughter.

Al's brother nicknamed Pick was the foreman. I got along great with him. He was a body builder and it showed. He was an impressive guy. We used to go on fishing trips paid for by Al to the Coronado Islands off the coast of San Diego. The night before we would go and party in Tijuana, and arrive at the boat and sleep as the boat departed the harbor early the next day.

The drinking was heavy while we were in Tijuana. We used to like a place called the Long Bar ... there were about twenty of us and we kind of felt safe in those numbers. Pick used to arm-wrestle anyone that wanted to, loser paying for the beer. There was always some drunk that challenged him, and they always lost. Hemingway would have been proud. We used to catch plenty of yellowtail tuna in those days. Everyone brought fish back. You could trade your catch for already canned fish if you wanted, but the best was bringing it back whole in some ice. We used to have huge barbecues in Hermosa Beach with my catch. Usually there were three or four large fish weighing about 60 or 70 lbs. dressed out that was marinated and put on the barby. A lot of people showed up from the neighborhood and the Theatre Department at El Camino.

Al Pickering asked me to help steer his nephew Sonny, who worked with us, into the college scene. I did and he ended up living with us at the beach. We traveled to work together. It was good; Sonny was a good guy.

One of the guys we worked with had a small boat that was 16 or 18 feet long, and one night in a drunken stupor we decided to take it to Catalina. The guy who owned the boat, his wife, Sonny and I left early in the morning. We had little in the way of supplies but we did manage to include a keg of beer. The water was calm and we made it to the island with no problem. We camped north of the resort area in an area that is marked Boy Scout Camp on the map. Wrigley, the millionaire who owned the island, had given the Boy Scouts the use of the area. It hadn't been used for several years and only an old chimney rose up from the sand. There must have been a large house there at one time.

We arrived at night, pulled the boat up on the sand and went to sleep on the beach. We woke when we were startled by some crashing noises; it was pitch black and we couldn't see a thing, but something was moving close to us. As our eyes adjusted to the night we saw lots of red eyes darting about. A herd of wild boar surrounded us! They had shiny tusks and looked like they meant business. They started to charge us and we ran like hell. I climbed up the rock chimney and hung on for dear life. Two people managed to get back to the boat. When it was safe I also made a dash for the boat. We found out later that there were herds of these pigs all over the island. We had made camp in an area that was used as a trash dump. We slept the remainder of the night on the boat. So much for the free campsite!

The next day we drank the rest of the beer and decided to head back to the mainland. We took off around one o'clock. Well, everyone knows the currents and the wind pick up in the Catalina straits in the afternoon … everyone, that is, except us. The waves were crashing over the bow of the boat. I was very seasick and stayed in the small cabin with the woman for most of the four hours it took to get back. We thought it was all over several times. We bailed a lot of water to keep from sinking. The boat was way to small for the trip we took it on. You live and learn. We turned in the empty keg and got the refund and never talked about trying that again. I lost track of Sonny at a certain point and haven't seen him since.

Black music had arrived, Ray Charles was mainstream and different from the R & B singers we were used to like Chubby Checker and Little Richard.

Don't get me wrong, I was a huge fan of the twist; you could learn it very quickly. Everyone was twisting the night away. Ray Charles took the world into a groove that was something new. His blindness was a way for us to see. I think it was the blues part of his music that was new to us. Soul music. What was soul? It was something you felt. You can tell when someone has it. If you connect with someone's soulfulness it can transform you. You understand the hardship, the hungry feeling of poverty, and the feeling of being a slave, or having your family ripped apart. Loneliness, hurt by love, scorned, whipped: you name it. It could also be the feelings you felt for your family: your brothers. There's a universal compassion you tap into, where all humans huddled on the earth, no matter what segregation has taught us, become related. I think the Righteous Brothers picked up on soul and turned it into their own thing, white soul. "You've Lost That Loving Feeling" was the song. Everyone was singing it. Soul had arrived. Motown turned soul into pop. They added the street corner doo-wop, some heavy bass and drums and Diana Ross and the Supremes. Where it would end nobody knew, but we were soon to find out. Ever hear of the Beatles?

I started trying out for small parts in the local theatres. I got the part of Jimmy in "The Rainmaker" at the Westchester Playhouse. This was a big moment for me; it was so professional. The cast was the best I had worked with, and they forced me to push myself. The role was suited to me. I was picked on and pushed around by a family of very assertive people. It took place in a rural setting on a farm. One day a guy showed up and claimed he could bring water to our drought-stricken existence. I believed him and so did my sister, who fell in love with the stranger. It's a great play. I became Jimmy, my character. It was what acting was all about, becoming your character. We performed that play to a packed audience every night and twice on Saturdays. At one point a fight breaks out in the living room, there are punches thrown and I get hit in the jaw. It's where the play finally takes a little turn. What has happened to this quiet little family? All the tensions come to the top. It doesn't matter about the rain. At least every other night the guy throwing the punch, (I think it was one of my brothers), missed and actually hit me. It made it seem more real, but it did hurt for a minute or two. The show was a local hit and ran for a couple of months. One night there was a group of young girls that approached me after the curtain call. They were aggressive and wanted my autograph. I was very thrilled to be at the center of so much attention. I was hooked; I had swallowed the bait.

In the final year at El Camino, I played the part of Balthazar in Romeo and Juliet. All of the class had some part in the play. There were a lot of parties. Drama instructor Howard Banks was in rare form as he directed us. The costumes had been hand sewn with the help of professionals. I had a small but significant part and was killed early on in the play. Everyone learned all the parts and Shakespeare became a part of my life. It was fun to read it in the meter and all, but I didn't always understand everything. There were tons of discussions about the interpretation of the various plays and their characters. This was valuable preparation for the work that lay ahead, understanding what you were doing.

First James Dean, and then Marlon Brando and Marilyn Monroe, were showing everyone the way to make it real. There were schools of acting springing up on the west and the east coasts that emphasized the method and theory of acting. It was a great time to be a student of acting. By the time we arrived at UCLA, we were ready. Classes on playwriting, public speaking, body movement, set construction and play production were pounded down our throats until we had been immersed in it so far that we walked around in a trance the rest of the curriculum.

My minor was in African studies. Don't ask me why; I don't exactly remember what I was thinking. I think it represented something very exotic and it helped to expand my horizon. I did descend from the likes of Christopher Columbus, you know. Literature class was also a well-embraced experience. The classics as well as the contemporary books were places where I could lose myself. People that don't read are missing out big-time.

The President of the United States had been assassinated. John F. Kennedy, the first Roman Catholic president. Kennedy had brought hope and the image of Camelot. Peace and Harmony. On November 22, 1963 he was killed in Texas by a sniper. It still isn't 100 percent clear what happened. The nation mourned, with images of his small children, watching as they buried him. It was a heavy time.

The Beatles and the Rolling Stones invaded America with their infectious music. They had taken the music of the black artists from the Mississippi delta and factory towns of Chicago and reinvented it. "(I Can't Get No) Satisfaction" by the Stones and "Please Please Me" and "Love Me Do" from the Beatles helped to bridge the dark political hole that was the landscape of America. It was just what we needed. It changed our lives forever. People waited in line to buy the records. Later the Americans began to retool and we had our own wave of rock music. Bob Dylan became popular as a political balladeer. His songs gave us a lot of food for thought, and we actually did start thinking. Some of my friends and I began to trace the origins of the songs coming out of England. We discovered the whole blues thing starting with Robert Johnson all the way to Chuck Berry; it happened right in our own backyard. The slaves of the southern U.S. were pleading, crying, asking for Jesus to help them. It came out of the spiritual arena of the churches and landed in the streets of poverty and trouble. Robert Johnson had done drugs and claimed to have sold his soul to the devil in exchange for the gift of singing and playing the guitar like he did.

UCLA FILM DEPARTMENT

Dave Pritchard, Victor Nastasia, and I all graduated from the Theatre Department of El Camino around the same time and headed for UCLA. UCLA had a very respected theatre department. I saw a new film called "La Dolce Vita" by Fellini, an Italian director. It was one of my first foreign films and I was taken by the magic that he created. It was the first time I ever concentrated on the directing aspect of a film. The camera work was brilliant. Storaro was Fellini's cameraman on a lot of films. When I got to UCLA I decided to enroll in the Film Department. I still kept classes in the acting division but I moved closer and closer to film. I thought I would like to act in films and I did several acting jobs for classmates. When it was my time to direct, the experience blew me away and I was again hooked.

My parents had bought me a new V.W. to go to college in. One day after school I was headed to court in downtown L.A. I had hurt my back at work and Pickering's insurance company was fighting about paying my medical bills. I was on the Santa Monica Freeway heading east toward downtown L.A. in heavy traffic, and had come to a stop along with the other cars in front of me. I heard a loud crash and looked into the rear view mirror to see the Ford Mustang behind me jump into the air and crash down on the rear of my car. My bug was totaled, my back was hurt again and I had to take a cab the rest of the way to court. I got a small settlement and bought a BSA motorcycle to get around. I had that motorcycle all through college and afterwards.

It was 1964 and I had moved out of my parents' house in Ladera Heights. I was sharing an apartment with an acquaintance from the film department named Richard Blackburn, right in the heart of Fraternity Row next to campus on Kelton Ave. in Westwood. I could walk or ride my motorcycle to campus, no problem. Richard was an east coast kind of guy. His family had lived in Grosse Pointe, Michigan and was now in the steel business in Fontana, California and well off. I went home with him a few times for dinner. I had to ride my motorcycle to Watts every night and build catering trucks until 2 a.m., then ride back to our apartment and sleep enough to get up in the morning and attend classes. Blackburn helped me with a lot of the academic stuff that was required. He used to help me write papers and sometimes actually wrote the whole thing.

The Film Department at that time was a vibrant thing. Film had only just become part of the curriculum for schools. Teaching the art, like the art itself, was in its infant state. Film had always been taken for granted as part of our culture. Now we were studying it and treating it as a legit form of expression, just like painting and literature. We had classes in old army barracks-style bungalows in the back corner of the campus. The funky nature of our surroundings helped fuel our creativity. We learned a guerilla style approach to filmmaking that was popular at the time in Europe called verite: cinema verite. Truffaut, Fellini, Antonioni, and Godard were our heroes. We saw every film that Europe produced at the time. The theatres near Westwood had foreign films all the time; we were first to see them and proud of it. Our classes discussed them, films like "The 400 Blows," "Breathless," "Jules and Jim." These films were our teachers and inspiration. The professors were hip and some, like my favorite, Colin Young, wrote for the European film magazines. Among all the teachers there, he affected me the most.

We used to attend parties and drink wine all night and discuss the nature of everything with him. Professor Young had parties at his house in Topanga Canyon. Plenty of wine. He was so hip. I remember after the debut of my film that I had made in his 170 Production class, he came up to me and told me I had saved the day with my project. "The End of Summer" was my first film and it starred Dick Blackburn and Jeannie Appel. He encouraged me no end with his comments. Ray Manzarek was in the same class and his film "Evergreen," and my film "End of Summer" were chosen for the showing in Royce Hall. This meant we got to cut the negative and get a print with sound attached. It was quite an honor. My parents showed up and were quite impressed.

I had completed most of my requirements in Jr. College and had a lot of electives available once I arrived at UCLA. I took photography almost every semester. I had also enrolled in the music ethnomusicology department. I had an interest in the African music I had been hearing in my African studies classes. The "Missa Luba" album was a choir of Africans singing all sorts of stuff from tribal chants to classical and religious standards, tunes you would recognize. It was very popular and we listened to it over and over. Maybe I was looking for the roots of the soul sound. I started a class to learn Indian music. East Indian. The sitar was the instrument of Ravi Shankar … that was soul. I met a lot of people in the Art Department while taking photography classes.

I started dating an artist girl with an apartment near Venice Beach on the corner of Washington and Ocean Park. She met some guy and decided to get married. I wanted her apartment. It was one of the old original buildings and had four apartments, two on the first floor and two on the second, divided by a hallway and staircase. It was two blocks from the beach and the front of the building faced west toward the ocean. Its glass enclosed front porch offered a view of the ocean if you looked between two rooftops. I got lucky and the place became mine for forty dollars a month. The people in those days that inhabited the area were mostly old and Jewish, and looked the other way to the antics of the new artist /hippie crowd that lived sandwiched in between them. Upstairs from me were two people from the UCLA art department. It was a friendly place to live, cheap and safe.

Not far from my apartment on Main Street there was a small storefront restaurant run by a wonderful black couple. Olivia's had the best soul food in the world. The lady was more like a mother than a restaurant owner. She fed people in need and was cool about running a tab. They served corn bread and chili with coffee for a dollar, and it was a true bargain. Everybody went there. It was a favorite of Jim Morrison's as well as Ray's, mine, David Thompson's and all my other friends. This was the first place I met Mary Werbelow, Jim's girlfriend. She was in high school when she met Jim and had followed him to California from Clearwater Beach, Florida. She had dark hair with screaming blue eyes and a body to die for. Jim used to bring her to the Friday screenings at the UCLA Film Department. They were inseparable for a long time.

I was starting to get high with my friends more and more. Ron Ellis, my old Embassy brother, was living with his older brother and another dude near where the Venice Beach Pier is now. We were still close and I spent a lot of time there at his house that looked like a castle. A short walk from his house was Hamburger Square. A bar in that square became our hangout: Hinano's, as it was called then and still is today. The majority of its customers were sailors and bohemians. The owner's son eventually took it over. He was a sailor and had a large sailboat that he kept in the harbor, which later became the Marina del Rey. In those days Venice and the old marina area was a sleepy little place. After years of hanging out in Hinano's I learned that Little J was a smuggler. He used to sail to Mexico and bring back kilos of pot. He trusted me, and once I actually accompanied him to a small garage near Hinano's where he had about a thousand kilos of marijuana stacked.

I was part of a crowd of people that were pretty close in those days, and between UCLA and Hinano's I kept pretty busy. Babe met me in Hinano's one night to drink and catch up. We were playing pool, double or nothing. I was winning that night and I had Babe down about 100 bucks. He was pissed and frustrated. There were some people sitting around the table drinking and watching us play. One of the guys was really drunk and started to harass Babe. I knew Babe's angry side and was hoping for the best. Babe lost again and the guy kept it up, asking Babe if he was ever going to finish etc. Babe turned, flipped his pool cue into batting position and cracked the fiberglass stick across the dude's head. He dropped like a stone, bleeding from the ear. Babe wanted to move in for the kill. I told him the guy could already be dead and persuaded him to leave before the cops came. He agreed and split.

I became good friends with Carol, the artist that lived over the garage, in the alley, next to Ron's house. She liked to smoke pot and paint, and I helped her get smoke from time to time. Once she was having a party and her best girlfriend brought her boyfriend, Clint. Clint Eastwood. He was on TV at the time playing Rowdy Yates on "Gunsmoke." He smoked and drank wine and was a regular guy. I slept with Carol from time to time and considered her a good friend. She was older and had a regular job somewhere. Duke was a tall thin English dude that had spent his life sailing in the Caribbean. He was the first guy I saw wearing an earring; I think he was a pirate in a previous life. Duke eventually moved in with Carol, got cancer and died. Little J would sell me kilos of pot. I then took it home and divided it into small amounts for sale to my friends at school. I had the perfect connection and I managed to keep the two worlds, UCLA and Venice, separate.

I was still working at Pickering Sheet Metal at nights, I started making stainless steel paintings with scraps, (and sometimes, not scraps) of sheet metal. They were three or four foot squares of mirror-like stainless steel with grooves that I pressed into them like sunbursts and rays emanating from the corners out across the space. I masked them off and sprayed the sections with candy apple colors: beautiful, but heavy. They were on display at Steve Richmond's store on the Venice Beach boardwalk, the Earth Rose. When he was selling the place, he called me asking what I wanted to do with my paintings. Foolishly, I told him to give or throw them away. I regret that, but I had no place to store them and I guess it was time to move on.

On a bright summer day as I was returning from a swim at the beach not far from my apartment, I noticed a young woman walking on the opposite side of the street heading in the same direction. She smiled as she noticed me and that was all it took. I crossed the street and walked along side her. She was in her late thirties, still very attractive. She had on a bikini top and a sarong around her waist and beautiful skin that was bronzed by the sun. She had a body built for fun. I told her I lived right there and pointed to my apartment. She said she just lived two blocks up and that made us neighbors. She asked if I wanted to get high. That's the way it was in those days. I invited her in and she pulled out some small pills she had in her bag. She said they were Disoxyn, some kind of very pure speed used for depression. We smoked a joint and dropped the pills. About an hour later we were higher than hell, and she told me she was a high priced call girl in Beverly Hills. She became very affectionate under the influence of the pills and asked if we could take a shower together. I had an old claw foot bathtub and got in first, adjusting the water. She got in behind me and started washing my back and washed my front and back thoroughly. She reached around my waist and soaped up my groin. I was hard as a rock. No one had ever done that to me. I turned around and she French kissed me deep. She kissed my nipples and worked her way down and proceeded to give me an expert blowjob. All the while, the shower was spilling over my shoulders and bouncing off her head.

She visited me from time to time off and on for two years. She would call late at night or in the early morning and ask if she could come over. It was always the same: take the speed and fuck until the sun came up. Later I found out she was living with some guy but who cared, as long as she came to see me. She had this trick she had learned in her escort business. She would sit on top of me in a cowgirl position, grinding away. Slowly she would lift her legs one at a time and pivot around to a reverse cowgirl position and continue on until she faced me again without missing a stroke. Ah, youth! Eventually we would nod off and when I awoke she would be gone. This happened over and over. She was a great teacher / partner for me. I had a lot of sexual energy in those days and it was good to spend it. It kept me calm and focused.

On the campus of UCLA near the Theatre Arts Department was a small catering wagon with tables arranged around it. We called it the Gypsy Wagon. People from the Art Department, the Theatre and Film Departments all gathered there between classes. It became a famous meeting place. All sorts of life were played out at the Gypsy Wagon: arguments, discussions, connections, love and breakups … you name it, it happened there. Some of us used to bring small bottles of alcohol onto the campus and mix it with the cokes from the Gypsy Wagon. Joints were rolled and smoked; we had a lot of parties there.

I was one of the first to discover the Lucky U, a beer bar and greasy spoon near Sepulveda and Wilshire. At that time in Westwood there was an ordinance against serving alcohol near the university. The bar was just outside the restricted area. It was frequented by old farts, from the V.A. hospital nearby in Westwood. Most of the time it was a friendly place. Times sure have changed, huh? Now there are bars lined up from one end of Westwood to the other. I would park my BSA motorcycle near the Gypsy Wagon and shoot over to the Lucky U when the opportunity presented itself. I loved hanging out with the slightly damaged. There are not a lot of pretensions; things are pretty much what they are.

After a while there was a small crowd of people from the Film Department that used to frequent that place. Felix Venable, Jim Morrison, Jose Gonzales and I were some of the core group. The pitchers of beer were cheap and the food didn't make you sick. There were a couple of pool tables and we were welcome when we walked in.

My first film project was a short about some guys in hoods that ride around on motor scooters and terrorize the old bums that hang around the Westwood Cemetery, a veteran's cemetery located next to the freeway near Wilshire and Sepulveda. Living and playing in that neighborhood, it was just natural that we would cruise through the cemetery to impress girls and stuff. Anyway that was the idea of my film. There was an old character that I used to drink with a lot at the Lucky U. I bought him beers and convinced him that he should act in my short film. He was aware of the idea of film, and I convinced him to play the lead. The story line was the bums are relentlessly pursued by an anonymous gang of scooter people. The music I cut the film to was "Ride of the Valkyries." It was weird; it held your attention, but not much payoff. The tension was the dynamic that worked the best.

LSD was first studied in Westwood, both at the Wadsworth V.A. center and the UCLA Psychology Department. At one point there was an ad in the campus paper asking for volunteers to try acid and be paid for the experience. A lot of people tried it, including Jose Gonzales. LSD was a funny drug. Some people tried it and saw the Promised Land, while others flipped out and saw monsters. Good trips and bad trips. My experience tells me that taking any drug only amplifies where you are naturally. If you're in a good place, you have a good trip. If you're in a bad place, then you might easily have a bad trip.

Jose was a volatile guy, sweet but just a little bit strange. He came from somewhere in South America. In a private moment, Jose told me that his mother had molested him as a child, had sex with him. He couldn't remember it being all that bad, which gave him another set of problems.

I shot films for several people in my time at that school, including Jose. I had ability and a knack for photography was developing. Jose's film was about a guy much like the legendary Sisyphus who keeps struggling against the tide up the mountain, only to fall back down and begin again. Jose went to his girlfriend's apartment one day and found her having sex with one of his friends. He flipped out. He stabbed her thirty or forty times as his friend ran for his life. He stabbed her repeatedly in her eyes. He told me he was trying to kill her soul. He said he was experiencing flashbacks to his mother's abuse and saw his mother in her eyes. He was proven guilty of the crime and sent to Atascadero State Hospital near Camarillo, the same place that Timothy Leary was sent to.

I hadn't heard from Jose for a long time. Years later I was living with my second wife Lorraine in Encino, California when I received a phone call from him. He had been released on a government technicality and was driving a cab in L.A. He was lonely and he wanted to see me. Oh my god! I made excuses until I ran out of them. I finally blamed it on my wife; I said that she was scared of him. He understood, but he needed somebody. What could I do? I felt scared.

Felix Venable was an older student, pushing forty. He had a huge capacity for drugs and alcohol that eventually killed him. While he was alive, he led the drunken party brigade. His knowledge of literature and philosophy was way ahead of ours. He was in transition from the beat generation to the hippie generation, as were a lot of people. He was a friend to many of us including Jim Morrison, Phil O'Leno and John DeBella, and we looked to him for direction. We often thought Felix knew which way to go but it proved to be wrong many times, and we had to learn to listen to ourselves.

The book that changed my life was "Siddartha" by Hermann Hesse. Its main theme is that try as you will, it is hard to impart the lesson of first-hand experience to someone. Experience is the best teacher. Hendrix asked, 'Are you experienced?' We were all trying to become experienced. Meanwhile, we were enrolled in film school. Could the adventure be combined into an overall experience that produced filmmakers that had something experienced to say? Only time would tell.

Dave Pritchard and I still hung out. He found a fun thing to do and he included me. We would drive around upper Brentwood around Sunset Boulevard on trash day and search for cool stuff that the rich people were throwing away. You would be surprised at the stuff we found. We sold it second hand and generated some money.

I had my pad in Ocean Park fixed up pretty good and it was a meeting place for our small crowd. The apartment was one room wide and you had to walk through each room to reach the kitchen and the back porch that I had turned into a dark room. I bought some beautiful material, dark green with a paisley design, that I draped over the windows in the parlor and the bedroom. In the parlor was a hookah, it was a traditional water pipe from the Middle East with a flexible pipe that you could pass around. I had one that I bought at an Indian store in Hollywood. It filtered the smoke through a bowl of water and thus cooled it off. I kept it filled with water and plenty of Mexican weed.

One day a guy named Norm from the Film Department showed up at my door. He had a beautiful, petite blonde with him who he introduced as Shelly. They had been lovers but now were just friends. He said he had to leave, and Shelly asked if she could stay. She stayed for about three months! Shelly's parents were newly arrived to Beverly Hills; she needed some space.

Shelly was an artist, a sculptor-in-training. She showed me how to mix a batch of plaster and form it into a block that could be sculpted. I did it big: I cast the stuff in a huge box. We put an armature in it that stood on a base. I proceeded to whack, chisel, and file that block into a rather graceful dolphin in mid-jump.

I remember days at the beach in summer with Ray Manzarek, his girlfriend Dorothy, Shelly and I. We drove in Ray's V W bug all the way down Main Street through Venice, past the canals and the oil wells to the huge stretch of sand next to the marina jetty. We usually drank some wine and smoked a joint.

Shelly was a willing love partner. It was the first time I had ever lived with someone. We spent a lot of time stoned on acid, naked, listening to music and making love. We got into a fight one day that escalated into me slapping her lightly. It freaked her out. I think she over-reacted a little; anyway, she left. I tried to apologize for a long time, asking for another chance. It didn't work out and I gave up.

One of the teachers in the Art Department put together a blues-oriented band called City Lights. Some of our friends played in the band. Rob Lewine, a fellow film student, played bass. I helped Peter Kleinert, an artist that shared a co-op studio space near Main Street in Venice, put on underground rock concerts in deserted buildings and artists' lofts in downtown Santa Monica. The concerts were like mini Love-Ins complete with free LSD at the door.

I put together a light show that mimicked the commercial rock shows of the day. I bought some micro switches from the local electronics store and arranged them into a keyboard. I ran wires from the keyboard out to banks of colored lights mounted in front of the band. The operator played the keyboard as he watched the band and tried to stay in beat as the lights flickered in syncopation. It was fun to do and people volunteered all the time. Some played the keyboard better than others. It was fun to sit so close to the music and be a part of the show. The lights kept burning out and we needed a constant supply. They were the same lights used to light the fronts of the apartment buildings all around Westwood and Santa Monica. Those expensive lights were the objective of many late night early morning raids.

Joan Churchill drove as we slowly cased the building and then struck with precision. The lights were ours. The next concert was lit.

The war in Viet Nam was raging. The French colonialists had really started something. They were being driven out by Ho Chi Minh who was backed by the Chinese communists. The American government feared the entire area of Southeast Asia would become communist. We backed a puppet government in South Viet Nam in the hopes we could block their advance from the north. All the males at UCLA of proper draft age were fearful of being sent to Viet Nam. We saw the body bags coming back from the war every night on the evening news. I received a deferment, first for my back and second for being a student. It was a good reason to keep your grades up.

I became very good friends with Kip Stevens, a fellow film student. He played guitar and we played our guitars together on a regular basis. We produced music similar to Sandy Bull's sound. It was a mix of eastern and western rhythms with jams that went on for as long as they felt good. We were composing and improvising as we went.

Our small group of buddies had grown to include; J. David Wyles, David Thompson, Kit Gray, Joan Churchill, Katie Miller, Tim Wawsiniak, Peter Belsito, Kip, me, and others I'm sure I've forgotten. We all lived near 3rd Street in Ocean Park and could walk to each other's houses. David Wyles had rented a large old Victorian beach house on the corner of 19th and Pacific.

We were all there one afternoon; Kip and I were jamming. David Wyles walked in with a woman on his arm he had met at the coffee shop. He introduced her as Susanne. She was the ex-wife of Bobby Driscoll, the child actor busted for being the cat burglar of Malibu. He had been arrested and was doing time. She was lonely and just wandering around the beach area. She asked if we wanted to get high. She had a thick French accent; it sounded so good. We had been smoking pot but were open to some more. She pulled out a little black case and opened it. She had crystal methedrine, a syringe, spoon and matches; she was a traveling shooting gallery. We all wanted to try it but the needle was a first for us. She was so sweet, like your mother as she tied off your arm. My veins are big to begin with but when you tie off my arm, well, they almost exploded up under the skin. She had no trouble slipping the needle into my arm. The crystals had been soaked and boiled in some water on the spoon and sucked up into the syringe. Once the needle was into my vein she pushed on the plunger. As she injected the meth into my blood I could feel its effect almost immediately; a warm sensation was rushing up from my feet to my head. I had never felt pure euphoria before. My only experience was with LSD and that had a lot of mental stuff attached. This was different; it was pure feeling, no brain games. She shot us up, one by one. She seemed to enjoy turning us on. We gave her some money to cover the cost of the meth.

Kip and I played our guitars for maybe eight hours. Our fingers were sore and about to bleed. The sun was coming up. Wow, the night had passed away and we were still high and wired. We all went for a long walk on the boardwalk by the beach. No one could sleep. The comedown is a little rough: you're tired but cannot sleep. Susanne came back the next day with the same stuff. We did it for three or four days. Meth is very addictive. It is so good in the early stages but with long-term usage you get skinny, your teeth fall out and there is permanent brain damage. Susanne and a lot of other people were strung out on it. I could understand why.

Most of the time we were content to just smoke pot in the hookah, then travel as a group into Westwood to see a foreign film at the Nuart Theatre or to an all-night deli to satisfy our munchies. A side effect of smoking pot is that it makes you so hungry you just want to munch something, anything.

I was still working at Pickering nights. I drove my motorcycle in the morning on the freeway from Venice to Westwood. After the day at school I rode to Watts and put in as many hours as I could. The shift ended at 2 am, then it was back to Venice for some sleep before the next day of school. My grades were not terrific but I graduated. We all took editing, camera, lighting and production classes and at the end of each semester, had a showing of everyone's production class work. Ray Manzarek was in the same class as me; we shared many classes. I acted in his films and he helped with my projects.

My 170 film project "The End of Summer," starred my ex-roommate Dick Blackburn and my old girlfriend from El Camino, Jeannie A. Colin Young was the instructor in charge of my class. Under his tutorship I put together a story of two young people who go for a bike ride at the beach and stumble upon a mysterious house. The house was the castle near Hamburger Square # 11 ½ Anchorage in Venice Beach where Ron Ellis lived. They find the door open and go in. They are alone. They explore. They put on some music. It was bossa nova, "The Girl from Ipanema," and they dance. They sink to the floor. They make out.

SHOOTING MY 170 PROJECT "END OF SUMMER" FROM
LEFT TO RIGHT: ME, STANTON KAY, CHRIS WOODS, STEVEN
LARNER AND COLIN YOUNG.
PHOTO BY LLOYD "BUTCH" ELLIS

Previously in our class discussion Colin Young and Stanton Kay, my cameraman, suggested that it was too easy. What if they don't make love? What if there's some problem? The new script was a secret. I told Blackburn and Jeannie that I would talk them through the love scene. When he would have naturally leaned in for the kiss, I stopped the scene again and again until he became confused and frustrated. I told him to take out a cigarette and light it. His confusion came across as his inability to complete the lovemaking. Blackburn never really forgave me for the trick I played on him and Jeannie. At the last moment the guy turns away for some reason. The moment is embarrassing. Is he gay or what? Jeannie was so hot. What happened? We never really find out. We find them later in a quiet scene sitting at a table eating some ice cream. As Blackburn eats his cone he gets some ice cream on his nose and the girl laughs and wipes it off for him, breaking the tension. The camera pulls back, the music score rises up and the situation is defused. The film was well received.

Jim's student film from our UCLA years had caused a buzz that wasn't necessarily all good. His print had fallen apart during the screening. In essence, the professor claimed that Jim was a bad filmmaker because of this faulty editing. In retrospect, I would have to say that it was a bad call on the teacher's part to come down on him so heavy. The visuals of Jim's film are vivid in my mind today. He turned the camera on his own crew. They were in Phil O'Leno's parents' house, drinking and smoking grass. Someone rolled a joint and they passed it around. They were high and the camera was hand held. The girlfriend of one of the crew stripped down to her undies and climbed on top of the T.V. She was dancing slowly and was threatening to take it all off. The program on the television just happened to be a documentary on Hitler's army marching into Paris. The combination of the semi-nude girl dancing and the Nazis marching is unforgettable. He was being free, letting the situation develop and capturing the moments on film. It was so pure. So his editing was not so good: his eye and his creativity made up for it.

Ray's autobiographical film was "Evergreen." I played the guy who steals his girlfriend. He finds a new girl in the Art Department. His new girlfriend was actually his real-life live-in girlfriend Dorothy playing the art student. Dorothy Fugikawa and Ray had a small apartment near me in Ocean Park. Ray was the first in our crowd to discover acid. He told me he had something I would like. They invited me to join them on Saturday morning in their apartment over the garage. He had scored three sugar cubes laced with LSD, and he and Dorothy wanted to share the experience with me. We took them first thing in the morning with some tea and honey. We listened to Japanese flute music for hours as we sank down on the floor and went into a sort of slumber.

LSD, commonly called acid or LSD-25, is a powerful semi-synthetic psychedelic drug. A typical dose of LSD is only 100 micrograms, a tiny amount equal roughly to one-tenth the weight of a grain of sand. It causes powerful intensification and alteration of senses, feelings, memories, and self-awareness for 6 to 14 hours. In addition, LSD usually produces visual effects such as moving geometric patterns, "trails" behind moving objects, and brilliant colors, illusions and vivid daydream-like fantasies. At higher concentrations it can cause long-lasting or even permanent changes in a user's psychology, point of view, and personality. Jim Morrison was one of the people that took a lot of doses. He was always pushing the envelope; He would take four or five hits at a time. He did change.

Dr. Albert Hofmann, a chemist at Sandoz Laboratories, returned to work on a chemical he hadn't touched for five years. Something had happened to the formula; it had changed. He attributed the discovery to absorption through the skin of a microscopic amount of the 25th batch (hence the precise name "LSD 25"). That and psilocybin were provided by Sandoz free of charge to interested scientists. The CIA conducted extensive research on it. Harvard psychology professors Drs. Timothy Leary and Richard Alpert became convinced of LSD's potential as a tool for spiritual growth. The CIA actually supplied these gurus with the drug for a time. Private persons such as Owsley from San Francisco started manufacturing it and it spread through the counter-culture like manna from heaven. The drug was banned in the United States in 1967.

The Japanese flute music faded into the distance as I traveled into my subconscious. Images and experiences from my past flashed by like a movie. Small things like a twinkle of light coming through the fish bowl would trigger a light show that seemed to last forever. I woke from that first LSD slumber thinking how positive it was and that somehow I was on the right path. There was more to life. I was willing to explore my mind. I remember telling Ray that "I knew I had been right about things." There must have been questions about myself that had been answered.

I made a film in my apartment that was trying to recreate the colors and sounds I had heard on my trip. I placed crumpled-up color gels with pieces of mirror on a turntable. I placed it in the sunroom and turned on the revolving table. I aimed the camera at the revolving materials and placed the lens slightly out of focus; the result was a dancing sparkling color feast for the eyes. I actually ended up taking it to the Wadsworth Psych Department and showing it to a doctor who had written an article about his research with LSD. He enjoyed the film.

At Ray and Dorothy's that morning we all stood up around the same time. There were smiles on our faces. About two hours had passed and we were hungry and thirsty. Dorothy prepared some fruit while I stared out the window. I could feel the salt air on my face. There was a little girl in the next yard bouncing her ball. I watched her for a while; the repetition of the ball going up and down was hypnotic. We ate the fruit and went for a walk along the beach. We didn't come down from the trip for about twelve hours.

When LSD was legal and it was kind of easy to get, we experimented a lot. Transcendental experience was the objective. Ravi Shankar's ragas were our theme songs. Eastern philosophy had always been stoned, immaculate, and serene. Ravi's music seemed to parallel the psychedelic experience with a quiet sleepy beginning, a ferocious middle, and with some degree of tranquility toward the end. Jimi Hendrix came out with an album, "Are You Experienced?" That was what he was talking about. Have you been there? The cover of Hendrix's album was a large psychedelic mandala painting.

Ray and his brothers had a cover band named Rick and the Ravens; they played small clubs and parties. Ray played a mean keyboard even then. We all showed up to cheer them on whenever they played in our area. One night at the Turkey Joint West in downtown Santa Monica they were playing late into the night. The club was about to close and most of the patrons had left. There were a handful of us from the Film Department, sitting around drunk as skunks. Ray invited us up onstage to join in on the final song. Some of us did: Jim Morrison and a few others gathered around and snorted into the mike. Jim grabbed the microphone and wouldn't let go. He was improvising sounds like Yea, Yea, and Whoa! This was a glimpse into the future, but we didn't know it at the time. Jim was a few semesters behind us. He got a lot of attention one semester when his first film project fell apart in the projection machine. He was humiliated and he stormed out of the classroom as the

72

professor tore him up for his sloppy preparation. I knew him only casually through Felix, who was one of his friends. Jim used to score pot from me and re-sell it. I don't think he actually smoked that much. He told me on several occasions that he didn't like pot.

I was enrolled in Playwriting 101 and set about finding something to write about in my first real one-act play. The professor told us to write about something we knew about, something that had happened to us. After much thought I settled on an incident that had happened at my parents house some years earlier.

My uncle Fonsie had two sons, Richard and Ronnie. Ronnie was retarded and a handful. Fonsie's wife had run off with the neighborhood Catholic priest. Man, was that an eye opener! Uncle Fonsie was left to care for his boys. One day while he was visiting our house, Ronnie stole my 10-year-old sister's doll and locked himself in the bathroom. My sister noticed the doll missing. Ronnie said he didn't have the doll but my sister later discovered it under the sink in the bathroom. It was torn apart and covered in semen. He was reaching puberty and the problem was escalating. Everyone turned to Fonsie. What are you going to do about this? Fonsie replied ...

THE DOOR TO THE DEN (my first attempt at writing a play)
Fonsie:
"Shut up, will you please shut up? It's easy for you to say put him in the hospital, but he's my kid, I know why he's like he is. Ever since he was a little kid, the other kids used to pick on him because he wasn't so bright. You think a father doesn't know how he feels being followed home and yelled after? It ain't no wonder when he started growing up he started getting back. So he put a couple of them in the hospital. Well maybe it serves them right, maybe it does. Think about Patricia, how about if she wasn't as bright as the rest of her friends, what would you do? It ain't easy to understand unless it happens to someone you love. And then his mother left. He changed. He was even different to me, like it was my fault or something. Ritchie started bring all those girls around the house and teasing Ronnie so sure, he started wondering about girls. I tried to tell him about girls but he just wanted to find out for himself. It got him into trouble but I got him out of it okay, didn't I? I'm all he's got. It's different now with him and me. We talk about cars and

engines and hunting and that kind of crap, and he's real smart. The doctors keep saying he's going to hurt somebody, but I love him and I'm not going to desert him. We're going to open a gas station and were going to make a go of it. We're going to build up a steady business and sit back and let the world run away from itself. Not us, not Lonnie and me, we have each other and that's all that counts. I mean, I love that kid. I don't care what anybody says. He's a good mechanic. You just watch and see, we'll make it, we will. We're all we've got. We will, I know we will...."

Patricia (the little girl):

Mommy, I found my doll, I knew he took it. It's all ugly now and broken and there are no arms and legs. The hair is all over the bathroom and it's stuck to the walls. Mommy, why did he do it? I didn't do anything to him. She walks up to her uncle Fonsie, Ronnie's father: "You ought to punish Lonnie, he was very mean to do that to my doll."

I was active in the UCLA Theatre Department and took part in its productions in some way or another, and sometimes I actually got parts. I remember doing a one-man play that Mike somebody directed where I played a leprechaun who appeared and played the trumpet with his mouth. It was actually a talent I always had. I think that when Mike heard it, he was inspired to write a play using it.

I became good friends with Tim McIntire, a young man in the Theatre Department. His mother and father were both well-known actors. His father was John McIntire who was on TV in the Wagon Train series. His mother was Jeanette Nolan, whose last role was as Robert Redford's mother in "The Horse Whisperer." Tim played the guitar and had played the violin since he was a little boy. He went on to compose the film score for the Robert Redford film, "Jeremiah Johnson." He used his violin and his voice to create the definitive high lonesome sound so important to the film. Tim liked to party and ride motorcycles. We connected on several levels and I remained friends with him until his untimely death years later.

The times were hectic to say the least. The Cuban missile crisis, the Watts riots, Kennedy's assassination, Viet Nam, Flower Power, music bursting into our consciousness in a new way, a way that was totally hypnotic. Instant fans, devotees ready to stand in line to worship. Who had time to think? We did the best we could under the conditions.

TIM MACINTIRE   1967

Paul Ferrara

We partied a lot. It wasn't always a party; there were accidents. People got hurt. Our parents disowned us. We were a minority. There were protests, civil rights marches against injustice, Chicago and the conventions, the Black Panthers, Kent State. Just to the north of us in Berkeley at another University of California campus, the kids got heavy into the politics. There was always something happening in Isla Vista. Marches and riots and then-Governor Ronald Reagan's heavy-handed use of the National Guard and use of violent force to break it up.

At our little film school in Westwood, we just wanted to make films about the problems. I don't think I have ever felt a part of the political stuff happening around me. I always have divorced myself from the masses and their petty, materialistic foolishness. Only lately has it dawned on me that I am a part of the greater society whether I like it or not. Anyway, each semester we had a production class and everyone in the class had to complete a short film. There were seven students to each group and about five groups. I was lucky to draw Colin Young's group. He was a progressive guy from the European school of new wave. He wrote articles for the Cahiers du Cinéma, a French film quarterly. He was our friend.

That semester Stevan Larner, a cameraman known for his award-winning documentary cinematography in Europe, was Colin's teaching assistant. I used his professional camera on my shoot; it was an Eclair. I kept in contact with him for a long time. He ended up shooting a T.V. show, the "Twilight Zone" episode where Director John Landis, demanded that the helicopter keep coming lower and lower until it crashed, killing the principal actors and a couple of children. What a fate. Stevan didn't work for a long time. They associated him with the tragic deaths on the film and he was blackballed along with Landis. Things finally cooled off several years later and he started to get work again. Sadly, Stevan died in an automobile accident in 2005.

Each person had to come up with a script idea. We took turns directing, photographing, and assisting each other until everyone's project was shot. After that we were given hours of editing time in the barracks, actual Army barracks left over from the last war. They were on the campus and had been converted into classrooms. Each small space in the editing barracks had a 16mm Moviola. We were assigned certain days and hours that we could edit our films. I found if you had a very late hour, in fact, the last available, you could edit all night long. The small group of people that figured that out became nighttime movie soldiers and we bonded. Many nights I fell asleep on the floor, and in the morning someone would wake me up and kick me out because it was their turn.

The Moviola had two sets of reels, one for the movie and one for the sound. Pushing on the appropriate handles and foot pedals controlled the reels. This stops the reels from spooling the film through a series of sprocketed gates and behind the viewing glass. When you stopped the film you could pop the view glass and mark directly on the film with a grease pencil. This was just a work print, mind you; the negative was safe. The mark would indicate a cut or a sound point or something. If it was to be a cut, you disengaged the film from the sprockets enough to lay it across a chopping block. A razor was pushed down and severed the film into two pieces. You now could add, subtract or alter the film. When your edit was done you put the opposing two pieces of film back into the chopping block and laid a piece of tape across the joint. The tape was made for this use and had sprocket holes that fit across the film and lined up with the pegs on the cutting block exactly. Another piece of metal came down to hold this joint while you severed the tape to its necessary length.

In a short film there could be no cuts, like Andy Warhol's films, or there could be thousands of cuts like Sergei Eisenstein's. We studied them both; anything was possible. We had screenings and hoped the splices were strong enough to pass through a projector. If you were lucky, your film got selected at the end of the semester and you got to cut the negative. The process was very surgical; we wore white gloves, trying not to damage the only negative that existed. It was then sent to CFI Laboratories in Hollywood for the first answer print. If everything was ok, they made a print ready for projection.

Every time I shot a film for myself or anyone else, I was at the lab the first moment I could be there to see the developed film. I am the same way today. The spontaneous shooting of film has a lag time after the fact that makes you wait to see the results. That is gone now with digital. I was uncertain of the results until I saw the image on the film. Was it recorded properly? And what about that fantastic feeling I had when the moment flashed in front of the camera?

PRODUCTION STILLS FROM DAVID THOMPSON'S 170
PROJ. 'GUNFIGHT AT OK CORRAL' TOP RT. KIP STEVENS

ME AND BILL NORTON   PHOTOS BY
                          CHRISTOPHER GRAY

I am a natural born photographer; I see stuff that others don't. I see architecture as form and am constantly aware of someone's good angle. The light is so important; I have learned to use the light that is available to best illuminate the subject. Néstor Almendros wrote a great book about learning to photograph films in Cuba with the barest of equipment. His book called "A Man with a Camera" was a great inspiration to me. I intuitively arrived at similar conclusions.

When I shot Kip's film we were in an old house in Venice. It had plenty of windows but little light inside to balance the light pouring through them. I took mirrors from everywhere in the house and placed them outside the windows. They reflected the sun into the windows and onto the ceiling. The result was bounced light from the ceiling, that wasn't perfect, but what the hell was the alternative? We shot black and white in those days and it looked pretty good.

A beautiful young East Indian lady was teaching the sitar class downstairs in the Music Building that I was enrolled in. The concept was hard because there were no frets, as on a guitar. You had to find the note with your touch and your ear. I was progressing the best I could. The scales I learned then are still in my mind now: Sar Ri Ga Ma and so on. It's like Do Re Mi, but in Indian. The sitar class followed my still photography class, and I always had my Mamiya camera in my backpack. One evening she introduced a friend that was visiting; he would be teaching that evening's class: it was Ravi Shankar. Holy shit, he was my idol. I didn't get much of his music lesson, but I did manage to whip out my camera and shoot the one roll of film I had. I took the roll home and developed it myself in my darkroom. I had his image. Amazing. In a rare euphoric mood I put on his music and began to print some pictures of him.

I had saved a piece of glass from a trashcan that caught my eye; it was part of a shower door and had little star-like images etched into it so you could not see through it. I laid the piece of glass across the printing paper and projected the negative through it and onto the paper. The result was really cool, and I printed it in high contrast. It was an album cover if I ever saw one! I found his record label's address in Hollywood and took a copy to them. They liked it; how could they not? They accepted it and paid me 150 dollars. I thought that was a lot of money. It was used for the cover of his album entitled "Three Ragas" on the World Pacific label. The cover is all white with a huge shot of Ravi's head in black that is composed of the tiny starbursts. It was perfect for the times.

In those days it was customary to invite movie dignitaries to teach classes. Sometimes it was for several semesters; in some cases it was for one semester or maybe just a one-time lecture. I was lucky enough to enroll in Josef von Sternberg's class. He was famous in Germany and the rest of the world. He was the man that discovered Marlene Dietrich and made several films with her. "Blonde Venus" was made in 1932 so he must have been in his 70's when he taught that class. He would start the class out trying to teach some film principle, then someone would interrupt and ask him a question regarding his films or about Marlene Dietrich. This would send him back in time and the hour was filled with anecdotes from his life and career. We watched the films "Blonde Venus" and "The Scarlet Empress" over and over, and he would answer questions about his style of lighting, his cameraman or his editing technique. His films were heavily influenced by early German impressionism, a style he and his various cameramen pushed to the limit: a lot of dark space with bright shafts of light streaming through, always with a pool of soft light on the actress's face.

"The Blue Angel" was his masterpiece, made in Germany in 1930 and starring Emil Jannings and Marlene Dietrich. It was a story of an aging, stuffy professor and his love for a beautiful cabaret singer, and his subsequent shattering humiliation when she dumped him. Von Sternberg wrote most of his films; he was a genius. He had fallen for Marlene, his leading lady, and she was his paramour for years in a widely publicized romance. After watching one of his films he would be talking about the lighting, and drift off in his mind to feelings for Marlene. We watched in awe as he reminisced; the class was always over too soon. That was rare. It's the thing that every star struck person dreams of. We were in the room with him week after week; it made the whole experience magical. There were other famous people that came, but none compared to Josef von Sternberg.

Kip and I met Dawson Hayward. He played bass and had a drummer and was looking for guitars to form a band. It was a very casual formation. Dawson had a good job and didn't need the money. We all had other stuff going on in our lives and we played for the joy and love of it. We practiced in Dawson's storefront building on Washington Boulevard. He was a special type of person, very artistic. His house was perfectly decorated in a minimalist style with an Asian motif, very white. There was bamboo and redwood fencing in the alleyway entrance. He had put some work into his surroundings, it was very conscious. After months of practice we started to sound pretty good. Someone gave Dawson a peanut butter jar full of LSD. We proceeded to take doses every day, practice, and generally trip out. Dawson seemed to get further out each trip and it was harder and harder for him to come back to reality. He lost his job and disappeared for weeks at a time.

One day we went to his house to see him and the place was empty of furniture and his things. There were huge scrawlings on the walls about Jesus and the devil with crosses and numbers painted in red paint. He vanished! Years later he told us he had a revelation and flushed the remaining acid down the toilet. Watch out, you fishes! He packed up his stuff and left it at his parents' house in Palm Springs and moved to New Mexico where he became Buddhist. He went to India and was seen as a saint by someone, which started this whole thing for him. He was a celebrity; he said people were kissing his feet. He came back and instantly had a following. He was the first to start an Ashram in Santa Fe. His Ashram grew to such a huge size that it overwhelmed him, and he left. He was there when I eventually ended up in New Mexico myself.

I graduated with a BA in Film Studies, but for some reason I didn't attend the graduation ceremony. Maybe I had gone skiing or something; it didn't seem important at the time. I started my graduate studies the next semester.

81

BUSTED

The summer of 1965 was the Summer of Love. There was plenty of music being invented in Europe and in the U.S. to keep everybody dancing. There was a plentiful supply of LSD and hemp was still pretty cheap. This is the summer that Ray meets Jim on the beach in Venice and Jim sings Ray some songs he had written. The words to "Moonlight Drive" are spectacular and poetic. Jim was always a poet. Ray's band with his brothers, Rick and the Ravens, were not playing that much and Ray saw a new band in Jim's words and his angelic face. Ray took Jim under his wing, gave him a place to sleep and eat. They worked on the songs for a few months and felt they were ready to build a band.

Ray met Robby at a meditation class. Robby played flamenco guitar but was in love with rock. They jammed for a while and when Robby pulled out his bottleneck and slid it up the strings of his electric guitar, Ray and Jim were sold. It was the sound that was to become The Doors signature. Needless to say, he was in. He said he knew a drummer and would bring him to the next day's rehearsal. He showed up with John Densmore, a jazz drummer who also was digging the new rock sounds. A flamenco guitar, jazz drums and a blues-influenced keyboard: add to that Jim and his angelic, childlike face and the dark poetry that he was turning into song lyrics, and The Doors were born. They wrote and practiced and started playing out.

They were not the only band rehearsing in Venice Beach. There was Canned Heat, the hottest blues band on the west coast. They had space near Main Street in Venice. Canned Heat practiced pretty much every night, and we followed their progress as well. Then there was the City Lights, a group formed in the UCLA Art Department. They played blues and rock and were good. They played at all the free functions, at parties, and always had impromptu concerts in someone's studio space.

The Doors, of course, were special to me and the others from the Film Department at UCLA. We supported them anywhere they played. Ray rented a large two-story house that was on the road to the Venice jetty; it was right on the beach. What a location! The band was set up in the front room and they usually practiced every day. They had no bass player; Ray bought a left hand bass keyboard and set it on top of his organ. That's why the keyboard never really plays rhythm in the early stuff: the left hand chord progressions are missing. Listen to "Break on Through." Ray's left hand on his new bass keyboard rocked. The Doors never played with a bass until later. Robby and Ray traded off solos just like a jazz band. As it turned out, Jim had a beautiful voice. He told me he had always liked Sinatra, and at times he crooned like him. There were also times when he went insane and screamed and jumped and tried to outdo Mick Jagger's style. The more Jim was stoned, the more he acted out on stage. The Stones were doing something that Jim liked and he tried to do the bad boy thing as much as the others in the band would allow. He had a tremendous hunger for being stoned, and it seemed to fuel his creativity. The more Jim's singing and performing improved, the more confidence he gained. He became known for being stoned during performances, and that was because most of the time he was.

Ray was the leader and tried to be the father figure to them all. His wife Dorothy was always there, adding the tenderness that was needed for not only Ray but for Jim as well. She had that stoic Asian quality; she never seemed to get stressed. When she had to, she went to work and supported Ray and the band in any way she could. I have always loved Dorothy, ever since that time in the apartment when the three of us took acid. She cut the fruit and placed some on my tongue. It brought me back into reality, the taste was intensified, magnified and sensual and I've never forgotten that moment. Ray was a lucky man to find Dorothy. He was into Eastern philosophy way before the rest of us. He was kind of scholarly and Ivy League and was into meditation. He came from Illinois, wore button down shirts with sport coats, and drove a VW. Dorothy was first generation Japanese-American. Dorothy added worldliness to the situation, and she was the inspiration for some of Jim's early images of women. She was a 20th Century Fox.

Jim came from a strict military upbringing living with his father, the Admiral. He was running from that authority as fast as he could. Imagine your dad is the Admiral. I know he loved his mother because he told me he did, but he refused to see her when she tried to visit him backstage at a concert. When I told Jim she was at the door and wanted to see him, he told me to make an excuse why he couldn't see her, which I did. It was sad to experience, but who knows the story of their life? How could I judge? Jim took much pleasure in singing the Oedipus part of "The End" where he sang 'Mother I want to fuck you, Father I want to kill you.' He performed that song so many times, each time with variations on those two lines: sometimes angry, sometimes sensual. By 1966 The Doors had a local following and were on the map. Their reputation had spread and occasionally they played in Hollywood. We followed them, helped carry equipment, and generally supported our friends anyway we could.

While we had the band with Dawson we attracted a small following, some of them being young girls you might call groupies. Leslie was a cute little blonde that loved all of us. She used to come to my apartment a lot. She was maybe 16 years old. She gave herself to the band. She melted into your arms, a true lover. She was so beautiful and committed to making you feel good. She wanted nothing in return. She just wanted to be next to you, smothering you with her sex, her love. God, that is what the true flower child groupie had: a love so deep that sex was the only expression that came close to what she felt. Well, that was okay with me. I loved her but I think I could never really fully understand her.

Leslie had been out of sight since Dawson's flip-out. She called me one night out of the blue. She had a new boyfriend at school and wanted to score some pot so they could party. It was late and I didn't really want to help her, but I did. I didn't have anything for sale but I agreed to sell her ten dollars worth of my personal stash. That's a small handful. She came to the door, gave me the ten dollars and disappeared into the night, and I went to bed.

Jim Morrison used to show up at my door at all hours wanting to borrow something from my record collection, usually a Muddy Waters or Howling Wolf album that had a song on it that he was learning. Sometimes he just wanted to get high or buy a small amount of weed for someone. It was about 5:30 a.m. and someone was knocking on my door. I heard a voice. "Paul, it's me." I think that it's Morrison or some other friend, and I got out of bed in my underwear and went to the front door. No one else would be wandering around that early. Jim did all-nighters and frequently showed up at my door at insane hours. I was used to it. When I opened the door, four plainclothes cops burst in with their guns drawn. They pushed me back against the opposite wall, spun me around and cuffed me, read me my rights and I watched them tear my apartment apart. They sat me in a chair; I asked what it was they were looking for. Someone held the warrant in front of my nose. It had my name on it, all right. Someone let out a yell from the back porch darkroom. They came walking toward us with a mason jar that had a few assorted goodies in it: a couple of tabs of mescaline, a water pipe, a small handful of marijuana and that was it. One of the guys held up my Mamiya camera and admired it.

So there I was, sitting handcuffed in the back of a police car in front of my apartment. It was raining softly as they drove me the six blocks to the Santa Monica Police Station. I was booked on the charge of selling marijuana to a minor with a possible sentence of 20 years to life. The story was on the front page of the local Santa Monica paper: 'Dope ring busted at Santa Monica High School.' They put me into a cell and locked the door. There I sat, trying to figure out what had happened. I had pretty much forgotten the small handful of pot I had sold to Leslie a month earlier. When I was given my one phone call, I called my girlfriend, Joan Churchill. I tried to explain to her what had happened and hoped she could get some information that would help me get out of this mess. I was alone in the cell. Night came and I didn't sleep much.

The next day I was loaded onto a bus with other prisoners and taken downtown to County Jail. That was where the entire county of L.A. funneled their prisoners to await further proceedings or spend short sentences for misdemeanors. Every large county has a main jail facility; this was one of the worst, located downtown near Olvera Street. In the sixties the gang thing wasn't that noticeable and it was a fairly peaceful population of bad guys. At least, that is what I experienced. As we stepped from the bus it was still raining; I was so depressed. 25 years to life: that was the rest of time. I was doomed. It was over, all the creation, the music, the films, the progress I had made in my life. What were my parents going to think? Selling pot to a minor was a big deal back then.

The bus pulled up in front of the biggest, cement-iest buildings I ever saw; it was like a fortress. We filed out of the bus in our street clothes and entered the main door. There were already fifty or sixty guys lined up along the walls; some were sitting, some were standing. The group from our bus took our place in the line. This is where we were to be processed: photographed, numbered, and relieved of our clothing and identification. We were walked nude through a shower area one by one and sprayed for lice and stuff. We were issued some blue clothes with L.A. County Jail stenciled across the back of the shirts and a non-removable plastic wristband with a barcode ID. We were allowed to keep a small amount of money, around five dollars.

Everyone was interested in what you were doing there. What were you in for? Some had stolen cars and got a GTA, which translates to Grand Theft Auto. Others had beaten their wives, but most of the guys were in for drug charges. When they asked me what I was in for and I told them selling pot to a minor, the look in their eyes told it all. It didn't look good for me. Shit.

We were given cell assignments and I was put into a cell with three other guys. There were four bunks to a cell. I tried to look everyone in the eyes and make my entrance as the iron gate slid closed, making a sound that made time stand still for me. It was the sound of finality. Locked up. There was a certain safety that also came with confinement. It reduced everything to a very common denominator: at least you're alive. The guys were pretty cool to me. The compassion for someone that suffers the same is there. It can be violent because of the frustration and stir crazy nature of confinement but for the most part, it's us against them. You've seen the prison movies; people band together. There was obviously one bunk open on the top right side. I climbed up and lay down. My eyes were two feet from the ceiling. People had scratched their initials and poems and letters to their girlfriends all over the ceiling area. The walls had been painted over, but you could see the last few generations of writings with naked ladies and tattoo type art mixed in. An inmate came by issuing blankets and he charged me fifty cents. The older black dude across from me said to just give the money to him. The lights went out around nine o'clock. I stared at the ceiling for hours. I finally fell asleep.

In the morning when the doors were opened, we filed out and fell into a line headed for the cafeteria. It was breakfast time and a welcomed relief from the small crowded cell. This would be a daily ritual. I must say that the food wasn't all that bad. The cooks were inmates, all big, fat and black. You have to love a fat chef. The food was southern and delicious: fried chicken, mashed potatoes and greens, ribs soaked in some Cajun sauce. Not too bad. Meals were the high point of the day: the walk, seeing other people ... then it was back to the cell.

The county jail is where the cadets from the Sheriff's Department start out. They are green and scared and they didn't want to be there. Nobody wanted to be there, but there we were. It was still raining. What was happening with Joan, my only hope at this point? The twenty years to life thing was hard to deal with, it was hard to keep any hope alive. I was feeling low. I mean, low.

I shared my cell with a black guy named Dog Man. I assumed that was his name because he was so ugly. He had that bumpy skin thing that some black dudes have, and he was not too good looking. He was there because he had committed murder. There was a Spanish guy that was in for rape, and a young white guy from Pasadena who was in for a bank robbery. Pretty good company for a guy like me: a film student and musician who liked to get high.

The guy from Pasadena and I talked a lot. He was young and good-looking, blonde with blue eyes, and he was glad to have someone white to talk to. And talk he did! He had taken acid and decided to walk into a bank with an empty bag and ask for some money. They gave it to him and he walked out. Amazed, he did it again and again about a dozen times before they caught him. He said he had about thirty thousand dollars buried somewhere. I called him the LSD bandit. He said he was going to tell me where he buried the money so that if I got out before him, I could dig it up and hire him a good lawyer.

The desperation inside a prison is a feeling that colors everything. Is someone going to remember me? It's the only way you're going to get help. Someone else has to do it; you have no chance of helping yourself. It is so lonely. I brushed my teeth a lot, did pushups and slept. Time stopped and the moments took forever.

It was still dark and raining outside. There were three or four tiers of cells along one side of the building. The opposite wall had a row of narrow windows, one tier of cells up from me. If you jumped up, you could grab the next level and pull yourself up, and then you could look out the narrow window and catch a glimpse of the world outside. Occasionally a girl would walk by a block away; it was all we had.

It finally stopped raining. It lifted everyone's spirit. They opened the doors to the cells and we went out on the walkway. I pulled myself up to the next level to look at the sunshine when suddenly the bell for door closure went off unexpectedly. I didn't quite know which way to go. I was alone up there, so I grabbed the railing with one hand and jumped over and landed with a crash on my level. I landed next to one of the old guards who was standing below me and scared the hell out of him. He spun around and there I was; he freaked out and attacked me. The guys in my cell witnessed the whole thing. The guard called for help and within a few seconds I was on the floor with several cadets on top of me. The older guard grabbed my wrist and read on my wristband that I was in for selling drugs, and he accused me of being on the tier above selling drugs. They roughed me up and threw me back into my cell.

About an hour later my cell door opened up and I was led out and taken to solitary lockup, my punishment for being in the wrong place at the wrong time. We descended in an elevator even further into the building and arrived at another row of smaller one-man cells with no windows, only artificial neon light.

We stopped at a cell that was occupied. The guard opened the door and told me to go in; I would have to double up. There was only one bed and a toilet. The guy already in the cell was bent over the toilet heaving. When he finished, he informed me he was going through heroin withdrawal. We took turns sleeping on the cot and sitting on the toilet. He wasn't violent, just sick. The lights were not turned off at night and you lost track of time. By the time the food was delivered to the cells in solitary, it was cold. It was very difficult eating cold food that had begun to harden up, and most of the time we just drank the liquids and nibbled on the food. By the time the ordeal in County Jail was over, I would lose 16 lbs.

My roomie's heaving was getting less and less. On the second evening he was removed and I was alone. Wow, I was finally alone and when you're alone, all you have are your thoughts. Besides worrying about my current situation, I was lonely. Really lonely. My mind drifted back and I seemed to remember every girlfriend I had ever had, girls I had totally forgotten. I masturbated. It was hard to sleep with the lights blazing. Along with my lack of interest for the food by the time it reached me in its condition, I started to get very weak by the fifth day. I was staring at the layers of graffiti on the wall and I actually hallucinated for the first time without drugs. It wasn't good, either. I saw scary witch-like creatures that appeared in the scratchings on the wall; they left the wall and started moving toward me. I was losing it. Twenty too life. It haunted me. Was it over? Was this it? It was the lowest point in my entire life. I was close to giving up. I had not heard anything from anyone since I had arrived at County. Was Joan trying to help? Did anyone give a shit? Could I be helped?

I remembered Jeanne Roop, a girl John Waid had turned me onto. She was the sweetest girl you could meet and had a killer body. She lived in Inglewood and had a roommate that slept in the same bedroom. I remember sleeping with Jeanne with her roommate sleeping four feet from us. We still had a lot of sex; her roommate didn't seem to mind. I remembered girls I had met in bars. Affairs that came and went were revisited like they had just happened. I think all the memories became a defense mechanism for the lonely place I was at. I tried to count the girls I was remembering and it was around thirty-five or forty. I had been a busy guy.

Just when I thought I couldn't take any more, a guard approached and opened the door. It had been five days, five very long days. I was beat. I dragged myself out of the cell and was led back to my old cell with Dog Man and the others. It was Baker row; I forget the cell number. Those guys looked good to me. They greeted me and looked at me like I was a ghost. Dog Man showed me the metal mirror and I looked like shit. I was thin and had a five-day beard. He offered me his razor and I cleaned up a little. I felt like Steve McQueen in "Papillon," the prison movie. You take what you're given. They comforted me, having an idea of what I had just gone through. When we went down to the cafeteria for dinner, it was really something. I ate like a horse. It was all good: mashed potatoes with gravy, fried chicken, hot veggies.

Another week passed and nothing, no word. Finally after fourteen days I had visitors: my mother and father. I was never so glad to see anyone in my whole life. Joan had not been able to come up with enough money to help me and had eventually gone to my parents. They put up the money to hire a lawyer. Joan helped them hire Peter Knecht, the same lawyer that was doing Peter Fonda's pot bust. They paid him his five thousand dollar retainer. My mother and father looked at me through the small window in the visiting room. My mother tried to get me to promise that I would not smoke pot, ever again. I told her I couldn't promise that, and to please just get me out of there. We could talk about everything else later. They posted my bail on day sixteen and I was released on day seventeen. I said goodbye to my cellmates and promised to try to help them the best I could. I feel a little guilty still that I was unable to figure out a way to help anybody inside.

It was late on the seventeenth day that I was finally processed out. My parents were there to pick me up, bless their hearts. I asked my mother to drive me to Olvera Street for a Mexican meal. She did, we didn't talk much on the way home.

When I got back to my apartment, the place had been tossed. My camera, the one the narc had admired on the day of my arrest, was gone. It was the only camera I had, the Mamiya, and it was the one I took my Ravi Shankar album cover with. That place on Washington Street in Ocean Park, my forty dollar a month apartment where my friends and I had spent so many stoned hours, where we listened to every new album we could get our hands on, somehow had lost its appeal. I straightened it up but it would never again to be the same, where we could smoke pot, listen to Jimi Hendrix blasting on the stereo, and sit in the sun porch and dream as the sun set over the Pacific Ocean.

I could walk out my door and be on the boardwalk of Venice Beach in seconds, walking or riding a bike in the fresh ocean breeze. In those days we could walk around safely at night, which we did many times. We'd walk to a friend's house or down to the Santa Monica Pier for some fish and chips.

When I acted in Kit Gray's film, his 171 project, we shot a cool scene on the Santa Monica pier where I read Jeannie A.'s palm. My old girlfriend from El Camino acted in my film and in Christopher's film. I think I still loved her. She had a serious boyfriend, but we were still good friends.

If you headed the other way going south, you could get lucky and Canned Heat were rehearsing, jamming, and allowing people to gather in their studio to listen. If I walked far enough or hitched a ride, I was at Hinano's Bar on

Washington Boulevard, my old hangout. Stopping along the way I could visit any number of friends that had studios or apartments in the area.

We were all incubating. We had experienced the introduction to knowledge at the universities, now we were trying to figure out what to do with it. For me getting stoned opened up an area in my brain that was so creative. I was not the only one experiencing that feeling. It was what Jim was going to write about. "The Doors of Perception" by Aldous Huxley was about breaking on through to a new place in your brain, a place where you could think outside the box. We were all so pigeonholed; we actually believed there were limitations. It was a renaissance, an explosion of new thought. It goes on today, thanks to that period. We were inventing. Out on a limb. Sometimes the limb broke, people freaked out, but for the most part we kept climbing higher and higher.

One of the first things I had to do was visit with my lawyer. Peter Knecht had an office on Sunset Boulevard. It was white and had pillars in front like the White House. He was a cool guy and made me feel comfortable. He had a confidence about him. I was not free yet, only out on bail awaiting my trial. He asked me if they had found any pot in my apartment at the time of the arrest. I told him no; maybe they found about a joint's worth, some paraphernalia and some caps of mescaline. I'm not sure they ever figured out what that was. I had been arrested for selling pot. They had expected to find a kilo or two at least. He asked me about Leslie, the girl that I had sold the pot to.

While I awaited my trial I was very paranoid. In fact to this day, I feel paranoia. I'm very careful about obeying the law; I don't ever want to go inside again. I totally understand guys who, take their own life, in the face of being arrested. Nobody wants to go back into jail. Well, maybe some guys want to go back. I have heard about and seen hardcore guys who prefer the life inside where they have some ranking and order.

About two months later we went to court. Those were a long two months. Who knew how it would turn out? Finally, the day came for the trial. I was early, and I was nervous. My parents accompanied me, and we were waiting in the hall when Peter Knecht walked up and greeted us. He saw the District Attorney with Leslie. He excused himself and walked down the hall toward them. I lost sight of him. We were let into the courtroom. Where was my lawyer? Just before my trial was about to begin he entered and took his seat next to me. He whispered in my ear that he had talked to Leslie and everything was going to be ok.

Court was in session; we all took our seats as the Judge sat down. The District Attorney of Santa Monica called his first witness, Leslie. She was sworn in. The first thing out of her mouth after she was asked a question was that she had been advised that because she was incarcerated at the present time, she didn't have to testify. "I refuse to testify." Holy shit! The D.A. jumped out of his seat and protested. The Judge asked him if he had any other witnesses. His case rested on her testimony. He was screwed and he knew it. The judge slammed the gavel down and said, "Case dismissed." That was it. As fast as it had begun, it was over. It ended. Somehow, Peter had gotten to Leslie: totally illegal, but totally cool. I was given two years probation. If I was arrested again within that two years I would go to jail for a long, long time.

Leslie had been arrested for something else and was serving two years at Sybil Brand Institute, a women's prison in the L.A. area. Upstairs at the Whisky A Go Go years later she approached me in a dark crowded space and I freaked out. Still paranoid. It was like the witch from solitary suddenly appeared, and I turned and vanished into the crowd. I think she probably wanted to apologize. She had been sweet. I still regret I didn't finish it with her, but that was how it went. I wasn't ready to go there, and I ran away as fast as I could.

One of the conditions of my probation was that I find a job and start a regular life. My love of the university student life had come to an end. The only place film students could find work was in the commercial production houses scattered around Hollywood, and I started making the rounds. I went for an interview at John Urie's on Sunset Boulevard across from Channel 5, the old Columbia Studios. John took the interview himself. He was a nice man. He asked me why I wanted a job and I told him that I had been forced into it by my probation officer. He looked at some of my photos that I had in a portfolio such as my Ravi Shankar album cover, a topless photo of a beautiful black girl I had met in Watts and a few other shots. I got the job.

Bill Norton, a fellow classmate from UCLA, was working there in the writing department. I knew Bill well; he had acted in the Kip Stevens film that I shot and I also knew his sister well. I said hello. He was working on his own script that would later be produced as "Cisco Pike" starring a young

Kris Kristofferson. I was assigned to the Art Department and I was officially an Assistant Art Director. I picked up samples of wallpaper and fabric and paint for Chuy Elizondo, the Art Director. Later we ended up working on "Becker" together: he was a camera operator and I was a Key Grip. John Urie had married Chuy's sister and helped Chuy get into the camera local. I told you he was cool.

Richard Bailey was one of the staff directors at John Urie's. He was in his thirties and was the 'hot' director with a hip look about him. One day he came to me and asked if I knew where there was any good pot. I had to tell him that I was on probation and a little paranoid of any discussion with strangers. We gradually became better friends and I helped him to score some marijuana. Eventually we became good friends.

A girl who worked at John Urie's turned me on to the apartment next to hers in a Hollywood bungalow type building. Her friend was moving out and I was the first to hear about it. It was on Laurel Canyon just south of Sunset Boulevard, pretty cheap and very convenient. At the time I was driving a 1949 Hudson Hornet and my BSA motorcycle. The Hornet didn't always start in the morning. I had to park on a hill so I could roll a little bit and pop the clutch. When I moved to the new apartment on Laurel I sold the Hudson Hornet for scrap and just had the motorcycle. The girl from work lived across from me in the courtyard. She thought because she helped me find the place I was obligated to be her boyfriend. I played with her when I could, but I had bigger fish to fry. Two nurses lived at the back of the courtyard. One of them loved music and gave B12 shots to a lot of musicians. She shot me up with B12 on several occasions.

Bailey lived on Harper and Fountain in a beautiful Spanish apartment building. There was a courtyard with a fountain, Spanish tiles everywhere and beautiful greenery. I could walk to his place from mine in 10 minutes and I started to hang out there more and more. He had a lot of friends and was very well connected. We did a lot of stuff together, and we shared acquaintances and girlfriends on many occasions. In the time I knew him Bailey became quite the druggie; he had a Merck Manual on his coffee table.

Bailey had one of the upstairs apartments. If you looked out his bathroom window and down to the neighboring apartments, you could see into the window of a bathroom belonging to this gorgeous girl who loved to walk around nude. We used to continually check for the times she would appear.

Downstairs and across the courtyard from Bailey lived a couple of ladies in separate apartments. They became friends of ours and eventually Bailey moved in with one of them, Jill Donahue. She was a tall beautiful blonde and a sometime actress. Her father was Jack Donohue, the producer & director. Between the two of them they had enough marginally famous friends to fill their apartment on a nightly basis. I met Denny Doherty and Michelle Phillips, Harrison Ford and Dennis Hopper, as well as hundreds of other people. You probably wouldn't recognize their names, but their faces were always in commercials or B-movies and you would have seen them at some time. Bailey's was pretty much the meeting place to get high and continue on to your destination. Eventually Bailey started dealing and the flow of people got even denser and scarier.

Once someone brought him three hundred mature marijuana plants from northern California. He got a great deal on the plants. They were freshly picked and needed curing. He hung them from the ceiling in one of the bedrooms and had to tape the windows because of the smell. We eventually bagged it all up and he sold it.

I continued to take pictures of people with any camera I could use. One of the art directors at Urie's liked the nude I had taken a few years back of a black girl I met in Watts. He made a Xerox copy and hung it on his wall. I had met her at an all black bar with topless waitresses near Pickering Sheet Metal. She was a beautiful girl with the most perfect tits I had ever seen. I asked her if she would do some pictures with me. She agreed and I took her to the Ocean Park apartment. We took pictures against a white background I had hung. She stayed for the night and we had the most delicious sex. Black women are so uninhibited. Sex is like dancing; they enjoy it. I took her home on the way to work the next day and never saw her again. I still have one of the shots I took. It's the same one the art director liked. That photo came with a price: a week later I got the crabs.

Anne was Jack Nicholson's secretary and she lived next door to Jill. Anne was a tall slender redhead. We became good friends and we hung out when we could. Jack was working more and more, thanks to "Easy Rider." She was very guarded with her sexuality and actually somewhat kinky about it. She liked me to sleep with her but never took off her clothes.

Next to Anne lived a beautiful brunette actress about twenty years old. She had some emotional issues and one day she committed suicide in her room. She had given me an antique mirror two days before. She took it from the wall and said I might as well take it, which I did. I still have it today. What a waste. Sudden death robs the system, the friends, and the loved ones. Some cultures believe the souls linger for a long time when the death comes prematurely. We all mourned for her. She was not going to be the only casualty we would know.

GAMMA LTD

Bailey had a friend named Ron Joy who was starting a photo agency. Ron rented a large building on Santa Monica Boulevard, two doors from the world famous Troubadour nightclub. Bailey and I went to see the place. It was a cool space, large and with alley access to bring cars in. It must have been a small market or something before; it had an open ceiling with big exposed struts. I hit it off with Ron, and he offered me a job helping him to get his studio going. Ron said he couldn't pay me much, but would give me money when he could and help me to get going as a photographer.

I quit John Urie's and put on my construction clothes for several months. I had seen the David Hemmings film "Blow-Up," a few years before. I tried to copy the white feeling of the studio in that film. We built a darkroom in the back and Ron hired a European guy with a thick Middle Eastern accent to work it. Ron came up with the name Gamma Ltd. The darkroom operation accepted work from outside photographers, so there was a constant flow of working photographers streaming through. I met a lot of cool people.

Ron's girlfriend was Nancy Sinatra, so he had a steady gig doing her publicity and album covers. She was hot at the time and had a hit with the "These Boots Are Made For Walkin'" single. There were two other photographers who worked there on a permanent basis. Bruce McBroom who I think still shoots stills for major motion pictures. The other guy was Larry Raphael, a semi-famous headshot guy from Hollywood with his own following.

In the front of the studio space was a large office. That's where the three people Ron had gathered wrote copy, made copies of the photos that were produced, and sent them to all the magazines in the world. Nancy was big in Europe and they sold a lot of photos that Ron shot in the studio. I had hung several backings against one wall and you could choose the color you wanted. I helped Ron shoot most of his sessions. I helped Larry Raphael a lot, as well. I was learning. Many times at night after everyone went home, I shot projects and worked in the dark room. Little by little I was given assignments nobody else wanted because they paid very little, if anything. Usually it was a spec job.

I shot Leonard Nimoy at his home at the beginning of "Star Trek" and Peggy Lipton before "Mod Squad," to name a few, as well as several medium level rock bands. Once in a while I got a small check, my share of the sale of various photos. Nancy was a very nice lady and treated me very well, even inviting me to her house for dinner several times.

One night Ann-Margret, The Beatles' publicist Derek, Ron, Nancy and I shared an intimate dinner at Nancy's house. Nancy was planning a T.V. special that would be directed by Jack Haley Jr. It was going to be a big deal and take two weeks to shoot. The production would move up and down California shooting songs against various backgrounds. Ron gave me the assignment of being the still photographer on the shoot. That night I was asked to drop Derek, the Beatles guy, off at his place. He invited me in to have a smoke. We got very high. He wanted to fuck me and he asked me to spend the night. I was gone!

I did shoots with several girls who responded to an ad Gamma had placed for nude models for magazine articles, and one of them sold. Cavalier was a man's magazine that was like a B-movie version of Playboy, and they wanted her for the centerfold. They asked me to shoot a larger negative version of the overhead on the fur rug shot. I rented a Hassalblad and shot it hanging from the overhead struts. I placed her on the large circular fur rug and put her in a Marilyn Monroe pose.

Nancy's television special was written by Tom Mankiewicz and directed by Jack Haley Jr. Jack's father had been the Tin Man in The Wizard of Oz and his wife was Liza Minnelli. He had his hand in a lot of Hollywood deals as producer, but he was going to direct this one. The famous Hollywood restaurant, the Brown Derby, did the catering. That was reason enough to want to be there. We started the shoot with a couple days at Pacific Ocean Park. In those days it was a large 1950s style amusement park. We started with a dance number, sort of á la "West Side Story."

Paul Ferrara

THE NANCY SINATRA SPECIAL.   PHOTOS BY STEVE NORTH

We then proceeded up the coast to the next location, Limekiln Creek at Big Sur. A few miles from the highway up Limekiln Canyon there's a cool waterfall. Nancy lip-synced a song with the waterfall as the backdrop. It took the better part of the day just to get the equipment up there; it had to be hand carried. Nancy looked beautiful as usual against the raging white water and the idyllic background.

The next stop was under the Golden Gate Bridge. I made friends with one of the other young guys on the crew; I think he was an assistant producer or something. His name was Steve North and we kept up a sporadic relationship for several years. We rented a car and drove back from Frisco together. We were both film buffs and had plenty to talk about. I visited Steve a few times at his house on Beverly Glen Boulevard where he lived with his parents. His dad was none other than Alex North, a composer of some renown who had scored some of my favorite films. Some were legendary. How about "Cleopatra," "Spartacus," "Who's Afraid of Virginia Woolf?," "The Misfits," and "Viva Zapata"? The list went on, but that was enough to impress me. He was Hollywood royalty, and there I was.

There was a sequence in Nancy's special that was shot in the Gamma Ltd. studio. Nancy was posing for photos and singing. Sammy Davis Jr. played the photographer. He was a very cool guy. Since I was the photographer covering the shoot, he related to me and asked me about my cameras. He actually was a camera bug. He was playing a hippie type guy and told me I needed some beads, so he took a strand from his neck and placed them over my head. Frank Sinatra, Dean Martin and Frank Sinatra Jr. all had scenes with Nancy in various locations. There was usually some banter followed by a song duet. It has become a camp piece of film.

Many years later I was on a rooftop in downtown Memphis when Jim Jarmusch told me one of his favorite all time songs is "These Boots Are Made for Walkin'." Just to prove it, he whipped out a tape and played it during an early morning party after shooting "Mystery Train" all night long.

Regardless of what people thought about Nancy and the pop sort of trash she was involved in, she could sing. She had inherited those pipes from the Man himself. Her brother Frank Jr. sounded like his dad, as well. When the shoot ended there was a party at Jack Haley's house. I think I was on an early date with Georgia Newton, who later became my first wife, but I can't be sure. Anyway, my date and I danced the night away next to Liza and company. It was a real Hollywood party in the real Hollywood Hills, and I was stylin'. A short time earlier I had been in L.A. County Jail in solitary confinement looking at a sentence of life in prison. I felt good!

Larry Raphael was shooting a motorcycle ad and asked me to assist him. I did. The casting for that shot called for a Tarzan & Jane type of girl, and the Gamma Ltd. studio was swamped with beautiful young ladies. The line of girls went out the door and down the street. I was in heaven; every beautiful girl in Hollywood was there. One of them caught my eye. She was dressed in leather buckskin and looked like a nasty Bo Derek. After her interview I followed her out the door and asked her if she would like to go to a movie sometime. She listened to my offer, thought about it, said OK, wrote her phone number down, and left. Wow, that was easy! I called her the next day and set a date for the weekend.

She lived off Fountain in a small apartment with a large beautiful German shepherd. Her place was sort of temporary looking with half-empty boxes of books and things strewn about. After the movie she invited me up to her place. We smoked a joint and she went into the bathroom. When she came out a few minutes later, she was completely nude and had the largest breasts I had ever seen. Oh my god! She came over to where I was sitting on the bed and put her legs between mine and said she wanted to pay me back for the movie. Those were the first breast implants I had ever touched. I must admit I was a little freaked by them. They were large and hard. She had a beautiful body, a deep bikini tan line and long flowing blonde hair. Bo Derek. We fucked the night away with the dog watching. It was freaky. She told me she was hiding from the mob, that they had paid for her tits and she was kind of indebted to them. They wanted her to work for them as a call girl or something. A few days later I tried to call her and her line had been disconnected. I went to her apartment and she was gone. The place was completely empty.

I met Peggy Lipton through a girlfriend of Bailey's. I was invited to her place in Topanga Canyon. We were supposed to shoot some photos, but all I remember is I fell in love with her. She wasn't having any of my affection and was only sweet and sympathetic to my advances. She led me on but was untouchable. This was the same girl who would be on the "Mod Squad" TV show and later married Quincy Jones. You don't win them all!

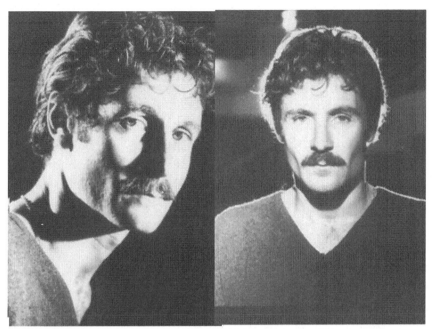

YOURS TRULY   PHOTOS BY LARRY RAPHAEL

GAMMA LTD.   CAROL LYNLEY

Carol Lynley needed some fresh headshots and Ron was busy, so he suggested I shoot her. Yeaaa. She was a twenty-something starlet who was quite beautiful. I shot her in the studio just like Ron would have set it up. I put a small light behind the gray backing and punched a hole through to backlight her, added a wind machine, and away I went. Those shots were some of the best she had ever seen. I got a lot of respect for the job as well as a few bucks and the chance to hang out with her for a day.

Meanwhile, Ray and Jim's group were playing nightly at the London Fog, a small club on the Sunset Strip a block west of the Whisky A Go Go. They called themselves The Doors after Huxley's "Doors of Perception." I still saw all my old friends from Venice and UCLA, and we all went to as many shows at the London Fog as we could. It was a narrow space and it was dark. The band's area was elevated about six or seven feet and you had to look up at them. I think Jim's performance style was invented up there where he felt safe. He got stoned a lot. It freed him of his inhibitions and allowed him to dance wildly, inventing very spontaneous moves. Sometimes he nearly fell. He was always on the edge of hurting himself. Right up to the very end, he was trying to hurt himself.

I picked up a spec job from a magazine that wanted pictures of Donovan. He was riding high with his hit "Sunshine Superman" and was playing up and down the Strip. I was to meet a girl named Ronnie Harran. She worked for The Whisky and was taking care of Donovan while he was in town. Her office was upstairs at the Whisky. As I climbed the stairs to her office, there was a group of guys sitting on the stairs who told me they were waiting to see her also. We waited. They told me they were the Buffalo Springfield band and were talking about playing the Whisky. Ronnie was the person who booked the bands. My meeting with her was about where to find Donovan and when to show up at a mansion in the hills where all the big bands stayed. The Beatles, Stones, you name it!

I was about to leave and she asked me if I knew of any good bands. I said, "As it turns out, I do. My best college friends call themselves The Doors and are playing right up the street." She said she would check them out. I guess she did, and she fell in love with Jim. He moved into her place for a while and The Doors started playing the Whisky as the second band.

My experience with Donovan went very well. Too well. There was a guy in his entourage named Gypsy. They had just gotten back from Jamaica and he was rolling giant joints from the Jamaican weed they had smuggled into the U.S. These giant joints that looked like cigars were called spliffs in Jamaica. Gypsy passed the fresh rolled cigar to me. I took a few tokes and don't remember much after that. I did manage to get a few good shots of Donovan, however.

Frank Sinatra was doing one of his many TV shows. The main photographer on the job needed a second camera for a particular performance piece on a sound stage, and I got the job. I think I was paid in cash and had to turn the negatives over to him after the shoot. Anyway, what a gig! I was onstage shooting the close shots, just a few feet from Old Blue Eyes as he went through a few songs. I remember "Old Man River." It was pure magic. I don't know what that guy had, but all you had to do was hear him sing and you felt it. There was a certain amount of swagger and confidence and pure musical ability, with seemingly effortless delivery. He was the cool. Like Miles Davis, like Jimi Hendrix and Ray Charles, they were on a mission: blessed with a talent that comes from above the human experience. Call it what you want, I will never forget the experience.

Ron Joy's silent partner in the studio was Blake Edwards. I never completely understood the connection. Blake was hitting his stride with the "Pink Panther" series and riding high. One day Ron asked me to deliver some photos to Blake at the Formosa Studios. I said sure. He was in the process of casting his latest Peter Sellers film called "The Party," and there was a part for a young photographer. I delivered the photos and as Blake thanked me, he asked if I had ever done any acting. I replied sure and rattled off my history. I was cast in his film. Ron took credit for it, saying he owed me for all the work I had put into the studio. Regardless of why I got the part, I got it, and I thank anyone who had a part in that.

I had to join S.A.G., the actors union. I was paid seven hundred and fifty dollars per week. That was a lot for me. I took my BSA motorcycle into a place on Highland that Tim McIntire had recommended and had it completely redone. It was now very beautiful, re-chromed and painted black lacquer. Tim and I rode together a lot after that.

Bruce McBroom was to be the still photographer on the set. I could supplement his photos with the ones I would be shooting acting as a photographer with a camera around my neck. My character was named Ronnie Smith. I wore a black tux for the entire film, which takes place mainly at a big Hollywood party at a producer's house during the course of one night.

Paul Ferrara

"THE PARTY' TOP, PETER SELLERS, BOTTOM LEFT CAROL
WAYNE, RT. BLAKE EDWARDS. PHOTOS BY:
BRUCE MCBROOM

I had come to the party with a beautiful Hollywood starlet played by Carol Wayne, Hollywood's latest ditsy blonde. She was actually very intellectual; she just played the dumb blonde. We became very close, so close that her photographer boyfriend, Barry Feinstein, was jealous. She used to bring three or four joints to work everyday. Sometimes she shared. It was the most potent stuff I had ever smoked. Acapulco Gold.

Peter Sellers was to play a bumbling film extra that is mistakenly invited to an exclusive Hollywood party. Claudine Longet played the young starlet who sings at the party. Her character is attracted to the Sellers character, an East Indian. Peter's bungling manages to bring the party to utter chaos through a series of stupid slapstick scenes.

One day there was a shooting break when Ravi Shankar visited the set with his entourage. I guess there was some connection because Peter Sellers was playing an Indian. There was an exterior part to the set outside the main house that had a large yard complete with pool. After a tour of the set, the group was by the pool surrounding Peter and Ravi. There was a lull in the conversation and Peter asked Ravi what he thought of all this make-believe. There was a short silence and Ravi replied 'Plastic grass.' That was why he was staring at the ground; he was taken with the fake grass. I didn't tell Mr. Shankar that I had shot his latest album cover, but I thought about the coincidence.

I had one complete scene with Peter Sellers. It got cut from the version I last saw but in essence, he asked me for a light. With camera in hand I answered in a British accent that I didn't have one, and that was it. He did remark after the cut that my accent was very good. I thanked him. Those were seven very cool weeks.

Carol Wayne was a vegetarian and was doing the macrobiotic diet routine. She described it and I decided to try it. Several of the cast went to lunch a few blocks from the studio every few days to a large health food store with a great restaurant inside that served macrobiotic dishes. It was a Japanese diet that tried to achieve a harmony between Yin and Yang. It starts with a three day water-only fast. On the third day you eat brown rice. Three days of brown rice and you slowly add vegetables. The two food groups, Grains and Vegetables, have the most Yin and Yang qualities. In the macrobiotic diet, the forces of Yin and Yang must be kept in balance to achieve good health. It was a fun exercise. The discipline of the diet was the most rewarding. I think it enhanced the high I was getting from smoking hemp. I have never forgotten the brown rice thing and I eat it often, now with vegetables and fish.

During the final scene, soap gets dumped into the waterfall that leads to the pool and a baby elephant enters with some teenagers. Bruce, the Gamma Ltd. photographer doing the stills for "The Party," had planted remote cameras everywhere to capture the spectacle as it happened. The scene was the last to be shot and it destroyed the set. Needless to say, they only shot it once. Bruce took several shots of me with the female characters in the film and gave me the contact sheets that you see in this book.

Bruce developed a relationship with Frances Davis who played the maid. She was the ex-wife of Miles Davis and told some very interesting stories about him. She was still wounded from the experience. She took Bruce on quite a ride until one night when he ended up stoned and in bed with another couple. When the guy came on to him, he said that was where he called it quits. Frances was a very sweet person, but I never saw her again after that film.

Years later on the set of "Becker" I met Al Checco, an actor from "The Party." When I introduced myself he gave me a big hug. He is very distinctive looking and once you have seen him, you will never forget his face. Bless his heart, he is still going strong.

About twelve years later I was walking with a gang of grips on the lot of Universal Studios when Carol Wayne walked by. I approached her and re-introduced myself. She said "Oh my god" and pulled me into her trailer. We had a great visit. She kissed me goodbye and I left feeling really high. She was a goddess, and she died some years later from an overdose surrounded by suspicious circumstances. She reminded me of Marilyn Monroe. What earth mothers, what sexual awakening. They both will be remembered forever.

Blake Edwards and Peter Sellers had collaborated to shoot a good part of the film using the technique of improvisation. Peter was good at that and Blake wanted to let him run with it. Their idea was to shoot video of each shot parallel with the film camera. That allowed them to instantly review the video to see if they had achieved their goal and the scene had actually worked. This was the beginning of a technical trend that would eventually develop into instant playback made famous by Francis Ford Coppola on the set of "One From the Heart." It allowed filmmakers to judge the success of the scene or shot. They could determine whether they were happy with what they captured on film, and they didn't even have to be on the set!

The story goes that Coppola would sit outside the sound stage in a converted trailer and literally run the shooting of the film while seated in front of a video monitor. Many commercials are shot with a group of art directors and producers huddled around a playback to correct or adjust the image or the dialogue. It has turned filmmaking into a debate, which is not always appreciated by those people who are waiting for the debate to dictate the course of action. So much of filmmaking is waiting: waiting for the lighting, the actors, the directors, the sun, the sound. Waiting, then moments of explosive human energy, then waiting again. This process repeats itself over and over for days on end. Ah, show biz.

Most days we ate across the street at the Formosa Café in our tuxedos and gowns. It was a good time for me because I was with actors. We shared this love for life thing, life and all its circumstance. It's the well of experiences you draw on to help you understand the characters you play.

Not long after I had finished "The Party," I was shooting some clothing shots for a young lady designer named Ola Hudson. She had a shop on the corner just west of the Troubadour, and she wanted photos of her latest creations. One of the models was a slight waif type redhead named Pamela. She had porcelain skin and soft blue eyes. As we talked during the shoot, she said her boyfriend was a singer in a rock band. Curious, I listened as she explained that his name was Jim Morrison. Whoa! I told her I had gone to school with Jim.

The Doors had progressed to the house band at the Whisky, were signed by Elektra Records and had recorded their first album. They had been fired from the Whisky by Elmer Valentine, the club owner, for using the "f" word in their performances. The Doors had management and they were on their way. Pamela told me that Jim was having trouble posing for the list of photographers that the magazines were sending; he was not showing up. She made a phone call and set up a meeting with the guys for me. What did I have to lose? I went to see my old friends.

It was like old home week. I had known these guys before their success and they knew I wasn't there to rip them off. It was a trust thing and it was what Jim had needed, a friend. Their managers, Sal and Asher, set me up to fly with them to San Francisco for a couple of concerts. I was supposed to shoot as much as I could, but it was too dark in the Fillmore to shoot. We did some sightseeing and along the way, I managed to get the group together for a pose or two.

One of the hardest things about shooting groups is to first get them all together, and then to hold their attention long enough for everyone to have their eyes open and decent looks on their faces. I used to shoot thirty or forty shots to get one or two good ones. As I progressed I was able to get a better percentage of usable shots. I added a motorized rewind to my new Nikon, which allowed me to grab more shots at the right moments. Ray lent me his Nikon F and together with mine, I had two camera bodies with a small assortment of lenses.

We flew back to L.A. and I developed the negatives. They were black and white and one roll of color. I dropped the proofs off at their managers' office. A few days later I was asked to visit with The Doors at their office and was offered a job shooting exclusively for them. I would get a percentage of the sale of any posters and concert books I produced. I would also supply all the teen magazines with shots for the articles they were doing on The Doors.

THE DOORS

I was put on the payroll. This was a new thing for me, steady money. It wasn't a lot of money compared to today's standards, but it was a start. Since I had worked for Gamma the money had been sporadic. The Doors paid me $275 a week plus I got some money from the magazines when they used my shots. Part of the deal we worked out in contract form was that I would produce a concert booklet plus posters that could be sold at concerts. I would receive 15 percent of the profits from sales of these items. When that was factored in I would make a little money.

I set to work getting the shots I needed for the concert book and supplying the magazines and newspapers with the shots they needed. I went to each of the band member's houses and took intimate shots. I followed them from concert to concert trying to gather enough to build a book. Ron Joy let me use the studio. I took Jim and his new leather/snake skin clothes there for some portrait shots. Those may be some of the only posed serious shots Jim ever did outside the band.

I hired a mutual friend to help me lay out the pages of the booklet. There was one shoot at a concert where Jim was handed a sparkler. He lit it up. I went crazy and shot as much film as I could get. One of those sparkler shots became the high contrast cover of the concert book I was to make.

CONCERT BOOK COVER

JIM AND STONE DOG

LMF POSTER

I also made a black and white poster called 'Light My Fire.' Jim was dressed in black leather pants and he was in his prime. A dozen shots from the same roll of film were ribboned down the left side of the poster. If you imagined it, you could see the action of his performance with the rapid viewing of this sequence of shots. For many months I traveled with them every time they went on tour. Their tours never lasted more than a week or two at a time, and then back to L.A. We went to San Francisco again and again. There were east coast tours where we would play up and down the coast from Florida to Massachusetts, from Ohio to New York.

After a concert in Boston we went to a restaurant on the pier in the Boston Harbor for a late night dinner celebration. There was a long banquet table and we were by ourselves in a private area. It was winter and outside snowflakes were falling. There was a huge fireplace roaring with a warm fire. Someone made a toast. I finished my drink and couldn't resist throwing my empty champagne glass into the fire. The headwaiter came over and made a big fuss. I explained to him the special ness of the occasion, the royalty of Jim and the Doors. As he protested my action, one by one everyone else threw his glass. When this happened he backed off and they served the biggest lobsters we ever saw.

As we traveled north to another concert, we convoyed in large rented Ford station wagons. Bill Siddons was road manager at that time. After one concert he asked me to accompany him to the front of the theatre to help pick up the payment for the show. It was to be paid in cash and he wanted company. He stepped into a small ticket booth for a few moments and emerged with two large shopping bags stuffed full of money. He said it was about 50,000 dollars. I walked back to the cars with him and we continued on to the next gig.

We eventually crossed over the border into Canada. While we were in Montreal for a show, we were led on a tour of the hip section of the city. The Doors attracted a small group of admirers as we walked along. One of the people we met was Richie Furay, who would later end up in the Buffalo Springfield. He told us we had to check out this chick that was singing up the street in a tiny coffeehouse. We entered and took our seats as Joni Mitchell sang her heart out. We all immediately recognized her talent.

It was beautiful weather and some of us decided to drive back down the coast to New York City where there was one last gig. I had the guys up in the Empire State Building, to Central Park, in the subways. I was grabbing as many group shots as I could. Sometimes I ended up with just one or two guys from the group and I took shots the best I could. We did the same routine in Washington D.C. Jim had an 8mm camera at the time. My shots show him shooting away but the footage was never seen. What happened to that footage? The Lincoln Memorial was one of the few places we had time to visit. It was hostile territory at the time with Viet Nam raging and us all being anti-war. I was glad to be out of there when we boarded the plane back to L.A.

The Doors did a two-day tour to San Francisco: two nights at the Fillmore with Steppenwolf opening for them. This was the famous club of the sixties for the hippies and was run by Bill Graham. Boy, was he a piece of work! Jim went onstage wearing a black velvet shirt and black leather pants. This was the sparkler concert. I lifted some beads off my neck and placed them around Jim's neck. They were cheap clear glass and brass beads that I had bought in the Haight-Ashbury district the night before. They were all different colors and they reflected the light. I got good pictures that night. He was wearing his traditional handmade leather pants that rode down on his slender hips. He dressed for effect but pulled off an 'I don't care how I look' thing. He was hippy chic.

About halfway through the show he was getting loose. He pulled the beads off in a slow motion sweep and threw them into the audience. What the fuck! I loved those beads. I ran into the audience who were standing at the apron and worked my way to the beads. Some kids were holding them, gushing themselves silly. I yelled, "Those beads are mine" and I reached out and snagged them. The fan held onto them, and the strand of beads broke. I was left with only the ones in my hand, and I still have them today. They're on a small strand together with the puka beads John Densmore and I collected on the beach in Hawaii.

Tim McIntire's friend Dean Goodhill was having a dinner party at his hideaway off Mulholland in the Hollywood Hills and invited me. During the evening I became acquainted with one of his guests. Ruth was a dark, beautiful, Mediterranean looking lady. She was alone with a small child and needed some loving. I think her baby was fathered by one of the guys from the group The Byrds. She had a small cabin type house off Woodrow Wilson Drive not too far from Dean's house, and she asked me for a ride home. She was still nursing her baby and her breasts were swollen; she was definitely an earth mother type. She had inherited the cabin from The Byrds, who had used it as a crash pad. An eccentric named John Compton owned the cabin, and maintained it just enough so the blackberry bushes and the cactus didn't overrun it. Other than that, the tenant was on his or her own. Ruth told me she was leaving the place and I wanted to live there! We drank some wine and sexed it up all night long. I helped her move out and it was mine.

I had bought a Rambler station wagon to haul my photo gear around and used it to move my stuff up from my apartment on lower Laurel Canyon. If you hung a right at Mulholland at the top of Laurel Canyon heading north and took another right, you ended up on Woodrow Wilson Drive. This was to become my new place. I loved it. David Carradine lived across the little road from me, and Frank Zappa was up the street and to the right. Hoyt Axton and his wife lived not too far up the street and I became friends with them.

We went to New York City for another couple of gigs. After one of the performances Jim and I ended up together, as was usually the case. The others went their own ways with their wives or girlfriends. We drank a lot that night and were driven by a chauffeur that had been hired to stay with us. We ended up at Steve Paul's downstairs nightclub. Jimi Hendrix did a late set; the place was packed. We were sitting in the booth next to Hendrix before his set. Some of Hendrix's girls saw Jim, and slid across and joined us. We were styling!

Jim was at the point of intoxication I had seen quite often. The next phase was usually something radical, then face down on the table. I hoped for the best. Hendrix was midway through his set when Jim joined him on the stage. This could get ugly and it did. Morrison was singing and Hendrix was playing guitar. Jim started to fall and grabbed Hendrix, and they both started struggling to remain standing. The roadies and management sensed some danger and started moving in, then a couple of fans in the audience started pulling at Jim, who held on to Hendrix's leg. Jim could get hurt here! I excused myself from the girls at the table and made my way to the stage. No one else knew where Jim's head was at. They probably thought he was insane. I grabbed him in a bear hug and whispered in his ear that it was me and we had to get out of there. He went limp and I carried him to the limo. By the time we got back to the hotel where we were staying, he was out. I carried him to his room and put him to bed. I was sober by then and took the limo back to the club to see some more of Hendrix. The manager of the club and the door people were so glad I had diffused the earlier situation that the rest of the night was on them. Hendrix thanked me and I sat at his table with his stable of chicks the rest of the night.

Back in L.A., The Doors were in the studio a lot working on their third album. I managed to get into the sessions most every day, sometimes bringing Jim from wherever we had ended up the night before. There were good vibes on this album. I was filming in the studio during the recording of "Wild Child."

By this time Babe had come to live with me up on Woodrow Wilson. He converted the old shed area behind the house into a bedroom. He was always comfortable wherever he was. Babe and I had been friends for twenty years. We went through some very interesting times together. We both grew up in what is now called South Central, an area in Los Angeles that is bordered on the north by Florence and Normandie. We used to hang out at Art's Chili Dog stand at Florence and Normandie, the same corner that became famous for the riot footage of the near-fatal beating of the cement truck driver Reginald Denny after the Rodney King beating. "Cant we all just get along". First I taught Babe how to put his hands into a changing bag and load film, which freed me up to keep the camera rolling. I also taught him how to use a nagra tape recorder and he became my sound man as I started to shoot 16 mm film footage of the band. Babe managed to record a lot of stuff that would otherwise have not seen the light of day. Babe was in the studio recording the interaction of the guys working out the details of the music. He had left Diane, his wife and their two girls. He told me he had enough and that Diane was crazy. He wanted to learn about L.S.D. He was ready to turn on.

At the Woodrow Wilson cabin we had a half-acre of cul-de-sac that was fenced off and at our disposal. Babe and I decided we wanted to get a dog and agreed to rescue one from a pound. We visited every pound and shelter from Santa Monica to Culver City and didn't think we would ever find the right dog. We were ready to give up for the time being when there in the next cage sat a large black lab mix. He looked up and saw us and he sort of sat up at attention. His look was one of "Well, you finally came. I have been waiting for you." Babe looked at me. "Now that's a stoned dog," he said.

When they opened the cage, he stepped out and greeted us without licking or too much fanfare. God, he was so cool! That was that, he was coming with us! He was about four years old and set in his ways. He fit in and we were family for a long time after that. It was destined: Stone dog became part of our life. He stepped into the Rambler, took his place on the back seat and we went back to the cabin. Stone loved that place: room to move around. Free, free, free at last. He never roamed too far, but he did visit as many bitches that came into heat as he could. David Carradine's girlfriend at the time was a young starlet named Barbara Hershey. She had a female dog that she would sometimes bring to visit. She told me she saw Stone dog mate with her dog, and sure enough, a few months later her dog gave birth to a litter. She invited me over to see them. The pups were very cute, but she was even cuter in her bikini that she was wearing as she greeted me at the door.

We were taking a short break in the Elektra studio during a recording session, when a message for Ray came in that someone wanted to see him. Ray left for a few minutes and when he returned, he was holding his eye. He started mumbling about some guy that had just attacked him in the hallway. I had Stone dog with me that day and the both of us headed for the hallway. I asked the receptionist about the guy. "He went out the front door." I asked who he was, but she didn't know. "How did he get in? She didn't know. Great.

I went out the front door onto La Cienega. Across the street heading for The Doors office I saw a dude that fit the description. Stone and I ran across the street. I let the leash go on Stone and grabbed the guy from the back in a reverse bear hug. He was a big guy and I was not that heavy, maybe 180 pounds at the most. We fell to the ground and there we were, with me holding on for dear life. I looked over and Stone was now sitting and watching us. Finally Babe came and I asked for his help. We held the guy until the police came. Ray ended up not pressing charges. The guy had traveled from his Midwest home looking for The Doors. One of The Doors songs had inspired his girlfriend to run off with someone else. He was pissed and wanted to kick some ass. Ray finally calmed him down and explained how they were just songs and they didn't want anyone to get hurt, blah blah blah. Ray had a pretty good shiner. The guy ended up working as a roadie for The Doors for a while. It was a little spooky for me to be around him and I avoided him the best I could.

Paul Ferrara

Paul Rothchild always had a stash of the best hash and pot that could be found. He liked the stoned atmosphere, but within that he liked to keep a control. With the help of Bruce Botnick, he guided The Doors sound and realized their potential as recording artists. Jim was a handful. Sometimes he brought a few girls with him. They had been partying and the party continued right into the studio session. The other Doors, Ray, Robby and John, tried to keep their cool as Jim would sometimes progress to the point of stupid drunk, when Paul Rothchild would be forced to call it a night. Jim was at his best when he reached just the right high. He was struggling with self-consciousness; he needed to be free of that and being high did it. It does that for a lot of people.

In the concert book I made there are a couple of pages devoted to the recording experience. It was very passionate, more concentrated than the live audience performances, yet they were trying to feel it like they did when they performed. They were a great live band when Jim was "on." When he was not having a great night, the reviews the next day were awful. When Jim hit the proper level of performance, the reviews the next day were sensational. I think most people that met Jim would agree that he was truly unique. The other three guys were easier to understand; Jim took some work. I was with him a lot for a couple of years and saw many sides to him. He was struggling to maintain the image of the stoned singer that he had developed. The other three guys didn't get it. They couldn't think outside their box. Why wasn't Jim like them, focused and interested in the money? He was so rebellious.

Jim carried around a briefcase, an old beat up piece of leather type of thing in which he kept his scribbled journals, poems he was working on and books he was reading at the time. He was very well read. He loved the French poets and Rimbaud was one of his favorites and mine as well. Rimbaud's book about his experiences as a young poet, "A Season in Hell," was a favorite of both of ours. The poet describes his descent into a hellish life of drugs and sex and debauchery leading him deeper and deeper inside himself and freeing up thoughts that had been suppressed for his entire life: thoughts about his childhood, his relationship with his mother and his sister, and about how the memories helped to form his thoughts and dreams. He described a process the other writers of the times were also discussing, one of experimenting with absinthe and other drugs. Aldous Huxley was writing about his experiments with psychotropic drugs, mushrooms and peyote, as a way of opening doors within the mind that would lead you to the unconscious thoughts you kept hidden. This was the path that Jim was on.

Almost no one around Jim 'got it.' They fought with him about his journey. His partying, as they called it, was infringing on their music and business life. He was a disruption and at the same time the very creation of what it was they were doing. Ray wrote in his book that Jim's friends kept him from his art. "How many poems and songs were not written because Jim was partying with the hangers on?" as he called them. Well, how many were written because of his partying and plumbing the depths of his soul in drunken intoxication? Many times I would see Jim scribbling in between the partying, or the morning after face down on the bar scribbling on a napkin. Jim being somewhat out of control was some of the mystique of The Doors. He became known for freaking out at his performances. People came to see him get crazy, and he did.

Once after a concert in Georgia, Jim and I were standing together waiting for our limo. A car full of young kids pulled up and offered us some smoke. They said they were headed to a big pool party somewhere outside of town, and asked if we would like to come along. It was a hot summer night; Jim looked at me, I looked at him, and we jumped into the van. They passed a bong to us, I smoked, Jim made a gesture to hit it but he didn't like weed that much. He did down the acid they gave him and so did I. What a night it was. There were about a hundred kids partying their ass'es off. Booze everywhere, a keg, wine; you name it, it was there. These kids knew how to party. Where were their parents? We had a great time. People were swimming in the pool, jumping off the garage roof landing in the water. The music was blasting. It was hot and a lot of the kids took their clothes off to swim. We followed suit. No one seemed to complain about the noise. The acid seemed to last all night; it was very pure stuff. Where did these kids in the middle of no where score such great drugs? The party was winding down as the sun came up. We had a flight to catch. The kids sat around Jim on the floor of the front room as the sun came up. There was quiet admiration going on. They were in heaven. It was a unique experience. They treated Jim like a brother, like he was one of them. He totally connected with the reality of his celebrity for once: not just the hype, but also the real people that bought his records. They delivered us to the hotel the next morning, and we packed quickly and joined up with the rest to leave for the airport. We were still stoned. It felt good.

David Schwarber, my graphics guy, and I completed both a poster and a concert book layout that everyone seemed to be in agreement on and I had them printed at Western Lithograph in L.A. Twenty-five thousand copies of each were delivered to the office at 8512 Santa Monica Boulevard, The Doors office / rehearsal space. I had a meeting with Jim and Ray where we discussed the completion of the book and poster. I mentioned to my two UCLA Film School friends that what was happening at the concerts, the performances as well as the audience reaction, was really something we should be capturing on film. They agreed and I was given a small budget to rent a camera and buy some black & white film stock and try it out. I began shooting 16mm film instead of stills and was getting some good stuff.

We were somewhere in the south. There was a violent storm between the next gig and us and all the airlines were grounded. Bill Siddons arranged for a small private plane to carry us to meet the concert date. Linda Ronstadt was opening for The Doors on several gigs, and she and some of her group boarded as well. We took off and for a while it was an easy flight. I was sitting next to Linda; we started talking and hit it off. She had a hit song on the radio called 'Different Drum' with a group called The Stone Ponys. Later we became a couple for about six months. They told us to buckle our seats because we were approaching some turbulence, the reason they had grounded the major airlines. The plane started to shake, the lights went out and came back on and flickered. The plane dropped about five hundred feet and then caught itself. We were being bounced around like dolls; it felt like the end. People were crying and holding on to one another. This went on for about fifteen minutes, then all of a sudden it became still. It was like we had passed through. No one said a word. The plane continued on to the city we were to play in and everyone made the concert in time.

As I followed the group into the theatre or stadium I was always asked who I was. It was explained that I was with the band; that was that and I got a pass. To the fans that approached me and asked if I was with the band, I replied yes. They thought I was the bass player. I found it amusing, and it did get me into a lot of places and next to a lot of girls. There was this joke about being the fifth Door sometimes. We eventually ended up back in L.A. and I started seeing Linda a lot for a while. She had a cool beach house in Ocean Park. By coincidence, it was very close to where both Ray and I had lived. She was very cute and in her early twenties. She was also very starved for attention. She was labor intensive. She loved sex and was very determined to have her way with me. No love involved. I did the best I could, but it was very mechanical and to the point. Sometimes after she fell asleep, Babe, who was usually with me and resting on the couch in the front room, would get up and we would go for a drink at Hinano's.

I introduced Babe to Tim McIntire and the rest of my friends like Bailey, etc. Babe fit right in. He was an existential type dude with no belongings to speak of. He didn't care about tomorrow; he lived in the moment. He was always reading a book; quiet yet explosive. Ever since we were kids in the Embassy, Babe could drink anyone under the table. Jim loved him from the start as I did, and they became good friends. We were a three some for some time until Jim started living with Pam more like boyfriend and girlfriend. Jim would disappear to be with Pam for days on end, eventually regrouping with us to continue his bachelor type life. We partied all over the place with Eric Burdon, Timothy Leary; anyone who was partying, we were there!

We were back in San Francisco and met up with January Jansen, one of the people Jim had met who designed his leather clothes. Jan was a very cool guy and the four of us hung out a lot. He took us to his friends' places where we got to meet the people of Haight-Ashbury: the artists, the musicians, the store-owners. There was an old brick building about four stories high; it was an artists' cooperative, of sorts. The center of the building had been hollowed out, and we could see top to bottom. The roof was fitted with a large skylight. It was so cool.

We decided to drive back down the coast to L.A. and we rented a car. Jan joined Jim, Babe and I as we took some acid that Jan supplied. We pulled over in Big Sur and tried to sleep in the car at a campsite. It was a little chilly and we couldn't sleep, so we started a campfire and continued to drink. At one point Jim had a stick he was holding and pushed it into the coals. It caught on fire and he was waving it like a torch. He pushed it higher and higher until it touched the pine tree that was next to us, which caught on fire. Babe and I sprang into action; we were good at that. We grabbed the branch and broke it off, admonished Jim, and he settled down.

In the morning we went into town for some coffee. The four of us were at a booth when Jan passed out and his head hit the table; he just went limp. Jan wore a large curly Afro type 'do, and at one point, Jim lit a match and held it to Jan's hair. It started crackling and hissing while Jan just lay there, passed out. Babe and I put out that fire, also. What was wrong with Jim? Sometimes he did stuff that was so stupid! It was like he was testing Babe and I to see how much we could handle. Jim was always testing people, pushing them to see what his limits were. Sometimes he could act like a little kid. God, he must have been a handful for his parents!

His dad was actually a Rear Admiral in the Navy, although everyone generally believes he was an Admiral. There was strict discipline at home. Jim didn't want to see his mother when she tried to see him at a concert once. I had to tell her he was ill and couldn't see her. She must have watched the concert. Stunned, I'll bet. Who was this wild performer? She was sad when I told her. I felt bad for the both of them. He never quite explained why he hated his parents so much. Anyway, he was running from authority as fast as he could. An Admiral for a dad. He had never even had a car. He was late to grow up and he was doing a lot of it right in front of us.

The next day we got going and stopped for some breakfast at Napenthe, a restaurant right on the highway that hangs out over the ocean on a cliff in Big Sur, before we headed south to L.A. We were outside sitting on a bench soaking up some warmth from the sun. A guy next to us struck up a conversation. He lived across the highway and made furniture out of large redwood trees. He asked if we would like to check it out and maybe smoke some good pot. We followed him to his place. His name was Richard Rutowski. He was married to Bettina, a beautiful German girl. We stayed for several hours and promised to visit him again. His furniture was beautiful.

Jan stayed in L.A. for a few days and then flew back up to San Francisco to take care of his various businesses. Jan had made Jim some new clothes made of exotic animal skins. Exotic snake skins sown into beautiful suits. I took Jim to the Gamma studios and shot some fancy shots with him modeling his new clothes.

Around this time I ran into Mary Werbelow who was trying to get into modeling. She and Jim were old news; Jim was with Pam by this time. I started helping Mary with photos; she photographed beautifully. I took some pictures of her without her top on. She had the most beautiful breasts. I saw her often. She had taken a cab to the studio and after we finished taking pictures I offered to give her a ride home. She told me she was broke and didn't have any food at her house; otherwise she would cook dinner for me. I swung into a grocery store and we went shopping. We bought enough so she was going to have food for some time. She was very thankful. She started to kiss me and soon we were naked on her bed. This was the first time we made love. She was a strange girl, something I couldn't put my finger on like she was in a world of her own. I left her sleeping that night. When her pictures were done I gave her copies for her portfolio. She got into the Maharishi and meditation after that and left for India to study with her guru. Jim and I lost track of her.

There was a break in The Doors touring schedule and they all headed off for vacations. Babe and I had nothing to do for these short periods of time. Harrison Ford, who I had met at Bailey's apartment, lived a quarter of a mile from Babe and me on Mulholland Drive. At that time Harrison was still acting, doing a small T.V. role here and there, and was supporting his family with carpentry. He specialized in remodel and design of recording studios and catered to the people of the Hollywood community. He had built The Mama & the Papas' recording studio. He asked Babe and me if we would like to pick up some extra cash. We agreed and occasionally worked on his various jobs.

There were various girls that grouped around The Doors at the time, and one by one they made their way to the cabin. One was Donna Port, a large size but shapely brunette with a very voluptuous body. She stayed with me on occasion. One day I noticed her car was still parked up on the road near the cabin. I inquired and found out that Robby had taken her and some other girl on a late night run to Mexico to buy some shrimp. They must have been very stoned. Robby fell asleep driving his Porsche and they had a very bad accident that left Donna paralyzed from the waist down. No wonder her car hadn't moved for so long; she was still in the hospital. Finally her dad came for the car. Donna was permanently paralyzed, and Robby took care of her finances for years and maybe still to this day, for all I know.

Harrison Ford and I were heading out in my Rambler to do an errand. As I backed up to head out, Stone indicated that he wanted to come along so I opened the back door and he jumped in. We turned onto Woodrow Wilson and Harrison swung his arm up to place it across the top of the seat. Stone must have thought he was going to strike me because he went for Harrison's arm; it was in his mouth. He didn't try to hurt him or anything, but he did have a firm grip on it. Harrison didn't freak and one word from me to Stone about letting go did the trick.

Stone was always earning his keep one way or another. He went on shoots with Jim and I, and he posed with Jim for a particular sequence that ended up on posters and other various forms of media. People always thought that was Sage, the dog that Pamela and Jim had, but Sage was blond and completely different looking. Stone was a big lanky black lab/blue tick hound mix. Babe made him a cool leather neckband that he hung a small Tibetan bronze bell on. It wasn't loud but it made a clink that let you know Stone dog's whereabouts.

It was the best of times. Babe and I were in NYC with The Doors and we were doing behind the scenes coverage. We traveled in a limo with Jim and Albert Goldman, a writer for the Times. Later on Goldman would entertain the idea of a Jim Morrison book but he died before he could write it. It was a good thing, because he never wrote kind things about Jim. Babe and I were crouched at their feet as they talked on the way to a concert somewhere. When we pulled up at the gig the fans, mostly girls, rushed the limo to say hello to Jim. Jim started to lower the window and they reached in and tried to touch him. One girl rested her hand on Jim's crotch. Jim got out and a few girls kissed him as he made his way into the concert. That was a small sequence in the film entitled "Feast of Friends."

The next day The Doors had a photo shoot with Richard Avedon. I had admired his fashion photography forever and was thrilled to meet him. He gave advance notice to Siddons that the film crew would not be allowed in his studio, but I decided to try to smash my way in. I hid in the middle of the group and entered the studio with the film camera rolling. The footage showed him freaking out and rushing me and covering the lens with his hand. "What was he doing in here?" He was such an asshole about it. I toured the rest of his place and saw his staff and the machinery they needed to make every client as beautiful as they could look. Airbrush, fading and dodging: you name it, they did it!

As we drove around in the limos on that trip in NYC, "Light My Fire" was being played a lot on the radio. It sounded so good. Everyone was basking in the gloriousness. The Doors had arrived in a big Number One type of way. The song was the all-time coolest song. It had touches of jazz, rock and flamenco. What more could you ask for? It lasted on the charts in America for a long time and firmly established The Doors as a monster group. The concerts got bigger and bigger. Jim was proclaimed a Sex Symbol. It was getting wild. Jim started to sense his power and began to use it to lead his young fans on a rebellious journey. He took his audiences to the point of riot repeatedly. I managed to get some of that on film.

In Ohio the stage was barricaded against the fans by a group of security guards that were totally on edge as Jim egged the audience to join him on stage. They started climbing up the front of the apron where the security guys grabbed them and threw them back into the audience. There were so many kids on the stage that Siddons, fearing for Jim's life, ran out and grabbed him at the end of the concert and carried him off. In "Feast of Friends," over the music of 'Five To One' it clearly shows the incoherent Morrison caught up in the frenzy and swinging his fist at the camera I was holding. I have never really been clear whether he was swinging at the camera or at me. After the film came out, it was one of the sequences most discussed as the first footage ever of The Doors or, for that matter, of any group, involved in the madness that could envelope a concert.

That night after a wild concert we arrived back at the hotel. There were kids everywhere and a lot of girls in the hallway. At first it was a little frightening and Jim barricaded himself in his room. We had adjoining rooms, and I went to him and discussed a strategy. I would go into the hall and pick the best. Once in my room if they were ready for the experience, I knocked on Jim's door and introduced them. Jim could never have kept up with the demand, so I helped him out. The girls were literally fucking me to get in line to fuck Jim. They all thought I was the bass player and I didn't tell them anything different. What a night! The heartland of America has proved to be a rich holding pen for the frustrated corn fed blonde, blue-eyed teenager looking to break free of the restrictions that the Bible Belt put on them. They all wanted to tell their stories of boredom and needed to touch - or in this case, fuck - someone famous. We did as many as we could and then it was morning. Thank god Siddons had again placed a wake up call for everyone. We packed and caught the plane.

I would take the film to CFI Laboratories for processing as soon as I could after returning to L.A. I had rented a small 16mm Moviola and was assembling the footage as I went, not really having any overall structure in mind. There was no MTV at the time and no outlet for what I was doing. I would edit and string small sequences together. Jim visited me at the Moviola quite often. He was truly interested in the process of film. He didn't have a home life and he spent hours with me down there. I bought a 16mm projector and once a week I would show the most recent footage in The Doors rehearsal room under the office where I had placed a large screen against one wall. Usually a lot of people would attend the screenings. They started yelling and screaming during the riot parts.

After the day's work we went out partying. We went to the Whisky a lot where the doorman would let us in and we were shown to Jim's booth. Many nights Jim would pass out there and I would take him home, leaving Vito and his troupe of very stoned dancers spinning madly on the dance floor. They appeared at every club on the strip from time to time, dressed in the wildest clothes you can imagine and the girls wore very little. There were always girls that joined us at our table that usually followed us home for the night if Jim hadn't gotten too drunk.

In New York Jim met up with Andy Warhol and his group. One of Andy's actors was Nico, a tall wispy blonde who looked like she was on Quaaludes all the time. Jim and Nico had an on-again, off-again relationship for some time.

Through all of his romances, Jim managed to keep a relationship with Pam. It was rocky to say the least, but it was there. She put up with a lot, but she retaliated in her own promiscuous way. She was a seductress. She knew how to use her girlish sexuality to get what she wanted. Jim was away on a short tour with The Doors, I think in NYC. I had stayed behind this time. Pam knew about Nico and in fact, knew about a lot of Jim's girlfriends. I met her in The Doors office and she asked me for a ride home. I delivered her to the Laurel Canyon house she shared with Jim. She asked if I wanted to come in for a drink; I said sure. A girl Pam employed to take care of the house opened the door, and Pam and I went in. After the girl left, Pam brought out the hash pipe. It was very good stuff. We drank some wine; we were both very stoned and I was lying on some very large pillows. She knelt down beside me and told me she knew Jim was with his other girlfriend. Would I stay for dinner? She was so seductive. She leaned closer and kissed me on the lips. It was a quick kiss. Nothing serious, but it was the first time she had kissed me, ever. One thing led to another and soon we were naked. She used her lips to make me hard and climbed on board. She was like the Energizer Bunny; I asked her to slow down. She said, " that's how Jim likes it". I told her I wasn't Jim. She had the cutest little body with small but perfectly shaped breasts, red hair that fell down onto my chest, light green doe eyes, porcelain skin dusted with freckles and not an ounce of fat. She was only maybe 5' 2" tall. Petite. I felt guilty but it was like a duty fuck. A friend needs it and you give it. When Jim returned Pam immediately told him, like she was gloating and rubbing it in his face. Jim asked me if it was true. I told him how it happened, that she had seduced me. He said he understood. We had shared girls before.

Jim was not jealous. It is an amazing quality for a person to have at least he didn't show it. He was truly unique. He had an elevated sense of his self that is rarely seen among people. Like his dislike for possessions, his generosity the way he tempted life. Playing with the circumstances. His confidence was so strong. He was a prince among men. Perfect in the poet/rock star role that he was born into. He didn't fit any mold. The critics stretched to interpret what was happening with Jim and The Doors. It was so natural it was hard to see it happening. Ray called it a visitation I call it a gift, whatever. You hardly noticed it day to day. Only when his songs, his words, his poems, his performances are analyzed or experienced first hand do you feel the power. There was no one else like Jim.

Jim always financed Pam's apartments and her business. She started a small hippie-type boutique around the corner from The Doors office, also in the Clear Thoughts Building. She called it Themis. Jim poured a lot of money into that place. Pam traveled all over the world buying stuff: Morocco, London, Paris, India. She brought back handmade clothing and incense and rugs and jewelry that she sold to the lucky people that found the shop.

Themis was the Grecian goddess of law and justice, the titan daughter of Gaia and Uranus. She was said to be the mother of the Three Fates and the caretaker of the young Apollo and Artemis. And care-take she did, almost to the point of smothering Jim. Periodically Jim would bolt. Pam knew he had other girlfriends; it was a constant point of contention. When I first met Jim he had bolted from his parents. He was disgusted by the older generation. We were all pissed. James Dean had immortalized our anger and frustration in "Rebel Without a Cause." Pam supplied some sense of normality to an otherwise hectic rock star existence.

At times I was invited for dinner. Pam would have set a large table set and had been cooking all day. Stoned, and with jewels and flowers in her hair, she was the perfect hostess for Jim and his house. She came from Orange

County, the daughter of a high school principal. She had some authority issues as well; she was always stoned or in a state of bliss. She treated me quite well, although she was a little jealous of Jim's small band of friends. We were the ones that took him away; we provided something she couldn't provide: brotherhood.

Babe and Jim and I were a pretty good partying team. Once in a moment of downtime, the three of us were at the Woodrow Wilson house. We took some acid and proceeded to cook some steaks while we were waiting to trip. Babe and I both took our steaks off the grill and went inside to eat. After a while we realized Jim wasn't with us. We walked outside and Jim was stoned, staring at the burnt steak on the barbecue. He was a million miles away. When we spoke he came to a little and we led him inside and shared our meal with him. We ate, drank some beers, and then headed down the mountain to the Strip.

Sugar Bear, an actor friend of ours that just happened to be a dwarf, met us at the door of the Whisky and showed us to our table. Sugar Bear used to hook up with us every once and awhile after the Whisky closed, and spend the night usually visiting three or four different parties. He hung out on the Strip and knew what was happening. When Eric Burdon and the Animals played the Whisky, after the club closed one night, the four of us went back to Eric's hotel and drank some whiskey, smoked some pot and stayed stoned until morning. Jim and Eric admired each other, as we did them. It was a cool time. Eric was doing the song 'Gloria' in his sets and later Jim did live versions of 'Gloria'; you remember the one where the letters are spelled out G-L-O-R-I-A.

We met everyone from Timothy Leary to Norman Mailer. The Doors were going to play a few concerts in Bakersfield, California. I hired Harrison Ford to be my grip/helper and he traveled with me Babe and the rest of the group in rented station wagons. Harrison needed some money. He was cool to hang with, and besides, he threw work to Babe and I when he could. I told him I didn't know what to expect and couldn't give him the details, but I assured him he would enjoy himself. I didn't know exactly what to expect. I never did. It turned out the concerts were lit so poorly that I was not able to photograph them. After the last of two concerts there was a lot of partying going on in the motel where we were staying. For some reason, John and Robby left right after the concert and headed back to L.A.

Robby was dating Lynne from New York at the time and he just left her there. She was hurt by him and got really drunk and crawled into bed with me and fucked me until she passed out. The first time I met Lynne she was with Jim at the Lucky U in Westwood. She was dressed in black leather clothes, just like Jim. He had met her in NYC and she had flown out to see him. Jim called and asked me to meet them there. Eventually she ended up with Robby and they remain together today. They have a son named Waylon who is now all grown up and has been following a musical path like his father.

The next morning we all awoke in Bakersfield rather hung over. From the look on Harrison's face, he had gotten laid as well. We heard from some of the local kids that there was a really cool spot on the Kern River to swim and party. I think there were two wagons full of equipment and us that headed for the swimming hole. It was hot and the water was great. There was a sandy beach area where the coolers and towels were placed. Lynne and her friend Peggy took off their clothes and sunbathed. Jim loved swimming. He took off across the river to a large rock outcropping that hung over the water. It was deep in that spot and people were jumping off. Jim stripped down to nothing, stood on the diving spot and did a very nice swan dive. There was a nice smooth rockslide that people would lay in and be swept along. Harrison, Babe and I got as much of it on film as we could, but we still managed to have some fun. Later, Jim was so self-conscious about the sequence of him in full frontal nudity that after seeing the dailies that week, he made me destroy the footage of him. Was this the same guy that would later destroy The Doors by allegedly exposing himself?

The first ever Pleasure Faire was about to be held in Calabasas and I decided to film the event. Jim, Babe, Harrison and I took the equipment that I hadn't returned yet from the previous week of shooting. They weren't open on the weekend, which meant we had free equipment. I bought some film and we drove to Calabasas. We had to hike in from the road about a half-mile to an ancient oak grove where there was a small city set up with booths and displays. There were jugglers, musicians, belly dancers, knife throwers, people reciting poetry. The theme was Renaissance England and everyone was dressed in authentic Elizabethan costume, totally in character. A lot of the people who attended the festival also dressed in costume. There was plenty of booze and drugs. It turned into an overnighter. There were small camps of people gathered around large fires, drinking and smoking. We ended up with some people from Hollywood that Harrison knew, Severn Darden and his crew.

There was plenty of free love to be had. The drugs in those days made sex easy and uninhibited. You saw somebody, took a blanket, and just walked into the bushes a little ways and had sex. It happened several times that night. There were thousands of people there. I shot the opening procession where everyone paraded by the camera dressed in costume; drums and bells accompanied the procession. I shot a lot of close-ups of the belly dancer's glittering costume. People were beginning to recognize Jim more but for the moment at the Faire, he blended into the crowd. We all had a great time.

The Pleasure Faire has changed over the years from something wild and uninhibited to a very organized commercial operation. We were lucky to have been at the first one. Ray used some of my footage in the compilation videos he directed. I never said anything, but that footage was my personal stuff that just got scooped up in the pandemonium after Jim's death.

I noticed subtle changes in Jim's personality as he became more famous. I am not so sure he was ready for the pressure of stardom. He was drinking more steadily.

We flew to Seattle for a concert. Babe and I managed to film the group visiting the monorail exhibit at the site of the World's Fair that had taken place a few years before. On the monorail was an old guy that Jim started talking with. He was very talkative about the Viet Nam war. As we sailed across the skyline of Seattle, he asked the question, "What the fuck are we doing over there?"

After the concert a minister of the Evangelical Church ended up backstage. He asked Jim some questions about his intentions: "There are questions in the community about what you are trying to pull off," referring to Jim's reference to fucking his mother and killing his father. He wanted to know about the anarchic theme of his words. Jim gave him some double talk about it was just showbiz; he seemed humble in front of the minister. They laughed it off and the minister left with no new information.

There was another riot at the Singer Bowl in New York. It was sort of a circular stage and lined with guards who were fully ready for a riot. Jim hurled himself into the air and landed on the stage in a prone position. He still had the microphone in his hand and was singing on the floor of the stage. The people in the audience started hurling bottles and chairs at the group as they played on. I tried to cover the camera and myself by crouching down beside the drums. It was insane. Jim was digging his power to incite riots. After the show in the dressing room Jim comforted a teenage girl who was struck by a chair. She had blood dripping down her head, and Jim had a towel and tried to soak up the blood. He explained to the camera that she was just an innocent bystander.

We flew to Hawaii for a couple of concerts and managed some sightseeing and photography in and around the shows. We visited the volcano; it looked like the moon. We flew a small plane to Maui for a few days of R & R where I filmed Jim riding a bicycle at the Lahina Pier. The entire group went on a sailboat ride. The sun was setting and Jim fell asleep on the sail. We sail off into the sunset. It was beautiful. That was one of the first sequences I cut before Frank came to work with us. It later ended up that it was the last sequence in the film later known as "Feast of Friends." I used music from the album by Gustav Holst called 'The Planets.' It still has a magic quality to it when seen. Robby was with Lynne, Ray and Dorothy, John and Babe and of course, Jim. It was a rare moment of tranquility in an otherwise hectic journey.

After the sailboat ride we were all sitting around the pool at our hotel. As the evening progressed everyone got pretty drunk. A young couple from a room near ours joined us. They were enjoying their time together: he was on leave from the war in Viet Nam and they were partying like there was no tomorrow. They found out I was filming The Doors and asked me quietly if I would photograph them having sex. I wasn't ready for that and declined their offer.

The war was making everybody crazy: the people fighting it and the people not fighting it. Everybody was involved. Students were rioting. Soldiers were deserting. It polarized everyone. Like the guy in Seattle said, "What the fuck are we doing over there?" Jim, Babe and I took some THC and we joined the rest of The Doors for a planned visit to a luau. They served barbecued turtle and pig and danced with fire and swords. The drug made me semi-incoherent, but I do remember imagining they were cannibals and that the turtle meat was human flesh. I got a little sick down by the surf later on. Booze and drugs do not always mix well. Oh well, you take your chances and you truck on, trying to get as high as you can and still maintain.

BABE, JIM AND PAUL   PHOTO BY © FRANK LISCIANDRO

SINGER BOWL   PHOTO BY DAVID SYGALL

One beach that we visited had a white stretch of sand that was littered with small white shells with perfect holes in the middle of them. It was like they were ready to string up. John and I both noticed the shells and took the time to gather a couple of bags full. These were the famous puka beads of Hawaii. Later I made a necklace of mine and in a few more years, everyone was wearing them. The next morning we were at the black sand beach where there was a rock outcropping that pushed down into the surf. Babe was barefoot and making his way across the rocks when a large wave came up suddenly and swept him off the rocks. He landed on some poisonous coral that he had to climb on to get back up, and it tore up the souls of his feet. We took him to the local hospital where they treated him. His feet were pretty much bandaged up and he hobbled the next morning as we boarded the jet back to L.A. The concert was a good one and the local reviews were very good.

The next big thing on the horizon for The Doors was a concert to be held at the world famous Hollywood Bowl. It was to be The Doors' big showing in their hometown. All of their friends would be there: their producers, the record executives, other famous rock performers, the media, everyone. The posters and the concert book were ready and were to be sold at this concert.

We decided to shoot the concert. Bruce Botnick and Paul Rothchild brought mobile equipment to the rear of the stage area and ran cable to the stage. It was a big deal. I was still working on a small budget. At the last moment we were told that we would have to pay 5 thousand dollars to the stagehands union to shoot in the Bowl. There was some discussion about spending that much money. The filming of the concert was on, then off, and then finally on. I had a total of four cameras. One was a master shot in the center of the seating area that I operated. It captured the whole stage and I was able to zoom in to the individual performers and then back out again. Frank Lisciandro was shooting a camera that was at the foot of the stage. David Thompson, my friend from UCLA, was shooting the one handheld camera that was on stage and Steve Wax operated the ultra high speed camera. Nowadays, film crews have as many as 10 or 20 cameras, cranes and dollies, and full crews of film runners. Nobody realized at the time that what I was doing would become the basis for a Doors archive of photography.

Backstage before the concert there was quite a crowd of people jammed into the dressing rooms. Mick Jagger was sitting next to Jim. Richie Havens had a video camera and was recording it. He says he doesn't know what happened to the footage. I was busy getting all the cameras in front of the stage ready. I wish I had captured some of the backstage, but it just didn't work out.

Tim McIntire, who had become friends with Robby and Jim through Babe and I, volunteered to announce the band. He stood to the side of the stage with a mike in his hand. In his rich baritone voice he said, "Ladies and Gentlemen, The Doors." Jim had taken acid and was a little bit off that night. Robby's guitar was not always in tune and the crowd was not pleased. They wanted some action; they had read the reviews about Jim's wild antics. As John started the drum sequence that leads into 'The End,' Jim asked for the lights to be turned down. If they turned down the lights I would be screwed: I was already all the way open on the lenses and it would ruin the footage. Luckily for everyone, Jim's request to have the lights turned down was not granted. He finally got off the light trip and started the song.

My little crew did great. We didn't have a lot of film magazines and the film had to be unloaded and reloaded on the spot. We managed to shoot enough footage for The Doors to release "Live at the Hollywood Bowl" later on. At that point in time I included 'The End', one of the sequences we had edited, in what became "Feast of Friends."

After the concert everyone went back to The Doors office for a party. The tension had been let out and it was time to party. I wrapped all the equipment and packaged all the spent film. By the time I joined the party it was winding down. Behind the office was a parking area that the party had spilled into. Georgia Newton, a friend of Robby and then Jim, was puking her guts out. I had seen her around for some time and I thought she was beautiful. She was 19 or 20 years old at the time. I offered her some comfort; I held her head as she heaved until there was nothing left. She came up to the cabin that night and slept it off. She went home and came back the next night. We made love, and soon after that she moved in.

I had been writing music and playing the guitar for some time. When Georgia came into my life, we discovered she had an amazing voice and could harmonize with anything I could sing. She eventually even wrote some lyrics to music I wrote. Jim knew Georgia from before and it didn't stop him from hanging around at the cabin and jamming with me and now Georgia. Babe still lived up there as well; we were a happy stoned little group; a family, you might say. Jim bought a Nagra tape recorder and Babe used it to record all the sound he could for the documentary we were shooting. He kept it at the Woodrow Wilson cabin, and a lot of the songs we wrote were recorded in the bedroom of that little cabin. One night when we were jamming, Jim wrote some lyrics down and sang them to a song I had been writing on the guitar. He started to sing the lyrics: 'At first flash of Eden ... We raced down to the shore.' He wrote more and sang more until he had almost the whole song. We played it over and over and it eventually became 'Waiting For the Sun.' John wrote about it in his book "Riders on the Storm." Babe swears he recorded Jim and I but to this day, the tape is missing.

John wrote that one day he walked in on Jim and Robby arguing: "Jim wanted to give credit to an old UCLA film school buddy for helping him pen a song." Jim says "Paul Ferrara wrote that melody, Robby ...the part where I sing At first flash of Eden, we raced down to the shore, Jim snapped. Robbie speaks..." No he didn't ...That's my melody. I know you originally wrote those lyrics to one of Paul's melodies, but that was an old one. I know my melodies." So much for sharing.

I had a sweet little Porsche at the time, a '59 tub convertible that I had painted dark green. Larry Raphael had a car just like it. He helped to fashion some of what I considered my style, and I thank him publicly for that. Georgia borrowed it one day and blew the engine up. She called her dad for help and it was towed to his friend's garage in Westwood where it was rebuilt.

Georgia came from a family that was composed of old California aristocracy. Her grandfather was a Bard and her mother was a Bard. The Bards were landowners and ranchers in Ventura County. Her father was a veteran of W.W. II and a little shell-shocked. Her mother was the financier and the matriarch of the family. They had a beautiful house in Beverly Glen, a canyon snuggled in the heart of the Beverly Hills mountains next door to the gated community where the movie stars lived. Georgia had been a rebellious young child and was constantly hitchhiking down the canyon and over the hill to the Sunset Strip.

FALLEN LEAF   STONE, GEORGIA, ME AND BABE

WEDDING DAY   PHOTOS BY JOANNA NEWTON

I was given the job of photographing the "Waiting For The Sun" album cover. I wanted to do something that showed them in a glamour type portrait for their third cover. They had one album with four heads and the second with a juggler. I wanted the sunrise behind them, which was kind of hard on the west coast. The easiest thing to accomplish was a sunset that doubled for a sunrise. Late one afternoon Babe and I rounded up the four suspects and loaded them into the Rambler station wagon. We arrived in Malibu just before sunset and drove to the top of a canyon. I placed a couple of shiny boards in front of them that reflected the setting sun behind them back onto their faces. I needed some height to see the pink of the sunset, so I climbed on top of my car and shot from there with a Hasselblad camera I had rented. Babe had the smarts to grab a couple of shots from behind us with a small camera he had. Of all the album covers they did, I still think it is the most flattering. I was very pleased with and proud of the result.

Jim, Babe, me and our dates all took acid one night and went to see Kubrick's new film "2001: A Space Odyssey." We sat in the first row of the Cinerama Dome Theatre. It was a wraparound screen with state of the art sound, and quite a place to be stoned! It was a real interesting night. Later we ended up at the cabin with nothing to do and we were still all very wide-awake.

We cruised around a lot at night after the clubs closed. Sometimes we went to Canters on Fairfax or Bob's on Wilshire and ate. One night we all piled into someone's car and drove up to Mulholland Drive to see the city lights. There was a road that led to the towers above the Hollywood sign that I always wondered about. We decided to drive up it and came to some sort of communications installation. You can still see those antennas from Hollywood today. We parked and started to snoop around. We opened the door and to our surprise there was a dude sitting by himself, manning tons of electronic equipment. He was startled at first but then welcomed our company. We hung out with him for a while and watched the monitors and equipment that was transmitting signals all over L.A. County. This is where the radio and television stations were being relayed out of the city to the surrounding areas. Eventually we all fell asleep somewhere, awoke the next day and went to The Doors office.

Jim was out of town when an offer came in to use the song "Light My Fire" in a Buick commercial. The three Doors that were in town jumped at the chance to make some easy money and they signed the contract without Jim. When he got back there was a meeting in Bill Siddons' office that I attended where Jim threw a tantrum and the shit hit the fan about them making a decision without him. He was totally against the corporate use of their art. It blew up in all their faces, about how it was supposed to be all for one and one for all. He never trusted them again after that. He threatened to burn a Buick on Sunset Boulevard. It was a harbinger of what was to follow: the eventual split that would be the end of The Doors. To this day the surviving members of The Doors are still disagreeing about the commercial use of their music. John has stepped up to protect what he calls Jim's legacy. John has changed more than anyone in recent times. Ray and Robby are still out there making Doors music. I can't say I blame them; performing is a powerful narcotic.

Someone got tickets for a play at the Shrine Auditorium called the "Living Theatre." The group of actors, was led by Julien Beck. The play was about freedom and Paradise Now. The actors got almost naked and came down into the audience and confronted us. It was at first a semi-frightening experience as the crazed actors climbed out into the audience. They were reciting lines about social restrictions, anti-war rhetoric, and sexual liberation. We were all really affected by the performance. Soon after that night, The Doors left for a concert in Miami. Bill Siddons informed me that the film crew would not go on this trip. There was some concern about money and the importance of filming another concert so soon after the Hollywood Bowl shoot.

That trip was to change the course of everything. It's well known what happened in Miami but for those of you who do not know what happened: Jim was very intoxicated and encouraged the audience to join him on stage. Typical, but at one point he asked the audience if they wanted to see his cock. He asked them over and over until there was frenzy. From Ray's account, Jim took off his shirt and held it in front of his crotch, and mimed unzipping his fly and exposing himself. He did it so convincingly that many believed they actually saw Jim's penis. Some swear they actually saw him pull his Johnson out and wave it around.

It made the Miami newspapers the next day. There were no photos of the incident but plenty of first hand accounts. This was the same guy that was embarrassed about the footage of him in the nude diving off a rock. He was reliving the experience of Julien Beck's Living Theatre. Nudity, it was everywhere: on the screen, on billboards, sex was implied in everything we experienced. He knew the audience wanted something sensational and he fed on their need for it. He taunted them and they responded, he taunted them some more and finally there was chaos. When the concert ended, the group went to the Caribbean Islands for a vacation.

A few days later Bill Siddons called with the news that Dade County had issued arrest warrants for The Doors for public nudity. Siddons told them to come back to L.A. What about the rest of the tour? All the dates had been canceled, the biggest tour they had ever planned. The public performance permits for The Doors were revoked. It was front-page news in every city they were about to play. The entire country rejected them. That was it. They came back to L.A. What a concert to not have documented on film! If my crew had been allowed to travel to Miami and film that show, the footage could have made all the difference in the world regarding Dade County's charges and the subsequent trial. I was so pissed. I will never forgive Bill Siddons for not sending the crew on that mission. The Doors became personas non grata. They couldn't get a gig. "The Soft Parade," their next album, didn't make a big splash and there they were. It was Jim they held responsible for the Miami problem. He was out on 5 thousand dollars bond. Max Fink was Jim's main lawyer and handled the trial. It was a heavy load for Jim to carry. He could get jail time, and Dade County was famous for its strict penal system.

The Doors management halted the documentary filming that I had been shooting of the band. Bill Siddons informed me that since the incident in Miami, all the future live concert dates were cancelled. They were going to stop extra expenditures, and that meant the film project I was heading was cancelled. Siddons had made the call to not send the film crew to Miami, perhaps to save money. He never really understood what I was doing. Years later when the Doors revival began, they came to appreciate what I had done. They pored through the footage and found they had the basis for three videos for commercial release. Danny Sugerman gave me plaques for the first two that proclaimed they had gone platinum, which meant they sold a lot of them.

I always thought Bill Siddons was jealous of our creative interaction with Jim. All the other Doors plus the staff and Jim's girlfriend Pam, were jealous of the camaraderie we had with Jim. We were his posse and we hung with him through thick and thin. We partied with him, we put him to bed and we took care of him like bros are supposed to.

I joined in on the next Doors meeting and asked what was to become of the footage I had been shooting. At the time they pulled the plug, we had roughly forty minutes of film cut. They told me that the project was on hold; in fact, a lot of stuff was on hold. I went down to the editing room and told Frank what had happened. We looked at each other and felt empty. We had sunk a lot of time and energy into the project. That film was like our baby. There was a whole room full of exposed film; I had shot around fifty thousand feet of film, and there was so much more to do.

Babe, Frank and I went to Jim and had a talk. He was the one who believed in the film the most and was having fun putting the film together with us. He stood over our shoulders and watched and made comments. Jim hadn't heard about the decision to stop production. He called Siddons, and Siddons confirmed the other three's decision to stop production. Jim hung up and looked at Babe and Frank and me. In those days there was no MTV. What were we going to do with the film?

We ordered breakfast at Jim's motel. He wasn't staying at the Alta Cienega; he was at a more luxurious place on Doheny Drive called the Beverly Terrace. We sat by the pool and ate and Jim thought about it. A shortsighted person would not have realized the importance of what we were doing. Jim was not shortsighted. He told us he was going to push to finish up what we had cut into a short film. He suggested we call it "Feast of Friends." We finished it up and added titles. I remember there was an objection to me getting directors credit. I don't know why, there was no one telling me what to do. Anyway I settled for "Photographed and Designed by". We were proud of what it was; it fully captured the experience of The Doors in concert and at play. We entered it into a few festivals, and it won an award at the Atlanta Film Festival. The reviews of the film were quite good for the most part. Jim became the spokesman for the film, which established him as a rock star who was also interested in cinema. He gave interviews based on the film, and it got The Doors a lot of press.

Georgia was pregnant and we decided to get married. Well, we were in love, why not? Besides, her grandfather was pressuring her. The ceremony was held at her grandmother's house in Ventura outside in the backyard. It was a beautiful, sunny day and the Ojai Mountains were the backdrop. I had sold my Porsche and bought a V.W. van, getting ready for a family. It was roomy enough for everybody including Stone dog, who went everywhere with Babe and us.

Georgia and I started taking trips to Big Sur and camping at the state parks. We visited Richard Rutowski and his wife Bettina. Richard had a large blonde dog he called Bandit. I think Bandit had some mastiff in him because he looked like a brick shithouse. He was thicker than Stone and his jaw was wide and menacing. Stone and he didn't like each other from the moment they saw each other; they paced around the house and yard. When they came close, their movements became slow and they kept an eye on one another: two large male dogs in their prime. We managed it for a while and then one day down on Phiffer Beach they got into it. The fight was ferocious. Richard and I had taken mescaline and were a little stoned. Stone and Bandit fought for what seemed like 15 minutes. They had a firm grip on each other and they dragged each other into the surf. The blood was flowing; I thought they were going to kill each other. Richard and I followed them into the surf and tried to break them up. Richard had Bandit's tail and I had Stone's. Neither dog wished to be the first to give up; I am not sure they would have ever given up. Finally we were pulling so hard that we had the two dogs suspended in the air when a large wave came in and smacked us all. It knocked us around and the dogs released their grip, fearing they might drown.

Georgia and I decided to camp out at Big Sur State Park and give the dog situation at Richard's house a break. We built a campfire and ate some food and tied Stone to the back of the blue bus. I had dressed all of his wounds; he was torn up pretty good. We were asleep on the ground in our sleeping bags I was awakened by Stone growling softly. It persisted until it got loud enough that I knew I had to check it out. I reached for a flashlight and saw a circle of glowing red eyes we were surrounded by raccoons! Raccoons know about campers and their scraps, and they were very aggressive about trying to reach our leftover food from the night before. Stone was at the end of his leash and they had advanced just up to where Stone couldn't reach them. I secured the scraps of food they were after and we all climbed into the bus and slept there the rest of the night. We were learning: don't leave food out near your sleeping area.

Back in L.A., The Doors were experiencing a low time. There were no concerts being booked, they had been banned. They went into the studio at

Elektra to record the "Morrison Hotel" album. Like I mentioned, "Feast of Friends" was only 42 minutes long, an odd length. "Feast" was just the tip of the iceberg, there was so much more. We showed it at a small theatre on Sunset Boulevard to our friends and the other three band members. They complained it concentrated too much on Jim and they thought it looked incomplete. Duh. Didn't they remember they had pulled the plug on the editing? What had they expected? Jim was the only one that paid any interest in the project. Anyway, we were proud of what we had assembled in spite of the other Doors and their lack of interest.

Jim, Babe, Frank and I took the film to the San Francisco Film Festival where it was well received. At the time, Francis Ford Coppola was running his filmmaking operation out of a studio he started called Zoetrope Studios. He invited us back to his studios after the screening for a party; after all, we were UCLA alumni. We toured the studio; it was beautiful. He was riding high on his success with the "Godfather" trilogy. We all sat at a long baronial table, and the food and drink kept coming.

Next to Jim and I and the gang sat a guy smoking a cigar who struck up a conversation. He knew who Jim was. He was Milos Forman, a Czechoslovakian who had studied film in Prague. He had directed a string of European films in the early sixties. Being film students, we knew who he was and he was impressed with our knowledge of his work. Milos asked Jim if he had ever acted; he wanted to do something with him. This was the beginning of the offers to act in film that Jim would receive. Forman had liked our film and that was good enough for us. Milos would later become famous in this country for directing "One Flew Over the Cuckoo's Nest."

Jerry Hopkins, the writer who would later co-write "No One Here Gets Out Alive," wrote in Rolling Stone magazine that "Many filmed dramas and documentaries about rock have shown the clutching hands and ecstatic faces that confront the musician or singer, but no film before 'Feast' has captured in so exciting a manner what actually takes place during a near-riot."

Everyone except the other three Doors knew it was powerful stuff. All they could see was they were not featured enough. Let's face it: Jim was The Doors. He was the inspiration. When they performed, Robby was for the most part motionless and introspective. Ray sat at the keyboard with his head rocking. John would spin his sticks in the air on occasion, but all the focus was on what Jim was doing. The three guys had a lot of trouble recognizing what was happening with Jim and his growth as a human being. Sure, he was troubled as all of us are, but put it into the context of being a super rock god and his troubles became even more huge and relentless. Jim tried to drown them in the booze and the downers. All that the other Doors members could see was that Jim was ruining their trip. After the group would finish with the day's work, they all fled as fast as they could to their domestic activities. On the other hand, Jim was left alone. Sure, we became his friends. He needed some friends that would stick with him through thick and thin. Babe and I did this; then Frank came along, and then Tom Baker. The support group for Jim's journey became complete. He didn't talk about his problems a lot but they manifested themselves in his completely outlandish social behavior.

Tom Baker was another of Andy Warhol's actors. Jim had struck up a friendship with the actor in New York. Tom came to visit in L.A. and stayed for a long time. He took our groups drinking and partying to another level. Another Irishman. Between Jim and Babe, who could party with the best of them, and now Baker...I kind of got left behind. Baker directed a film starring someone he had met on the Strip named Bongo Wolf and I shot it for him. Bongo was a strange kind of dorky guy that wore fake fangs on his teeth and carried around a pair of bongo drums. He was strange to say the least, but he had a lot of offbeat friends in common with Baker. This film is where I met the Gemini Twins. They later acted in a film I did called "Rada the Child".

We attended the opening night of Blood Sweat and Tears at the Troubadour. David Clayton-Thomas was about to step up to the mike to begin the show when Jim let out a blood-curdling scream. We had all been partying for some time and Jim was drunker than the rest of us, which was normal. Pam was there, Georgia and I, Babe, and Tom Baker. We were upstairs in the balcony. The lights dimmed and the set began. The first song was good but by the second Jim was shouting Yea...Yea at the top of his lungs. He upset the performance to the point that security came up behind him and grabbed him by his hair. It was long and provided the perfect handle for them to lift him up and escort him out. I was so sad for him. We were all embarrassed for him but tried to act like we didn't know him so we weren't ejected also.

Later we found Jim asleep in the back of my car. I know that Jim was not consciously trying to ruin the show, but when he was drunk, he was totally insane and his enthusiasm became distorted and obnoxious. Ray calls Jim's drunken persona Jimbo in his book, but never gets that Jim's 'Jimbo' character was the link to an alter-ego, a multiple personality, that I saw emerge many times. His personalities ran the gamut from angelic to devilish.

Jim had a talent so outstanding and undeniable; it seemed to come from somewhere else. I think it even amazed him, and it would be the thing that tried to drive him mad. It was like he could see the shooting star, he knew it was him, and he was smart enough to know that every shooting star burns itself out. He was not afraid of death, however; he taunted it and he pushed it. He did things that took him to the edge all the time. Sometimes he took us with him, like taking 30 downers and drinking Jack Daniels, then trying to record.

Paul Rothchild recognized Jim's threshold, his point of intoxication that rendered him useless in the studio. He recorded as much as he could and then called it a night. Sometimes the intoxication worked for the song and the vibe made a magical moment.

Sometimes when Jim was drinking he liked to drive his car. He drove his Mustang from the Whiskey A Go Go down Sunset Boulevard at 100 miles an hour. He didn't stop for one sign, trusting the circumstance to something else. I saw cars crossing in front of us. We missed them all by some divine chance. The Shelby left the pavement and sailed through the air as we crested the hill. It was just like the chase sequences in "Bullitt," the Steve McQueen movie. We headed down Holloway, hung a right on La Cienega, past the Alta Cienega Motel and across Santa Monica to the office.

Mustangs were fast enough to begin with. Carroll Shelby was a racecar mechanic that made a business of tricking out Mustangs. He made them as fast as he could and still remain legal. He installed a thick roll bar that didn't leave room for a back seat. This was Jim's first car; I was with him when he picked it up. Someone dropped us off. He didn't even know how to use a clutch. I drove it back to the office. I drove it quite often, and it was the fastest thing I had ever driven on the streets since the days of drag racing my hot rods. It got him in trouble over and over again. Once, Jim and Babe and a couple of girls crashed into the Beverly Hills Police Station. They had spun out of control and jumped the curb, and slid up onto the lawn next to the main entrance.

Now that "Feast of Friends" had been terminated and made into a short film, I had the time to shoot some film for myself. I was shooting some personal footage, small sequences, bits and pieces. Kit Gray, a fellow film student from UCLA, was my soundman. We used Jim's Nagra and we shot my father in a sequence on a yacht in Newport Harbor. He talked about his good fortune to live in the same area as John Wayne. He described his encounter with him at a grocery store. His admiration for Wayne, the movie star, was almost embarrassing. My mother was on the boat and I shot some footage of her, but it got lost.

We went to the Long Beach drag strip. The dragsters at night took on a mythic quality as the smoke from the tires enveloped them. The sound was incredible, their open exhausts belching out fire. We went up to Houdini's mansion in Laurel Canyon where the Gemini Twins were living. The actual mansion burned down in 1959 but there was still a French-style mansion across the street with an old lady living in the house. She rented out portions of the house to actors and musician-type people. The place was spooky; some claimed it was haunted.

The Gemini Twins were very cute girls that dressed in very sexy hippy outfits. They were aspiring actresses and had done small parts in a lot of Hollywood films. They were in Joe Namath films; does that give you an idea? I wanted to capture their life style: a stoned, living for the moment, waiting for their big break to happen, type of life. Kit and I arrived the night before filming and set up some lights and cameras. We came back the next morning before any one was awake and started shooting. The two girls were in bed with Richard Fortunato sandwiched between them. Richard was the boyfriend of one of the twins and was a local undiscovered lead guitarist who played with various bands. They woke up and started their day with chatter and singing songs, and Richard read the newspaper. When they finally got up they had on very thin nighties. They were so sexy. Georgia was in some of the footage as the girls thumbed through their theatrical scrapbook. The film later got edited at night in the Clear Thoughts Building. Frank Gardoni, a documentary filmmaker, was generous enough to allow me the use of his room and Moviola at night when he went home for the day. I called the film "Rada the Child," a name I had gotten from one of my East Indian books.

I was almost finished with the editing and Jim was watching over my shoulder as it ran through the Moviola. He knew I didn't have the money to finish the film, and he liked what he saw. The next day there was a check for me at The Doors office for five thousand dollars. Jim was like that, spontaneous and generous. I saw him give people clothes off his back, money to strangers. He always had time for people, especially his fans. Some of The Doors thought Jim was being used by people, hangers-on they called them. I don't think they were considering how smart Jim was. He wasn't being used; he was being generous. That's a precious quality for a man to have. What a man he was!

Jim liked to visit the Army Navy store on Santa Monica and Vine Street to shop for tee shirts and Levis. It is still there. Every time I drive by I think of Jim for a moment. After buying some new clothes we would return to the office. Jim would change into his new clothes pile his old clothes outside in the alley and set them on fire. I know I'm reading into it, but in retrospect it was as if he was shedding his skin. Reptilian. He had few possessions. He pretty much carried everything of value in his beat-up leather briefcase that was always with him: mostly books, poems and writings he was working on. He was always writing stuff down. Their were several napkins scribbled with poetry and songs stuffed into the side pockets of the briefcase.

Mary Werbelow, Jim's old girlfriend from Florida, wrote me a letter and asked me to give Jim a message. She had gotten sick in India and was in a hospital. She asked Jim to send her some money but for some reason, he flat out refused. He asked me to answer her letter. I did, and sent her a small amount of money. We didn't hear from her for a long time after that.

HWY

An American Pastoral

Jim's fame and good looks excited Hollywood. There were offers of scripts and possible acting jobs. Jim was stressed out about his lack of experience in front of a camera. I suggested he write a short script that we could shoot as a screen test. He came back a couple of days later with "THE HITCHIKER." That is what his original ten page script was called. Jim's script would turn into the movie "HWY." 'Wow, cool idea' I said, as Jim looked at me waiting for a reaction to his short script. But everything Jim did was intense. I suggested we shoot the hitchhiking scene as a test for now. Jim approved the idea and I went to scout some locations with my girlfriend Georgia near her uncle's house in Palm Springs. I was looking for a lonely stretch of desert highway.

Jim's script starts out with the main character Billy crossing the border into Mexico. He propositions an attractive Mexican girl, a waitress, a whore, into running away back across the border and marrying him. She tolerates him. She is working and has to listen to him ... but there is something she likes about him, he interests her. He leaves the scene drunk and threatening to get a lot of money and come back for her. A title appears here in the script: The Hitchhiker (An American Pastoral). We next see him hitchhiking on the highway, various shots of him on the American desert. The cars glide by in slow motion. After several cars drift through the frame, one stops and he gets in. The driver is a middle-aged man in a business suit. There is some small

146

talk and Billy dozes off. We see the man reaching over to touch the crotch of the sleeping Billy character. Billy wakes up instantly and produces a .38 pistol. The scene cuts to a long shot where we see the car and hear a gunshot. We see Billy taking the man's money and throwing his body on the side of the road. Billy drives off. The car breaks down and he is picked up by a state patrolman. Billy eventually pulls a gun on him and orders him into the trunk of the patrol car. Later, as we find him hitchhiking again, a family of four picks him up. Billy fights with the father inside a convenience store and manages to get the family back to the car. The next morning someone finds the car and its dead occupants. There is blood everywhere.

The film jumps forward to a television reporter interviewing Billy's father. He is old and an obvious alcoholic. He enjoys the spotlight. It's raining and Billy drives through the night listening to gospel music. He flashes back to a scene from his childhood. His father is teaching him how to shoot a gun. He has a rabbit in his sight ... next, he is at his high school, and then at the local drive-in where he is very aware of the carhop and her ass. Billy and the carhop end up in his car, cruising around, parking and having fun. They exit the car and disappear behind some rocks. Moments later, we hear three gunshots. Billy wanders around in L.A. He shaves in a gas station. He enters an arcade and plays pinball. He steps into a photo booth. Next scene, he is eating at a hamburger stand when the cops approach him from behind. They cuff him. The police kick and beat him and a struggle ensues in the back seat of the police car as they drive off.

Here the script takes a jump. There is a montage of old footage depicting death: Che Guevera's body, animals killing one another, etc. We see the front of the Hall of Justice. The hitchhiker floats dreamlike out of the door and by the camera and out across a deserted city. Next we are in an auto junkyard. Billy meets up with some hobos that seem to recognize him and call him by name. There is Doc, an older man. Blue Lady, a funky, glamorous woman. The third character is a young boy in white makeup. Clown Boy, Jim called him. They sit around a fire. The sun is rising the characters are talking. Doc puts out the fire and asks Billy to leave with them. He tells Billy the rest of the gang will be real glad to see him. Doc and Blue Lady head off toward the rising sun with Clown Boy dancing and waving goodbye. Billy, the hitchhiker, the kid, the lover, the killer, sits next to the smoldering fire. THE END.

Tom Baker found out about a party in the San Fernando Valley and took Jim, Babe and me along for the ride. Baker was an occasional lover of Janis Joplin like a lot of people were, and she was going to be at the party. She had just done a concert somewhere and was letting off some steam. She had a quart of Southern Comfort in her hand. Jim and Janis were drinking heavily and playing pool. We played doubles. Janis was like a guy. She shot pool and swore like a sailor. Not great looking, but she was sexy. She had a way about her that was so relaxed. I don't know if that was because she was drunk or what. She liked sex and wasn't ashamed to ask for it. Just like a guy. She could sing; everybody respected her pipes. She sang better than anyone. Today people still try to sing like Janis. The pool game broke up and we lost track of them for a while. Someone came running in the front door and yelled, "They are going to kill each other." Babe and I ran outside and found the two rock stars in the front seat of a Mercedes. Janis was beating Jim with the empty Southern Comfort bottle. Jim had her by her hair and neither was going to let go. We got them apart. Jim was bleeding a little but nothing to worry about. I never figured out what they were fighting about. Paul Rothchild produced them both. Small world.

During Easter week of 1969 I rented a 35mm Arriflex movie camera and bought several thousand feet of color negative film. Babe brought the Nagra and Frank came along for encouragement and company. We headed to the location Georgia and I had found in Palm Springs. It was brisk in the early mornings. I also brought an 8mm film camera along and the footage behind the scenes shows us all wearing coats while the cold wind is blowing in our hair. We had come to shoot the hitchhiking scene from the movie Jim had written. We expanded the scene to include improvisational stuff. Jim got into it; he was a natural. Acting was easy for him. It is only the self-consciousness that was a problem. He discovered what actors call business: he found a stick and carried it along. He was relating to the side of the road like a true hitchhiker would. He drew in the sand with the stick and mimed drawing a gun and firing it into the sky. I shot several takes of every setup. If something looked good I would ask for a repeat of the action and try to refine my shot. I was doing my own focus and sometimes it took a few tries to get the coordination between the pans, tilt, and the zoom just right. The shots were looking cool. The long-lens shots of Jim in the open desert with the snow-covered San Jacinto mountains as a backdrop were great and I shot that scene four or five times.

Finally a car came up over the hill and pulled to a stop to pick him up. The car that pulled over is Jim's brand new custom Shelby Mustang, the one Babe poetically named the "Blue Lady" after one of the characters in Jim's script. In a long telephoto shot, the Mustang pulls over to pick up the Hitchhiker, Jim. Babe is driving but he is not recognizable. Jim gets in and the car drives off. I got into the car and shot through the windshield as Jim drove. One great shot of Jim driving the car shows him throwing an empty can of Budweiser beer out the window. His head tilted back, his eyes were on fire, and he let out a tremendous scream. Right then, he had become the killer on the road. He was experiencing the acting thing. That's what this whole thing had been about. He knew it had happened after the fact. He smiled. That night at the hotel we took a handful of THC (synthetic cannabis) and decided to continue shooting as the unexposed film and our time allowed, improvising and giving Jim more time in front of the camera. That's what this experience was intended to do, give Jim screen time.

The next morning I take everyone up into Tahquitz Canyon. At the top of the canyon is Tahquitz Falls, a beautiful desert oasis. Georgia and I had hiked there several times. The water is crystal clear. Jim dove in and swam to where the waterfall was splashing into the pool of water. He dove under and he emerged from under the waterfall and swam toward us. He's lean and wearing only his black leather pants and he walked toward the camera, dripping wet. He laid down on a huge granite rock and took a nap. Later we followed him down and out of the canyon, back to the highway.

We were ex-film students, high on drugs, killing time and having fun. We shot all the film we had, improvising various scenes as they happened. We were driving on the highway when we stumbled upon the "coyote scene." A car had hit a coyote, a seemingly benign event that turned into a big deal with helicopters flying overhead, policemen and spectators on the side of the road. The lady that had hit the coyote was crying. The wild dog wasn't dead, but mortally wounded. He was struggling to breathe and whimpering. We instinctively jumped from the car and I started shooting over Jim's shoulder as he leaned over the coyote and attempted to console it. It became a two-shot, Jim and the dying dog. People that have seen "HWY" have expressed concern over that particular scene, trying to understand its significance, to interpret it's meaning. It was just an improvised scene on the side of the highway. Read into it what you want.

One night after the day's shooting I did some spontaneous interviewing on the Nagra in the motel room. During this session Jim recounted an incident on the highway when he was a little boy. There was an accident on the road and his grandfather was driving. He was in the back seat and could see out of his window. There was an overturned truck with dead Indians flung everywhere. As he recalled that sight, Jim sounded like he had remembered it for the first time. It was exciting. That recording ended up in the movie as a voice over. He later used the story in one of his songs.

Later that night we called a friend from Hollywood that was now staying in Palm Springs. We all knew her; her name was Linda O. She asked Jim if he wanted some reds (super downers.) Of course Jim invited her over. Booze and Tuinols together can be deadly. The next morning I awoke first and went downstairs to call room service. Linda was sleeping on the couch. She was completely nude and looked quite serene. Her legs were spread and there was a napkin on top of her genitals.

On our way back to L.A. we took a detour into my old neighborhood. The scenes in the film, drifting through suburbia while the soundtrack from "The Misfits" plays underneath, were shot on my childhood block in the Vermont Knolls. "The Misfits" was on TV in the motel room and we recorded some of the scenes between Monroe and Gable. Jim once told me he had felt like Marilyn Monroe in a way, selling himself and not being comfortable doing it. He felt like he was living his life in front of everyone. What once seemed like art, poetry and music had somehow become a nightmare of celebrity and business, with constant problems with the other members of the band, his girlfriend Pam and all the other girlfriends that came and went, the police, the arrests, the drunken performances, the constant pushing of the envelope in the name of creativity.

The last part of the shoot took place in front of The Doors office by the bus stop across from the strip club we frequented all too often, the Phone Booth. In real life Jim's favorite place to crash was the Alta Cienega Motel, which was right next to the Phone Booth. We used the location to film Jim's character making a phone call. He explains to someone how he had to kill someone. We later found out he was talking to Michael McClure. Michael played along with the call. He went upstairs to his room and took a piss.

We see him from behind but clearly hear his urine hit the water. That scene troubled the Coursons so much that I do believe it held up the progress of the film after Jim and Pam died. Then he went up on the roof of the 9000 Building on Sunset Boulevard. John Patk worked in the building and let us in and accompanied us to the roof. Jim walked along the parapet of the building, silhouetted by the landscape of L.A. Every time I turned the camera on or off, a few frames of flashing would occur because the shutter remained open and let in too much light. These frames were later incorporated into the film to go along with the sounds of explosions. It was night and the city looked brilliant and sparkling. Several people had gathered by now and they watched as Jim walked along the parapet. He teetered as his arms searched for a balance. The spectators held their breath and so did I.

The footage was developed and ready for viewing at the CSI Film Laboratory. We had a nice size screening room. It was beautiful. Jim looked fantastic. The camera liked him. With some acting lessons, he could have been the next James Dean. This was the first 35mm film I had shot. It's amazing how sharp and clear it looked. Jim, Babe, Frank and I were elated. We gathered up the boxes of the work print. Work print is the quick printing of the negative, with no color timing or any corrections. It is used to edit and gets beat up in the editing process. It is on the wall, in the machine, on the floor, in the bin. It gets scratched up and bent, cut apart and reassembled. We took the stack of boxes to the Clear Thoughts Building and went out on the town. We hit all our favorite spots, ending up at the Whisky.

Jim had rented his own office space next to Gardoni's, upstairs from Pamela's Themis boutique and directly across from Elektra's recording studio on La Cienega Boulevard. It was a convenient location for Jim. Frank Lisciandro took on the editing of "HWY" along with Jim. They lost themselves in the editing room for months and months. The film morphed into a compilation of the stuff we had shot spontaneously in the desert. Jim and Frank continued with the improvising we had started during the filming and found a groove as they edited the footage. It had nothing to do with Jim's script any longer; it became a new invention. Finally there was a work print to look at and there was a scheduled screening. I wasn't too happy with the choice of the graphics for the titles, but once the film got started the mood changed to a more serious vibe. It was clear it wasn't going to be your normal Hollywood film. It had art house written all over it. They had taken every take of particular scenes, such as the hitchhiking part, and repeated the action over and over. It worked. Jim looked so good: his hair blowing, the San Jacinto Mountains in the background. Jim had included a song written by Georgia and I called 'Bald Mountain' as the music under the driving scenes in the Blue Lady. That sounded good to have a song of ours on the track.

BALD MOUNTAIN

I BEEN DRIVIN UP BALD MOUNTAIN
I BEEN DRIVIN ALL MY DAYS
MY OLD HORSE HE'S LONG AND LEAN
LONG AND LEAN AIN'T GOT NO SHOES
WELL HE'S MEAN I GOT THE BLUES

UP BALD MOUNTAIN WE DID RIDE
SIXTEEN HOURS WE DID RIDE
OVERLAND RIDE HOW I CRIED

UP IN THE SKY
WHAT DID I SEE
CIRCLING OVER ME
STRANGE BLACKBIRD
GONNA SET ME FREE

The film was tedious, but for a reason. It wandered with no objective like the character did. It had a very unique presence. I don't think I had ever seen anything like it except maybe early Warhol. The camera lingered on Jim no matter what he did. So many of the scenes were art we found lying by the highway: junk cars, dying coyotes, the old woman at the Santa Monica pier in her wheel chair, the Cheetah nightclub in the background before it burnt down. The Doors had played there in the early days. Those were good times. The film ends on an old lady and some children as the camera floats around her 360 degrees. The film was done. It was timed and a release print was made.

At the first showing on Sunset Boulevard, the theatre was packed with friends, associates, and as many reviewers as we could get. The subsequent reviews were all over the place. Some thought it was great; others got up and walked out halfway through. It was compared to an Antonioni film by one reviewer. The Italian director had just released "Zabriskie Point," and the two films had similar style and subject matter.

Jim wrote about film, thought about film, talked about film. He had been a film student and we had come up with something unique. There was no pigeonhole it fit in. He took the print of HWY to every festival that would have him. He was proud of the film. Thirty years later it still struggles to be seen. It is a huge bootleg favorite, mostly in Europe. Every Doors fan has seen it and there are plenty. There is constant dialogue as to its meaning and people have focused on its every detail.

There was a Jim Morrison film festival in March of 1970 in Vancouver, British Columbia. Harvey Perr quotes Jim from something Jim had written dealing with cinema contained in The Lords 'Notes on Vision: "Oswald escaped into a movie house after killing Kennedy." "The ancient tradition of shadow shows the beginning of film." "The shadow show was aligned with religious ritual aligned with celebrations which centered around cremation of the dead." Other quotes included stuff like: "In the film HWY, he is the archetypical American loner, friendless and family-less, without seeing it. We sense it but we do not see it". "Jim has made a film, a real film." Perhaps the ultimate outlet for Jim's genius is film." "You talk about his film, for example, and he wants you to know that film is a team effort." You recall the credits of "HWY." It was a film by Jim Morrison, Frank Lisciandro, Paul Ferrara and Babe Hill. They all worked together before on 'Feast of Friends', the cinema-verite documentary." The voice singing the haunting song 'Bald Mountain' on the soundtrack was Paul Ferrara's wife Georgia." These are some quotes from a rave review in Poppin, a rock magazine, by Dorio Lucich: "The photography is beautiful...Morrison is beautiful as the hitchhiking killer... The movie wasted no time sinking deep ... a great film, one which should be shown in every city of Amerika but which probably will not be picked up by any large distribution house. It is perhaps too real."

Jim got tired of the problems associated with fame: struggling with the other Doors over selling out, receiving a conviction in the Miami trial and facing possible jail time, no privacy. He decided to go to France and take a breather. He would join Pam, who was already there, and pursue his writing career in the land of writers. France didn't extradite to America for this kind of indecency thing. Roman Polanski had escaped trial in America for sex with a minor by moving to France. Jim landed in Paris with his leather brief case and two films under his arm. Thirty years later, Europe is riddled with bootleg copies of both "Feast" and "HWY" that probably stemmed from Jim's copies. Rest in peace, old buddy, we've never forgotten. "HWY" lives forever, along with all your other creative endeavors. Yes, your life was interesting enough to base a movie on.

In between "HWY" and when Jim left for Paris, there was an amazing amount of activity that consisted of recording "LA Woman," publishing a book of poems, "The Lords and the New Creatures," some prestigious appearances, and concerts. The Doors were coming back from the Miami thing. There was hope, except for the fact that Jim was burnt out. He wanted out. He had never been in it for the money and fame. His star was falling, still bright but flickering as it started to descend. He wanted to write poetry. He didn't feel healthy. Pam had been living in Paris and encouraged Jim to join her. He missed his little mama. Most of all he needed to change his life style. There was no hope for that in L.A. as the lead singer of The Doors. And there was always the impending doom of the trial that was approaching in Miami. If he was convicted there was jail time involved.

When I had completed shooting "HWY," I took a job at Encyclopedia Brittanica's film division writing and directing a series of children's films. I had met Warren Brown, the department head, at a party and he had asked to see a copy of "Feast of Friends." I showed it to him and he really liked it. He said, "I'm proud to know you" and offered me a job. I also was finishing up a script I had been writing entitled "Solatium."

"Solatium" is Latin for the money paid to a family that loses a son to the military. In olden times the king would compensate the families that lost their sons in battle and I think it is the same today. It was autobiographical. A student gets busted for drugs, goes to jail, and when he gets released has a paranoid fantasy that imagines a time in the future when the cops are hunting longhaired hippies in the Hollywood Hills. There's a tremendous shoot-out at the end that awakens the lead character back to reality. He and his wife have just had a baby and he needs a job. He is confronted by the reality of life in the world of responsibility. He is forced to sell out and get a job. It wasn't bad for a first script. David Thompson helped me edit and finish it.

Georgia and I were at a New Year's Eve party at John Densmore's house to ring in 1970. We got home late and a few hours later Georgia went into labor. We had done the Lamaze classes and a plan was in place. We just were a little groggy from the party to remember it fully. We finally got to the hospital and we had a little boy. I wanted to name him River. I had an idea about the flow of life and it looked like a river to me. Everyone thought I was crazy but let me have my way about the name. Georgia chose the middle name Jesse. I don't think anyone got the name River, including my son, until River Phoenix became popular twenty years later. His parents were hippies also. Oh well, we were parents. The cabin was a nice pleasant place to hold a baby in your arms.

Years later I got a phone call from a writer who was doing an article on Jim. He had asked Jim if he ever had a son what would he name him, and Jim had answered River. The writer wanted to know if I was really River's dad or could it have been Jim. I looked at Georgia, knowing she had loved Jim for a long time. She assured me River was ours and we laughed it off. Knowing my son for all these years, I am convinced he is mine.

We were very cramped in the small cabin. We decided to take David Thompson's offer to share the big house he had on 3rd Street in Santa Monica. We moved into the large bedroom in the back and he slept in the front. David's house was just three blocks to the boardwalk on Santa Monica's beach. I took Stone on long walks along the water as often as I could. We were enjoying our time. We were saving some of the money I was making at Encyclopedia Brittanica. I was back to the beach with my old friends. Stone loved running on the beach. David was a good friend and he loved my small family. Babe was living at Tim McIntire's house and was doing well. It was a good time.

RETURN TO EARTH

After having been in the center of the hurricane that was called The Doors, life now seemed so dull. I felt empty and unfinished: all that work, excitement, the future of The Doors was uncertain. I went on with my life, but I never did see any money from the concert book and poster I had created. The documentary had been put on hold. The music business had been the problem not the music. The music is the thing that is pure: the writing, the exploring, stumbling through the musical ideas, discovering the magic when it all comes together. A song is born, and it can live forever. Not really thinking about the results, the monetary gain. It's the part that sets you free, and being free is what it is all about. Everything we do is about setting ourselves free: the thing that delivers you from the humdrum, the complexities and the obligations of your daily life. It was the world of corporate considerations that started to control everything. How many bands broke up? How many were cheated out of their share of the profits from their creativity? How many artists have to die in the process? I don't really know all the answers but something seems wrong. Nowadays it's all computerized anyway and if it isn't, it will become computerized. Re-mixes, Snoop Dog and Jim.

Georgia, Rio and I began a new phase. The children's films I was creating became important. Everyday I drove into Hollywood from David's house in Santa Monica to work on them.

David Thompson was a rebel and he is still fighting the establishment today. In UCLA he had made a film about the gunfight at the OK Corral. I played Wyatt Earp. It was a very thought out, detailed, moment by moment account of the actual gunfight down to the last bullet shot. He cut and re-cut it and was never really happy with it, but it was a great accomplishment. It had a million fast cuts and resembled the early Russian film style or what later Peckinpah did in "The Wild Bunch." It was in black & white and the costumes were very authentic. I remember going to Western Costume in Hollywood to pick out the costumes and gun stuff.

David was very literate and was always working on some script or another. He was a gentle person and helped me in my early days of fatherhood. I remember him bringing Georgia flowers on occasion. David turned me on to Neil Young, who he worshiped. "After the Gold Rush" was an anthem in that house on 3rd Street. It was an old Victorian style house. Most of them are now gone, torn down to build the condos you see everywhere. It had a large front room with an adjoining dining area. In the front room there was a fireplace that we kept burning through the winter as we listened to music every night. In those days the winter storms washed a lot of wood up onto the sand. After every big storm we gathered as much as we could and stacked it in the back. When it dried out, it was excellent wood for burning. David was also into camping and exploring the earth, especially hot springs. We bought a book that listed every hot spring in the U.S.

The Whole Earth Catalog was a great stimulus to us. We read every page and a return to the land seemed our goal. As Neil Young so aptly put it in "After the Gold Rush," Mother Nature was surely on the run in the 1970's. Our environment suddenly became important. Maybe having a child and thinking of his future was influencing us, but we all collectively began dropping out and contemplating the return to nature. This movement had been going on for a while but it took us film students a little while to get on board. We planned trips to the wilderness whenever we could. There was a large dining table made of old dark wood which served as the eating, discussion and general getting high area.

Steve Dragon was a friend from college who returned from Peru after disappearing for months. He had stopped in the mountains of Mexico and got strung out on magic mushrooms but snapped out of it long enough to escape and ended up in Peru. He discovered cocaine, a drug that was starting to show up in Hollywood. It was the beginning of a new era. The Indians of South America had been using it as a drug for centuries. Steve showed up one day, opened his suitcase and placed several small statues on the table. We thought they were beautiful. Steve laughed as he broke one across the edge of the table and emptied the contents onto a piece of paper. It was the most pure cocaine anyone of us would ever see: large yellow flakes that shined. He showed us how to dry it under a light so you could chop it up with a razor blade to make it into a fine powder. It was the most incredible high: euphoria without the mind games of LSD.

Around the same time, Richard B. showed up with a couple kilos of Acapulco Gold, a mythological strain of hemp from somewhere near Acapulco, Mexico, I assume. It was golden in color and obviously all flowers and buds. I only saw it in that form that one time in David's house. Our plan had been to invest in a pound, split it up, and try to sell some ounces to friends. I think we became greedy and kept almost all of it for ourselves. Between the pure cocaine and the Acapulco Gold it was some of the most stoned time I have ever experienced.

Rio, the nickname we gave River, wasn't walking yet and we got him a jolly jumper that hung from the ceiling. And jump he did! He still was jumping last time I looked. It was early spring and we were planning a trip to a hot spring in the mountains near Modesto. If you drove to a certain spot near a lake and hiked in for several hours you came to a place called Blaney Meadows. In our book it showed a wild, untended hot spring near the South Fork of the San Joaquin River. Kip had married Sally Norton, sister of our classmate Bill, and they had an infant named Deva. We both packed our infants on our backs. We were accompanied by Babe, David Thompson, and David Wyles.

Luckily, I brought my 8mm camera with me and recorded some good moments. One such moment was David Thompson crossing the swollen springtime river wearing a 70-pound backpack. He had elected not to cross with the rest of us, thinking he would find a better crossing place later. It turned out it became more difficult as he hiked on. We waited on the other side for him and he decided it was now or never. He rolled up his pants, took off his shoes and began to cross. The river was running fast and up to his knees. It was snow run-off and cold; his feet must have been numb. It was difficult for him to maintain a balance with the backpack and the swollen river moving so fast. Thank goodness he had a walking stick for balance. There were some scary moments but he made it across. In the film I shot his crossing lasted for several minutes. It was such a Zen kind of moment.

We made a camp. David Thompson broke out his fishing gear and brought back several large trout for dinner. As it got dark it started to snow. Go figure. We built the best shelters we could and crawled in and fell asleep. In the morning at least a foot of snow had fallen. We had brought small Primus type cooking kits and we lived inside our tents for at least a day until the storm broke and the sun came out to melt the snow around us. The hot spring we had come to visit was located in the middle of a small meadow. It wasn't very big and only three or four could soak at a time. We enjoyed the warmth and were constantly scheduled to take our turns. It taught us all about the uncertainty of camping in the wilderness. Snow. Who would have thought? Spring time in the Sierras. Stone dog chased some deer through the camp. Babe held on to Rio's hand and dipped him through a hole in a rock into the raging waters and we christened him officially, River.

I was reading the "Book of the Hopi" by Frank Waters, which chronicled the ancient history of the Indians of the Southwest. It was a mind-expanding experience to know what had happened on the land I was living on. In my official education, the Indians had been glossed over and painted by Hollywood to make their experience only known from an Anglo perspective. Then I read "Black Elk Speaks" and I started to understand some of my anger and frustration: my pathetic lack of understanding of my ancestors, and what they had done. I longed for the Indian spirituality expressed in their thoughts about life and creation. Respect for the land. They called it Mother Earth. They worshiped all life; even the animals they ate were worshiped. They had a sense of belonging to all things, an interconnectedness. They saw stories in the stars and worshiped the sun.

Before Rio was born Georgia and I took a trip to Mesa Verde. It's a state park now in the four corners area of Arizona, but in the ancient times it was the city of the original tribes of the Anazazi. We took some mescaline and hiked down a hill to an unguarded Kiva, which was a large diameter hole dug into the earth. It had a bench around its circumference on the inside and they were covered with poles and earth. This was the most sacred spot in their culture, where all the decisions and ceremonies and prayers took place. We crawled down into the Kiva and sat in a sunny spot (the wooden roof had long since vanished) and closed our eyes. We were tripping out for a long time when we became aware of others with us. I opened my eyes and the entire Kiva was ringed with Hopi and Navajo Indians dressed in

State Park Ranger uniforms. They didn't have to say a word. We got up and politely excused ourselves and headed back up the hill to the parking area. I think they appreciated that we were not harming anything, but respectfully experiencing a secret moment. They melted back into the scenery and we drove off.

On the walks along the Santa Monica shoreline with Stone, he and I sometimes made it all the way to the Venice Jetty where the ships would access the harbor. The jetty was formed by boulders that stretched out a half mile on either side into the ocean. Stone would swim out to the end and chase the seals that sunbathed on the rocks. He would chase them for hours. God, he could swim! A few times people in small boats would haul him on board and bring him back to the shore, and I would thank them. After they left, he went back out through the surf to chase those seals some more. If you listened closely, you could hear Stone barking at the seals over the sounds of the surf. Eventually Stone would give up and return exhausted, and then we would walk back to Santa Monica. He usually would sleep for hours after that.

I wrote several short scripts for Warren Brown's Encyclopedia film division. They all dealt with everyday affairs for small children: keeping clean, watching out for traffic, etc. I put the stories into allegorical terms. "The Dirt Witch" was a character that enjoyed putting spells on kids. She caused them to fall into the mud and created messy situations whenever she could. A little girl in the film finally busted her. The little girl convinced the witch to take a bubble bath. The bubbles rise up and cover the screen and the witch turned into a beautiful little girl. Tim McIntire's wife Kelly Jean was a very accomplished actress. I asked her to play the witch, and she took the time from her busy acting career to help me out. The film worked on a subliminal level; it was good.

The "Traffic Safety" film is about a world where the streets are inhabited by cars that lunged like tigers and sharks and made sounds like tigers and lions. The film followed a small band of children on safari and dressed in safari gear. They spot a city from a mountaintop and venture closer for a look. They have to watch out for dangers, and are confronted by Cobras and Mustangs and other cars that speed by. The cars make the sounds of animals, like it's a jungle out there. They had to pay attention to the signals or else they would surely perish. I submitted several scripts, and these two were chosen for production.

I struck up a friendship with a young man named Bob Angers we became friends and still are today. Our paths continue to cross. who was a graduate of Antioch. He was working as the janitor / fix it guy at the Encyclopedia film offices. When it came time to shoot my scripts, I used my pull to get him on my productions as a grip. When Warren asked who would clean the place, I told him to hire someone new. He smiled and agreed. They hired a good cameraman and the shooting began. It wasn't what I had been used to on the road with Jim, but it had its intense moments. The shooting took two weeks. It was a small crew. We used 16mm cameras, sync sound. When the footage came back, they liked it. The concepts I was trying to achieve actually were ones to be found in the editing and sound effects. They wanted to set me up in an editing room somewhere so I could continue my ideas to completion.

Around this time Georgia's parents decided to take a trip to Europe. They would be gone from four to six months and they asked us to house sit. We said goodbye to David's house and moved into Beverly Glen. The house was quite a ways up the canyon, just before the cafe where James Dean and later Dean Stockwell hung out. I had a Moviola delivered to one of the bottom bedrooms. The editing began and was going quite well.

We still went on weekend hikes into the Big Sur wilderness. Babe, Georgia, Rio, Stone and I took a really good hike. After an all day hike, we made camp and fell asleep. In the morning we took some very fine mescaline. We stopped on a sunny hill just above the trail, took off our packs and took a rest as the drug began its effect. It was hot and the large ancient live oak trees surrounded us. I felt something hard under my back; the ground was usually soft from years and years of oak leaves forming a carpet of decaying humus. I rolled over and dug a little to find the source of my discomfort and uncovered a mortal and pestle in perfect condition. The pestle rested in the curve of the square stone, the mortal. I knew that I had found something last touched by an Indian and I thought it was a sign. What are the chances you lay down on the side of a mountain and hit the exact spot some Indian had left his tools? The Indians of that area were mostly gatherers. There were plenty of acorns from the giant oak trees. I still have the pestle today, but the mortal was too heavy to carry out and my pack was already huge. I made the decision, an easy one, to leave it behind. The odds of those coordinates!

I was almost finished with the editing of the children's films when Richard Rutowski from Big Sur asked me if I would help him edit a short 8mm film he had shot. He had it converted to 16mm and we edited the film downstairs at Georgia's parents house on Chrysanthemum Lane. His film was very interesting: it was about a woodcutter in the woods going about his business. He cut the wood into small pieces with an axe. He was obviously very experienced; his moves were not wasted. Suddenly as he reached down for the next piece of wood to cut, a snake leaped out of a dark hole and bit his hand. This snake was special and known to the woodcutter as being lethal. The point of the whole piece was that without hesitation, he grabbed his axe and amputated his hand. No panic, no indecisiveness, only a Zen-like reaction. He covered his bloody stump with his shirt and ran for help. The moment he amputates his hand is the essence of his film. I still remember his short film to this day.

Richard eventually hooked up with Oliver Stone and became part of his production team. I know he played the strange Indian guy that keeps appearing in Oliver's film about The Doors. He is credited with several associate producer titles with Oliver and his films. Around the time I was helping Richard edit his film, he told me they had found cancer in his wife's body. Bettina was a beautiful German girl in her late twenties. I have one picture of the two of them together. I never learned what kind of cancer she had, but within one year she was gone. Richard changed, as well he should; he was grieving heavily. He left Big Sur and headed for the Southwest to live with the Navajos in Second Mesa, Arizona. I didn't see him for a long time.

Georgia had received a letter from her cousin Za in Canada inviting us to visit her and her boyfriend. They were in the mountains growing a small patch of weed. The photograph looked good. We planned a trip as soon as I finished the films. By the time I did finish, Babe asked to accompany us. Sure! I still had the blue V.W. bus. We made a bed in the back and headed up the west coast toward Canada: Babe, Stone dog, Rio, Georgia and me. It was crowded but it was a friendly crowd. When we got to the Columbia River in Washington, we took a break and camped long enough to cook some warm food. The river was the largest I had ever seen. It must have been a mile or two across and moving deep and quiet. Stone took this to mean a swim break, waded in and soon was swimming away from shore. It looked okay for a while but then the main current picked him up and swept him away. We freaked out. He looked like he was lost forever. Much to his credit, Babe grabbed a kid's bicycle and rode off in pursuit. A long time passed, maybe two hours. First we saw Babe and the bike coming toward us, then fifty feet behind him Stone, who was exhausted, his tongue hanging from his mouth. He lay down and slept as we finished our lunch. Stone had been swept maybe two or three miles down river to a bend, where he had managed to swim ashore. He met up with Babe, who somehow had never lost sight of him. Babe was like that all his life: he couldn't handle the daily chores too well, couldn't pay his taxes, couldn't stay sober when he drove, but he always rose to the occasion when the situation was desperate or it needed him. For years we had each other's back. I hope he's well. We put a leash on him after that (Stone the dog, that is.)

Our plan was to drive to Idaho and cross into Canada near Coeur d'Alene. The countryside was flat as we drove east through the state of Washington. Babe was driving and we were drinking a few bottles of beer. I rolled the window down and decided to throw an empty bottle at the garbage can that was mounted to lean toward the highway about forty feet from the pavement. We were driving around 65 mph so I had to release the bottle enough in advance to compensate. I launched it and by god, it went in. Babe looked at me; I was laughing. What luck! He said I couldn't do that again in a million years. I finished the next beer and as we approached another garbage can I said, "Let's see." I rolled down the window, picked my spot and let her go. It went right into the can. We were both silent after that. I didn't try it again; we just drove on.

There was a beautiful small lake along side the highway heading north to the border where we pulled over and rolled a big joint. We had heard about the strict searches at the border and decided to bury the small stash of pot we had. We dug a hole near our camp and placed it in a jar, and would come back for it later. Some fellow campers came back from fishing the lake and offered us two huge trout; I had never seen trout that big! We ate well that night and the next morning crossed the border into Canada. Those border search rumors were right; they tore our bus apart and searched our bodies.

British Columbia is essentially a series of high mountain valleys running north to south. We were in the eastern-most valley. Its eastern side was an extension of the Bitterroot Range that ends in Idaho. In the 1860's there had been a gold rush similar to the one that happened in the lower 48. Za was living in the area near Golden. We headed north on the only road that went there. We pulled off the highway at the designated spot and headed up the lower range of hills on the east. Za and her boyfriend were easy to find; there were not that many people in the area. They had leased a small piece of land in the foothills and built a cabin-like affair on the top of a small meadow. It faced south and west and got the best sun. They were growing pot on the hill up behind the cabin and wanted us to go in on some land. There were a couple of problems with that! We would have to give up our American citizenship. Not to mention, the winters were severe and lasted at least nine months. Now, we were L.A. people and used to good weather. It was too extreme.

While we were there they took us on several day excursions. There was still snow at the top of the mountains in late June. As the heat of the summer days got more intense, there were rivers of great force and size streaming and crashing down off both sides of the alpine valley. These rivers were once the focus of the gold miners. As we walked up a small canyon near a river we spotted a cabin through the trees and stopped to explore the abandoned building. Inside it was like a time warp, exactly like the miners had left it about eighty years ago. I mean, there were plates on the table! And beautiful wood burning stoves and assorted pots and pans. They must have pulled out rather fast.

We found one hot spring on the bank of a river that was marked on a map in a remote canyon. The water was very hot. There was a log cabin that extended out over it. It must have been a tavern or a lodge way back when. Anyway, we enjoyed that soak. Southern B.C. was primitive and the land was cheap and for sale. The locals were mostly descendants of the early settlers, pioneers and gold miners. We decided to look at the Peace River area in Alberta following tips and hearsay from people that we met who were also searching for land.

We said good-bye to Za and her boyfriend and headed north. At a fork in the road, we could either go to the right towards the border and Alberta, or go to the left and the highway leading back to Vancouver. We made a unanimous decision that we had seen enough of the North Country. Heading back to Vancouver, we drove by glaciers on the Kamloops Highway. Vancouver was having a small renaissance with the draft deserters from the Viet Nam war and the drug culture people who migrated there for a more free and open society. It was like a clean Haight-Ashbury district. We spent a couple of days exploring the city and smoking some hash before we headed south back to L.A.

Georgia's parents were returning from their European vacation and we needed to think about where to live. Georgia's grandmother still owned several properties. The family owned a huge cabin on Fallen Leaf Lake, just south of Lake Tahoe. When I visited the lake house for the first time, Georgia and I had been living together for some time in L.A. Her father still insisted that I sleep in one of the small guest cabins. Georgia crept down after her parents retired and we spent time together. The main cabin was huge with vaulted ceilings and it looked out over the lake. The property had a private pier and boathouse. It wasn't extravagant but it was real comfy. We returned the next summer by ourselves. Georgia was pregnant, that makes it 1969. We had managed to swing ourselves into the family schedule of reservations.

My parents came to visit. It was a nice time, and I took Super 8 footage of the visit. I had my amp and two mikes set up in the main room of the lodge because Georgia and I had been practicing and writing music. One day the women, Georgia, my sister and my mother, went into town. I asked my father if it was ok to smoke a joint with him or should I go outside? He said it was ok. I fired one up and took a few puffs and I offered it to him. He declined but he became so contact-high, he grabbed one of the microphones and did about a half hour of stand-up comedy. He was high but claimed to not remember the incident for the rest of his life.

Georgia and I continued to sharpen our singing act. We did songs from Muddy Waters, Bob Dylan and Mississippi John Hurt, along with a steady flow of new songs we were writing. During this time I wrote the words to 'Hopi' and 'One More Drink'.

Georgia had a beautiful pregnancy. She stopped taking any diet pills or other forms of drugs; it made her so conscious. She was a little scattered before and always high on diet pills. That strength pill is now very regulated but in those days the doctors handed them out quite easily.

There was a baby shower of sorts at The Doors office. They gave us a beautiful stroller. We were the first out of the Doors crowd to get pregnant. Later, Robby and Ray both had little boys. Rio was born the second day of January 1970. The summer of 1970 Georgia and I were left with the Fallen Leaf cabin for about three months. We just got lucky and no one else wanted to visit and it became our home. That summer, Tim McIntire, Kelly his wife, Dick Bailey and Jill, and Babe all visited at the same time. We had a blast, high and having fun. L.A. is quite a place and it seems to numb people. When you actually get free of the city, your spirits soar.

After that summer we moved back to Beverly Glen. This time Georgia's father allowed her and Rio to live in the guest room, but not me. I found a small garage apartment down the street and moved in. It was walking distance to the Newton's house and worked out ok. Of all people to have as my next-door neighbor were Linda Lovelace and her boyfriend. She had a huge porno hit with a film called "Deep Throat." She was ordinary Midwest pretty, had a good body and had the ability to put seven or eight inches of cock into her mouth without gagging. She was a star for that, whether she liked it or not. She claimed they forced her to do it, that she had been a slave of the Mafia. She did look like she was enjoying it in the movie. She had just had a baby and was trying to sue people, get an acting career going and getting high a lot. I became friends with them and we partied a lot. I felt compelled to read the book about her. Wow. "Deep Throat" and "Behind the Green Door" started an industry rolling that is now bigger than the so-called Hollywood Dream factory. Pornography.

We knew that we wanted to live on some land somewhere, and we wanted to raise Rio in a clean environment. We took as many trips looking for land as we could. We pretty much ruled out the northern climates. We took a trip to southern Colorado passing through the Four Corners area again, and then on to Crested Butte. The area at the time was just a ghost town and there were hippies living everywhere. They had patched up the old mining town and were living the best they could. Later that area would be developed into a ski resort.

In early summer there was still snow on the ground. We thought maybe we would swing down to Taos, New Mexico and look at the land further south. Along the way we saw land in southern Colorado for a hundred dollars or less per acre. Mostly it was stark, uninhabitable land with natural gas vents popping up along an underground pipeline. We crossed into New Mexico and things started to look better. There were more Indians and Mexicans in the populations and the land seemed more hospitable. We ended up in Taos where a hippie girl told of us a valley on the other side of the mountains called Mora. It was green and beautiful and there were a lot of places for rent. We drove over the mountain pass and looked at Mora. It was an alpine valley and mostly deserted by the younger people who had gone in search of jobs. That left a lot of older people. It looked European, like Spain or someplace untouched by the modern world. We were sold. We were also broke. We headed back to L.A. to gather up our stuff and get some money.

Around this time Jim Morrison left for Paris and the three remaining Doors were playing and trying to write some new songs in the old Doors rehearsal space below the office on Santa Monica Boulevard. We sang them 'Hopi' and 'One More Drink' and asked if they would back us on a couple of demos, and they agreed. We rehearsed those songs a couple of times at The Doors office, then carried the instruments to the studio. We recorded the tracks on the first or second pass. At that point, they still thought Jim would return and their spirits were still intact. They were generous to play on our songs. Believe me, they never played on anyone else's demo.

Jim's decision to use 'Bald Mountain' in the soundtrack of "HWY" was another blessed event. It was something so rare, and it can never be taken away. I was friends with Paul Rothchild, The Doors producer, from all the recording sessions I had attended. He heard those two demos and liked the songs, and he invited Georgia and I up to his Laurel Canyon house to discuss our music. We were honored! We sang about six songs for him. He liked 'One More Drink for the Road' the most. He repeated the line, "the keys to the horses." He wanted to place our songs and we were interested. He said he wanted 50%, or half the publishing. Georgia and I thought that was a huge chunk to give away but in reality it was a standard deal. Those songs were like our babies. Now Rothchild was producing not only The Doors, but also Janis Joplin, Paul Butterfield and Love. He could have put one of our songs on a Joplin album. 'One More Drink' would have been perfect for her. We declined his offer. We were so young and stupid.

MORA

I bought Captain Jack's 1953 GMC truck. He lived in Beverly Glen and when I saw his truck, I had to have it. It was powder blue, original color, and a one-piece windshield. I packed everything into the pickup and covered it with a tarp. I bought a second old truck, a 1951 Chevy. I drove one and Georgia drove the other all the way to Mora.

On our first trip to Mora we met Nick and Sally Dimas as we explored the furthest, most dead end valley we could find on the map. The wind was blowing hard as we drove along a narrow mountain road in the Chacon Valley. We spotted two people holding up a cinderblock wall; it was the beginning of their house and it was coming apart. I figured out what they were doing and hit the brakes. I backed up, ran up to them and helped them get some braces in place. I think it finally did fall down sometime later. However, the gratitude they showed us grew into full-fledged membership into their family. Sally was a Valencia, one of the oldest and most influential Spanish families in Chacon. Her father, Manuel, had been the sheriff. Sally and Nick had just returned from working in California and introduced us as friends from Los Angeles. We were invited to live in downtown Mora with Nick and Sally and their children.

As summer progressed Sally's father, Manuel, suggested we might want to explore some land he owned up in the mountains. We had a picnic one day. It was remote and beautiful, at the end of a long winding canyon: an alpine meadow with a stream running through it. A spring burst from the mountain and sweet water flowed. There was an old hunting cabin that had long since fallen into disrepair. He offered us the cabin to stay in while we looked for land. Our life in New Mexico started way up in the mountains at the top of Cañada del Carro.

We didn't realize it then, but we were part of a larger exodus. Young people had been leaving the cities and returning to the land all over the place. They became what were termed hippies. Now, I don't really know what hippie means: maybe hip, I don't know. The drug culture struck some with lofty ideals like caring about the environment, and peace and love as ideas to build a philosophy on. It followed that people formed communes. Land cost money and most kids were broke. Several people went in on land and lived on it. Commune was a term that developed from the original idea of communism, where everybody lived and worked together. There were several communes on the Taos side of the Sangre de Cristo Mountains, but on the Mora side there were none. We really didn't know this at the time but later it became clear. There had been rapes and fights between the locals and the hippies for about a year in Taos. We didn't know that either. There were just a few Anglos in Mora when we arrived. We sort of mixed right in with Sally and her family and never really associated with other white people for a long time. It turns out the history of the area was quite complex, to say the least.

The closest town to do our shopping was Las Vegas (New Mexico, not "Sin City"). It was about thirty miles south of Mora on what was then Route 3. The road from Las Vegas to Mora had only been paved some forty years earlier; Mora was still asleep in the twentieth century. We were the first wave of people bringing in new ideas. Most of the young people had left the mountain valley in search of jobs. There were deserted houses and ranches everywhere. I had saved about 4 thousand dollars and we were looking for land to purchase. We knew there were places for sale but nobody would talk to us about them. We were outsiders. Las Vegas was a town that had been built as a cargo station for the Santa Fe Trail. It was a frontier town like no other. Its history is legendary. Billy the Kid and Doc Holliday and Wyatt Earp had spent time there.

(From the) Las Vegas Optic, New Mexico
April 8, 1880

TO MURDERERS, CONFIDENCE MEN, THIEVES:

The citizens of Las Vegas have tired of robbery, murder, and other crimes, that have made this town a byword in every civilized community. They have resolved to put a stop to crime, if in attaining that end they have to forget the law, and resort to a speedier justice than it will afford. All such characters are therefore, hereby notified, that they must either leave this town or conform themselves to the requirements of the law. The flow of blood must and shall be stopped in this community, and the good citizens of both the old and new towns have determined to stop it, if they have to HANG by the strong arm of FORCE every violator of the law in this country.

Mora had become a favorite hiding place for many undesirables fleeing the law. It had thousands of places to hide. Before the railroad brought trouble to Las Vegas, the valley had been an agricultural community raising a substantial amount of grains. The leftover families of the first European trappers built huge gristmills on the several rivers that flowed through the valley. They had names like the Saint Vrain, the Cassidy and other such European names. These mills supplied the army and other people who traveled the Santa Fe Trail with flour to make bread. The early frontier soldiers had a fort just outside of Las Vegas with thousands of soldiers stationed there. Mora had dance halls and prostitution.

The soldiers from Fort Union fought with the Comanches and the Apaches, who made it a practice to raid and kill the traders who traveled through the area bringing goods from the eastern U.S. to the settlers of Santa Fe. Santa Fe was a Spanish town of thousands, actually Mexican Indians who had come up from Mexico with conquistadors from Spain. The Spanish had captured and abducted Indians in Mexico and marched them to Santa Fe to be the workforce. The Spanish and the Mexicans mixed with the local and mostly peaceful Pueblo style Indians, and a new society was born: the mix being Spanish from Spain, Mexican Indians and the Indians that were already in the north. This three-way mix later would be called Chicano people of Aztlan.

Howard Bryan writes in his book "Wildest of the Wild West," 'Commercial and military traffic on the Santa Fe Trail increased in intensity during the Civil War era, with an estimated 3,000 wagons passing through Las Vegas in 1865 and some 5,000 in 1866. The Ox and Mule teams moved at a rate of ten to fifteen miles a day. By now most of the southbound Schooners were bypassing Santa Fe and proceeding south down the Chihuahua Trail through El Paso to richer markets in the interior of the Republic of Mexico." There had been Pueblo Indian revolts with resulting wars that went on for a time. The confederate war pushed right along through the Santa Fe area, and eventually the American forces took the whole area and annexed it to the U.S. Before New Mexico had become a state, the Texas state army marched on New Mexico looking to annex the territory to Texas. It didn't work. The Texans were defeated.

So here we come into this sleepy little area with a violent history. It didn't look violent. It was beautiful, with green forests with valleys broken up into narrow little farms that had been passed down for a long time from family to family. Elk and deer and wild turkeys were everywhere, and there were still bears roaming around in the mountains. There had been beaver in the day and it had been a favorite place for trappers. The rivers and streams were loaded with native trout. Everyone thought of it as God's country, or at least as close as we were going to get in present day America.

As we searched the area for some land to purchase, we found many small houses that had furniture, stoves and remnants of the previous tenants. By staying close to our host family, the Valencias, and the other neighboring Spanish people, we isolated ourselves from the other hippies that were slowly filtering into the valley, much in the same way we had come, mostly by accident. It was bound to happen. The hippies helped themselves to the stuff that had been left in the houses. There were skirmishes with the locals but it didn't affect us for a long time to come. The whole community was on food stamps; even people that didn't need them were collecting. When the hippies figured out the food stamp thing and started showing up in the line for federal assistance, that's when the locals got angry. They thought this new thing with the hippies might blow their good thing with the stamps. There were fights at the office on days when the stamps were issued. Who were these new people, outsiders, and most importantly, Anglos?

Mora had a history of rebellion. Again, I quote from Howard Bryan's book "Wildest of the Wild West." "Resentment against the foreign invader spread through towns and villages north of Santa Fe, however, exploding into open revolt at Taos during the early morning hours of January 19,1847. Throngs of Taos Hispanics and Indians from nearby Taos Pueblo swept through the snowy streets before dawn, dragging Americans and American sympathizers from their homes and killing them and burning and looting their homes and businesses. Their prize victim was Taos merchant Charles Bent, whom General Kearny had appointed governor of New Mexico a few months before. The revolt spread quickly south to Mora, thirty miles north of Las Vegas, where insurgents under the leadership of Manuel Cortez, on the morning of January 20, captured a small American wagon train as it was entering the town and executed the seven or eight Santa Fe traders accompanying it. The rebellion was meant "to shake off the yoke bound on us by a foreign government." Meaning the United States. "Leading eighty men, Hendley moved north out of Las Vegas the following day and headed for Mora. Reaching the outskirts of Mora on January 25, they found an estimated one hundred and fifty insurrectionists under arms and preparing to defend the town. The soldiers stormed into the town, and close-range fighting raged through the streets and into the houses, until the insurgents sought refuge in a two-story fort with portholes that served the mountain valley as a safeguard against Indian attacks. A battering ram was brought to bear against one door of the fort, and Hendley rushed into a small, smoke-filled room. A bullet fired from an adjoining room struck the captain, causing his death within a few minutes. With the death of their captain the Missouri Volunteers retreated to Las Vegas with the body of their captain."

So there we were in the Cañada del Carro. I fixed the roof and windows and rebuilt the door on the small shack and we had a temporary home. Rio was starting to walk and he had some little boots to help him navigate the rough terrain. We didn't see a lot of people; our only visitors were the Valencia family. Manuel and Wilford, two of Manuel Valencia's sons, came a lot for firewood, hunting and just visiting. When Manuel senior came, he always took me on walks where he would point out the local herbs that grew everywhere. After a while I became pretty good at finding herbs and identifying them.

I bought a small chainsaw at Joe's service station, and on the way home saw a dead tree next to the road. I stopped and tried out the saw as Georgia and Rio watched from a safe distance. It was sharp and cut through the dry tree fast. It started to fall, and it was falling straight for the truck. Oh my god! The first tree I cut fell across the roof of the truck. I was real quiet as I chopped it up and loaded it in the back of the truck. I think even Stone dog thought I was stupid. I never made that mistake again. I learned to put a directional cut, a wedge type slice, at the base and then move around to the other side to cut down to it. The first cut gave the tree a void to fall into and hopefully direct its fall.

We would have campfires down by the stream and Manuel would bring food and beer and his friends and their wives. Georgia and I would entertain them with our songs. During this time in the canyon I wrote 'Black Jack Pine,' 'Sweet Wine' and 'Nuilena.' We sang our songs a lot, there wasn't much else to do. Another frequent visitor was Manuel de Herrera, a rancher from down below near the entrance to the canyon. He rented the land from Valencia to pasture his cattle in the summers. He and his son Ivan would ride the horses up and check on their cows. They were sweet people. His family was from Indian blood and they were all quite tall. I don't know what kind of Indian they were, maybe more Plains than Pueblo.

The summer progressed at a slow beautiful pace and we were quite comfortable. A letter came for us at the Mora post office from Babe. We didn't open it till we got home from our day in town. In the letter Babe informed us that Jim was dead and he gave us what information he had. When Jim died, the rumors about the circumstances were so confusing. Even Bill Siddons, who had gone to Paris to help Pam with the arrangements, hadn't actually seen the body. Having known Jim so intimately, I knew his death was probable. We were both devastated. Georgia and I cried a lot. We both loved Jim very much, and our lives along with many others' were going to be different from then on. I wrote a song called "James, James."

JAMES, JAMES

Took us up, took us down

Had a party all over town

Riding through the alley

Screaming in the night

Foot on the floor

We're running thru the light

You say you don't care

If you live too long

Just so someone hears your song

Poet, prince and lover

Angel in disguise

Born on fire

With the devil in his eyes

Balancing on a roof top

With a bottle in his hand

Something's pulling him under

No one understands

From out of nowhere

Given the part

Destroy their minds

Steal their hearts

You say you don't care

If you live too long

Just so someone hears your song

In that neighborhood summer turned into fall around the end of July. A horrendous rain came around that time, and at that altitude it got cold and turned to hail. The hailstones were the size of golf balls and were knocking branches off the trees; we could hear them snapping. The lightning came right down into our canyon. The crack of the thunder was so loud, even Stone dog was shivering at my leg. The road became impassable and Manuel de Herrera offered us one of the small and unoccupied houses on his land at the bottom of the canyon, next to the highway. We accepted and moved everything down to a more civilized area. We had several leads on different pieces of property but nothing was working out. One of Wilford Valencia's friends named Ruben had accompanied him up the canyon and told us of his father-in-law's property that was for sale. However, he described it as way up on the side of a mountain, which didn't sound very appealing.

Georgia's mom sent her a ticket to bring herself and Rio to L.A. for a visit. I would remain and continue my search for land. I kept busy making wood for the coming winter and helping Manuel de Herrera work his ranch. We were harvesting hay and storing it in the barn. The cows would soon come down from the high country and live on the fields we had cut and eventually would stand outside the barn in the dead of winter and eat the hay. Cutting wood and tending to livestock was pretty much it.

I remembered Ruben's story of the land on the side of a mountain and decided to check it out. I found his father-in-law and he agreed to show me the place. He was renting a house at the bottom of the Rio de la Casa, a canyon that went up to the west from the Mora highway around Cleveland. I visited and introduced myself and we got into the '53 GMC and started the trip up the canyon. The road crossed the river several times and the bridges were in bad repair. Once we crossed the river next to a bridge that had fallen and we drove through the water. After about three miles I asked, "where is this place, anyway?" He told me just a little more. Well, exactly 5 miles from the highway we came to a bend in the road with a gate on the right side. He opened the simple barbed wire fence and we entered. This was it! The place was at around 8,500 feet elevation.

From the road I could see some structures that were in bad repair. There was a large house and a small log cabin about a hundred feet apart. There were cows all over the place, including inside the houses. The doors and windows were gone. A stream, or I should say an acequia, rippled not far from the houses. He explained that the acequia was the property's front boundary and we proceeded to walk the property. We went down alongside the acequia and entered a small canyon where the water made small waterfalls as it plummeted along. When we came to a fence, we turned a sharp left and climbed up a steep embankment. We came to several small meadows that had overgrown with beautiful scrub oak that reached up maybe thirty or forty feet. We crossed another small acequia that he explained cut through the center of the property. We continued up into the pine trees and followed the top fence back to the road we had driven up on. It was about 38 acres. It was perfect. He wanted 8000 dollars for it, which came to about two hundred an acre. A little high I thought, but worth it. Only one catch: someone had already agreed to buy it, and he was waiting for him to get the money together.

While Georgia and Rio were gone, I visited the Valdez's house a lot waiting to hear about the people trying to buy the place. The story was Fulgensio had married Clorinda, a member of the Trujillo family. When her mother died, Clorinda inherited the 38 acres. It had been part of a bigger piece that had been the Trujillo ranch. When they got old, they moved down the hill to be closer to the highway: a typical story.

We drove back down the road, it didn't seem so long going down. I dropped him off at his house. That was the place. I had 4000 dollars left and we needed another 4000. I immediately called Georgia and told her I had found paradise. She asked her mother and father for a loan and headed back with the money. When I took her up there, she agreed it was the perfect piece of paradise. We courted the Valdez's for about five more months. I was now taking my wife and child with me on the visits to Clorinda and Fulgensio Valdez's house and we were getting very friendly. Finally I took Clorinda aside and asked what was happening with the land. Why wasn't her husband talking about it? She confided to me that the other people had not been able to come up with the money. Fulgensio, her husband, was embarrassed to tell me he had borrowed against the place and did not possess the papers for the property. I asked her how much he owed; she replied two thousand dollars to the Bank of Las Vegas. I said: "No problem." I put everybody into the car and we went to the bank. I paid off his loan, he got the papers, and we bought the place!

Winter was coming and we couldn't wait to move in. I brought all the wood from Herrera's place I had been cutting and tried to make our new home as livable as I could. I got rid of the cows and put plastic on the windows. There were some old interior doors that came with the place and I put them into three doors leading to the outside. There was no running water, but there was electricity. There was an old outhouse that we used until I could build a new one.

Troutman's was a place halfway between Mora and Las Vegas. He fixed guns and I went to him about buying a used rifle. I found a beautiful black and chrome Majestic wood cook stove there that we paid him 35 dollars for. What a buy! I hooked it up in the kitchen area. It really roared when stoked up; it was perfect.

We had to go to the acequia for water. For those who don't know what an acequia is, it is a man-made ditch that takes water from the river and diverts it to the various farms along its path. Our ditch was one hundred and thirty years old and provided water year around, as long as it didn't freeze too solid. We bought a tin bathtub, and that's where we all took our baths in the winter. We heated water on the stove and placed the tub in front of the oven, and we could take nice baths. Usually one of us would pour water from the stove over the head of the person taking the bath. This was how the old timers had done it and it was what I was really interested in. How had our ancestors survived without modern conveniences? Surviving ... this was the real test. Mother Nature can be a beautiful thing. She can also make it real hard on you; she can kick your ass if she wants, and don't ever forget that.

I felt that times in the world were going to get difficult: not Armageddon, but close. A lot of people felt that way. That's why the counter-culture press, i.e., Whole Earth Catalog, was selling the survival gear and publishing the info books. The end seemed imminent, what with pollution, overpopulation, war and politics. We had the right idea but we didn't know the end was going to take so long. It seems to be a much slower decay than we had imagined.

I only had the old Chevy and the GMC pickup. I bought a set of chains and stacked wood in the back of the truck and was actually able to get through on the road most of the winter. It snowed a lot that first year. We had to dig a trail to the outhouse. It was hard on Georgia. I think I was more into the survival thing than she was; I needed to prove something to myself. I wanted to be independent, free of the system and the pushbutton life we were all so addicted to.

Each generation passes on its hardship to the next. My parents impressed upon me how lucky I was. They had to walk to school in the snow. Times were tough and they lived through the Great Depression. We were all lucky. There was new prosperity after the war. Guys got out of the military and bought houses in the subdivisions of America. That's what L.A. was a lot of factories: government factories turning out military equipment. The Valencias had all come to L.A. in the fifties to work in the factories. That's what I had in common with the people of Mora Valley. I was second generation Italian and was raised Catholic. They were all third and fourth generation Spanish. Their culture was close to mine. A lot of my friends in high school were Hispanics. Dave and Danny Martinez were actually descendents of families that lived in Mora. If that doesn't connect the dots, I don't know what does.

We gathered wood and lived on food stamps. We wrote and sang a lot. It was a long winter and I think Georgia got pneumonia for the first time. I stayed up and stoked the fire all night long. We needed a second stove, so I sent for an Ashley from an ad in the Whole Earth catalog. It came to the railroad station in Las Vegas. It was the most modern wood stove you could buy for the bucks. It had a revolutionary damper system and an airtight burning compartment. I hooked it up in the kitchen at the opposite end from the Majestic stove. I had heat at both ends of a fifteen by thirty foot space; that was half the house. I kept the other side closed for the first winter. Somehow we made it through that first winter. Even Stone dog was happy to see the snow thaw and melt, and green return to the land.

What a first spring and summer we had. It was beautiful. It was what we had come for. Below our property was a beautiful clearing with a small lake at the bottom. We watched the herds of deer feed in the mornings. Flocks of wild turkeys started to roam through, scratching the softening earth for worms and other things below the surface. We met the Fresques family, our neighbors, as they rode their horses by our house passing through to their property. Florintino and Agatha were in their late fifties and still used the horses a lot. They were the salt of the area. They knew no other life; they were truly mountain people. Floyd, as everyone called Florintino, was also in charge of the acequia. They called him the Mayor-domo. He and Aggie were caretakers of the five thousand acre ranch down in the valley, the next inhabited ranch to the south. It was owned by H.O. Grace, but at one time had been owned by a Congressman or something and was somewhat famous for its fishing and hunting. Ernest Hemingway was a frequent visitor. It also was a source of much logging in the old days.

Floyd invited me to the first ditch meeting of the spring. I had to pay about four years of dues, the money owed by Fulgensio, the man I bought from. Then we set about to clean the ditch, as everyone referred to it. It was already about three miles long by the time it reached our place. After us it went down the small canyon to a valley just below us called Vallecitos.

Vallecitos used to be a thriving little community with a schoolhouse, a church, and several families that had lived there. It was now a ghost town but there were hayfields owned by different people that depended on the water. It also was our only source of water. There were two good springs that I got our drinking water from. One was halfway up our canyon's road, called the Cartwright Spring. Excellent water. The other spring was down through the little canyon on our property just above the acequia on the next piece of property. It was only approachable on foot or horseback. There was a trail and a hand gate connecting the properties. It was a favorite hike for us. You could sink your face into a large holding tank with crystal clear water that flowed from the inside of the mountain and drink your fill. The water was actually sweet. Everyone always remarked about the sweetness of the water. In the dead of winter I would walk down the trail to the spring, no matter how deep the snow, and carry back containers of water.

We ate very healthy in those days. The food stamps were enough if you bought in bulk to get you through. We ate a lot of rice and grains. We found a place in Las Vegas that was selling health foods; it's still there today.

The first winter taught us many lessons about what it was going to take to live at this altitude. I couldn't afford a 4-wheel drive vehicle, so I thought how did the old timers do it? Well, they used horses. Wilford located a horse for sale in the early spring and I went down to take a look. We drove to his friend's house in Chacon and they saddled up a red horse. We were pulled over alongside the narrow road that heads up to Chacon. There was grass alongside the road, and every so often there was a driveway that left the road and took the people to their properties. Each driveway had a culvert passing under it to keep the runoff heading down along the road.

I guess they were playing a joke on me. I had no experience with horses and I think Wilford knew that. I climbed on. Someone said to be easy with the reins and give him some room. I kicked his flank to give the signal to go. The next thing I knew, I was traveling at a fast pace alongside the highway. I tried to rein the horse in but he was running and there was no stopping him. We came to the driveways and somehow he negotiated them without breaking his stride. I was hanging on for dear life. My knees were locked into a grip on the horse's neck. He ran and he ran and he ran. Somehow I survived and he finally started getting tired. I managed to slow down enough to get off. The horse was breathing hard; there was steam coming from his nostrils. The guys followed behind in the trucks and slowly approached the horse and me. We had run about two miles. I was in awe. I was a little bit mad at the joke that had been played on me, the greenhorn, but it was a great lesson. I now knew there were differences in horses.

I found an old Indian packhorse named Charlie at the local gas station that was for sale and I bought him. He came from the Navajo reservation somewhere near Farmington. He was old but good, and Stone seemed to get along with Charlie. We needed a gentle horse to learn on and use at this stage of our development. Now I could pack water up from the spring on a packsaddle I bought. The warmth of springtime in the Rockies is something to behold. When the breeze stops and the sun hit's the south facing slopes, the air is warm and fragrant. The wild flowers started to appear: first the iris, in a brilliant lavender color. They were plentiful. Then for a time the grass was covered with dandelion flowers, and the color of yellow took over. One by one the plants and trees started to show life. The oak trees that grew everywhere started to get a soft green glow as the leaves opened up. Charlie was in heaven. We all were in heaven.

That first summer my neighbor Timmy, Floyd's son, brought his bulldozer over and dug us a pond above the designated garden area. I figured I could store water to be used to irrigate the garden. I buried a pipe in the low side of the dam and capped it off. Having no water in the houses made it difficult to stay clean. I built a small diving platform on the pond so we could avoid the mud around the edge of the pond and dive into the water. I made it a routine in the early morning sun to dive in and swim across. The water was cold but it was worth it. That muddy pond was the source of much fun. We had inner tubes that the kids could float on and they had a ball.

In the immediate vicinity of the houses were about a dozen or so wrecked cars. They had been used for parts so long ago that they were mere skeletons, and they had to go. As I became friends with Timmy, I told him I wanted to get rid of the junk sitting everywhere. He offered the use of his acetylene torch; I just had to buy my own gas. I said of course. It took a long time to cut those cars into pieces that could be lifted by hand and put in the back of my truck. I drove the pieces into Las Vegas on our weekly shopping trips and dumped them in the landfill.

Halfway up the canyon to our property there was a small group of cabins on either side of the road that ran along the river. An old Anglo couple lived there named Jerry and Stella Linville and they owned the cabins. The place was well known and every summer visitors came from all over to rent the cabins and fish the river. It was the only place in the canyon that had a telephone. We became very good friends with them. They loved little Rio and treated him like he was their own grandson. We used their phone from time to time and people would leave messages for us. Stella always had a fire going in their house, even in the summer. Most women in the area were the same about keeping their stoves hot. They kept peacocks and guinea hens. The hens put up a racket when someone approached; they were a good warning system. They also kept a lot of chickens and had a very cool bird barn across from their house.

Jerry had come west from somewhere in Kansas to save his life. He had been given only a few months to live, and they packed up and headed west. That had been thirty years earlier. They found the land by the river and had been there ever since. The old 1929 Ford coupe they came in was still in the barn. It still ran and sometimes Jerry would drive it down to the post office on a clear day. They were a shining example of survival. Jerry was an expert wood carver. He spent the winters by the potbelly stove carving the most intricate patterns into some exotic piece of wood someone had sent him. He made chain links carved from exotic woods that looked and moved just like a real chain. I still have two of them today.

At our property there was a large chicken house that needed repair. I fixed it up a little and we started some chickens. It later turned into a barn type place that I could keep Charlie's food in for the winter. I added a small corral that attached to it and our horse facilities took shape.

Timmy Fresques had a younger brother named Richard. He and his best friend Leroy Martinez became constant visitors. They were wild kids but we got along good. Leroy wanted to learn about carpentry and I put him to work on his first job helping me rebuild the barn building. They were both in high school and into as much trouble as they could find. When I first came to Mora all the kids had conservative haircuts. As time went on they started to mimic the hippies and grew their hair longer and started to smoke pot, etc. Leroy had an Afro, if you can imagine that. Leroy now has seven kids and is an old man but in those days he was footloose, wild, and like his father, he played the guitar and had a beautiful voice. I later gave him a guitar and he would sing for us for hours on end. People still admire his vocal talents today.

Richard had talent with horseshoeing and raising ponies. He had a small herd of four or five horses at that time. His father Floyd raised cows and Richard owned a couple of those as well. Both boys liked to get high; they liked it a lot. They visited often for dinner and we would smoke around the campfire. Leroy would sing and I would accompany him with my guitar. I am godfather to his fourth child, Amber Marie. I consider myself part of his family. I know his mother and father well, and stop to see them often.

That first summer we received a visit by three people who arrived on horseback. They approached the house from the forest and introduced themselves as the hippies that used to live in our house: Waylan Peaker, Tony Schramm and Sharon. They were now living in the second canyon north of us called La Sierra. That would become a favorite place for young white people to visit and sometimes take up residence. The three visitors had been raising pot not far from the house we now lived in. They had harvested a couple of pounds before they were forced to leave when we bought. We became friends. Waylan was a dropped-out psychology teacher from Oklahoma, Schramm was a half-German, half-Mexican from Santa Fe, and Sharon was from San Francisco. Vagabonds on horseback, stoned and colorful. They were hanging out like a lot of us, just enjoying life.

Once again, Mora was to become a hiding place. There was a freedom from the world and its problems, a place where you could concentrate more on your lifestyle and rejection of the mainstream. We wanted to live the purity of life like it had been, before the complications of modern man took over. The Indians of the Americas were our role models. But again, the undesirable element of people running from the law found our hiding spot.

During a bright evening snowstorm that winter, I heard the dogs barking and looked out the kitchen window. The clouds were thin enough to allow the moon to illuminate the freshly fallen snow. I saw a group of horsemen with heavy cloths and blankets wrapped around them that were dusted with fresh fallen snow. They had lined up in front of our gate and appeared motionless. I could make out five horses, and it looked like three men and two women. I could see one child sitting in front of one of the women. It was very cold, maybe around 30 degrees. It was so bizarre. I put on my jacket and went outside to see what they wanted. They were young white people, maybe in their mid-twenties. They had long hair, wore beads and leather clothing and were wrapped in blankets like the Taos Indians. They simply said they were cold and asked if they could get warm. It was spooky but I felt sorry for the women and children. They pulled their horses in and tied them up near the barn and then poured into our toasty kitchen.

Georgia made them some warm tea and gave them some cookies. They were traveling towards the south when the storm had set in. They got caught at Walker Flats in a heavy snow and had headed down the road. They said they were from New York. Go figure. I let them sleep in the cabin that night. It was outfitted with a stove but not much else. In the morning they came back to our house for some coffee. The conversation drifted into this grifter-type dialogue, about how everything should be shared. They thought I should share my place with them. Could they have some food? It got threatening. I looked at Georgia and I could tell she was scared. There we were, nine people standing in this small kitchen. I felt surrounded. I asked them to leave. I told them there was a ruin down the trail by the creek, and they could stay there but, they didn't want to leave. It got into a pushing and shoving situation, with one of the women actually hitting me on the chest. Somehow I got them out the door and they left, but they stayed in the ruin down below us for two weeks. In that time they made their way up to our place and usually demanded food. They wouldn't take no for an answer. They finally rode off down toward Vegas. We were glad to be over that.

It turns out there were several bands of people from New York riding around on horseback. There were some in La Sierra, some in Taos, some in Vegas. They finally settled about five miles south of us in the Seven Room house, a huge old Spanish adobe situated at the end of a old mountain road. They were heroin junkies and thieves. There were thirty or forty people including children, and they became know as the Banditos. According to the local rumors, they were armed. There had been burglaries. There were herds of cows in the mountains for summer pasture, and cattle were going missing in the high country. There was plenty of poaching going on. Deer, elk and turkey were disappearing from the neighborhood. There was a rumor that someone had died of gunshot wounds up there and they had cremated him. The Banditos were the first to file for food stamps and their presence at the office in Mora set the tone for the rest of us for a long time. Hippies!

The people of Mora had heard enough. Finally early one morning, the Fish & Game along with the State Police surrounded the place on horseback. They rounded the Banditos up and took them down to Las Vegas. When it was all said and done, a lot of those people were wanted for crimes in other states. Serious crimes. Most of them got shipped off, and the remaining few loaded all their belongings including horses into a semi-tractor trailer and headed for parts unknown. I heard they were in Idaho. I didn't care as long as they were gone.

Things returned to normal a little bit, but the damage had been done. Anglos were bad people and were probably going to rip something off. We could no longer hide; the world now knew about the stoned mountain lifestyle we were leading. Airplane flights began looking for pot fields. People were getting pulled over and searched on the way through Mora.

There were problems similar to what Taos had experienced a few years earlier: fights, confrontations, rapes. Where once I had been a Flower Child, now I was carrying a gun. Now that we had found a paradise, we were going to have to be strong enough to stay. It was tricky because I had many local friends and I had to maintain my relationship with them, yet still guard against the Chicano next door that would love to blow my head off.

Babe had moved into Tim McIntire's house on Beverly Glen after Jim's death. Babe was a good companion, Tim liked to party hard, and they hit it off. Tim had his house remodeled by some guy that had taken a liking to Babe and offered him a job. Babe followed him all over the place to different building sites. Babe liked cement; he learned to build forms and build houses on top of them.

He took some time off that summer and visited us and he helped me a lot. It was nice to have my old friend around. He was like Rio's uncle. Georgia loved Babe as well; we had been on many adventures together. Babe fell in love with the ranch like we had. He helped me with some cement projects and we partied a lot. He was a very free spirit. He loved being free from society. In all the time I knew Babe, he never paid taxes. He was more anti-establishment than me. We had been rebelling since we were young and in Jr. high.

Babe and I started to hunt turkeys. Every morning they were in the back of our property. They were hard to sneak up on; they detected any movement. We had to get there early and wait for them to arrive, lay still and hope they wandered close enough to get off a shot. Once the shot went off, they scattered like leaves in the wind so we only had one chance. Once I shot a turkey and he didn't die. He tried to drag his wounded leg and get away. I ended up clubbing him with the butt of my rifle and smashing his head in, but I broke the rifle. It was an expensive turkey, but it was my first! Babe went back to California before winter and did cement work again.

I had a bigger chainsaw that fall and I must say I became a fanatic about my woodpile. I tried to mimic what I saw in the Spanish people's yards: mountains of wood. Until you have been really cold, you won't understand.

I wrote Kip and Sally and told them about Mora and the property we bought. They visited that next winter. I remember them fighting their way up the snow-covered road. Kip had a ¾- ton Dodge 4-wheel drive truck. God, it was powerful. They moved into the cabin, and Kip fixed it up enough to house his wife and Deva. He fixed the roof and bought a stove. It was nice to have friends close by. The next spring Kip wanted to grow some pot. I was scared. I still had nightmares of prison. I agreed but didn't help. They dug a huge pit up from the house on the mountain slope, filled it with perfect ingredients and planted their seeds. I started getting cold feet and we argued about it. They thought I was being paranoid. Unless you have ever experienced the prison system, you don't really know what paranoia is. They decided to move out. I couldn't stop them. They wanted to raise pot and I didn't. They found another house just down the hill near the highway and left. I visited often.

Around the same time Bob Angers, Bob Gondell and Carol Supriano arrived from L.A. They were all involved in the commercial film production business in one way or another. Angers was the guy I had moved up to grip at Brittanica Films; he had been working at a commercial house with Bob and Carol. They hung around with us for a while and eventually moved in with Kip and Sally. After a while they had trouble with their Spanish landlords and moved to Chacon. Kip found a large house on a remote dirt road up in Chacon Canyon. It was beautiful in the summer but it drifted over with snow the first winter, and they had to fight their way in and out. They had it hard. One by one they returned to Los Angeles.

Soon after that period, some people from Louisiana started partying around Mora. I saw them hitchhiking up from Las Vegas one day and gave them a ride in the back of the '53 GMC. It was winter and I said I would take them to their house in Holman. The road was drifted over and of course, I got stuck. Well, we dug it out and in the process we became friends. They had come up to the mountains to escape the deep southern heat of summer: some left and some stayed. The next thing I knew they had moved into the cabin by the spring below us. Margie, her brother Michael and his girlfriend Jan walked up the spring trail to our house all the time. We ate and played music; Michael played guitar also.

Babe visited again the next summer. He fell in love with Margie and they became close. He was living in our cabin at the time. Babe would hike down the trail and either return or come back the next day, depending on how she felt. He told me he always knew when she was feeling like sex, because she would come to bed naked. He was passive with women and I never saw him chase after a woman; he would rather be without. He had deep scars from Diane, his first wife, but when Margie showed up it was different. I was so happy for him.

Margie and Michael's last name was Pousson. They were Cajun through and through and were huge music fans. We got along great. They hung out with musicians and went to all the big music festivals in the south. They had been to Willie Nelson's ranch for a party. When Babe went back to work, they moved up to our place and they lived in the cabin for a couple of years. They loved to get stoned and play and listen to music. Margie was pregnant when she came to the valley. When Babe went back to work the next winter, she gave birth. By the time she moved up to our house she was nursing. She had a beautiful body and she liked to walk around naked in the morning. She and Georgia got along great and we spent a few great winters together.

In the springtime Michael and I, accompanied by the women and the children, would drive up from our place to Walker Flats in the national forest to cut oak and ponderosa from the sides of the road. We were some of the first people to cut the big old dead oak. It was gray and thick, maybe 2 feet across at the base. It made our saw chains dull very quickly, and we had to learn to keep the chains sharp. That gray oak burned hot. The stoves glowed red as long as we had a constant source of oak. I bought a giant old ¾-ton Ford truck from an old man down on the highway and we called it the Gobbler, the big red Gobbler. We built wooden sides for the bed and could stack nearly a cord of wood in it. It was fun. We took food and had picnics alongside our work.

Babe had bought a '49 Chevy delivery truck and his brother Dale installed a new Chevy V-8 in it. Babe drove back and forth a lot. One time he told me late at night on one of his all night driving trips he hit a deer somewhere on a back road in Arizona. He felt so bad that he stopped, built a fire, and ate some of it. While the Poussons were living in the cabin, Babe brought Tim and Kelly Jean to the ranch. We had a blast; they helped me dig a long shallow ditch to bring water to the field next to us. Tim played his violin at the campfires every night. The times were good. He was working on the "Jeremiah Johnson" score and he played us all the tunes he had written.

Tony Schramm from La Sierra started taking us to Taos and Santa Fe and introducing us to his acquaintances. We met Clarence from Santa Fe, in Taos where he was living. He was part Spanish and had a beautiful girlfriend, Donna, who he eventually married. Clarence was a trader, like Schramm. They made their money by connecting people with what it was they wanted. It was an age-old profession; they had picked it up by osmosis. They could always get pot or anything else you needed.

Waylan eventually moved to a place west of Taos near Abiquiu. He started to visit Mexico every summer and returned with turquoise. He always had stones for sale. The town closest to the turn-off to his house was Coyote. It was arid land. The house he rented was near another set of houses that he rented and turned into pot farms. You took a short hike from his front door, climbed through the fence that separated the properties and approached what looked like an abandoned farmhouse. In that country the roofs were flat. Dirt was piled on top of the latillas that spanned the vigas, and that was the roof and ceiling. There was a ladder that led up to the roof and it was a place to dry food for the winter: chilies, corn, you name it and it was dried up there. Waylan had opened up the roof of the neighboring house and planted about two hundred pot plants. Once while visiting, he took me over there and showed his crop to me. It was incredible. You didn't know what was in there until you passed through some chicken coops and opened the door. He financed his life for years like that.

Waylan always had women around him. He had several children with different women. Once he and his pregnant girlfriend threw a giant Thanksgiving party; there must have been a hundred people there. Coyote was in the middle of nowhere, a magical place, with the Piedre Nal rising up in the foreground. That mountain was famous for many reasons and it can be seen from Taos looking south. It is a classic flat-topped mountain and it had some mystic Indian relevance. It was always a good trip to visit Waylan's.

The locals that visited his house were wild, with wild looks in their eyes. They were descendants of Indian Mestizos. They would bring fresh killed deer and drop it on the kitchen table. Waylon smoked his pot with them. It was a precarious situation with his neighbors; they knew too much. He was robbed from time to time. Nothing serious was lost, but nevertheless, it was an intrusion. His interaction with the natives of Coyote was eventually the thing that ended his stay there.

Schramm had met a lady who was known by her last name, Potts. He rented some land in La Sierra and built a huge Kiva style house that they had their only child in. They named him Mountain. Potts wanted to have a natural birth. She was laying on the table in the huge round underground Kiva in contractions, but the baby wasn't coming out as planned. She was near death when someone finally took her to the hospital. Later she moved over to our place and lived in her tipi when she and Schramm broke up. We dressed in leather and made beads and visited with Indians. Who knew this would happen? God, those times were special.

Once while Babe and I were driving to Las Vegas for supplies in his Chevy, I spotted a large bird hanging from a fence on the side of the road. He stopped and backed up. Sure enough, it was a large golden eagle strung up by his wings. We put it in our truck and took it home. We learned later it was a protected species and it was a federal crime to have it in our possession. At that time, Indians could possess the feathers for ceremonial dances and stuff so we thought, "Cool. We'll take it to the Taos Pueblo Indians."

Georgia and Rio went with us, and we got to the pueblo a couple of days later. The bird was stretched out in the back of Babe's delivery truck and starting to smell. We found our way to a medicine man to show him what we had. When Babe threw open the back doors of the truck, a gasp was let out by the crowd of Indians who had gathered in the rear. It turns out that the golden eagle is revered as one of their brothers on earth. It is sacred and they wanted it. We said we would like to have some peyote that they were rumored to have. The main man offered us six old dry peyote buttons and some buffalo hides he had been tanning. We stepped into the small house next to his that he used for drying the skins. As I helped him get them down from the loft, he put his hands on Georgia's tits. They were, by the way, large and admired by all. She told me later he had grabbed her breasts helping her up a small ladder. We returned to the Walker Flats house with items from the pueblo; that kept us floating for some time. I did have the idea to keep three tail feathers and a couple of the claws, which measured about two inches in length. I still have the feathers and the claws today. They are hanging above my head as I type this story.

Around this time a couple from the east coast moved into a house down along the highway: Pooh and Annie. Pooh was a nickname for James Byres, a bright young man from Pennsylvania. It came from Winnie the Pooh, of course. He was gentle and easy to get along with. He wore braids and made jewelry, and was an easy target for the neighboring kids who ripped him off every time he went to town. Annie was a tall, young, Nordic blonde. They made quite a picture in little Mora. Once when we visited them, Pooh told us of his troubles with his neighbors. We offered him the cabin and a little protection from the locals, so he moved up to our place. He built a porch in the front of the cabin that became his shop.

Pooh had developed a style of making jewelry that was more modern than the traditional Indian designs. He made channeled and inlaid types of bracelets, and the stores in Santa Fe gobbled them up. They took a long time to make; it was very labor intensive. He made and sold enough to support a simple life. Once a week he and Annie would drive to Santa Fe and sell. Sometimes beautiful Annie would visit the high-end hotels and enter the bar area and sell strands of beads and Pooh's bracelets.

TOP: BABE, GOLDEN EAGLE AND RIO
RIGHT: RIO AND ME, FALLEN LEAF

PHOTO CREDIT: GEORGIA PULOS

The basic steps in the making of the bracelets was a cutting and soldering process not unlike what I had experienced in the sheet metal world of Pickering Sheet Metal. I have always been good with my hands, and it was only a matter of time before I tried it. I started to make a little and bought some equipment of my own. Pooh was making lapis jewelry. Schramm brought around a guy that had Afghanistan lapis by the pound in the back of his Volvo. He was Middle Eastern and had some connections for the stone. Pooh also showed me how to make Indian turquoise beads. They sold very well. We bought pieces of stone and shell in Santa Fe and cut them into small pieces that could be drilled through and wired onto some tough piano wire. After stringing it up to a length approximating a necklace, we'd take the small square pieces and run them across the front of a grinding wheel. The squares started spinning and eventually the corners came off. The end result was round beads that then needed to be sanded from coarse to fine grit until smooth. They were buffed to a shine and restrung onto bead string. I finished them off with clasps that I fashioned from silver wire. Pooh taught me that trick as well. My jewelry always sold.

Georgia learned to help, like Annie did for Pooh. She even inlaid some of the bracelets. Inlaying the bracelets was like laying a cobblestone road. We would take pieces of raw stone and grind them into plates or bricks, if you will, and place them one by one into the silver channel. When we had several pieces fitting into the channel, we stopped and used epoxy to cement them in. When the whole channel was full of pieces of stone, we took the bracelet that had been formed into a wrist-sized circle to the stone-grinding wheel: smoother and smoother on finer and finer sandpaper, and eventually to the buffing wheel. The wheel was lubricated with a constant stream of water to keep the stones from getting too hot.

Pooh had helped me to find a way to make some money. He never had to pay us rent and was welcomed as a neighbor. Sometimes the stones we purchased were of such good quality that we just shaped them and made nugget necklaces. We made small silver beads and placed them at intervals on the nugget necklaces. It was similar to what the Indians had done for a thousand years. We had several Arizona Highway magazines from the sixties that had explored the Indian turquoise art. Those magazines were our constant inspiration for designs.

Pooh was a very inventive person. He had made his own heating system out of two 55-gallon barrels hooked together, one on top of the other. The heat rose from the bottom barrel where the fire was, to the top barrel creating a second space to store hot air. It really worked well.

He also came up with a sweat lodge down by the ditch. He cut willow stalks and stuck the sharp ends in a circle he had drawn on the ground. He bent the top of the sticks to the center and tied them together, creating a framework on which he placed blankets and plastic and mud. Inside the small enclosure he dug a pit. Outside he built a fire of oak. He gathered some volcanic rocks from the Taos area and placed them into the glowing ashes. Once they were red hot, he pitchforked them into the pit. It got very hot in there once the front entrance was sealed. We had a bucket of water that could be poured onto the glowing rocks causing steam and heat to engulf us. It took some getting used to; it was so hot that many people couldn't take it. We did sweat lodges all year long, especially when it was winter and there was snow on the ground. The ritual was to step from the heat down to the ditch and pour a bucket of ice-cold water over your head. Once you got over that, you could think about going back in for another round of sweat. The lodge held about six people, but that was a little tight. Everyone was naked, Annie and Georgia included. It was a very stimulating experience.

Once Pooh and Annie had moved up to the ranch, it freed us up to go back to L.A. for visits. Rio was getting older and needed to see his grandparents. I bought a V.W. bug from a German kid passing through Mora. We packed it up and headed to the west coast. Stone stayed with Pooh that year. We visited Tim McIntire in Beverly Glen; he lived very close to Georgia's parents. We sang him some of the songs we had been writing in New Mexico and he wanted to use some of his recording time to record them. He sort of produced them and he added his talents for playing guitar and violin on them. Strangely enough, it was at Elektra Studios on La Cienega, the same studio The Doors had recorded at. We recorded 'Black Jack Pine' and 'Sweet Wine,' among others. Tim's playing and his love made it all the more cool. The executive in charge of the studio at the time was a friend of Tim's. When he heard our recordings, he offered Georgia and I a contract. He asked if we would be willing to go out on the road and promote our songs for three or four years. We looked at each other; it wasn't possible with Rio and the ranch, plus we had seen what life on the road did to people. Once again, we turned down a good offer.

Around this time we had a huge party with about a hundred people from all over New Mexico. The network was forming! Everyone brought good drugs and drink. It was late at night and people were all over the place. The bonfires were huge and people were dancing. Stone came up to me shivering; there was something wrong. I think I was too stoned to recognize the seriousness of his situation. I stroked him and then something pulled me away. We didn't see him for three days after the party. I figured he had gone on one of his journeys; more than once he had been seen in small villages in the next canyons. His hound nose could smell a bitch in heat, and he would travel until he was weak to be near her. He always came back. I was climbing the steps that led into the house when I saw something under the porch. It was Stone dog and he was dead, stiff as a board. He must have died soon after I saw him during the party. Man, we were sad. I'm still sad, but what a great thing to have known a dog like him. He lives forever in the photographs I took of Morrison where he posed so willingly. Babe and I built a funeral pyre and kept it burning for three days. Stone didn't go easily. We buried the ashes. Years later after a rain I found his skull and have kept it ever since.

Much later I learned that Richard's dad Floyd poisoned many animals in the area. He was famous for poisoning coyotes and dogs that bothered him or his animals, so I now suspect that Stone died from poisoning rather than natural causes.

The second winter Pooh lived there my sister called. She and my mother had a restaurant uniform business, they had landed a few big accounts, and she said they could use some help. We packed up and headed for Newport Beach; we needed to make some fast money. At first we slept on the floor of the factory. Later we moved into my parents' apartment where all three of us were living in a very small guest bedroom and finally, we rented a small apartment in Costa Mesa.

I cut the fabric. There was a large table that I placed the fabric on. I rolled it back and forth until there were maybe thirty layers. I put the patterns onto the fabric, traced the outline in white chalk, and used an electric shear to cut them out. It was not far from the work I did with sheet metal: patterns and cutting. Same thing. We tried to save some of the money.

We found a small recording studio on Balboa Island. Our songs were changing; they were getting world-wearier. 'Nuilena,' 'James,' and 'How Have You Been.' We just put them down as fast as we could, mostly first takes. All our stuff was recorded mostly in first takes. Even with the three Doors we knocked them out with not much fanfare, and especially when we were paying for the studio ourselves.

Some real Doors fans inhabited the apartment we lived in. I rented a projector and showed them "Feast of Friends." One or two of the girls in that apartment were hooker/massage ladies. Once one of the pretty young things told me what she did was a fairly innocent experience most of the time. She described how one of the guys wanted her to take off her pink angora sweater and jack him off with it. I came real close to giving in to temptation a couple of times.

Rio was the nickname that stuck with River in New Mexico. The locals couldn't say River too well. Rio was Spanish for river. It was all good. In Costa Mesa, Rio experienced what having a lot of kids around was like. We enrolled him in kindergarten and he had a blast. He was getting older and was lacking companionship at the ranch. The next summer we even took one of the kids back to the ranch for the summer. They had a blast together. They built a fort up on the hill overlooking the house, played war, cowboys and Indians, and swam in the pond. It was hot that summer. We tied several inner tubes together and we floated about. The water was cold because it came from the river that came from the snow pack. We finally had some horses that we could saddle and ride. I had a red sorrel that I purchased behind the bar in Holman. She was pregnant when I bought her, and young and strong. I called her Serrana, which meant lady mountain.

The man who came to install our phone, finally, was Jake Regansburg. He was a horseman and lived in Guadalapita: he raised horses, he bred horses, and he raced horses. We got to know him well. He sold Georgia an albino gelding; well-trained, but a little spooky looking. In the snow he couldn't see that well and would run right up to a wire fence and slam on the brakes. As long as you knew these things, it was ok. His bad eyesight could be compensated for with good judgment. Jake came up and shoed our horses for years. We visited him and his son at their home. He was going through a divorce at the time. We went for rides with him up onto the mountain by his ranch, the Sera Montosa. He was an outfitter, which means he took people from Texas on pack trips in deer and elk season. He had several brothers; they were all not only horse people, but influential in the politics of Mora.

Georgia, Rio and I started taking horseback trips into the mountains just up from our ranch. Schramm was the first person to show me a trail leading to the high country. There were at least ten lakes scattered along the ridge. The mountains behind us were called the Sangre de Cristo range, which meant the blood of Christ. The name has been interpreted many times. Some think it means that the water flowing into the valleys and fields brings life in the summer. Others think it is a much more literal meaning, the bloodshed by the white settlers at the hands of the Indians. All I know is, it was beautiful up there. The lakes had trout in them. We could camp anywhere we wanted. It was only approachable by horse, which meant it was not well traveled like the campsites in Big Sur, for example. If we rode from our small ranch up the Walker Flats road and up the trail from there, it was about a three to four hour ride. We did it a lot in the early days. We were young and high. In the early summer there was usually still snow up there.

One year Georgia and Rio were on Blanco and the horse stumbled in a drift. Down they went and they tumbled in the snow for quite a ways. The horse missed them as he slid to a stop. They were all ok. We helped them up and continued on. It was twelve thousand feet up there and the air was thin and crisp. It was such a cleansing experience.

Serrana had a young female horse, commonly called a filly. She was to be Rio's horse and we called her Rosy. She came right up to him. It was our first experience with horses and their babies. The young horse from birth stays by its mother. If you ride its mother off a cliff it follows. Rosy followed us into the mountains and knew the trails before she was one year old. Jerry Linville gave me an old axle off a Model A truck and I made a cart for hauling stuff. I put some thin poles on it that stuck out in the front. I bought a harness set from Jake, the kind used for working horses that pulled wagons and logs and stuff and attached the poles to the side of the harness. Serrana didn't get it at first but soon figured it out. She was an intelligent horse. I could bring in wood in all kinds of weather. It looked cool. I was so proud.

Floyd Fresques brought his big black workhorse Smoky over and I plowed the garden in the spring with a hand held plow. When Smoky slowed down with the weight of the plow digging in, Floyd would hit him with a piece of leather. Floyd was a very small man, and he compensated for that with an attitude of brute force. He hit his horses and tied them into knots, if he had to. Once I saw him hit Smoky with a board across the head. The horse tolerated him. For many years Smoky was a part of my life as I helped Floyd drag logs to his house in the winter for firewood. We worked in two feet of snow with Smoky. That's how they had done it, with horses. Sometimes Smoky would be hooked up to a log and we would be coaxing him to move. All of a sudden he would lunge past us, almost crushing us on the small trail we had cut in the snow ... somehow, nobody got hurt.

When I first moved up the mountain, Floyd and Agatha were alone in the canyon taking care of H.O. Grace's place. Later their daughter Idene and her Anglo husband from California moved back. Idene's husband eventually left her there and went back to the city somewhere. Their youngest, Richard, finally graduated high school and they became a family unit again, working the ranch together.

Henry Trujillo made contact around this time and he started to visit with Dennis, his young son. Henry was born at our ranch; his father built the house we lived in. We developed a deep lasting relationship. Henry's nickname in Mora was Polia, which is Spanish for moth. He had been a logger, a road builder, a heavy equipment operator, and finally landed a job on the high school maintenance crew. One day he was in a dark area of the building and he fell, causing much injury to his head and back. He was on a disability program that sent him a monthly check, which meant he had a lot of time on his hands. He showed me all the trails and roads in the U.S. forest that surrounded our small ranch. He taught me how to read signs in the forest and on the ground, use a chainsaw and maintain it. Most of all, he taught me how to hunt.

Georgia's dad Travers had been in W.W. ll and brought home a German sniper rifle, a 8mm Mauser known for its accuracy. The guts of that gun were used in many American hunting rifles; however, it was heavy. I hunted a lot in the early days. I bagged a couple of turkeys, but the deer and elk eluded me. I would see the tracks and follow them endlessly without ever seeing the animals. The tracks were very visible in the snow and those first few winters I chased them for hours and hours. It kept me busy and kept me in great condition. In the deep snow I had to use leggings to keep my legs and feet warm and dry. On the occasion when I got too wet and cold, I had to stop and take off my boots and socks and try to get warm or the frost would bite, and then you had a big problem. If your feet have ever been cold, so cold they hurt, you know what I mean.

Rio was around three or four years old when I got up one morning and headed to the outhouse. Just beyond the garden and up on the small hill behind it was a beautiful large deer. He had dug through the snow and found some clover and was busy eating, and he was not aware of me. I froze when I saw him. I was halfway to the outhouse, and I backed up slowly to the house and grabbed the Mauser. I returned and got closer and closer to the deer. I laid the rifle across one of the poles on the corral and took steady aim. I shot. The deer went straight up in the air and landed back on the ground. It had been a perfect shot. He didn't suffer. I went back to get help. Georgia, Rio and I took a large hunting knife and headed for the dead animal.

I had read the book on dressing out a deer one thousand times. First, you cut the back legs just above the hoof. It releases some gland that would otherwise cause the meat to taste bad. You then insert the knife in the stomach just ahead of the genitals. This deer was maybe two or three years old and a male. You open the stomach cavity all the way to the rib and remove the guts. The smell that comes from the stomach area is quite overwhelming. We all gasped and continued on. We ate the entire animal the best we could. We got a few steaks off his back, some roasts, and the rest we dried with salt and made into jerky.

I think I was having more fun than Georgia and Rio. They seemed to be getting bored or restless with living such an austere life. At times Rio would stand by the gate when a truck was approaching, and hope it was a visiting kid or two. There were no kids around his age and he was lonely.

Georgia's brother, Travers Jr., visited and his artistic talents led him to sculpt a solid oak mantle for the Kiva style fireplace that Kent Featheringill and I had built.

After Stone dog died we got a beautiful husky mix and raised him up to almost full size. Georgia and her brother decided to ride horses down to the highway. The dog followed and the first thing he did when he saw the highway was to run onto it, where a truck hit and killed him instantly. They came back with very long faces. They should have never taken him to the highway. Lesson learned.

Georgia's parents visited in the early years, as did my mother. Her parents worked in the garden and hiked. My mother was born in a rural landscape and enjoyed the ranch. I had built a bathing place down by the acequia. It consisted of a 55-gallon barrel on top of a fire with a faucet that released the water into an old claw legged bathtub. It was large and two people could sit in it. You bucketed the water into the barrel and built an oak fire and in a couple hours you had a bath / Jacuzzi. We even used it in the winter. My mother got a very hot bath and quite a kick out of it. Many times I sat in the tub soaking as snow fell on my face and the moon lit up the meadow and its small lake below, shining in the dark.

Kent and I were building the Kiva fireplace in the front room. I had found a large deposit of petrified wood on the hill above the acequia and brought back enough to cover the fireplace. It had been some time since Kip and Sally planted the pot and then moved out. After Kip left, I had dug up the patch and destroyed all the small plants that were starting to come up. In the early fall we were finishing the fireplace and on a hike through the oak trees I noticed three pot plants. They had persisted, and with the summer rains had grown to around six or seven feet high. A female on horseback rode by and happened to see us as I was cutting them down. I didn't think much of it at the time. Kent and I decided to try to dry the three plants and have something to smoke. Well, the female rider was one of the daughters of H.O. Grace and she must have told the Fresques, who called the Sheriff. Richard visited late at night to warn me.

The next day while we were disposing of the plants, the sheriff and three State Police cars arrived. They caught us red-handed. Kent and I were cuffed in the kitchen with the old Sheriff of Mora, Palamone, watching us. I knew him and he didn't like busting us, but it was out of his control. The state troopers had taken over and they were searching the house. On the table in a small container sat the last of the best piece of hash from Afghanistan I had ever smoked, and I didn't want it to get taken. Since it was Palamone's job to watch us, I talked to him as I backed up to the table. I grabbed the small package, backed over to the wood box by the stove, and dropped it in. They never found it. They were done searching the house and had found the three plants. We were exiting the house and being loaded into the State Police cars when Georgia and Rio came walking up the path from the spring. They had been visiting the Poussons. Rio started to cry. Thank goodness Georgia saw what happened; otherwise, she wouldn't have known where we had gone.

Kent and I went to the Mora Jail. It was old and run down but still functioning. Everybody came to visit; somehow, they managed to bring us a six-pack of beer and a guitar. It was like a scene out of a B-movie. Georgia went to the District Attorney's office in Las Vegas. He was a well-known liberal and probably smoked pot himself. He always let the locals off the hook. His office was staffed with young good-looking girls, and they took a liking to little Rio and beautiful Georgia. I think, the District Attorney, Tiny Martinez, liked Georgia as well. Anyway, he released us on bail and we went back up to the ranch. We were in the jail for about four days. Babe had arrived just after we left with the police. Somehow he found the hash I had dropped into the wood box and he was smoking it when Kent and I got back to the ranch.

Two weeks later Tiny paid a visit to the ranch and asked what had happened. I told him the story about how I had pulled them out from a place I had discovered on the property: they weren't even my plants. I hoped that they wouldn't contact California and find out I had been arrested before. He dropped the charges and I had to pay a 10-dollar fine. That was it!

Things quieted down as it turned into winter. The fireplace we built worked great; it was the center of activity. Margie, Jan Marie (her baby), Jan and Michael visited almost every day. We had a pretty good stereo and a lot of records. We sang, played music and had an experience that people dream of. We eventually got a small black and white TV that picked up a weak signal from Albuquerque. Rio watched 'Sesame Street' through the bad reception. We also started to get the news. In the winter we listened to a lot of music. We had the new albums from Joni Mitchell: "Court and Spark;" The Allman Brothers: "Eat a Peach;" and others. Jan and Michael got married in the Mora Courthouse with Georgia, Rio and I as their witnesses.

Rio was getting older and Georgia started thinking about school. She didn't want to put him into the Mora school system, and she was probably right. What to do? We started to question the future, our relationship and our individual goals. I didn't want to leave. She did. It's that simple. We argued, the arguments grew into fights and we started to drift away from each other. We decided to split up. I would accompany them back to L.A. and get them going in some apartment and eventually file for divorce.

Pooh was still in the cabin and Babe was staying in the big house. Pooh had discovered cocaine and was drinking a lot and partying in Santa Fe most of the time. He and Babe got into a fight over fifty dollars and Babe decked the little Pooh bear. Pooh left.

It was early spring and Babe's daughter Kelly was staying with him. Babe found some green celery stalk type plant down by the ditch and ate six or seven of them. It turns out it was hemlock and he had eaten enough to kill a cow. He went into convulsions and Kelly didn't know what to do. Babe went into a coma-like state and was unable to communicate. He was dying.

Meanwhile, Pooh had contacted the State Police about Babe hitting him and got them to accompany him up to the ranch to get his things. They arrived as Babe was flat on his back. Kelly was never so happy to see the police! She ran to the gate to greet them. They called the ambulance and Babe was taken to Las Vegas emergency. They thought he was acting like an alcoholic and going through some kind of seizure related to alcohol. Finally, Babe came to enough to tell them he had eaten the hemlock and they pumped his stomach.

Pooh moved to Santa Fe and began his party life. The consumption of hemlock produces nervousness, trembling, poor coordination, birth defects, depression, coma, and death. Babe was a lucky man. If he had not punched Pooh and if Pooh had not gone to the police, Babe probably would have died.

.

BACK TO L.A.

Georgia, Rio and I lived together for a while on Dickins Street in Sherman Oaks. It was an older building with only eight units, mostly single mothers. I set up my jewelry equipment in the back porch and tried to support us. Georgia and I were still sleeping together. When she started dating someone, I saw the hopelessness of the situation. I started seeing one of the pretty neighbors who sometimes dated the drummer for Tom Petty and the Heartbreakers.

I eventually learned who Georgia was dating: it was Sally's brother Bill Norton, who I had known quite well in college. He was doing well; he had written and directed a film with Kris Kristofferson. He went on to write and direct George Lucas's next installment of "American Graffiti": "More American Graffiti." I went down to his house in Venice Beach and had a friendly meeting with him about maybe being the still photographer on the shoot. I never got the job, obviously because Georgia was flying up to his locations and staying with him for weekends. He was not the only friend my ex-wife was seeing. I won't go into details, but it was so totally un-cool.

I moved into a storefront at the corner of Laurel Canyon Boulevard and Burbank Boulevard and started my photography thing again. I advertised and was mostly shooting headshots for actors. It was fun to be shooting again, but I wasn't making any money. Georgia wanted her share of the ranch. I had no money and didn't want to lose the only thing I had ever loved. The only thing of value I had was the contract with The Doors for a percentage of the profits from the stuff I had done for them. I went to Robby and told him

I would like to sell them my contract. We did it in two payments, one for 15 thousand dollars and another for 10 thousand dollars. I gave the money to Georgia, she signed over the deed, and that was that. I called Pooh and told him I had purchased the ranch, and not to pack up and leave. He watched the place for several years as I rebuilt my life again in L.A.

One day as I drove down Ventura Boulevard heading toward the studio, I noticed a girl on a moped next to me in traffic. She was young, blonde and beautiful: my next model! I flagged her down and we exchanged numbers. She was just a teen at the time. She started coming by the studio and we shot a lot of tests. As she grew into a young woman she started hanging out at the Playboy mansion, doing drugs and leading a fast life. She became more interested in behind the camera stuff and did makeup for me, etc. She also designed costumes that she and her friends modeled and I shot. I called her Tami, but her real name was Tamara Davis. She went back to college and I didn't see her for a few years. She studied photography and started shooting 8mm footage of any band she could. She put it together into videos that eventually got shown on MTV. She met one of the Beastie Boys while making their video and married him. Last I knew, she was living with him in the Silver Lake area of Los Angeles and occasionally directs a film. Her last was a Britney Spears film. I think her greatest feature was "Guncrazy" with Drew Barrymore.

The three remaining Doors were putting out an album called "Other Voices." I did some shots of them; I don't know if they ever used them or not, but they looked good.

I visited with Rio whenever I could. I brought him to the studio and we played. We found a beautiful old couch in the alley behind the studio. It was old; the rain had loosened all the veneer off, and the fabric and stuffing had long since washed away. We dragged it over to the studio. Over time we stripped it down and refinished it and had it re-upholstered in dark green velvet. It was elegant then and now. I still have it; it's in my garage, covered up.

There were several kids in the Dickins Street apartment that I befriended. I still know them today: Chuck Crivier, his brother Chris, and David Moore have been to the ranch and I have helped some of them become grips in the film business. They have married, had children and settled down.

HEAD SHOTS   1977

I was not making a lot of money shooting headshots and I was having trouble collecting money from clients. One girl that came through was very pretty and wanted some shots because she was thinking of modeling. As things go with models and photographers, she eventually took off her blouse and we shot some with her arms crossed covering her breasts. Well, I guess she went home and told her rock musician husband because he stormed down to the studio. I talked him down and we became friends. They even drove out to the ranch the next spring because they thought they might want to be caretakers.

Meanwhile, Bob Angers from my days of making children's films had progressed along as a grip and was running the night shift at Universal Studios, only two miles from my studio. He said I should come over and work with him. I could work nights and still pursue my photography in the day. I checked it out and before I knew it, I was working as a Permit Grip, building scaffolding and erecting sets on the stages of Universal Studios. I got my thirty days and paid the money to join Local 80. I was a Union #80 Grip. In those days the studio was working to full capacity. Including "Battlestar Galactica" and "The Dukes of Hazzard," there were a total of 32 stages at that time and they were booked year around. The first year I worked as a grip I made twenty five thousand dollars. It was a lot of overtime, but the money was good.

The good news was the film industry went down in the summertime everybody got laid off. I collected unemployment and headed for the ranch. I never missed one summer at the ranch for over thirty years. One day as my rigging gang and I walked between the stages heading for the next job, I saw Carol Wayne from "The Party" and called out her name. She recognized me and pulled me into her trailer, where we chatted and caught up with each other's life. She gave me a big wet kiss and I left her there. When I rejoined my gang, everyone was amazed. I never told too many people where I had been and who I had known. It was like I had been reborn with a new identity.

In those days Universal was very busy and a lot of people got into the workforce that would otherwise not have had a chance. I called Babe and he knew Bob Angers from New Mexico. Babe came to Universal and started working nights alongside me. There were maybe two hundred grips doing rigging at that time. Drugs were plentiful and we partied a lot in the darkness of that studio. At lunch we all ran across the street to the U Joint, the nearest bar, and threw down as many drinks as we could. It was difficult work and kicked the shit out of us. We had to stay happy and stoned or we would succumb to the misery of the task. It was our job to climb into the permanent rafter grid, anywhere from thirty to eighty feet above the sets, and rig scaffolding that ended up suspended one foot above the sets. It was heavy work, it was dangerous, and it wasn't for everyone. I kept my head down and did the work. I met another Grip who was also a photographer, and he started sharing the studio space with me. His father was a famous actor.

It was hard leaving Georgia and Rio even though I knew I had to. Just before the divorce was final I looked up Ray Manzarek. He had a band named Nite City; they sounded good but were having trouble getting gigs. They made an album and were kind of sitting around. It was Christmas time and they were all feeling kind of low. I asked Ray if they would back Georgia and me on a couple of songs for old time's sake. He said sure, and I agreed to give each of the guys a hundred bucks. They were happy to do it. We recorded 'Change' and 'Joyride'. We were done in two or three takes. Nite City broke up soon after that and Ray went on his merry way.

My divorce with Georgia was final. At that time Ray was renting a big house on Mulholland Drive for the band to use as a hangout. Danny Sugerman lived there. It was winter and cold in the studio; when Ray found out I was sleeping there, he offered me one of the extra bedrooms in that house. I moved in and Danny and I became reluctant roommates. It was a large Hollywood house with a Jacuzzi that looked out over the valley; I used it a lot. Danny was using heroin at that time and dating some cute young girls. A few times I found him nodded out with a needle dangling from his arm. I pulled it out, cleaned him up and helped him to lie down.

On the table downstairs was a manuscript written by Jerry Hopkins, the same guy we sat with in Barney's Beanery so many times as he interviewed Jim over and over. He had written a book about The Doors, but the publishers didn't want it. Danny suggested I read it and give an opinion, which I did: it was too long and too factual. It conveyed little of the excitement that The Doors had produced.

I moved out when I saved enough money from working at Universal to afford my own apartment. It was around the same time that Ray gave up the house on Mulholland. I still had the '73 Ford truck with the camper shell on it I had bought with money working for my sister. I gave Georgia money when I could. Time was marching on.

When Bob Angers left Universal and went to work for CBS Radford, I followed him over there. It was a smaller and friendlier lot. My life was starting to take on some kind of accidental structure. It wasn't the same as most of my contemporaries with a career and plans for retirement. The answer was truly 'blowin' in the wind.'

GRIPPING

'What is a Grip?' is a question that I have been asked at least a hundred times. John Huston, the famous director, once was asked in an interview: "If you were stranded on a desert island, who would you want to take with you?" He answered, "My Key Grip." Grips are people who are adventurous and daring, like the Special Forces of filmmaking. We build the structures that are necessary for the shooting of films. Grips are in charge of moving the camera on dollies and cranes. When the camera is perched on the side of a building, rigged on the hood of a car, or strapped to the side of an airplane or bridge, the Grips have rigged it.

In those days there was a strict pecking order in the Grip Union Local #80. No one moved up until someone died or retired. That's how the old guys had structured it so they had some security. First, you were a thirty-day Permit and then you were allowed to join the union. We all became Permits, the lowest rank you could hold. It weeded out a lot of people that wouldn't have made good Grips. We were paid around eight hundred dollars a week. I was a number three for several years. The industry was very busy in 1978 and that was when Bob Angers hired me, and then Babe, along with many others.

Working on the gang hanging scaffolding and moving walls was called Grip construction. We started out on night shift; that is when the shooting companies would go home. We would make changes to the sets that included adding new scaffolding above the sets. The scaffolding held the lights and sound people. We hung chain from the permanent rafters, called perms, at least thirty feet above the stage floor. At the bottom of the chains hung what we called a bale, a piece of scaffolding-like iron that held the ends of the wooden beds. The beds made up the flooring that was called the scaffolding. They were painted green and sometimes the scaffolding is referred to as the green beds. They were all tied together and braced with long boards that reached up into the rafters on a 45-degree slant to keep them from swaying.

I liked it up high and was good at it. We climbed up a long series of steps to get to the perms. The only time we came down was for lunch and breaks. A guy named Pat Campe took me under his wing and showed me the ropes, literally: he had come from a family of circus performers and had done high wire work before. I am forever indebted to him for his kindness.

I had a long hank of ¾-inch hemp rope that had a hook on it. I lowered it to the spot that would make the bale hang just over the set wall. A Grip on the floor would attach my hook to the chain on the bale, and we pulled it up hand over hand until the hook on the chain reached the grid of wood we were perched on. We slipped the hook over the wood perm and went on to the next hang. The beds that fit in between the hanger bales were anywhere from four feet to ten feet. They were stored outside in the back lot of most of the studios. When it rained they became soaked and very heavy. Two guys pulled a bed up to the bottom of the hanger and someone else landed it, hooking it in on both ends until eventually there was a walk- way just above the set.

I was in pretty good shape for a forty year old man; the ranch had kept me strong and trim. In the early days I didn't have a log splitter and chopped all the wood with an axe. Putting up hay was a good workout, as well. I had thrown my back out a couple of times and was seeing a good chiropractor in Westwood, trying to keep my back healthy. Almost every Grip in the business has back problems.

Once on the back lot of Universal Studios the Grips built a five or six-story scaffolding straight up. It's actually called camera steel; it's a platform six feet square for the camera to mount on to shoot high angle shots. It had to be braced off with cable every twenty feet as it rose up from the hillside. It was a big deal: special permits were issued and the inspectors were there most of the time. It took the better part of the day just hauling up the pieces and erecting it section by section. You had to climb a ladder that was attached to the steel. Finally it was done and all the Grips had come down. The camera crew arrived, took one look at the platform and said they were not going to climb up there. There was a big meeting and finally they offered them enough hazard pay to coax them up the ladder. Of course there was a hazard, but I guess not for the Grips who had been all over it for two days! That's how things went for Grips. The dangerous, the dirty, the difficult, it all fell onto the Grips.

The actual shooting of the movie was called Production. That is where the money was, mainly because of the long hours that a Production shoots and the overtime that is worked through the week. By the time I got to CBS Radford I was waiting to become a number two rank, which meant I would get to work on actual Production sometimes. The head of the small Grip department at that time was Joe Meshelski. He was a wonderful kind man, something I hadn't seen too much of at Universal where it was a large factory-type situation with little contact with the boss. Joe recognized my ability to understand Production; after all, I had been a filmmaker/ film student. I had a leg up on the rest of the Grips. I not only understood the needs of the cameraman, but also understood the effect his request would produce.

One day the department got a call for an extra hammer on a show called "The Lazarus Syndrome" starring Louis Gossett Jr. It was a hospital show and Lou was a doctor, sort of like "ER." The Key Grip on the show was Ron Woodward, who had been a famous Dolly Grip. That means that you had an exceptional ability to move the camera and were in demand by the Directors of Photography and Directors who saw the camera moves daily in the footage shot the day before. It was magic when the camera came to a stop just at the right moment when the actor stopped moving. It was all about timing and not everybody has that ability. Being the Dolly Grip eventually gets a little bit old. Ron moved into the role of the Key Grip with his cameraman. The Dolly Grip position is a job that wears you out because of the sheer amount of time needed to be on call and ready for the positioning and/or repositioning of the camera. There is little time to get away to visit the bathroom or the snack area because the Director or the cameraman is constantly repositioning the camera. The dollies used by Hollywood were built especially for the job. They weigh anywhere from five hundred to eight hundred pounds. Sometimes a dolly has to be carried upstairs to second story locations or put on top of a platform. It takes at least four guys to lift it, and a person can get hurt.

The dolly can move on a smooth floor but sometimes track has to be laid. Once the marks are on the floor and the track has been laid in a configuration that allows the lens to reach the desired position, you are ready to shoot. The track resembles a train track; the wheels of the dolly fit right on and allow it to glide smoothly from one position to another. When the actor enters the door, the dolly moves with the actor until he stops at his mark. At that same time, the dolly should be stopped at its mark. The Director asks the camera operator how it was and if it looked good they moved on. Usually there are several takes of a scene before everyone, including the actors, get it right. Nowadays there is a monitor and the Director can see and decide for himself if the move or the focus was good.

Ron, the Key Grip of the show, took a liking to me. I was attentive and knew how to handle myself. He told the department head, Joe Meshelski, that he wanted me full-time. Joe told him I was only a number two and that there were people ahead of me; Ron said he didn't care and he wanted Joe to bend the rules. Joe did, somehow, and I worked on the set of "The Lazarus Syndrome" for the rest of the season.

Ron taught me how to set flags and use C stands, which is what a Production Grip did. The Gaffer would set the lights according to the Director of Photography. It was then the Grip's job to cut the light from the lens of the camera and diffuse the lights off any walls and or people that were being bothered by too much light. Nets could be added to reduce the light in certain places as the cameraman deemed necessary, to achieve the desired look.

C stands are three-legged stands that telescope up and down and have an arm with a head that receives a pin from the flags. This allows you to place the flag or scrim strategically in front of the light to achieve the desired effect. The flags that cut the light and the scrims or nets that reduced the light were usually placed in front of the lights by rigging hardware off the green beds where the lights were placed, or off C stands in front of lights placed on the floor. Sometimes you could see the shadow on a wall or on the chest of the actors. The cameraman could say to give him two t's, which meant across the tits. A cowboy meant across the thighs where a holster and gun would hang. There was a lot of set slang that was used, and people are amazed when someone yells out 'hang a baby or a black over there' or 'kill the senior.' A baby is a small light, kill the senior means turn off the large light that is referred to as a senior, and a black is not a person.

Coppola had just released "Apocalypse Now" and I had bought two tickets to the opening at the Cinerama Dome in Hollywood. Coppola had used The Doors' "The End" in the movie. I couldn't resist. The "Godfather" series had been huge and he was one of my favorite directors. Never mind he was from UCLA, but how could that not count? I was standing in line at the CBS payroll window and behind me was Lorraine, the second assistant director from "Lazarus." She was a tall young Italian girl with beautiful blue eyes and dark hair, a perfect combination. I hadn't really talked to her except one time I had to check out with her when I needed to get off early to buy a little yellow Fiat sports car. Knowing she was Italian like me, we started talking and I bragged that I had two tickets to "Apocalypse Now." She asked if that was an offer, and I answered her question with a yes. We went to see the movie at the Cinerama Dome and went to her place after. She had an apartment in an old Hollywood style building a few blocks up Argyle. We got it on right away. She had been married and divorced and so had I; we had a lot in common. We kept our relationship quiet at work for the rest of the season. I don't know exactly why, but she wanted it that way. She moved into my apartment in Burbank soon after.

I was in the middle of writing another script at the time. It was to be called "Younghearts," a Romeo and Juliet type of story placed in present day Burbank with cars and the cruising scene that took place on Van Nuys Boulevard. Juliet, of course, was a beautiful white middle class girl and Romeo was a Hispanic named Danny. The drag racing sequences were some of my best writing; I knew about it from first hand involvement.

YOUNGHEARTS (the script)

INT. '39 CHEVY

We hear music from the tape deck as we see the '39 cruise down a residential street. Danny brings the car to a stop. He shifts to low, revs it up and slips the clutch. The rear wheels burn rubber as the clutch responds without a shudder. Danny tries it again, then drives off down the street

EXT. VAN NUYS BOULEVARD.

Danny whips a turn onto the Boulevard. It's a quiet night and there aren't many cops out. Danny drives alongside a '57 Chevy coupe. They cruise along for some time in second gear straining the engines but not racing. Then, as if by some secret signal, they both hit it hard at the same time. Danny double clutches and crams it into low gear watching the tach hit eight thousand. He pulls away from the '57 easy and when he shifts again increases his lead. A smile comes across his face as he shuts down just in time for the next signal.

Danny meets Julie. They fall in love. Julie gets pregnant. Their families fight and they both grow up and go their own ways. It is like a serious American Graffiti with racial tensions and real street racing and drama. She gets an illegal abortion and ends up in the hospital. Danny hears about it and is heading for the hospital when he runs into a roadblock. The police know him and his Chevy. He cannot wait for the search and stuff the cops are putting him through. He hands the wheel over to his friend and climbs out the window and into an open window of a parked Cadillac. The police notice his suspicious move.

INT. PARKED ' 70 CADILLAC

Danny lies on the floor of the front seat. He has his arms up under the dash and he's concentrating. He pulls himself up and looks out the window. The cops are looking for him in the other direction. His body is slouched down and barely visible. His right hand reaches under the dash and connects the two wires that hang loose. The old Caddy turns over. He pumps the gas pedal and the engine fires up. It's got a blown muffler and is loud. One of the cops still searching for Danny hears the Caddy and turns toward the car. Danny sees him and he sees Danny. Danny grabs the shift lever and crams it into the lowest gear. The Caddy squats down in the rear and the tires peel out from the curb.

EXT. ROAD BLOCK

COP

There he is!

(points with his flashlight)

ANOTHER ANGLE

Danny steers the big car into the traffic. The other cars are forced to stop as he lunges between them and hangs a right to head away from the roadblock and toward the hospital.

INT. ' 70 CADILLAC

Danny can see at least three police cars behind him, in the rearview mirror. Their pursuit lights flash and the sirens scream. A helicopter joins the chase.

INT. CADILLAC

The whole thing is way out of control. Danny's sweating and his face is tense. He's got the big Caddy going about sixty as he approaches a yellow signal. He floors the Caddy as it changes to red, just squeezing through as the cross traffic weaves a barricade for the approaching cops. They slide to a stop and are out of the race.

EXT. VAN NUYS BLVD.

The police cars converge on him from opposite directions. They are seconds late as the Cadillac roars between them and they slide toward one another, crashing. The Cad is hitting around ninety mph as a signal turns red on Danny. The cross traffic begins to flow. No way to stop. He rams the Cad into the center divider to slow down, but the big car flips up onto two wheels. He slides through the crossing traffic leaving a trail of sparks and metal. Near misses all around but somehow he is through. The remaining pursuit vehicle is defeated at the signal and Danny regains control of the Cad. He vanishes down the Boulevard with no one following him.

EXT. HOSPITAL ENTRANCE

The Cadillac creeps into the parking lot with its lights off. It has two flat tires and is considerably crunched but manages to limp into a dark corner and park.

He sees Julie and she is heavily sedated. He spends a tender moment with her and leaves. Julie's brothers and their gang are looking for Danny. There is a big fight and Danny is arrested. By the time he gets out of jail, Julie has run away and gets into drugs. She ends up in a halfway house. Time passes and Danny has a new girl friend. Julie sees him pass by in a crowd but is unable to reach him.

EXT. VENICE BOARDWALK - Day

Julie steps out into the sunlight. Danny and Mike and their dates have disappeared in the crowd. She starts to follow, but stops. There is a tear in her eye as we see her decide not to follow any further. Slowly her demeanor changes. She smiles, realizing it's over for Danny and her. She closes her eyes and feels the ocean breeze. It's the Fourth of July and someone lights a firecracker. A pantomimist dances up to Julie holding two sparklers. He gives her one and curtsies. Julie laughs and sits down on the doorstep of the halfway house as we PULL BACK AND UP. The sign over the doorway reads," IF YOU COME THROUGH THESE DOORS YOU ARE HALFWAY HOME. The shot soars higher and higher, finally including the whole beach.

We see the Fourth of July fireworks begin on the pier. The night explodes with color. THE END

Babe watched the ranch until Lorraine and I got there in the spring, then he left to go do cement in L.A. He was the perfect caretaker. A lot of people were scared of Babe. They had good reason to be; he had moments of uncontrollable rage. He loved to 'beat people up'. Lorraine seemed to love the ranch; she got right into it. She had loved horses all her life and we purchased some new horses and tack. We rode a lot that first summer. Rio came to visit and we had a great time.

It was a hot year. We put in a large garden. I dammed up the top irrigation ditch and had black plastic pipe running down about four hundred feet to the houses. As long as the ditch was running, we had water to the kitchens. When Lorraine arrived from L.A., there was a summer solar shower built down by the garden area in a teepee type structure. I had run the black plastic pipe down to it. Just before it got to the shower it flowed through a coil I had placed on black plastic. The sun hitting the coil heated the water up (sometimes too much) and delivered it to a bucket with holes punched in the bottom. The bucket hung above your head suspended from the intersecting teepee poles. It was a very fun experience and the kids loved it.

I identified all the herbs in the area for Lorraine. She took an interest in the wild flowers that grew all over the place. She made dry bouquets and cured the herbs all around the house. It was nice to have a woman around that loved to be there. She got into the wood stove and cooked breads regularly. She was a great camp cook. When we went on trail rides she always insisted on bringing gourmet foods like steaks and eggs, etc. That was something guys would never do, but really enjoyed.

Leroy became a constant trail companion. He had worked for the forest service as a teenager and knew the mountains above us like the back of his hand. We took at least one trip a year to the high country for as long as I can remember, and sometimes we went several times in one summer. Lorraine had a glow that first year; a lot of people got giddy at that altitude, and she was no different. It was a pristine paradise, unspoiled by the twentieth century. It was remote and off the beaten path.

Mora had a reputation for being a little rough. That kept the Texans away for the most part. The Winnebagos didn't stop in Mora; they kept moving right on through to Tres Ritos, Taos and beyond.

That first year Lorraine and I took the money from our tax returns and put in a well. I borrowed Jerry Linville's copper divining rods and I witched the place. It was an amazing thing: they bent toward each other as I neared a certain spot on the land every time. That's where we dug the well and by god, we struck good water. An outfit from Vegas drilled the well and we hit the first water at one hundred feet. The amount of water that a well could produce was measured by simply filling up a one-gallon bucket repeatedly for one minute. At a hundred feet deep we were getting three gallons a minute; this was very low and we kept drilling, which was costing 10 dollars a foot. At two hundred and fifty feet we hit the mother lode: so much water was gushing from the pipe that it knocked the bucket from my hand. We capped it off and waited till the next year to bring the electric to the well site, build the pressure system, and run pipe to all the structures.

That first year one of Floyd's daughters, Vangie (short for Evangeline), watched our place. She turned out to be somewhat of a witch and a thief. She removed everything that wasn't bolted down and hid it under a nearby neighbor's cabin. She was gone when we arrived the next spring. I eventually found most of our possessions. She and her small son had spent time dropping rocks into the well to hear the splash. We had to clean it out. The water was sweet to the taste but hard to the touch. We had it tested and it was fine.

The area up the road from us was called Walker Flats. It was the beginning of the state forest. People still had grazing rights for their cattle up there under an old agreement that was put in place when the Spanish land grants were purchased or stolen from the local people. The whole area was once part of a huge land grant. While the king of Spain owned the area all the way to California, he gave land as payment to the high ranking military and Governors of the area for their service. The movement in the sixties by several radical groups, namely the La Raza in our area, was an attempt to reclaim some of that land the grants had given away, land that rightfully belonged to the people. Dennis Banks in the Dakotas was fighting the same reservation type battle and he eventually lost in a huge gun battle with the FBI. The La Raza was later disbanded but the sentiment still remains today.

We pretty much had the Walker Flats area behind the house to ourselves; even the locals had forgotten about it. For example, most of them didn't know that a beautiful waterfall was tucked away in a small canyon off Walker Flats. It came from North Fork Lake and it had carved out a beautiful stone-lined path as it fell some 60 feet. There were pools of crystal clear water with shiny green fern and moss that clung to the smooth white granite. A refreshing mist rose up from the falling water. Henry and the guys that were born there visited often, but they were a small group; the rest were oblivious. It was called the high country up there. It was around 9,500 feet in elevation. We were a brotherhood of the horse; people you met on the trail could become friends for life.

Ricky Lucero was someone I met at the lakes one year and we are friends to this day. Ricky was a legend in the area as part of what they called the Mexican Mafia myth. In the sixties there was a small war between the locals and the forest rangers and the game wardens. There was a shootout in the high country between a game warden and one of Ricky's friends from childhood. It was a big deal. Soon after Ricky's friend was buried, the game warden who shot him was watering his lawn down along the highway and was shot from a distance with a high-powered rifle, killing him instantly. There was a huge investigation into who killed the state employee but no one was ever convicted. That murder is still talked about.

It was a tradition to feed the family by hunting in the local mountains. The laws of the U.S. Game and Fish are still not respected and probably never will be. It's just the way that it is, but at the same time folks have to be made aware of the need for conservation of the natural resources and that includes the wildlife. They have figured it out and are cautious of the law, but sometimes necessity takes over and a person kills to feed the family. I understand the government trying to protect the wildlife ... but when they turn around and sell a high priced hunting license to a person from New York who comes to kill a trophy elk and take only its head and hindquarters, it pisses off the people who need the meat to feed their families. I have to side with the locals about that.

Lorraine and I left at the end of the summer to start jobs in Hollywood. I was still working at CBS and that next season found me on a sitcom pushing a dolly for someone who was sick. I was still a number two but had enough skill and know-how to sub for the guy. It was a cold turkey experience for

215

me; I hadn't done it before. In those days there were four cameras mounted on Fisher 9 dollies that filmed the sitcom. The operator rode on the dolly as the focus puller walked alongside and adjusted the focus for the different positions that we moved to during the scene.

The Dolly Grip's job was to find the position on the floor that suited the camera operator's need to get the shot he wanted. Blocking was when the Director lined up his shots. We marked each position during the blocking of the scene with tape on the floor. In a sitcom there are usually four cameras running at once in front of a live audience. The Director decides the positions for the cameras that give him the proper coverage or shots to edit a smooth scene.

The master is the shot that sets the whole scene and usually includes the entire set where the action takes place. Another camera fills in with a medium or closer shot. The two outside cameras covered the dialog in what was described as overs or singles. During a scene there could be as many as ten or twelve positions that the dolly had to arrive at. I had a pad of paper on the handles in front of me that described the positions. Visuals determined the move, such as 'she enters the room and x's right.' Sometimes there was a line from the script called a line cue that the Director wanted the camera to move on. I got the hang of it fairly fast with the help of some generous brother Grips that would shout out help from behind the other dollies next to me.

Lorraine and I were married in Taos, New Mexico in the Sheriff's trailer. We had two deputies as witnesses. We spent the next summer at the ranch. It was our honeymoon. When we got back to L.A., we pooled our money, she two-thirds and me one-third, and we bought a small house in the cheap part of Encino; it was a real fixer-upper. It proved to be a worthwhile time-filler for me as the Grip business, with my number two, roster status, proved to be seasonal at best. Then, there were always the actors or teamsters unions that would sometimes strike. When I wasn't gripping, I was remodeling that house. Next door I could hear someone practicing electric guitar. After a while I met the neighbors and became friends with Louis, the guy who was practicing guitar. His girlfriend roommate waited tables in restaurants. He played in top forty bands for a living, and he gave me some lessons on lead guitar. I diagramed the neck of the guitar on paper and began to learn.

LORRAINE AND I   TAOS WEDDING

Around this time Ron Woodward, the Key Grip that had given me the job on "Lazarus" where I met Lorraine, was selling his equipment package. He was also a friend of Lorraine's before I met her. Lorraine and I decided to spend ten thousand dollars and buy his package. It came already stored in a lock-up in a suburb of the valley called Winnetka that Ron had used for years. He just handed me a key and that was that. Ron had done "Romancing the Stone" and other projects that took him and the equipment to remote locations like the Amazon. It was a well-seasoned pile of equipment that was still serviceable, and I started doing small jobs using it.

Dean Goodhill was my old friend from college days and a friend of Tim McIntire. I had introduced Dean to Ron Joy at Gamma during my time there. On occasion I used his darkroom that was located behind his parents' house in Beverly Hills below Sunset Boulevard. He was from a privileged Beverly Hills family; his father was a famous ear doctor to the stars. Dean had some photos of Mick Jagger and the Stones that he took on a visit to England, and it was enough to get him signed on as a contributing photographer at Gamma Ltd.

He phoned and asked my help making a small film he was producing and directing. Dean had adapted a novella titled "Vera" into a short film script that ran about thirty minutes and had mortgaged his house to finance it. He hired Stephen Poster, a friend of a friend, to be the Director of Photography. He offered to pay for the equipment and I think I even saw some wages. Lorraine was not working at the time and signed on to be the first Assistant Director. The film was a period piece with costumes and horses, etc. Dean procured the Disney Golden Oak Ranch just north of L.A. We converted an old cabin on the ranch into the interiors of the house Vera lived in when she meets her lover.

Stephen Poster was a pleasure to work for. On one shot that brought the characters from the house, I suggested that someone lie on their stomach and shut the gate as the crane arm pulled back, so that we appeared to move through the gate. The camera was extended over the gate with a crane arm. The crane drove away as the people approached. As the camera pulled back we saw the gate closed and our characters opening it and stepping out. It was cool and Poster was impressed. I have always had a good eye and a sense of visual styling, and movement of the camera is part of that. I was a physical person and gripping was a mostly non-pressure job that allowed me to be involved with the Director of Photography's artistic creation of a film. It was a good experience.

Lorraine and I wanted to be more involved in filmmaking and we decided to shoot a rock video. She would produce it and I would direct. I wrote a song and cast our neighbor Louis and a band we put together as the group featured in the video. The song was called "Children in Paradise."

Before I met her Lorraine had dated a camera operator who was trying to become a Director of Photography. His name was John Toll and he went on to win two Academy Awards in two years, back to back. Pretty impressive! He agreed to shoot the rock video for us.

I met George Halverson when I was gripping. He was managing a small studio on Fountain, just east of Sunset on the edge of Hollywood called the Max Sennett Studios. He talked his employer into giving me a stage on spec. That meant if I ever saw any money from the project, I would pay them. Thank you, George! I later used George as a Best Boy on a couple of my shows. But that comes later. The funny thing is that Jack Anderson from "Vera" was on the stage next door shooting a film with Lorenzo Lamas called "Body Rock." The cameraman was Robbie Müller, and that's when I first met Robbie.

There were two parts to the "Children in Paradise" video, the performance of the song and the drama story that intercut under the song. I found a young Chicano hottie to play Louis's love interest. They are in the bedroom of a small apartment; Louis is on the bed as his girlfriend pulls her fishnets on. She is dressing like a hooker and he is not happy. They argue. She hands him some money and he throws it into the air. It floats down in slow motion. A beautiful parrot perched on the bed grabs at the money with his beak as she exits. The other sequence is a dreamlike sequence with the girl on a horse that Louis leads along a sparkling slow moving river. At one point they are playing in the water and he kisses her as they roll in the water. Her dress was sheer and her young breasts were clearly visible.

Louis actually fell in love with her; he believed the dream sequence and started calling the actress. She asked me to stop him. He was convinced he was going to get some of her; maybe he did, for all I know.

Our friends all helped with the shoot. Louis's live-in girlfriend catered it. Audie Aragon pushed the dolly. He was the son of Art Aragon, the famous boxing star from L.A. He was a Grip and we worked together at Universal

Studios in the early days. He later visited the ranch in New Mexico and bought property nearby.

Tim Wawrzeniak, a UCLA classmate, pulled focus for John Toll. We shot about twenty hours straight. The crew was burnt. I needed more coverage, but Lorraine was the Producer / First Assistant Director and she pulled the plug at twenty hours. The sun was coming up as we left the stage. Most music videos are the same: a long intense shoot with plenty of music and plenty of smoke. After hearing the same song over and over, you no longer like it! It was a beautiful video and the music was Santana inspired. It was a success; it looked great but it didn't, however, prove to be the ticket to the big time for anyone. It was just another step in the dance.

Meanwhile, my first wife Georgia was working in Santa Monica at an antique store. Down the street from her was a Spaghetti Factory type restaurant. She said was going to find a millionaire and marry him, and she did: he owned the spaghetti restaurant. Georgia came from a family that had been living off old money from their grandfather's wealth. That's all they knew; there wasn't any motivation to work. Georgia's mother was living in Santa Barbara and bought Georgia a small house in Carpinteria, a surfside community south of Santa Barbara. I saw Rio on the weekends. We exchanged our boy halfway in Ventura somewhere for years until Georgia's relationship with her boyfriend heated up. They wanted to travel, so she put Rio in the best boarding school in Ojai.

I got a phone call one afternoon from Rio and he was sobbing. This was the first I knew of Georgia's decision to put Rio in a boarding school. He didn't understand and he felt abandoned. He filled me in on what had happened. I told him to stay put and I got in my car and drove to the school. I told them what was happening and they led me to him, where he was sitting on his bunk in a small dorm room. His roommate was also in the room and just happened to be the son of a famous actor. Rio was ten years old. Our divorce had been hard to digest and now he was left by himself. I told him to get his stuff and we drove back to L.A. The school didn't even question me, for some reason. Lorraine was great; she accepted Rio like he was her own and he lived with us until he was seventeen.

My mother, bless her heart, used to come and live with us when we needed her. She was the nurturing grandmother to my son, something I didn't experience.

Rio's friends from Dickins Street were still in the picture, Chuck and Chris Crivier. They lived with their father not far from us in the valley. A new kid my son met was Dave Moore; he was a single parent kid. His father was not in the picture too much and I did all I could to be father to all of them. We did surfing, Little League, and BMX bicycles. I had inherited the old Ford station wagon in my divorce with Georgia and it was perfect for transporting kids and equipment. In the summers we packed up and headed for the ranch. Sometimes one or more of Rio's friends joined us; it was a great place to let kids run. We camped a lot and had bonfires at night. We watched shooting stars and listened to music. Marshmallows turned into beer as they all got older. I taught Rio how to use a power lawn mower to make money in the neighborhood and when he was ready, bought him a mint condition set of Ludwig drums. He was a natural drummer. You could tell when he was small because he used to patter on surfaces with his hands, just like I did. Good rhythm. My guitar playing was getting better and we played music together for years like brothers. We still have a great relationship.

I got a phone call from Mary Werbelow. She was living in a studio apartment in a large building full of artists in downtown L.A. She was about to have her first one-woman show. Would I come? Of course I would! It was great to hear her voice; I had lost touch with her. I asked if I could visit her before her show and she said, of course. I told Lorraine I was going to interview one of Jim's old friends. It was a nasty part of downtown; I was afraid to leave my car on the street. Her space was lined with large canvases that she had painted with full-figure, life-size portraits. They were quite good.

I asked Mary if she was going to paint one of Jim. She said no, she didn't want to talk about Jim. She and I were about the only two people who hadn't blabbed our stories about Jim to the world. It was nice keeping the secret of our life with Jim; we were comrades about that much, anyway. She told me she was seeing someone and was probably going to marry him. We drank some wine and got sentimental, one thing led to another, and we made love for the second time in our lives. The love we had for one another was still strong. She was one sexy old girl and she gave me the royal sex treatment. No wonder Jim loved her so much as a young man. I promised to go to her art show and I did.

Things picked up again in the industry and I was working back at CBS. Lorraine moved to Sony and was First Assistant Director on a Lorimar show called "Knots Landing." I ran into Jack Anderson at CBS on a show called "Rhoda." He was a graduate of an east coast film school. He had pulled focus for Stephen Poster on "Vera" and we had become friends. While on "Rhoda" we became closer and he told me he was going to pull focus for the famous Robbie Müller again during his next hiatus from the studios. Was I interested in being the Key Grip? It was a non-union, low budget film being directed by Jim Jarmusch. It was a no-brainer! Of course I would like the chance to get creative again. Yea!!! I rented all the films I could by Robbie and Jarmusch and became a fan overnight. I wanted to work with these people.

A few weeks later Robbie Müller called and said Jack had recommended me, and that was good enough for him. I was hired over the phone by the famous Robbie Müller calling from Amsterdam, where he lived (he was Dutch) . I didn't care if it was non-union or not. The people from the production office in New York called and confirmed. They sent me tickets to New Orleans where the film was to shoot for six to seven weeks. The title of the film was "Down By Law" and it is now a cult classic.

Jim Jarmusch was a rogue filmmaker from New York. His first films were exciting. "Permanent Vacation" was an underground circuit film that won much praise. It had such power; it defined a whole new genre of filmmaking. I don't know that he set out to be a superstar in the underground film community, but that's what he had become. He was like a rock star; he had groupies and fans all over the world. This was to be his first commercial underground film and it was financed by foreign money.

It was a simple tale of three guys whose lives converged when they all found themselves incarcerated in the same jail cell. He cast Tom Waits, the Italian comic Roberto Benigni, and John Lurie, a New York jazz musician friend of Jarmusch's. What a team! It was like being on the road with The Doors again. Tom Waits was raised in the Lawndale – Inglewood area of California, close to where I was brought up. We sort of bonded on our past. He was an amazing performer and writer of songs; it was a privilege to work and play with him, Jim, Robbie, Benigni, and all the rest of the people who were gathered in the Bayou Plaza Motel. We were a couple of miles from the French Quarter and after shooting the film all day or night we commenced to play, party and experience New Orleans.

The place was usually pretty quiet by the time we got back. They had meals for us there and occasionally we snuck into the bar that was closed and started our own party. They brought in loads of crayfish and cooked them especially for us. There were a few local celebs in the film in smaller roles like Etta James, the famous blues singer; she showed us all the cool spots to hang. Sometimes we drove out of town to a small veteran's hall in the country where someone was playing blues ... and I mean, blues! This was the real shit. A few drunken patrons would be dancing real slowly in front of a bandstand in the corner of a large hall. The music was the purest I'd ever heard it.

We ate in every famous restaurant in the Quarter. The food was amazing and fun. The waiters cleaned off the white tablecloths with knives and the chefs were world-known. We were there for Christmas, and Lorraine flew in. Jim threw a beautiful Christmas dinner at one of the famous upstairs eateries on Bourbon Street. It was first class and elegant. Someone got a shipment of cocaine and on New Year's Eve, a lot of us took a riverboat cruise. It was cold outside on the deck as we smoked good pot and watched the moon dance on the water as the city lights drifted by. There was a concert and dancing in the ballroom of the boat; it was always blues music. That's easy to dance to, and everybody welcomed in the New Year together.

The next day it was back to work. We shot in the swamps, in the old turn of the century buildings that were once whorehouses and were now restaurants, hotels, the famous New Orleans Jail, the French Quarter, and country back roads in the middle of the piney woods. You name it, we used it as the canvas to tell the story of these three guys. The story is about three very different types of guys learning to get along during a prison break. We shot the prison stuff in the real New Orleans prison. They had emptied the homosexual wing and allowed us to shoot there. All the prisoners were moved to an exterior yard where they had tents for them to live in. They didn't like the conditions very much and sometimes would start banging their cups on the ground. That halted the shooting because of the sound.

When we first entered the facility we were given a speech about not getting into elevators with inmates, not becoming isolated, and not having contact with any prisoner. At first we were worried about being in the homo area of the prison; I felt weird touching stuff. By the time the week was up, we were sleeping in the cots and using prison blankets to cover up and no one caught any diseases. On the last day of the shoot I brought a joint to work and fired it up in the cell we had been shooting in and passed it around. It was a salute to the time I had spent in jail in L.A. for pot.

The characters in the movie find a way to escape. They go through a religious transformation and after successfully evading the prison guards and their dogs, end up becoming close friends. Eventually they all go their separate ways and the film ends just like it began: the three characters are alone again with just themselves. It is sort of a Zen-type experience; Jim is influenced by Asia a lot. In turn, the Asians really 'get' his films.

"Down By Law" is quiet like a Samurai film that is peaceful and serene until there is an eruption of emotion and bloodletting. They call his filmmaking style minimalist. It tries to describe his technique of telling the story in master shots with very few coverage shots and a minimal amount of camera movement. The scenes often are shot in one master that encompasses everything. The actors enter and walk into close-ups. We discover what the scene is about through dialogue. As the shot finishes the camera moves ever so slightly, and it ends.

I had rented Robbie Müller's most recent film before this one, entitled "Paris, Texas." The style that he developed working with Wim Wenders, the German filmmaker noted for his minimalism, was a perfect choice for Jarmusch. The story is that Jim went to Amsterdam and approached Robbie in his favorite bar, told him how much he admired his work, and that he wanted him to shoot this American film of his. Robbie 'got it' right away and became a fan of this new film director.

Jim was a huge fan of Nicholas Ray ("Rebel Without a Cause"), which just happened to be one of my favorite films. Jim was a tall, handsome guy with a wild amount of white hair on his head. He wore black a lot. He was a rebel, outside the Hollywood system. All these attributes matched Nicholas Ray to a 'T.' Ray even acted in a Wenders film, "The American Friend."

Jim's style was improvisational. He could sense what extra stuff the moment invented and incorporate it into the film. He had a script, but would write and adapt to the stuff the actors were giving him. He constantly had new dialogue that was inspired by something that happened on the set or after shooting in the daily wrap parties. He had a projector flown down from New York and screened the dailies or the previous day's footage. Everyone was invited and there was pizza and beer and children. Because everyone got to see the work on a daily basis, everyone was in sync with the progression of the shoot. It was a wonderful, artistic experience. You get close like a family on a shoot like that, and it is always hard to say goodbye.

Robbie came from old school European cinema where the camera was usually on sticks. More recently they started to use the Elemack type dolly; it has three wheels and a hydraulic post. You could move the camera around, raise it up and back yourself into a corner to take advantage of the entire space before you. It didn't move very well, however.

There was to be a chase scene in the film as they escaped from prison, a long running shot through the swamp. The Fisher 9 is the heaviest dolly in Hollywood, known for its powerful arm and its strong chassis and I had rented the only Fisher 9 dolly in the area for this scene. A Mafia-type guy named Little Joe or something kept it, and he delivered it to me in the swamps.

As I walked along the path the camera would follow with Robbie, I realized how stable the track would have to be. We would be moving as fast as we could. The swamp is made up of decaying matter that sits on a soft, wet water-filled marsh; our feet sank as we walked along. I ordered a load of plywood and laid a foundation, overlapped a second layer on top of that one, and then placed the round dolly track on top of that. With the help of every available body we carried the eight hundred pound dolly to the track and set its wheels onto it. We had to walk a hundred feet across soft swamp earth to the beginning of the track. Everyone got a quick lesson in the hardships of the craft of gripping. Jack carried the Arriflex camera that Robbie religiously used and mounted it on the dolly.

When everyone was set: Jarmusch, the actors, Robbie, Jack and me, "action" was called. Tom Waits, Roberto Benigni and John Lurie took off running through the swamps. I had a slight lead and was up to speed running alongside the dolly as fast as I could. The track was about a hundred feet long and we used every inch of it. As Robbie felt us stopping, he started a pan that followed the actors as they ran out of frame. We repeated this several times. For various reasons the more actors and elements that need to come together in a scene, the more difficult it is to put on film. We ran out of light and had to call it a day.

The next morning we came back fresh to start the running sequence again. The track and plywood platform had sunk overnight. It was a swamp. We fixed the level with shovels, apple boxes and cribbing. We started the running shot again, and six takes later we had it. My legs were on fire. I was wearing water boots and running was difficult. That kind of shooting kicks everyone's ass.

That night we went back to the hotel and took showers and later met across the street at the Chinese restaurant. Their steamed whole fish was to die for and I ate it often. Back at the hotel after dinner we broke into the bar area and started to drink ourselves to sleep. The high of filmmaking is not easy to turn off. Many a person has fallen into the pattern of drinking himself to sleep and in this case, that is what we did.

One of the Production Assistants was an Italian kid named Guido Chiesa. He found out about my Morrison days and he asked me questions for the entire shoot. What was Jim like? Tell me some stories, etc. I repeatedly get those types of questions. Sometimes in a genuine circumstance I am willing to reminisce but other times, I shy away from questions. He was sincerely interested and we talked about Jim. A few months after the shoot was over, Guido sent me a copy of an Italian film and music magazine that had printed the story that he wrote from our talks. It was very cool even though it's in Italian, and I'm not quite sure what it says.

The opening sequence in the film "Down By Law" floats by the poor neighborhoods, shotgun shacks, projects and abandoned buildings. This was accomplished by finding a large Ford station wagon and rigging plywood out onto the tailgate. The camera was on a high hat, a mounting that is on another piece of plywood. Those two pieces of plywood were screwed together and extended out the rear of the station wagon. Robbie was wearing a safety belt; he sort of hunched down over the eyepiece and hung on for the ride. I had to let some of the air out of the tires to make the camera float smoother, feeling the road as little as possible.

We would use this method many more times, including shooting the end scene. The two characters, now somewhat safe from the pursuit, walk down a country road. They are walking toward the camera as the Ford creeps slowly forward; it's called a walk and talk. It worked quite well.

What happened to the third character? For those of you who haven't seen "Down By Law," Roberto Benigni and the other two characters meet up with a beautiful Italian woman who just happens to be running a small cafe in the middle of nowhere. Her husband is dead and she is stranded. She and Roberto fall madly in love. All four characters spend a night dancing and drinking in this tiny cafe in the middle of Louisiana. Roberto's character chooses to stay with the beautiful woman, who, by the way, is his real life wife Nicoletta. Waits and Lurie leave in the morning and walk off together, and then choose different paths at a fork in the road. That is essentially the end of the film.

In the beginning of the film, Tom Waits plays a down and out disc jockey that is thrown out of his girlfriend's house, played by a very young Ellen Barkin. We shot in an upstairs apartment in the French Quarter. The Tom Waits character takes a job delivering a car for some shady character. It turns out to be stolen and he is arrested, and that's how he ends up in prison. It was a brand new Jaguar and the dealership sent a representative to oversee the use of the car. I had to rig car mounts all over the damn car. I didn't have much experience doing car mounts, but when the cases of mounts arrived from L.A., I figured it out the best I could. Robbie suggested using tape to take the final vibration out of the camera. I taped that camera with shipping tape in every which way I could trying to brace it off, and the shot came out great.

I was sweating for hours as I placed the heavy metal objects on top of the shiny new Jag while the dealer representative stood over my shoulder. I used as much padding as I could. Waits floats through the night in the Jag doing his DJ rap over the radio that's playing. It was classic. When we were in the boats in the swamps, we would wake up in the morning at the Bayou Plaza and be bused to a dock somewhere and placed in fast boats that took us to location. Again, I mounted the high hat to a seat in one of the boats and Robbie shot across to a second boat holding the actors. There was little current so the boats were very steady. There was no dialogue in these scenes, and the motors moved us slowly through the water.

Having been a still photographer previously, I carried a still camera in a case on my belt and managed to shoot a lot of good behind-the-camera stills. Years later when Criterion Films was releasing the film on DVD, they called to ask about the stills I took. I sent them what I had and they used several to show the behind-the-scenes stuff under the narrative of Jim's recollections. It was a welcomed surprise. I had kept the stills with my collection of other film I had shot for twenty years; now I know why.

I got back to L.A. and was basking in the glory of the experience I had just been through. Everyone left on a high mark. The weather had turned cold in Louisiana and the swamp was icy early in the mornings. As we finished shooting, a northern storm swept down across the bayou. We packed up our stuff and said goodbye.

At the Hollywood premiere I was standing in the lobby talking to Jack Anderson when Roberto Benigni came flying across the room and jumped into my arms. The cameras flashed. I felt honored that he even remembered me. Being Italian, he and his wife sort of befriended me and we corresponded for a while. I think I was in love with his wife, Nicoletta who had a small part in the film. Roberto is called the Italian Chaplin and went on to star and direct in many Italian films. He is a funny man. He won an Oscar in 1997 for his Italian film, "A Beautiful Life," about a holocaust victim and how his humor helps him and others to survive the dark experience.

It was nice and warm in Encino. I had fixed the backyard up and was growing about thirty super rose plants: mostly Mr. Lincolns for their fragrance, but there were some other colors mixed in. There was a beautiful old peach tree in the yard that I had pruned before I left. It was budding up and soon was in full bloom. Between the roses and the pink flowers on the peach tree, it was very sweet smelling. The large covered patio in the back had been neglected for some time. It was huge; the floor was covered in flagstone and in the corner was a fantastic fireplace / barbecue. The story goes that a professional baseball player, name unknown, had built it during his stay in the house. I refinished all the wood, put a new roof on it, and added some outdoor speakers and a Jacuzzi. When I got home Lorraine and I made wild love; being apart had some upsides. Like fighting, it's always good to make up. Show business is not always kind to relationships because of the periods of time spent apart.

I started working at CBS Radford again. I was bouncing around; I had no permanent show. I spent a few days on this show, on that show, a few days on the gang, whatever. One day I got a call from Stewart at the Grip union telling me he has good news and bad news. The good was, I had finally reached a number one status. The bad news was everyone else had been moved up, also. They abolished the seniority system. My luck! This meant I could work anywhere, but so could everyone else. Someone with thirty days in the business could now be eligible for the same job as someone with twenty years experience. It wasn't fair. Another deal struck with the producers! We were always giving something back, like higher dues and reduced health benefits. I hated the union from the very beginning. It was totally corrupt.

A bunch of Jabonies ran it and the Producers used their caveman mentality to manipulate them to their advantage. The Producers had orchestrated the whole thing because they wanted to break the seniority and they did; they essentially opened up a roster that had been closed for a long time. They were tired of the old guys with union seniority who thought they didn't have to work, could drink on the job, and generally didn't care about the production they were involved with. However, in came every son, nephew and other kid that knew someone, and within thirty days they could be working on the top films and T.V. jobs that were available.

I had to move fast. My background as a filmmaker gave me an advantage. I understood the process. Sometimes that became threatening to the Director of Photography I was working for. The ones that took advantage of my small and quiet suggestions actually helped their projects. I made small differences all through the day; I was proud to be an invisible contributor.

I was day playing on a show at CBS Radford called "Remington Steele" staring Pierce Brosnan. It was near the end of the production season and I was looking forward to the time I would have at the ranch; it was still a big part of my life. Ron Woodward had taken over as the head of the Grip Department and I got a message that he wanted to see me. He said he had a problem on the "Hill Street Blues" show. That morning they had fired the Key Grip for alcoholism which made him a risk to the production. It was a high profile shoot'em up type cop show and was a legend even while it was shooting. Every few days there were car chases, people jumping out of windows and general mayhem. The Key Grip is generally in charge of the safety on the set. He rigs a lot of the camera mounts and works with stunt men. The cameramen were often suspended on platforms that hung out from windows or on the rooftops of buildings ten stories high. He asked me if I thought I was ready to be the Key. I had just done "Down By Law"... it was a non-union show, but still. I said of course I'd give it a shot.

The next morning I showed up on the set of Hill Street Blues at six a.m., found the cameraman and introduced myself. His name was Jack Whitman. He welcomed me under very difficult circumstances; it was a heavy blow to have to fire someone who had been on a show for many years. The Key that had been fired had a devoted group of friends that let me know that they were not happy with me being there to replace their friend. It's understandable;

however, the cameraman was covering for him a lot and just couldn't do it any more.

The first scene was on the stage. It called for a moment by a wall leading into the squad room. Mr. Whitman asked if I could make some shadows on the wall. I jumped up and looked for one of my crew; I was going to need some stuff. Nobody. I looked at Whitman and he motioned it was par for the course. I went to the equipment area, grabbed some C stands and some flags, and arranged them under the scrutiny of the whole staff. I felt everyone was hoping I would fail but I didn't, my pattern of slashes on the wall was good. Whitman said so; he turned to the Assistant Director and said ready. He had turned the set over to the Director. The Assistant Director yelled out "Picture is up." I stepped back and took a position just behind Whitman and watched as the cameras rolled. After two or three takes we moved into the interrogation room and we worked again to make it ready for the cameras. This went on for maybe sixteen hours my first day and all the days. No wonder it drove Billy to drink.

After one week I was whipped. We came back on Monday and did it again. Most of the show was shot on the stage but every week there were two or three days when we would be loaded onto buses in the front of the studio and bused to downtown L.A.'s Main Street. It was dirty and hostile, and people used to throw bottles off rooftops at the crew. Shattering glass was common. We had to be careful: the bystanders that crowded nearby were potential threats to us. There was one alley we used a lot. The crew called it Shitters Alley because the bums used it to shit and piss on a regular basis. Before we shot, water trucks drove through and followed up with disinfectant, but it still stunk.

The equipment we handled was on the ground. There was a saying if some cable or piece of film equipment was being seen by the camera to "throw a drunk on it" which was a joke that meant hide it somehow. At lunchtime they fed us in a parking lot that had tables set up around a mobile catering truck. The only thing that separated us from the civilians was the wire chain link fence. They stood there in their rags and watched us eat steak that had been barbecued on the spot; it was awkward, to say the least. What could I do? Nobody liked it. It was like working in hell. When I went home, I took my clothes off outside and ran to the shower. Mentally, it was hard to concentrate on making a movie while seeing those kinds of conditions all day. I drank myself to sleep a lot.

There were only a few more shows left in the season. Jack Whitman appreciated what I did for him and soon the other people got it. He motioned for me to ride home from a downtown location in his personal car. He said "You earned it and from now on, you ride home with me." A very interesting bond forms between the Director of Photography and his Key Grip. I think it's a discussion for another book.

The principal set on the stage was a squad room. The show had established a look that was different from other shows. It looked real, more hand-held than people had seen on T.V. It was a combination of hand-held as well as a sandbag on the dolly instead of a solid mounting device; the camera operator just balanced his camera on the sand bag. It gave a unique look to the footage and that technique became a star in its own right: "the Hill Street Blues look." I finished off the season and that was the last I saw of that show. I think Jack Whitman connected with a Key he had worked with before, and that was that.

It was spring and I was getting ready to go to the ranch. It was always a lot of work and a lot of fun to open up the big house and get things running up to speed for the approaching summer. By the time Lorraine and Rio would get there, the horses were shod and the place cleaned up after a long winter season. We had great times in those years: a lot of trail rides and camping adventures. We were getting to know the high country pretty well. The lakes at the top provided a perfect destination. We camped near the lakes and fished and ate like kings. More often than not, Leroy and now his sons that were growing up started to join us.

Michael Grace, grandson to the owners of the four thousand acre H.O. Grace ranch just south of us, started hanging out and then living in his grandfather's house when he died. We became good friends, and he usually came on his three-wheeler at dinnertime to visit and hang out with us. We started hooking up with him on some of the trail rides. We used to cut through his property and pick him up, or simply say hello and continue up the trail that passed by his house heading for Middle Fork Lake.

There were three lakes just above us, about a three-hour ride: North Fork, Middle Fork and South Fork. They all had small streams that overflowed off the side heading down the separate canyons below them. The canyons were steep and the trails demanding of respect. The streams turned into pools of water and an occasional waterfall, like the one on North Fork that was accessible by vehicle from Walker Flats. We had many picnics at that waterfall and took every visitor we had for a look. My mother and father had a blast up there. My father loved Walker Flats so much he asked me to scatter his ashes when he died in a lilac patch just to the left of the road beneath some beautiful aspen trees. The three streams which could run very hard in severe weather made their way down to where all three intersected just in front of the main house at the H.O Grace grand lodge.

When the old man died Michael moved into the lodge and we spent a lot of time visiting him. There was a huge fireplace, trophies of elk and deer and bear were everywhere, and there were Indian rugs to die for all over the floor. Years before in the Bandit days, some of them rode from La Sierra on horseback and stole a lot of rugs. Old lady Fresques tracked them to where they were and got them all back. God, she was great. The main lodge was like something out of a Southwest architecture magazine. We drank and smoked and dreamed a lot. The converging streams by the lodge were full of native trout, and Mike let us fish them whenever we wanted. Leroy and Richard were the reigning champion fishermen in the area. In those days, they could catch fifty fish in a couple of hours. Richard's parents still lived in the caretaker's house just below the main lodge where Michael lived. Michael ate with the Fresques's and with us a lot. He had just gone through a nasty divorce and was in need of friendship.

Around this time Stella Linville was brutally raped by some kids from Guadalapita. Jerry had been down by the garden and didn't hear a thing. Stella kind of went mad after that, she was never the same.

After Jerry died, Stella sold the beautiful little resort they had built to someone who let it cave in on itself. The new owners never came back after they bought it. Stella refused to sell me her beautiful wood cook stove; I don't know why. She left the place furnished when she sold and moved to Kansas to live with her son. Every cabin had a cook stove and tables and chairs and beds. Within a week or two, everything had been stolen. I watched it happen as we drove up and down the road. I should have taken the stove but I didn't.

This year we put in a bathroom with Leroy's help. It extended off the kitchen of the main house; wow, did that change life at the ranch! I added a washer and dryer, and we were styling!

After Vangie had ripped off the ranch like she did we decided to put some effort into finding a good caretaker. Johnny Bonny, our neighbor down the hill, found two guys in Taos who were looking to care-take a place and he set up a meeting. They showed up at our place, a scraggly pair of drifters. It was comical in a way. Jeremiah was six foot three and had flaming red hair. His partner Rick was a good-looking guy with dark hair, shorter than Jeremiah. We felt we weren't going to find anything better so we agreed to give them the job.

We went back to L.A. Lorraine was given one of the "Knots Landing" shows to direct in return for her being First Assistant Director for another season. Rio was going to school in our neighborhood. I was having trouble finding work and was mainly bouncing around that season. I converted the small garage into a T.V. room. It was dark and cool, perfect for napping in the hot valley summers.

Christopher Porter, the Gaffer on "Down By Law," called me. He had been Frieder Hocheim's Best Boy and when Frieder couldn't do "Down By Law," Christopher moved up. He was good, a tall man with shocking blonde hair and an enormous body. We got along great; it was an instant bonding. He called me from Canada where he lived with his girlfriend. They had a building in downtown Toronto that they were renovating. Oliver Stapleton, the Director of Photography, gave him the job of Gaffer for an upcoming shoot about Chuck Berry's sixtieth birthday concert. Taylor Hackford, who had recently done a film called "La Bamba", was directing it. Christopher told me the job was mine if I wanted it. Of course! He hired me for Oliver. It was to shoot in St. Louis, Missouri where Chuck had a ranch just outside of town. Another film on the Mississippi: cool! I hired Audie Aragon to push the dolly for me.

HAIL! HAIL! ROCK 'N' ROLL 1987

This film turned out to be one of the highlights of my life. Of course, it was starring Chuck Berry as himself, Keith Richards was the on-camera Music Director, and Eric Clapton filled out as the third of three main characters. It doesn't get any better than that; I was in pig heaven. The film essentially is the rehearsal and planning for a sixtieth birthday concert in downtown St. Louis at the Fox, one of the classic old theatres in the country. I had the pleasure of buying Eric Clapton a drink. I thanked him for all the enjoyment he had given the world and we toasted.

ERIC CLAPTON, CHUCK BERRY, KEITH RICHARDS
"HAIL, HAIL ROCK AND ROLL"

The first two weeks of the shoot we were bused to Chuck Berry's ranch. In the old days his ranch was "the scene" in St. Louis. He had love-ins and parties for a lot of the local people, and he says that once he had sixty thousand people there. It was a legendary time, written about in all the local newspapers. Now it was a rusting, sprawling one-story living space with peeling paint. Its enormous guitar shaped swimming pool was empty and cracking from non-use. A large building with a kitchen, a stage and lots of seating resembling a nightclub was behind the pool and separated from the main house.

All the musicians that were to play in the concert were also brought in on a daily basis. We filmed them rehearsing and playing, arguing and getting along. There were two cameras going most of the time: Oliver operated one and Ed Lachman operated the other. We installed a basic lighting system that included fake columns on the side of the stage; they were hollowed out and contained a lighting package, and we shot everything that happened.

Taylor Hackford had come from documentary. Oliver made it possible for Taylor to shoot as he was accustomed, without interruptions to the flow for re-light chores. I was smart enough to bring my small camera and I shot a lot of stills. I promise to display all of them on my website at www. paulferrara.net .

What a treat to see Linda Ronstadt again. I walked up to her as she entered the rehearsal hall and re-introduced myself. She was surprised to see me and asked, "What are you doing here??" I told her that I was working on the film. We made small talk and laughed.

Every artist that showed up there had an entourage of several people. By the end of the two weeks of rehearsals, the club at Chuck's farm was full.

There was a scene with Chuck thumbing through his scrapbook that had been kept by his faithful secretary of 30 years. She was a blonde and you could tell that she was quite attractive when she was young. It was no secret that Chuck liked white women, although he was still married to his first wife.

When the Assistant Director called lunch, everyone left the room except Chuck and me. I pointed to a photo in the book and asked who it was, and he told me a story about the young girl. He kept on talking to me as he pointed to each photo or press release. God, I was beside myself. I told him what a fan I was and that I had an original 33 and 1/3 copy of Chuck Berry's

"Golden Hits" album. He was surprised and said it was probably worth some bucks, but I would never sell it. We both missed lunch that day and it was worth it. The scene didn't make it into the version of the film I saw, but it was priceless to me. I will never forget that brief time with him and his generosity to share it with me.

Chuck was a hard man to like; he constantly displayed his bitterness and his love for money. He came from a poor background and was proud to show us his collection of Cadillac cars. We fired up the old Cosmo Club in east side St. Louis where Chuck got his start. Its roof was falling in and it was very dirty. The Art Department did a great job: it looked like it must have in the old days. Original band member Johnny Johnson was on piano, and the room was packed with Berry's fans and family. A great time was had by all, and it shows in the film.

Taylor Hackford was one of the best Directors I had worked with so far. His skillful management of high-strung artists kept the show rolling. Chuck refused to shoot a couple of times. Little by little we worked our way to the final concert at the historic Fox theatre in downtown St. Louis. It had been completely restored and looked magnificent. It was just a few blocks from where Chuck Berry grew up and he remembered he wasn't allowed in because of his color: he had the last laugh. All of St. Louis showed up and most of them got in. The film is a testament to the power Chuck brought to rock and roll. Clapton, Richards, and Jerry Lee Lewis all claim their undying gratitude and respect to the man who shaped the future of rock and roll and gave them a road map to follow.

There was caretaker chaos when we returned to the ranch that year: Jeremiah had found kiddy porn in Rick's stuff; it was about little boys. Oh my god! During the winter they had invited a hippy lady up there, wired in a porch I had in progress next to the big house, and housed her goats there. They had eaten the yard down pretty good. She left when the kiddy porn was found; I think she might have had a kid up there. Rick had moved to Vegas and found work somewhere. Jeremiah stayed that summer and became quite friendly with us. He helped gather wood and do other chores.

When Babe came that year he didn't like something about Jeremiah, who was a tall red-haired geeky looking guy. He couldn't put his finger on why; he just didn't like him. Jeremiah watched the place that year while Babe, Lorraine, Rio and I all spent a week at the lakes. Babe had gotten stoned as we were saddling the horses to come home and put the bridle on wrong. It was lying across the horse's eye and he couldn't see. Babe got on the horse and it started bucking, trying to get Babe off. We were on the steep side of a mountain on a narrow little trail. I thought Babe was a goner but he managed to stay on. The horse got a little tired after three or four minutes of intense craziness; I managed to gain control of the horse and Babe got off. Was he pissed! When we discovered the harness across the horse's eye, Babe got quiet and didn't talk for a while as we started our descent from the mountains.

Later that summer Babe and his daughter Kelly were staying in the cabin, bunking with Jeremiah. Babe had gone to town and when he returned, he got into it with Kelly. He chased her around the yard in front of Lorraine, Rio and me. He caught her, she went down and he proceeded to give her a rather rough beating. Later he told me she had been messing around with Jeremiah and it had turned sexual. She was just a teenager at the time. We were eating dinner when Jeremiah showed up at the door. Babe ran from the table, threw open the door and started to beat the shit out of Jeremiah. We all followed the action out onto the porch. Babe had lost it. The red-haired geek was in a fetal position and Babe just kept pounding on him. I tried to break it up and I punched Babe in the face, trying to get his attention. He turned to me and said "Now we're even," alluding to the time when we were teenagers and he punched me in a gang fight, by mistake. Babe went back to beating on Jeremiah. I told him my back was hurting and I couldn't try to break it up any longer. He seemed to understand the pain I was in and he said, "You said the magic words". He stood up and walked off.

Poor Rio took it rather hard: he started crying and ran up the road. Lorraine was outraged; this was the second caretaker he had beaten up. I told Babe it would be better if he and Kelly moved in with our friend Papa Bear (as we called him), who had a large house in the next canyon to the south on Jack Nicholson's property. Jack had bought the property soon after "Easy Rider." The film crew had actually shot in Las Vegas, only thirty miles south. Some of Jack's friends had come to New Mexico tripping on acid, found this land and talked him into buying it. They were camped out on the side of the mountains waiting for space ships or something.

Years later I was roller-skating with Jill Donahue in Tarzana and she introduced me to Jack. I told him I had some land near his in New Mexico. He claimed he didn't know much about it. It was a beautiful piece of property with two parts to it. One was at the end of the road just under the peaks and the National Forest; there was plenty of wildlife up there, including bears. The lower half was referred to as thé lower farm. That's where James, or Papa Bear, and his wife and kids lived. James welcomed Babe and Kelly. He needed some company anyway, and Babe came in handy to him. He had been my right hand man for a long time. It was a sad thing I did, but it was necessary.

Lorraine and I concluded that we could attract a better type of caretaker if there was a bathroom and kitchen in the small cabin. We started saving and planning for the next summer's construction on the cabin. We all left to go back to work. Jeremiah waved goodbye as we pulled out of the gate. We crossed our fingers. What could we do?

Ron Woodward called me to ask if I would be interested in Keying on a show going to Kansas for two and a half months. I didn't want to go there, but I needed the work. It was a television mini-series entitled "Murder Ordained." The cameraman Terry Meade knew Ron and asked him for help finding a Key Grip. Ron told me it was a tough show, but that was why he had called me; it was a compliment. He told me I could use his ex-Best Boy and I agreed to the deal. It was October when I flew to Kansas City. I was bused along with other key persons arriving at the airport to a small town called Emporia. It was about three hours west of Kansas City and where the actual story had taken place.

When I got to the Holiday Inn in Emporia and checked in, I went down to the disco bar in the lobby area and was greeted by the cameraman. He was a sweetheart; I was lucky. The room was filled with young women in their teens and older. What was up? I asked. Terry said they had heard about Hollywood coming to their small community and wanted some action. Oh my god! I called Danny the Best Boy, and told him to hang onto his hat: there were a lot of girls waiting for the crew. I had Bumby on dolly, and Mike Hodges and Danny's friend Dave Serieka as extra hammers; we would pick up extra labor locally.

We were in the middle of the Bible Belt: there were more churches than people. The story we were shooting was about Pastor Tom Bird who fell in love with one of his parish ladies and killed his wife to be with her. The actual incident had rocked that small religious community. They still remembered it and weren't all that receptive to our being there to film a reenactment of the thing.

I was getting used to living in motels. This one was right off the main highway and across the highway was a meat packing plant. When the wind blew just right, we could smell meat and blood. My crew became like a fighting unit, partying and working most of the day with very little sleep. Danny received a shipment of cocaine and proceeded to sell it to the crew. The local people were way ahead of us and had their own supply of cocaine: in the middle of the country, in a little hick town. Go figure.

There was a real live disco in the town and every weekend the kids came from a hundred miles in every direction to get high and dance and fornicate until the sun came up. There were some colleges around there, one right in Emporia and one not too far away in Lawrence. They provided the atmosphere and the bodies for all the partying.

Terry Meade's style of photography was old school television: a big light over the camera, and shoot! It made our lives simple. We shot in a lot of locations and difficult positions. The most difficult was the bridge where the wife's car went off. It was an old trestle-type bridge with two narrow lanes where the road crossed a river. The car had been discovered in the swiftly running river below it. The logistics of crane, camera and lights up and down the steep bank resulted in many injuries. We shot in that location for several days. The weather can change quite suddenly in Kansas. The northern winds sweep down out of Canada and can change the temperature quickly, and we had to dress accordingly.

We were all getting a per diem allowance, a set amount of money paid out daily for living expenses etc. when you are away from home. One day one of the local hires came to me and told me Danny refused to give him his per diem. He wasn't making much as it was and needed the extra money; I told him I would look into it. That night after we all got back to the motel, I went to Danny's room and asked him about the per diem. There were baggie's and coke stuff, marijuana scales and god knows what else. He was being a little gangster. Danny told me, they could all get fucked, he wasn't paying them. I told him to pay them right away, and he finally said he would.

Danny started showing up late for work in the mornings and one morning he didn't show up at all. The guys tried to cover for him. The Best Boy is in charge of men and equipment and it's very crucial that those two things are in place for the Key Grip who is standing by the cameraman, listening to orders. When the Key asks for equipment and men to work the set, they must be there. It's like an army: when the commander asks for something on the front line, it has to arrive. It's critical. ` When I asked Serieka where Danny was, he replied that he was sick and decided not to come to work that day. He also decided not to tell me. O.k. He finally came back to work a couple of days later and asked me if he could go to Kansas City the next day to arrange a flight to L.A. for his wife's birthday that following Sunday. Then he got sick once again and didn't notify me. I made Michael Hodges the Best Boy and told Danny he could stay on as an extra hammer. He took offense at the demotion and quit. He left the next day and, according to Serieka, he was surfing by the next morning

Things smoothed out. Hodges had hooked up with the script supervisor, Serieka had a live-in girl, and I was not without company. Bumby had tied a rope across the inside of our grip truck with a collection of panties belonging to the girls we had been with. I introduced Bill Bumby to a girl across the room in the bar just out of fun and they hit it off. She was a tall beautiful Indian looking girl. Bumby was just out of a bad divorce and she was just what he needed. He actually brought her back with him to L.A. and eventually married her.

Dave Serieka and I were both married. Serieka had a great wife, but his girlfriend followed him home to L.A. and confronted Dave's wife at the front door. Serieka was a wild sort of biker / drug smuggler, a character right out of a book. His stories were great.

One cold day we were all in a garage of a house we were shooting in. Out of boredom, Bumby scribbled on the wall with a marker pen: "We have come for your children." We left the location around nine at night, grabbed some dinner and drank for a while. When we were back in our rooms I got a call. The local police had notified the producer that someone had written a threat on the wall of the house we were in that day. Bumby. Oh my god. He came forward and apologized and he had to paint the garage on his day off, Sunday. The local people thought that a Manson-like character was among us and they were freaked. Bumby, who called himself Salvador Dolly, was just messing around. He had a strange sense of humor. Most of the time he kept us laughing, but this time it crossed over the line.

When it started to turn into winter, it got really cold. I mean, ice on the trees. It started snowing. Winter clothing to the max, and I was <u>still</u> cold. Even the equipment had ice on it. I had to put on a parka and gloves to go outside and then take them off again to come back inside. It was adding fatigue to fatigue.

"BARFLY" 1987

Toward the end of the shoot in Kansas I got a message from Lorraine that Robbie had called from Amsterdam. I called him back and he told me about a film he was doing in L.A. The dates worked out almost perfect. We would wrap the Kansas shoot and begin the feature entitled "Barfly" almost the next day. I brought all my crew from Kansas to "Barfly." Christopher Porter was not gaffing this time; Frieder had opted to take the job because it was not on location, so he could stay in L.A. and see his wife and new children every night.

Charles Bukowski was a famous beat L.A. poet and icon, and "Barfly" was a screenplay that he had written from one of his novels. Mickey Rourke would play Bukowski as a young man. Barbet has given him the chance to play the role he was born for. He played the hardened ex-con, prizefighter actor role in real life and this role was perfect for him. He actually did fight professionally in Florida or somewhere. He took up acting in the jail system and when he was released, he looked up a drama coach and began.

Faye Dunaway was to play his love interest. She was getting older and was also in a slow period of her career. This was a comeback role for her and she got rave reviews. Now we're talking! Barbet Schroeder, a famous European filmmaker, was directing his first American film. "Barfly" was a story about people who drink. Bukowski's character is a brawler, a fighter, a drinker and a poet. There are several scenes where he and the bartender, played by Sly Stallone's brother Frank, step into the alley behind the bar to fight, trying to prove who is the better man. That's it. It isn't very deep but it is sentimental. Bukowski was present most of the time during the shooting.

The main location was, of course, a bar. It was in Culver City near the Sony Studios and we were to be there for a good portion of the shoot. Upon arrival there, who should I see sitting at the bar and drinking? Babe Hill! He worked at Sony and this was one of his watering holes. Come to think of it, Babe is like a character right out of one of Bukowski's novels.

The place was dark, even darker than most bars, and it had neon lights everywhere. One of Robbie's challenges was to light it and keep the look of the dark neon lighting. Frieder and he devised a method for building a neon type light that was controllable. The system they came up with was crude but it worked. A ballast controlled the intensity of the neon tube. I made foam core housings and we mounted them in C stands. I think the name C comes originally from Century stand. Maybe it was developed at Twentieth Century Fox. Makes sense! In this case we taped nail-on plates on the back of the foam core and mounted the new neon lights into the C stands. We brought several tubes of neon in closer to provide the fill light for the actors' overs and singles. We draped color gels across the lights; the overall lighting of the bar was accomplished with these lights. In close-ups, Mickey's make-up was a little extreme. Fay looked beautiful under this soft light. After this film, Frieder Hocheim actually refined these lights into what is now called Keno Flo. Everybody uses them and I'm sure he is profiting hugely.

Mickey Rourke was a true character. He drove his powder blue Harley to work accompanied by his entourage of twenty bikers, who also rode Harleys every day. His trailer parked near by the shoot was always rocking. There were always parties and the drugs flowed. Once he got into a battle with the studio heads that ran the show's finances, and demanded a Rolls Royce be given him as his personal car for the rest of the shoot. When it was delivered, Mickey destroyed it with the help of his biker crew. They jumped up and down on it until the roof caved in.

Mickey Rourke was a hot property in his early days with films like "The Pope of Greenwich Village," "Diner," and "Body Heat" as credits, but he was a hard person to work with and he fell from grace. He didn't work for a while, and then he did "Nine ½ Weeks," a soft-core film that opened in selected theatres.

Mickey was playful on the set. He loved to steal my knife that was in a sheath on my belt. When I would go to use it there was a big laugh from him; this went on for the whole shoot. Finally I made him a bet he would never get my knife again without me knowing. He took the bet; I put double face tape in the sheath and inserted the knife. It stuck; I couldn't get it out, and now I had him. I used another knife for my work and I waited. Soon I felt a tug at my side: I reached behind me and grabbed his arm. He was busted and I won the bet.

Mickey was known for being quite the ladies man. His steady girlfriend at the time was Terry Farrell, a model from New York. She later ended up an actress on the show "Becker" with me for six years. We talked about Mickey, and she said he was a rough person to live with.

Back to "Barfly" … so, there is the big scene where he and Faye Dunaway were taking a bath together. She was pretty much topless with the soapy water covering the rest. Mickey was supposed to get in with her but he started hyperventilating. He was given a paper bag to breath in and eventually calmed down enough to shoot the scene. Did Faye scare him? Was his partial nudity a problem? I know that nude scenes are hard with the whole crew watching. He had been fine with Kim Basinger in "Nine ½ Weeks," and there was plenty of sex stuff in that film. I don't know what happened; maybe it was something else. Maybe there was too much partying.

Barbet Schroeder was known for his documentary film called "Idi Amin Dada," a dangerous project that showed the vicious Uganda dictator for what he was. He also made "Koko, A Talking Gorilla" for Hollywood and now was doing "Barfly." He had been a huge fan of Bukowski for a long time. Barbet went on to direct many more films based on the success of "Barfly" including "Single White Female," an even bigger success. Bukowski was there for much of the shoot and we all got to know him. What an honor. He died a few years later. Bukowski was a sketch artist and he gave me one of his pen and inks drawings autographed to me. I still have it. There is a bar on Sunset called "Barfly" where the "Becker" cast used to have its Christmas parties. There are pictures of Bukowski, Faye Dunaway and Mickey Rourke on the walls. What a flow this life seems to have.

Robbie Müller had a childlike innocence to him. He chuckled a lot and nothing much seemed to upset him. He went about his work in a quiet confident way. When the lighting was done, he would step back and say we are now ready to shoot. He always operated the camera; he said so many decisions are made as the scene unfolds; it would be impossible not to be in control of the camera. He would hunch over the Arriflex and disappear into it. Sometimes after a scene he would say "bravo" to the actors, turn and smile. His involvement with the actors was very intense. He became part of the story, sometimes moving the camera ever so slightly. His artistic choices were always a part of the drama. He insisted on shooting the master for the scene when the light was just perfect. Everything else could be staged, but the landscape came first: usually early in the morning or late in the afternoon. The sun was low at these times and gave a natural edge to everything, as opposed to overhead light that makes shadows on everyone's faces.

Robbie and I spent a lot of time together, both when we were shooting and when we were not shooting. In an Idaho airport he told me his live-in wife of several years was leaving. He was sad but said that it wasn't the first divorce for him. I understood, as I was now married for a second time. He had a child with this lady and that was the part that was going to be hard. He was born in the Dutch Antilles on the island of Curacao off the coast of Venezuela. He grew up on a Dutch plantation in Indonesia where his father was involved in rubber. He remembers one particular time when he was very young, running through the fields with the natives chasing his family with machetes. There was some type of revolt and the Dutch settlers were on the run; he said he thought he was going to die. The natives in that area were descendants of headhunter cannibals. Later in his life he found his way to Holland and lived in Amsterdam. He had a good life, with a summer place on the Canary Islands. He was a small man, blonde with laughing eyes. He rolled his own cigarettes from damp French tobacco that he had flown in to him no matter where we were. I even got a little hooked on the smell and eventually was rolling my own. Shame on me; I had quit for so long.

Robbie was staying in a motel in Santa Monica right off the ocean near the pier. I picked him up on Super Bowl Sunday in the morning and drove him to our house in Encino where we were having some friends over for the game. He didn't know much about American football but like everything else, he got into it right away. He loved music and had a good knowledge of it. We talked music a lot. He loved Pink Floyd and American blues. He seemed to stay away from anything commercial.

He started shooting for Wim Wenders in 1969 when they made "Alabama: 2000 Light Years From Home." They did many films together, most notably "An American Friend" with Dennis Hopper and "Paris, Texas." "To Live and Die in L.A.," "Breaking Waves" and the Jarmusch films including "Ghost Dog" and "Barfly" were some of the films he did with other Directors. Robbie had a mystery girlfriend; she was young and totally devoted to him. He was eccentric and she was cool with that. I think she was from Kentucky or Tennessee; she would always show up no matter where we were, stay with Robbie for a while and then leave. We all loved her for the comfort she brought to him, and she became part of our group when she was there.

Robbie is the most sensitive cameraman I have ever worked for. He comes from a place that descends from the Dutch master painters: he's that intense! The Dutch were also the masters of the sea for many years. He was also a captain: a Captain of Cinematography. I miss him and the energy we had.

Rio was all grown up. He had a yellow V.W. wagon and his drumming was getting real good. We used to practice in the small bedroom on Collins Street in Encino where I draped some furniture pads over the windows for noise. One day when I bent over to adjust my amp, my left ear was very close to Rio's drums and he just happened to hit it rather hard. My ear started ringing and hasn't stopped yet. It's called tinnitus and it is caused by many things, most of them loud. It is a form of nerve damage that is untreatable.

Rio's mom Georgia had gotten re-married. She and her new husband, Andy Pulos … the guy she met in Santa Monica … were renting an apartment in Carpinteria while they shopped for a house in Santa Barbara. Carpinteria is a sleepy little town just south of Santa Barbara and it's where Georgia's grandmother kept a beach house for years. Georgia and I had lived there with Rio as a baby and we wrote the "Santa Barbara" song there. The surfing was great; when Rio found out about that, he was gone! He put his drums and surfboard into his yellow V.W., said goodbye and split. I couldn't blame him. I wasn't happy to see him leave but what could I do? He had lived with us for about six or seven years and he and Lorraine had gotten close. I remember once when she scolded him for something, he had replied, "You're not my mother." It was typical for step relationships and it hurt, but it is the truth. At a certain point you have to let go: it doesn't do any good not to and it actually can ruin a relationship. I have become good at letting go. It's not that it doesn't hurt, but the hurt seems to go away faster.

Georgia and Andy bought a house on the 'Riviera' of Santa Barbara. Their house looked out over the entire Santa Barbara Bay. Andy has been a good stepfather to Rio, and what more could I ask for? The year Rio moved to Santa Barbara with them, they left him alone in that extraordinary house while they took a three-week trip to India. I think Rio and his friends had a good time while they were gone.

ELVIRA 1988

I got a call from someone at NBC Productions based at the Warner Bros. Studios in Burbank. The cameraman they had hired was holding interviews for a Key Grip and he had requested an interview with me. His name was Hanania Baer and it turns out he was a fan of Jarmusch's film "Down by Law." I asked around and he was not an easy cameraman to work for: very demanding and he could be rude to people not something I am fond of. I got the job and I walked softly. All the preliminary meetings with Hanania were sweet. He was a quiet man, not large of stature but with an intense power about him. He had been raised in Israel and had been in the army, where he met and married his wife Shuli. Once I got to know him and understand where he was coming from I had some tools to work with and we got along great. He respected my previous work and me, all the way back to Morrison and film school. I think the people he had trouble with in the past were people he didn't respect. I respected his earnest quest for the best he could do and he respected me for understanding his passion and helping him achieve his goal.

The film was called "Elvira, Mistress of the Dark." Elvira was really Cassandra Peterson, an actress that had hosted a late night spooky movie T.V. show called "Movie Macabre." Cassandra and her boyfriend had come up with a script that sold and there we were. It was shot mostly on the back lot of Warner Brothers Burbank. At least half of the movie took place at night in the town square of a small town where Elvira's aunt has died and left her a haunted house. They find out she is a witch, or at least they think she is, and the townspeople strap her to a post in the town square and proceed to burn her at the stake. Of course it doesn't happen and she makes an escape.

In those days everyone was doing cocaine and we were no different. The actors, the directors and most of the crew were doing coke just to stay awake. It also made the drudgery of filmmaking more fun. It was a difficult shoot. Director James Signorelli was from New York. He directed the film segments of Saturday Night Live. No big deal in itself, except he had never done a feature film and had no experience. Hanania and he had trouble over that kind of inexperience, and he blamed Hanania when there were delays.

Mark Buckalew, the Gaffer, and I teamed up and managed to survive Hanania's wrath whenever it did surface. Hanania was under a great deal of pressure; he was caught in between the Director and the Producer. The Producer wanted him to go faster, but the Director's lack of experience was slowing us down. We managed to finish the outdoor sequence and were scheduled to move over the hill to Hollywood and a different studio to do the interiors. Well, we were essentially fired. A whole new crew was brought in. It was a bad thing but Hanania, who shot the majority of the film, was to be credited as the Director of Photography. Matt Leonetti, the cameraman that came in to finish the shoot, was given credit as additional photographer. After having worked for Jarmusch and some other stellar directors, this film was a joke. The money was good but it was typical Hollywood bulllshit. Elvira actually became somewhat of a cult figure and the film is still trotted out during Halloween almost every year. I think she even has action figure dolls that are supposed to be her. More power to her. I was happy to move on. Mark Buckalew kept in touch for a long time. I was to work with Hanania many more times during the next ten years.

After that film I had some time on my hands and I started to get serious about remodeling the house that Lorraine and I shared on Collins Street. I turned Rio's room into an office. The room Lorraine and I shared was turned into a guest room, and I added a large master bedroom onto the back of the house. Scott Oram used to live next door to me on Collins and was doing carpentry, and he took on the job. He and I managed to build a beautiful space.

Scott and I became close. Our relationship continued and he came to the ranch several times. When he was living next door he had a girlfriend and they had a rocky relationship. One year when Lorraine and I went to the ranch for the summer, Tamra Davis, the young model I used to take pictures of, offered to housesit and she brought her girlfriend. Scott said that they used to nude sunbathe in the backyard and that he and his buddies would climb onto the roof and check them out. His girlfriend also ended up in the yard with Tamra. I don't know what happened then, but I did find out later that Tamra was bi-sexual and the friend she had brought to live in our house was her lover. The neighbors across the street said there was an older man that used to visit the two and sometimes spend the night. Whatever, it sounds like I missed something!

Tamra told me she was going to art school and I didn't hear from her for years. When Lorraine was on location once I met Tamra in Westwood and we went to a movie. She had turned onto rap music and played some for me. She was so excited about the lyrics. She had picked up on it early on and started shooting 8mm film of various local rap groups. This progressed into the MTV explosion of rap music videos and she is credited with hundreds of videos in that time. Eventually she made a feature film starring Drew Barrymore called "Guncrazy." After she told me about the film I rented it, and I was impressed. This was the teenager I saw on a moped in the valley that became a model for me as well as a friend.

SUPERCARRIER 1988

I wasn't working steady at the time. An acquaintance called me up and said he was trying to replace himself on a show he was keying called "Supercarrier." It was first a feature and now a T.V. series. There were a couple of shows left and would I take it over? I said yes. It was shooting in Valencia. Studios had been built in a deserted factory and locations up and down the area behind Magic Mountain. a huge amusement park. I had to bring a couple of guy's and I asked Kenji, an old friend from my early Universal days, to come with me. He had worked on "Elvira" with me. The cameraman was Frank Raymond and we got along good. He was a still photographer, smoked a pipe and was a mellow type of guy.

The schedule was very hectic. The show took place inside a unit of the Navy that manned a large ship but also managed to get caught up in excursions into enemy territory on the land. There was a second unit going constantly and plenty of work for everyone: explosions, gunfights, car chases, you name it. Once we were in the San Pedro harbor shooting on a top classified, nuclear information ship. Everyone on the crew had to be screened and background checked.

On the sound stage in Valencia they had built a ships command post, a round room with radar and computer screens lining the walls; it looked good on screen. Near the end of the shoot we were on a late Friday night shooting schedule. The time was running out and we had to complete the day's shooting and get out before midnight. They gave us one last scene to shoot and told us we had to hurry. It was a hallway where two enlisted men were to have a conversation. The Assistant Director was on Frank to hurry.

Frank said it was going to take twenty minutes to light but the Assistant Director said he didn't have twenty minutes. Frank asked him how much time did he have and the Assistant Director replied: none. So Frank said, in that case, we're ready! We shot it with available light, two bare bulbs: that's what lit the scene. It didn't matter anyway. The show got poor reviews and ended with the ninth episode.

Frank and I parted on a good note and kept in touch for several years. Relationships come and go in the business of film production; you never know when you will work with someone again. Sometimes you show up on the first day of a production and spend a lot of time trying to figure out where you had worked with the familiar faces you see. The season ended for both Lorraine and I and we made plans to head to the ranch.

Jeremiah had sold my wood trailer to my next door neighbor, Fermin Pacheco, packed up whatever else he wanted like my 22 caliber rifle and pack saddle, and had run off. His story was that someone had shot at him. There were bullet holes that entered the kitchen window that were 22 caliber. Johnny Bonny and Rick set out to find him before we arrived and found him in a hippy camp on the Taos side of the mountains and they got my stuff back. The ranch was unattended for a while and it seemed to be intact as we pulled up to the gate. Babe had been right about Jeremiah, but he wasn't right about beating people up. I got the trailer back from Fermin who said he was shocked that Jeremiah had been so convincing.

Lorraine and I agreed we needed to pay someone more money and provide them with a comfortable house to watch our place. We hired Leroy to build the kitchen and bathroom that was to join up to the east side of the log cabin, the caretaker's house. Lorraine put an ad in the Caretakers Gazette and we also advertised locally. There were plenty of local Spanish people who wanted the job, but we thought they wouldn't spend much time up at the ranch because they had family in the area. In fact, several of the applicants wanted to just come up and check in on the place once a day. Nope, that wasn't what we needed; we needed someone who had no home. People called us from all over the country. That first year an older couple that were camped in Mora and looking for land came up, and it worked out great.

The Bagley's had one young son who came up and lived with them off and on. The father had a small mail order business making wood parts for MGs, the English sports car. Evidently there is a lot of wood built into them and anyone redoing a vintage model MG would order wood through Bagley. I thought it was very interesting what he did. He set up a shop in one of our outbuildings. They stayed one year and found their own property. The next year their son took the job; he was very quiet and very trustworthy. It was all good. Around the third year he also left and once again, Lorraine placed an ad in the Caretakers Gazette and the local papers.

Finally a lady called from Las Vegas. She was just passing through and saw the ad in the Las Vegas Optic. She came up and fell in love with the place. She had a dog that fit into our pack with no difficulty. She was in her early forties, had no family with her and was looking for a place in the country to be quiet and think. She seemed perfect but she was a woman, didn't have a 4-wheel drive and nobody knew her. Lorraine thought she was perfect. She actually moved in as Leroy was finishing up the work on the kitchen. Scott had come out to the ranch and did a lot of work on the project as well. I designed the room that faced south, southeast to have a lot of glass in the walls. I wanted to take advantage of the sun in the winter months. It worked out very well and we were able to keep some plants near the windows that thrived right through the cold periods of the winter

This lady's name was Leslie and she became close with all of us. She was especially good with the dogs and cat that lived on the ranch. She worked her way up to loving the horses as well and eventually she got one of her own. She was sent from heaven: someone else that could enjoy the beauty of the place without the thought of wanting to be somewhere else. She helped to varnish the wood in the kitchen addition to the cabin she was going to live in. It was all tongue and groove pine, with large beams spanning the ceiling. She was a large German woman, not fat but not thin either, and still beautiful in her forties. She owned a shotgun and knew how to use it. She bought a 4-wheel drive truck and that put her in very good shape to live there. That year as we left the ranch with Leslie in charge to go back to work, we felt comfortable for the first time in a while.

Lorraine was directing now and wanted to learn more about filmmaking. She bought books and asked me questions every night after her day's work. She asked questions about the lenses, such as; what was the effect of the length of the lens used? Lenses are calibrated into millimeters; the low numbers offer the widest view, and the higher number lenses result in a narrower field or what is called a telephoto. The depth of field becomes important. The field is everything included in the frame, from close to far. The longer the focal length of a lens, the less depth of focus there is. For example, it usually appears that the focus is on a person as the background becomes soft or out of focus. The wider lenses or the lower millimeter numbers would hold everything in focus, as in the background and the foreground. These are generally used for establishing shots or the masters where everything can be seen.

She also asked about a thing called the line and about what it meant to cross the line: it's an imaginary line between characters. Once the editor takes you from the master shot to the close-ups, you remember the master and expect the characters to be looking left or right depending on what you saw before. For instance, if a character is looking left in the master, he has to be looking left when his close-up comes for us to know he is still facing the same direction. This starts to get difficult in a scene where there are several characters; a scene with a dinner table is a good example. If the director or the cameraman crosses the line, it becomes awkward for the viewer and you lose the flow of the scene and you no longer feel comfortable with the logistics of the scene. It's a basic principal of filmmaking; it's hard to understand. You have to feel it and then you understand what it is. The whole thing of storytelling with film is so new; it's in its infant stage. I think the public has progressed with the advancement of technology and is staying even in understanding film technique. Take "Star Wars," the epitome of advanced filmmaking. Kids get it. Film lives beyond technology, much like music. It strikes you in a place between dreams and reality. It's a hard feeling to explain what music or film actually does to you.

Lorraine was a very smart person and she grasped the concepts that were new to her quickly. She had been an extra on the first "Godfather" movie when it was shooting in New York and had been bold enough to ask Francis Ford Coppola how she might be a director someday, like him. He told her to simply take the Directors Guild test. She did, and was third or fourth highest scoring person on her test in a field of five hundred. She told me the test was common sense, figuring out how to fix problems and make judgment calls. She was smart and had a burning desire to direct. I don't know why someone wants to go through that much agony; you have to really want it.

The demands put on a director are humongous. They have to deal with the script, its contents, the actors' temperaments and interpretation of the story, and the placement of the camera. And finally, they have to deal with the studio head or the producer who is relentlessly bothering them about the speed they are working at, the progress of the shoot, and a load of other problems. Sometimes directors are like traffic cops, just trying to insure that the people get from Point A to Point B without hurting anybody. A creative director can take a meaningless story and make it into a gem. The casting and the interpretation of the material are critical, that's why some directors are so sought after. It's the thing they bring to the table: they are artistic engineers. They make the art and technology merge, like a lion tamer in a circus. Lorraine used to think of herself as the Velvet Hammer, it's a good analogy.

I started writing another script entitled "To Love and Protect." It was a true story and it took place in the area where we lived in New Mexico. A friend of mine, we can call him Manuel, had to kill a man, a deranged psycho that was just out of a mental hospital and passing through. Manuel's wife was with the kids at the lake when she was attacked, by the psycho. She escaped and told her husband. Manuel found him still at the lake and confronted him. There was a fight and Manuel ended up shooting him with a rifle he had in the truck. Manuel stood trial and was acquitted in twenty minutes by his neighbors. There was some good writing in this script. Lorraine helped with the second draft and I included her name in the writing credits. I took meetings based on this script but they weren't looking for a revenge script at the moment. It would have been a great Charlie Bronson script. It is still a viable script today with so much about the right to bear arms in the news all the time.

They wanted me to pitch some other ideas. One idea I did pitch was a story idea I had for a reverse Dr. Jekyll and Mr. Hyde story. In this case, Dr. Jekyll was a woman. I called it "Dr. Jekyll and Ms. Hyde." It showed up years later and I always wondered if my pitching that story led to its actual production. That's the risk you run when you pitch ideas.

Lorraine was having some issues at work. There were only a few women directors in Hollywood. She was in a man's world and she thought she was getting beat up. After directing a largely male crew for fourteen hours, when she came home she became more and more demanding; I felt she treated me like the crew sometimes. She started seeing a therapist on the weekends; her name was Marilyn Ruman and she had several actors as her patients. Lorraine became very friendly with her and they actually started a film production company for a while. More of this later....

"MYSTERY TRAIN" 1989

I got a call from New York. Jim Jarmusch was doing another film, this time in Memphis, Tennessee. Of course, Robbie was shooting it and Christopher Porter was gaffing. It was perfect. This time I got my equipment on the shoot. They sent two guys to L.A., we loaded my stuff onto a 5-ton and they drove it to Memphis. The film was originally called "Tuesday Night in Memphis" but ended up being called "Mystery Train."

As I write this story I am listening to The Doors on their radio site over the internet. It's free and it was a great idea. It has a lot of interviews with Jim and Ray interspersed with music performed live, for the most part. As I think back, it is about a convergence of people that makes things so great or horrible. In the case of The Doors, what a wonderful meeting of souls! Even with the turbulence inside their band, they managed to create great music.

In the case of the film we were about to make, it was a convergence of three stories that all meet in the imaginary hotel in Memphis, Tennessee on a Tuesday night. By the way, the hotel manager was none other than Screamin' Jay Hawkins of "I Put a Spell On You." Jarmusch's last film "Down By Law" was such a hit in Japan that he got financing for this film from Sony in Japan. There was a guy from Japan that stayed with the production who handled the money, and sometimes showed up in full Japanese Kimono dress.

Memphis was a little different from New Orleans but still it was on the Mississippi: my third film on the river. Was this a pattern? Was something drawing me to that river? I doubt it. We stayed in the second best hotel in Memphis. It was three blocks from the famous Beale Street, the legendary street that attracted all the blues talent. It was lined with bars and speakeasies, restaurants that featured music and plenty of street people playing their asses off on whatever instrument they had. No place I had been in the south reeked of evil like this place. It was right on the river, and there were old slave quarters built along the river for sending and receiving fresh slaves. The unemployment rate was forty-something percent at the time of our shoot in 1989.

Lorraine came for a visit. As we were walking the three blocks to Beale Street, we were hit with rocks from across the street where several black teens were hanging out. We walked fast and got where we were going. It was hostile. This was the home of the King of Rock and Roll, Elvis Presley. Elvis's Graceland was the number one tourist destination in the area and there were buses that came into town heading for there. The tourists, usually mostly asian, rushed into the small antique stores looking for something that had Elvis's name on it. I was standing inside a shop when this happened. The customer bought an old autographed black and white photo in a cheap frame. The guy left thinking he had the real thing. As soon as the bus left the salesclerk reached under the counter and pulled up another identical picture and put it into a frame. He smiled and said it happens all day long.

Lorraine and I took the Graceland tour and let me tell you, the place was a 1950's, tasteless place. It was dark and full of ugly furniture, the kind you would find in a cheap motel. Go figure. It didn't fit my image of what Elvis meant to me musically; I was so disappointed. The legend of Elvis is huge in Memphis. His interaction with the local town was legendary. Everybody had seen him, gone to the movies with him, bowled with him or received presents from him. Everyone claimed to have known him and there were a lot of stories to be told. Some said they had seen him after he had died and claimed he was still alive. Fans from around the world visit there, especially on his birthday when the town becomes a zoo. Something like what happens in Pere Lachaise in Paris where Morrison is buried. I think my next book will be about a fan. They can really get "out there," you know.

"Mystery Train" is about two Japanese kids that come to America to visit the famous sites where rock history had taken place that they had read about in a magazine. They are following a guidebook that takes them to Graceland, Sun Studios and other points of interest in the U.S. There are three converging stories: the Japanese tourists, three American friends who get involved with a shooting and are fleeing the law; and a beautiful lady hiding from her lover.

The three guys are played by Joe Strummer from the band "The Clash;" Rick Aviles, an up-and-coming standup comedian; and Steve Buscemi, a popular New York actor. In the third story, the woman sees an appearance of Elvis in her room. Obviously it's a ghost, but it goes on for some time and we get caught up in the dream. It all comes to a head when there is a gunshot in one of the rooms and all the people in the hotel are instantly involved in a new story. After the shooting incident, the three groups all drift off on their separate ways. It's a strange film, but all of Jim's films are strange; some are just more successful.

"Permanent Vacation," his first film, was one of the most brilliant films I had seen since the early French stuff that had so consumed me. "Permanent Vacation" had a working-class sensibility, a gritty edge. In black and white, it was realism like you never saw. I was an instant fan. "Mystery Train" was a larger, more complex mainstream, almost Hollywood-type, production. It has since been called independent film production. Independent films have come a long way since then. Now with Sundance and other similar showcases, the independents compete with Hollywood on a financial level. The edge is actually being blurred as Hollywood now "gets it," picks up some of the better independent films and distributes them, and finances the next film from the hot new directors. There is a constant flow of new independent films. The Michael Moores of the world keep coming.

After each hot and dirty day of shooting, the crew came back to the hotel, showered, and met on the rooftop where there was a pool and hangout area. Most of the shoots were nights, which meant we were getting back to the hotel around three or four in the morning. It didn't matter to us; it was the end of our day and we partied. We smoked, drank and generally got high. When we saw the sun come up, it sort of signaled the party was winding down. People were hooking up in the hot tub etc., and the couples headed for their respective rooms. Tomorrow's call was around four or five p.m. and we would start all over again. We bonded so much, being the only people awake at that time. When the hotel across from us started to scream about the noise, we turned off our boom box and the party started to break up.

One of the motifs of the script was a gliding or floating-like camera that followed the Japanese couple through the city as they visited various landmarks. We had taken the station wagon rig from "Down By Law" and improved on it, so Robbie could sit on the tailgate and operate the camera that was mounted on a high hat. He always used a fluid head; he actually had never touched a gear head, the standard in Hollywood. The shots involved stopping and starting as the actors paused to exchange dialogue. The starts and stops are critical; because of sound, the station wagon's engine had to be turned off. Myself and whoever else was available had to push the giant station wagon like it was a dolly. I was usually reaching in and steering and pushing at the same time. After a while we got the hang of it. If my Hollywood brothers could have seen me, they would have laughed; however, the effect was very interesting. The camera had a floating effect as opposed to a rigid Hollywood dolly shot, which is usually very steady.

A lot of the hotel stuff was shot in an abandoned building one block from the actual hotel where Martin Luther King was shot. There were some very heavy vibes around that place. It was in the summer and it was hot. Jim had exterior air conditioning units brought in and piped the cool air into the building when we were not actually shooting. There is one scene where the ghost of Elvis appears. He was a pretty convincing actor/ impersonator. His costume was sequined from head to toe. Robbie used every light and every flag we had to light him just right. It was a jungle of lighting equipment that surrounded the poor guy.

There were several sequences around the train itself. They found a beautiful old silver train. We shot along the tracks as it passed by. We measured the distance very carefully with the train in place, but it was still a scary piece of camera operating. Robbie was seated very close to the tracks as the train flew by. He put a coin on the track. As the train passed, it flattened the coin. It was a good idea, and the whole crew did it! I still have my flattened coin today.

Inside the train they wanted the dolly to move down the aisle as we see the passengers one by one until we discover the Japanese kids. The aisle was too narrow so I had to remove all the seats on the opposite side. It was a hundred and ten degrees in the train car. When the train sat still it became hot, there was no air conditioning.

The sequence where the three guys are cruising around Memphis in their '54 Ford pickup had to be rigged so the camera could see all three people. The distance from the camera to the subjects using the lens that Robbie wanted was out in front of the bumper. No chance to slap a rig on the hood here; I had to build a platform. Ron Woodward's speed rail, ratchet straps, and a couple of pieces of wood did the trick. About four hours went into building the rig. It looked great. Triangles are the key to stability, you learn that quickly! We had a great wrap party in one of the best restaurants on Beale Street.

There was one female Production Assistant, a local, who made it her mission to fuck as many of the crew as she could, starting at the top and working her way down. She didn't get down to me. Oh well.

Once on a Sunday when Lorraine was visiting, the hotel fire alarm went off around seven in the morning. Everybody emptied down the stairwells and the elevators. Christopher Porter looked sleepy and so did the girl he was with, who wasn't his wife. It turns out President Bush was heading for the hotel and it was a Secret Service exercise to check the fire alarms.

There were constant rumors about a feature film that was based on the Jerry Hopkins / Danny Sugerman book, "No One Here Gets Out Alive." Who would direct such a film? Believe me, there was some serious negotiating going on between all The Doors parties concerned and any studio that wanted the project. It finally ended up in the hands of Oliver Stone. I was there at the preview. I sat next to Bruce Botnick, The Doors' longtime recording engineer/producer. The film was beautiful, it sounded beautiful. The concert parts were great. Val Kilmer was great as Jim. The only thing was that for Jim's personal friends, the ones that loved him, his soft side was gone. There was no love, only the sensational, the evil side of the character. It was weighted toward sensationalism. All of Oliver Stone's films are like that. I am not a fan; just recently he proved me right with his version of "Alexander." Another example was "JFK." It was so over the top. It doesn't matter except generations to come will know Jim as the character in the film. Just check out the chat rooms! But that kind of distortion is familiar with the myths that surrounds all icons, and Jim was no exception.

Billy Idol played my character in the film, Cat. Dennis Burkley played Babe, and we were referred to as Dog and Cat. The funny thing is that the guy we met in Big Sur, Richard Rutowski, was now working for Oliver Stone and had the part of the baldheaded Indian guy throughout the film. Man, life is weird. Oliver interviewed a lot of people including Georgia, my first wife. Everyone said he was an ass. It was obvious to me that he had studied my footage, and Val had probably studied the footage as well. The moves that Jim did live in my footage had been recreated perfectly by Val Kilmer. He was the one great thing in the film: him and the performance footage. The rest was bunk.

Bill Baker was a Grip I had met at CBS Radford. We became good friends. I went to his wedding. I worked for him and he worked for me, on occasion. He called me one day and asked if I could Key for one of his cameramen. He was busy and couldn't do it. I said of course. As it turned out, this is the same cameraman that Jack Anderson always told me I should meet. His name was Gregg Heschong; he was a graduate of UCLA and a cool guy. The show was a one-hour T.V. special starring Martin Short called "I, Martin Short, Goes Hollywood." Gregg had done the Tracy Ullman show at Fox, and she was doing a piece in this special. Eugene Levy the comedian was directing; it was his first time as a Director. Gregg and I hit it off. He had been a camera operator for years. He had been Sven Nyquist's operator, a very prestigious credit. Gregg was also a still photographer. His dedication to the lighting was old school: he was an artist. His father was an Art Director and had done many top-notch productions in the fifties: "Gunsmoke," "The Wild Wild West" and "Hawaii Five-O," to name a few.

Gregg remembers going to work with his dad and spending time on the sets of those productions. Gregg now has three children and brings his oldest son to work. I might add that his son could operate the wheels on a gear head at the age of six. We shot in Martin Short's house as well as locations all over Hollywood. It was glorified T.V. It was to be a movie of the week or a comedy special. We shot it fast and without much fanfare. When we finished the shoot, Gregg and I promised to work together again as soon as it was possible.

That summer, at the ranch, Lorraine and I built a large garage/studio space on a pad I prepared the year earlier. Leroy, Trini, and company built the structure. I bought six large four-foot by four-foot thermal pane windows from Leroy's wife Roma and placed them in the south facing walls. I put them up high enough so you couldn't look in from outside. I didn't want to tempt anyone with the contents. It turned out to be more a studio than a garage. You could put the tractor or the Dodge Power Wagon in the garage side and work on it. I found a large antique potbelly stove that kept the place warm in the dead of winter. It ate a lot of wood, but I had a lot of wood!

In the summers when Rio and Chuck came, we set up our instruments in the studio and jammed for hours on end. Those early jams turned into an album we made years later called "PlGRM The Child Returns"

We had a big Christmas party at the ranch the first year the studio was built. It was bad weather, cold and windy. I invited all the neighbors: Mike Grace and his wife Maria, Leroy, Roma, Johnny Bonny, you name em, they were all there. The kids of the families came too, if they were old enough. We had a decorated Christmas tree with blinking lights and also strung blinking lights along the ceiling and all over the walls. I brought my stereo from L.A. and the Yamaha speakers were magnificent; it was our disco. We had a huge bowl of Moon Juice: that's what Leroy and I called the vodka concoction we took to the lakes. It was pretty much just frozen juice, sliced fruit and a lot of vodka. Everyone brought beer and whatever else they wanted. I think Leroy brought some Mula, homemade whiskey from Les Duex. Someone he knew over there made a batch every year. It was precious.

It was one of the best parties anyone had been to in a long time. The main space of the studio was thirty-by-thirty and provided plenty of room. We danced and got drunk as skunks. The potbelly was raging and outside the weather was cold and snowing lightly. The snow is beautiful at night with the moon shining on it. When it got too hot from dancing you could step outside and feel the cold. It was sobering, the fresh night on your face. Sometimes as you were pissing (or throwing water, as it is called in that neck of the woods), your gaze would catch a horse that was close by standing in the darkness watching you. The dogs were always there. At that time of night they were curled up under the benches or anywhere they could find a spot.

The spring of 1990 Hanania called with a movie of the week that was going to Hawaii. Hawaii! I hadn't been there since the time I accompanied The Doors there in '68. It was a great gig after a cold winter. The show was to shoot for three weeks and end in Hawaii; that meant we could stay after and enjoy the islands and come back when we wanted. With this to offer, I called Cameron Phillips, my old friend from Universal and asked him to push dolly. Dana Van Auken took the job as my Best Boy and off we went.

What a blast! It was a bad TV script called "Murder In Paradise", but who cared? It did star Barbara Carrera; that was a treat just being near her. Hanania liked her a lot. It was the first time he ever asked me to take a picture of him with a star. A lot of the film took place in a beachfront shack. We lined the walls with muslin cloth. It has a slight beige tint to it and when you bounce the light into it, it was warmer. It was the look Hanania went for, it being Hawaii and all. We shot on the beach in front of the shack for days. At lunch we could run down and dive into the surf. The only problem with shooting outside is that it's mostly all grip work: shiny boards, 12 by 12 frames stretched with silks to cut the overhead sun, and bounce cards that reflected the sun. It was grip intensive and we didn't have much time to fuck around. We looked forward to the time we would spend once the show ended.

There is a famous mountain behind Honolulu that is steep and awesome to behold. It is supposedly where people committed suicide for romantic reasons in the ancient times. There was a scene where Barbara Carrera stands up there and communes with the gods of evil or something. We had to carry the equipment up in backpacks. The rest was carried by hand. We rigged a hand rope up the steep trail. It was beautiful once we got up there. The wind blew kind of hard, sweeping up from the ocean. It was like an updraft. You can stand very close to the sheer edge of the cliff and the wind will hold you there. It was blowing in Barbara's hair. It was very dramatic.

A few hours after we arrived up there, a large black mass of clouds appeared off in the distance. We could see the rain falling from them; the wind was blowing it straight at us. We could get very wet! Everyone looked toward the Unit Production Manager for his call to wrap up and get the hell out of there, but he wanted to get the sequence we had come for and was willing to risk the consequences. The clouds got closer and closer, the wind picked up, it started raining and we all got a little scared. Finally Bill Carroll, the Unit Production Manager, said it was a wrap. The only trouble was that the trail we had come up on, the one with the rope handrail, was slick and muddy now. We were carrying camera gear in one hand and holding onto the rope with the other as we slid down the muddy trail. People were scrambling to get down. We were scraped up and bruised and muddy as hell and a lot of us ended up at the local clinic that afternoon. Carroll had egg on his face as we all stood in line for medical attention. We all headed for the bar that night!

The next morning we loaded up onto airplanes and headed for the big island where we were to shoot for several days. My old friend Gary Beals and his wife Naomi lived there, so I called them and arranged to meet for drinks in the hotel bar where I was staying. Gary and I knew each other since Washington High School. We were pretty close, and it was great to see them. Gary went to college in Hawaii and majored in ocean biology. He had a great job teaching on the big island, went fishing out of Hilo all the time and was well connected. I'm going to look him up now that I am retired, I swear!

There is a great botanical park on the big island where we were scheduled to shoot. One of the world's most beautiful waterfalls was the backdrop for some dialogue we were to shoot. We had to wear rain gear and protect the equipment in full sunshine. The mist from the waterfall made rainbows as it drifted up from the bottom of the falls and made us all damp. If you have to be working, you might as well be in the midst of beauty. It is the most appealing thing about working on film crews: the chance you could end up in paradise. Then again, there is Shitters Alley. Oh well, you can't win them all. For sure, there is never a dull moment and it is kind of glam. You can sit across from Barbara Carrera or Faye Dunaway and eat lunch.

Gregg Heschong had a small feature shooting in northern California and Bill Baker couldn't do it. Again, I won. Thank you, Bill Baker. I signed on to do the film. It started shooting a week after the Hawaii show ended. Perfect. I could spend four or five days in Hawaii and then head back and load up for Gregg's show. Well, nothing is perfect. The day before we were to wrap in Hawaii, Bill Carroll made the announcement that the show was adding a week more of shooting to take place on the back lot of Warner Brothers. There was a lake there and it doubled for Hawaii. I looked at Cameron and Dana; they were as pissed as I was. We had really wanted the Hawaiian vacation more than anything. It also screwed up the next show I was to start. I had hired Dave Serieka as Best Boy on Gregg's show, so I called him from Hawaii to re-arrange the schedule.

To save money when we left Hawaii, the company chose to let the Hawaiian crew pack up everything while we headed back to L.A. Well, they didn't load up a lot of the expendables like tape, diffusion and gel rolls. When we opened the containers back in L. A. and the stuff wasn't there, we had to buy new materials. Bill Carroll didn't get it. Where was the stuff we had in Hawaii? It was like he was blaming us for the Hawaiian crew not putting the stuff on the plane. Hanania had a previous commitment and so did I. We both quit. We were not having a good time with the Director anyway; he was an ass. The finished product reflected his ability as a Director. Bill Carroll was pissed.

Serieka backed the five-ton truck that was going to work on Gregg's show, up to the ten-ton I had been working out of on "Murder In Paradise" and shifted my equipment from one to another while I continued keying the show with a new package of equipment that had been delivered. It was messy, but what could I do? Bill Carroll accused me of stealing the diffusion and gel and tape, etc. that was never sent from Hawaii and he wasn't going to pay me my last check. I eventually had to take him to a grievance type hearing with a representative from my local union representing me. He couldn't prove that I had taken it. My story was backed up by the other crewmembers and he eventually had to pay me. This was the only time in my career that I had to grieve someone.

"A CRY IN THE WILD" 1990

Roger Corman was a famous director from the early sixties who had parlayed his success into a production company. He produced many of the early shock films like "Pit and the Pendulum," "The Raven," etc., films that were usually starring Vincent Price. Coppola and many others had worked for him as they came up through the ranks of non-union low budget film. His wife was producing the film we were doing. It was her first project, a children's book entitled "Hatchet." It had been a very popular book and she bought the rights at the request of her children, or so the story goes. The story is about a young boy aged about ten or twelve with divorced parents. He is being flown in a small plane to a location where his dad lives and works. The pilot of the plane has a heart attack as they fly over a wilderness area, so the boy is forced to fly the plane and eventually crashes the plane into a lake. He survives the crash and retrieves a hatchet from the partially submerged plane. He uses it to survive in the wilderness, hence the name of the book, "Hatchet." He is finally rescued and returned to his parents. The story is his growth in the wilderness from a scared kid to a strong young boy.

This film version of the book was titled "A Cry in the Wild" and proved to be quite a challenge. First of all, there was no Gaffer; that meant Serieka and I lit everything with bounce, shiny boards and nets. Second, the film takes place on a lake in the wilderness. We weren't in the wilderness but it was way the hell at the top of the mountains above Quincy, California just north of Lake Tahoe. We used Buck Lake, a glacier lake, which was five miles up a dirt road. For the most part, the shore was littered with rocks, big and little. We had a peewee dolly, thank god, and we set track on top of the rocks all day long. We had masses of cribbing and apple boxes under the track to keep it level and strong. When I pushed the dolly I had to step on the struts in the track; I was too high off the ground to walk on it. I had to be careful: one wrong move and I could fall between the tracks and probably bust my nuts.

A small aluminum boat with an outboard engine that sometimes refused to start was how we moved the dolly and other equipment, as well as the crew, to various parts of the lake. This was work! Serieka and I never had worked so hard, but we had a lot of fun. We wanted to be there; it was beautiful. It didn't get any better: first Hawaii and then the Sierra Nevada Mountains.

The kid in the story encountered mountain lions, bears and other assorted critters. He swam back out to the floating wreckage of the plane to retrieve whatever he could. There was a hole in the side of the plane that the kid, played by Jared Rushton, crawled through to get inside the small compartment. The plane would move around and bob and weave with the small surges on the lake, and Jared was having trouble not getting hurt. They tried all kinds of anchoring devices: there was a crew of divers that rigged the plane to the bottom of the lake with ropes and wire. It didn't work.

Finally Gregg looked at me and asked if I had any ideas. I came up with a way of building a scaffold out of my speed rail that sat on the bottom of the lake and supported the plane just below the water line, like a cradle. The underwater crew anchored the structure to the bottom with weights. I built it on shore and we floated it out to the middle of the lake and pushed it over and it slowly sunk to the bottom. It took a day to get it together and it worked great. It stayed put for several weeks and held the plane rigid enough to get the shots we needed. We shot the rest of the water stuff in a swimming pool in Quincy. Any time Jared was submerged, we were in a pool.

The show was dangerous in many ways. Just walking up in that altitude was hairy. People had to stay hydrated. The rocks were difficult to navigate. Then there were the animals. The trainers that were doing the show had their own animals. It was such a low budget film that they were practically working for nothing. There was no medic on the crew. I brought this safety problem up several times to no avail.

There is a scene where the boy is running from a bear. He splashes into the water, the bear follows him and there is a struggle. Of course, Jared didn't do that part; the animal trainer dressed up like Jared did it. He had also become the stunt double. Just before we were to shoot, the bear was hanging out in the shade with the trainer/stunt double. The bear found a beehive under a log and got stung on the nose. The trainer didn't think anything much of it until they started doing the scene: I guess the pain kicked in and the bear went wild. He slashed at the trainer's body with his huge claws and gashed his arm pretty bad. The wife of the trainer rushed to his rescue and led the bear back to his cage. The guy was bleeding pretty badly and he started going into shock. We wrapped him the best we could and he left in a production van with the Unit Production Manager nervously driving as fast as he could. It was maybe a half hour down a long windy dirt road to the town and the nearest hospital. It turned out okay; the guy recovered and finished the show with his arm in a sling. This is precisely why the film industry has rules: a union show would have required a medic. What if the guy had gone past the shock into cardiac arrest? It could have been tragic, to say the least.

Later on the bear finds the boy again at night while he is sleeping in his little campsite. Of course we had to shoot that one scene in the dark. They flew a Gaffer guy in for two nights and we used a generator for power. The animal handlers had rigged an electric shock wire around the perimeter of the scene, just in case. Well, the bear never touched it because he knew from his training it would hurt. On the other hand, I couldn't see it and I tripped and landed on top of it; it tingled real good. I screamed as I struggled to get off the wire. I was already tired and I didn't need any other problems.

Ron Woodward had built a lathe track rig about eight feet long that a camera could mount on and slide from one end to the other. He used it to shoot outside the window of a vehicle as it drove down the street. The shot was from the driver's close-up to the person's face in the back seat. There was a scene in a low cave-like area where the action takes us right into the dark recess. I used that piece of track right on the ground to slide the camera in to Gregg, who took the handoff and continued the scene from his position inside the cave lying on his side. It worked great.

There was a scene that took us through the forest as Jared ran. I didn't have enough track for that length of running. There was a road near by and we staged the running just off the road. We used one of the production vans with the sliding door rigged open. We hung the camera in the opening with bungee straps. It was suspended by the rubber straps and floated there, absorbing the motion of the van as we drove alongside the action. It's amazing what you can do with a little bit if you put your mind to it.

Gregg was an accomplished cabinetmaker. He was very good with his hands and his ideas are always good. It is such a pleasure to work with someone who has an idea what is going on.

PLANE RIG, GREGG HESHONG, CAMERAMAN.   HAND HELD
CAMERA, HANANIA BAER.   ROBBIE MULLER AND I

There was a lengthy scene in the plane at the beginning of the film where the pilot, played by Ned Beatty, has his heart attack. This little film had attracted some good actors. We had no money to shoot in the plane while it was actually in the air. Besides, the cabin was too small to fit the two actors and the camera, etc. Gregg came up with the idea of shooting through the window into the cockpit while the plane was suspended from an industrial crane. Well, that was a good idea but how do we suspend the plane from the crane? This was a moment in my life where all my past skills came together in one moment of brilliance! There was a muffler shop in town that allowed me to work on the weekend. I welded I-beams through the plane and under it. From these beams I rigged speed rail that formed a cage-like affair that Gregg could sit in just outside the plane. I made a solid attaching point for the crane on top. Once it was lifted off the ground, my crew could spin it slowly in either direction with ropes they held. From Gregg's camera position, it appeared that the sky and the clouds were drifting by, simulating actual flight. Actually it was the plane moving that made the clouds appear to be drifting by. I took several photos of that rig.

Gregg had a beautiful large white dog named Nova that was with us the whole shoot. Most of the crew stayed at a Boy Scout facility. I refused to bunk with someone and they put me, Serieka and Jack Anderson, who also refused the Boy Scout accommodations, up in the local motel. Jack was the Second Unit Director of Photography / camera operator. By now we had become good friends. I had my amp and guitar with me, and I practiced most of my spare time. Sometimes Jared Rushton and his small posse of visitors used to visit my room and hang. I wasn't great at lead playing yet, but I could play my old style of strumming and picking chords with the best of them. Serieka hooked up with the costume lady and her trailer was rocking most of the time. She was a wild one, just like Serieka. She had a tattoo of an eagle across her butt. The talons hung down and held her ... well, you know. She showed me, that's how I know.

We partied a lot. One of the guys they hired locally was just out of high school. He was a big kid named Paul, just what we needed up there in the rocks. My other local hire was a friend of his and another big kid, an Indian from the local area. Quincy was right in the middle of the pot growing northern California scene. When Paul found out Dave and I smoked and needed some, he said no problem. The next day he brought two large shopping bags full of fresh bud. He gave one to Dave and the other to me. It was a lot and it stunk to high heaven. I finally ended up stashing it in a hole I cut in the bottom of one of the chairs in my room. I put many plastic bags around the package and you could still smell it a little bit. It was like living with a skunk. One day Dave was seen smoking a joint on the back of the truck. Someone reported it and the next thing we knew, the shit hit the fan. There was an announcement made at the lake that the local police were involved and our rooms were subject to search. I told Gregg I had to go down the hill for something, and Paul and I took the pot and stashed it at his mother's trailer. Dave and the Indian boy worked the set for the couple of hours that took.

The Script Supervisor is the person who holds the script, makes notes, helps the Director keep track of the scenes and dialogue, and helps if someone forgets their lines by yelling them out. The original Script Supervisor on the set was Liz Porter, a tall, thin, attractive young lady with an engagement ring on her finger. Well, that didn't stop Gregg. He fell in love with her. The Unit Production Manager also wanted her and this caused a little bit of friction. Still, the two of them - Liz and Gregg - became an item. She was having trouble with her fiancé, and Gregg was single and willing. Finally in a show of power, the Unit Production Manager fired Liz two weeks before the end of shooting. She left suddenly and a new young lady showed up to take her place. Guess what! Before you knew it, Gregg was hot and heavy with the new Script Supervisor. He was kind of on a rebound from his affair with Liz.

Lorraine came for a welcomed visit. She flew into Reno and drove up for the weekend. This was around the same time Liz got fired. Dave and the costume lady, the one with the eagle on her ass, went to Reno for the weekend and drove the costume truck full of clothes. Well, Dave ran into a friend in one of the casinos that sold them a fist full of meth. On the following Monday we all showed up for work at a picnic scene in one of the local parks where Jared is re-united with his family. There were a lot of actors. Where was the costume truck? We waited. I tried to call Serieka at the motel. No answer. The costumer was used to driving the truck to the locations. What happened? The production people started to panic and they called all the hospitals, police stations, etc. Finally they found the costume lady in jail in Reno where she had been busted for walking down the street completely nude. Meanwhile, Dave was passed out in a motel. They had smashed the top of the truck on a low hanging sign. They finally showed up five hours late and were both fired. I said goodbye and Dave left. He knew he had fucked up. What could you say? They brought me a semi-experienced person from Reno that helped me finish the show.

We had attracted quite a following of spectators; this was the biggest thing that had happened in Quincy since the Gold Rush. The wrap party took place in the bar and eatery we had frequented for the whole time. It was one of the only ones in town. The locals turned out. It was wild. Gregg was full on with his new girlfriend and they made quite a couple with their lovey, kissy, out in the open romance. It had been a hard show to shoot and we celebrated being finished by getting very fucked up that night. One of the extras the next day showed up at my room as I was packing and offered me a going-away massage. I couldn't refuse. I did tell her I had a pact with my wife. We did everything else but actually fuck. She told me my wife was a lucky lady as she proceeded to work her magic mouth between my legs. She was quite a good-looking lady, tall and blonde with a great body. She told me she danced topless to support herself and her little girl: lucky loggers and locals.

The Unit Production Manager told me in no uncertain terms that there was no plane ticket for me. I had driven with Serieka and we had been paid for the gas. He was actually going to make me pay for my own ticket home after I had worked so hard on the film since day one. Gregg didn't like him anyway after he fired Liz, so he called his bluff and publicly said he would pay for my ticket himself. It was a grand gesture on his part. I headed back to L.A. the next morning after getting one more massage from the blonde go-go dancer.

Gregg pursued Liz for another year or so. It was rocky, to say the least. She was still living with and engaged to a sound mixer she had been seeing for years. Finally she broke it off with him and agreed to marry Gregg. Gregg and Liz got married in a beautiful old L.A. church on Wilshire. Jack Anderson and I were both in tuxes that day. He stood with the wedding party and I ushered people to their seats. Many years have passed and they have three fine children: Alex, Elisa, and William. This was a classic location romance that ended in marriage. God bless them.

"BUT HE LOVES ME" 1991

Hanania started to get hot and we were working a lot. We did an after-school special. That's like a one-hour format T.V. show that airs in the afternoon when the young target audience is just home from school. It was about abuse between a young high school couple in a relationship. Hanania won an award for photography and was kind enough and appreciative enough to have an award printed up for me as well. He valued my help almost more than anyone. We had a very special relationship and I became good friends with both him and his wife Shuli.

The show was called "But He Loves Me" and starred a young Donovan Leitch. He was the son of Donovan, the sixties singer. Donovan of "Sunshine Superman." Donovan, the one I had photographed in the sixties that day up in the Hollywood hills with Gypsy and the huge spliffs he rolled with Jamaican pot. Wow, I am constantly amazed at the random interaction among peoples. I'm very interested in the migrations of peoples. I like to hear their stories; it fills in a picture of life I am drawing.

We were working for none other than Churchill Films. Joan Churchill was the girlfriend that had helped to get me out of jail, and this was her father's business. Joan was now a big time documentary film cameraperson. We met in the hallway of Churchill Films while we were using one of the offices as a set. She walked by and we noticed each other. "What are you doing here?" she asked. Well, having heard that question more than once, I simply replied, "I am with the crew". I should have told her I was the bass player. "We're shooting one of your father's productions." She had been married to a sound recordist she worked with and had a few children. She complained that he had left her to raise them by herself. She didn't look that happy. She was always sort of like that: serious, on a mission, her personal life was second. I think she finally found someone and is happy now that she is reaching the third act of her life. Every time I see her I remind her how grateful I am for her help when I needed it. Joan had been in the film school at UCLA and knew Jim Morrison, Ray and everybody else I knew. She was like a little sister from my past.

Lorraine was directing five, and sometimes six or seven, shows a season. She was finally on a roll. She changed agents every few months until she finally found someone she liked. That lasted for a while. She was becoming a feminist; her take on the people she had to work with was they didn't respect women. Well, you know, maybe she was right. It had been a man's world for so long. Old time Hollywood was built by the Mayers, the Goldbergs, you name them, they were men. She was in uncharted territory. There were groups of women banding together to talk and form an alliance. "Women in Film" was one of them.

She had optioned a book called "The Woman at Otowi Crossing." It was about a woman who had a Tea Shop at the base of the mountain where Los Alamos was built in New Mexico. The scientists used to go there for tea and fresh baked goodies to discuss their various projects. One of the projects, of course, was the atomic bomb. This woman becomes involved in the secrecy and intrigue surrounding the invention and the detonation of the first atomic bomb. Oppenheimer, the inventor of the bomb, was an interesting character to play a woman finding herself against. Lorraine asked me to read the book and give her an opinion: I liked it. She optioned the book. Marilyn Ruman was involved and I think at that time they were partners. They tried for a while to write a script but they didn't know where to start. They talked to writers but they wanted too much control of the project. They didn't know what to do. When I read the book, I saw the film. It is like that a lot with me; I am very visual, and words translate easily into images for me. I told them I had an idea how to write the script for "Otowi Crossing." They agreed; what did they have to lose?

I wrote the script and I must say if anything, I made it too commercial. It was good, but just then another film about the same atomic bomb was announced. It was a large feature and this was to be a small independent film. They took a lot of meetings with my version of the script under their arms. Another writer that also had read the book commented to Lorraine and me that I had actually found the film in that book!

Like I said, Lorraine's partner Marilyn was a shrink to several movie stars, and one of them was Dan Aykroyd. Some of the stories she told were real good, like the time he had an anxiety attack in the LAX baggage claim area. He had fallen down and was muttering to himself. She had to go and get him; he would only respond to her. What power she had over these people! Marilyn was a very powerful person and Lorraine listened to everything she said. She was in fact helping Lorraine to overcome her feelings of helplessness, helping to empower her. This was becoming more and more a problem for me, however. She would bring her hostility toward men home and into our bedroom, where sex became a negotiation. How much could I beg? It didn't help that it was sometimes months in between my jobs, which Lorraine constantly reminded me of. She discussed money a lot; she was making so much more than me.

I got a call from Ed Lachman, an up and coming young Director of Photography. He had seen "Mystery Train" and loved it. He asked how I got those floating shots on the city streets. I was almost embarrassed to tell him, but I did. He laughed and said it looked really good, and he asked if I would like to do a one-hour rock concert with him in Seattle. Of course, I said yes. It was the Fine Young Cannibals in concert in an old theatre in downtown Seattle. It was a four-day shoot and he said, "See you there." The production called me with info and sent me the plane tickets.

Ed Lachman had been the second unit Director of Photography on the "Hail! Hail! Rock 'n' Roll," Chuck Berry film. He had also been the cameraman on "The Lords of Flatbush," "Desperately Seeking Susan" and "Less than Zero." I was more than eager to work for him; all of those films were cutting edge. He did have a small reputation for being a hard person to work for. Oh well, there were plenty of them. You have to work with an asshole once in a while or you will starve to death. Ed wasn't an ass; he was just very self-centered. We had the first meeting in the green room of the old theatre we were to shoot in. There must have been forty camera operators and assistants gathered from all over the world and in most instances, they were the cream of the crop. There was a louma crane, which is a camera on an arm that is operated remotely from a screen and two joysticks. You must have seen them swinging in front of your favorite artist at some concert lately. There was a Steadicam a camera that is strapped to the front of the operator with an elaborate counter balance system that enables him to walk with the camera with little, if any, vibration or movement noticeable. It was invented by: Garrett Brown. It's only a decade old and is now a must on any show.

The rest of the cameras were scattered around the stage and auditorium, with two mounted on dollies. It was a big deal. They wanted a dolly shot that moved in and to the left side of the stage. This was kind of hard because the theatre had seats that went right up to the apron of the stage. There were a lot of meetings about how to accomplish this; it went back and forth for some time. The seats had been bolted down to the floor for eighty years. The hardware was brittle and broke with little effort. They were probably rusted, it being Seattle and all.

Finally I suggested that the easiest thing would be to leave the seats alone and build across the top of them. I sent for every apple box in Seattle and I placed them right on the seats, building them up like blocks until they reached above the backs of the seats. I did this to a pair of seats in each row. When they were all in place I screwed plywood across them and built a ramp-like affair. I had to get higher as we descended toward the stage because the audience floor dipped and then came up again to meet the stage. It got a little dicier as we did that, but it worked out okay. Next, I screwed the track down on top of this and then we lifted the Fisher 9 dolly up and onto the track. There were no other experienced Dolly Grips on the crew they had assembled for me in Seattle, so I was going to push that dolly. There was a second dolly moving just in front of the apron horizontal to the stage, typical of concert shooting design.

I remember when I shot the Hollywood Bowl for The Doors in 1968, I had four cameras: three were on sticks or tripods, and one handheld camera was on the stage: four angles. The Cannibals shoot had maybe eighteen cameras. Had I had a budget for that shoot, who knows what type of film we might have ended up with!

Oh well, there we were in Seattle. It was winter and it rained nonstop. I was put up with other crewmembers in a hotel that was fully enclosed with glass. The pool was on the ground floor in the center and the hotel smelled of chlorine. It was steamy everywhere; we got used to it. Outside it was always wet. The concert went off without a hitch; all the equipment worked perfect. The only problem was with the band: they were a very volatile group of people. They were paranoid and as it turns out, they didn't last very long. Some groups get along and others implode. It's just the nature of people, especially young rock stars.

When I got back in L.A., I got a call from N.Y. Ed Lachman wanted me to Key a film he was doing with Mira Nair. She had done a film I loved called "Salaam Bombay." She had a new film with Denzel Washington called "Mississippi Masala." They told me the schedule and we agreed. The film got pushed or postponed and when it finally did shoot, someone else had become the Key Grip. That was something Lachman was known for: loyalty was not his strong suit. I was disappointed and called N.Y. about it, and was told they simply had changed their mind: sorry. This would happen several times. It was one of the main reasons I didn't pursue an acting career. Rejection. I don't have a good time with it. Those that can suffer rejection or those who never experience it, become the actors.

"BABYFEVER" 1994

Hanania had a small film with an offbeat director named Henry Jaglom. I don't know where they met or how he got the job. Jaglom was a rare kind of dude. He had been one of the editors on "Easy Rider," which was the ground breaking smash film debut of Dennis Hopper and Peter Fonda. Jaglom had directed a film called "Always" that put him on the map, and now he was doing one called "Babyfever." This was a rare experience. Henry assembled his actors together, some experienced and some not so experienced. He proceeded to yell and berate them so intensely that many broke down and either stormed out of the room, or reached a place of such realism that the performances actually benefited. It was a brutal form of direction; it was hard to watch. Having been an actor myself, I wanted to strangle him. It was all we could do to just remain quiet. Actors would leave the set sobbing. He would go after them, and soon they would return to the set and we would start again. Somehow he had made it all right.

His films were a combination of storytelling and improvisational acting techniques. Hanania made his small film look beautiful. He and Jaglom had an artistic understanding. We did another in the following year called "Venice/ Venice." I hired Michael Hodges, the guy I got the job for at Universal, to help me. He couldn't believe Jaglom and he still talks about it today. I think Jaglom married one of his writing assistants and calmed down a little bit. He did seem like a fairly nice person when he wasn't directing, but when he was directing it was like watching something from the film "The Cuckoo's Nest."

Lorraine didn't go with me to the ranch that summer. She flew in a couple of times but for the most part, she was busy with agents, "Women in Film," Marilyn Ruman, etc. This was a pattern that was starting. I took our two dogs with me, Buster and Coco. Leslie was living in the cabin and we spent a lot of time together working, talking, and riding horses. I had built a large stone-lined fire pit just outside the big house where I lived. It was there for the thirty-two years I owned the property. One night when I was having my nightly fire, Leslie decided to join me and we had a few beers. She was tall, blonde, in her forties and still in good shape, and I always thought she was gay. As the night progressed we both got a little drunk. When she said she was going to turn in, I tried to give her a good night kiss. She pulled back and left to go to the cabin. I didn't think much of it. I lay back on the bench and looked up at the stars. At that altitude, you could see the Milky Way galaxy like it was just in front of your face. The constellations were very visible. Once when Bob Angers visited with his family, he pointed out Orion's Belt, Scorpio and a few others that had always been there but I had never seen. The shooting stars were so big and eventful that anyone witnessing them would let out a noise like wooooo!. Once I was alone by the fire as was often the case, and a ball of light came out of the east and headed straight for me. It was huge, the biggest shooting star I had ever seen. For a moment I thought it was a spaceship. It passed over my head and headed west over the mountains, and I fully expected to see a forest fire where it landed.

Back in L.A., Lorraine and I were talking about where we were headed. I was making the point that it was too lonely by myself at the ranch. I told her casually that even Leslie was starting to look good to me and about my attempted kiss goodnight. Well that was that: Leslie had to go! Why in god's name did I tell her that story? I think it was to emphasize my feelings about her not going to the ranch on a more frequent basis.

The next spring I was first to arrive at the ranch. Leslie was ready to leave and she offered to sell me all her horse tack. She had bought a maniac horse that threw her to the ground in the field just below the house and she sold him. I bought the gear and she left. We kept in touch for a few years but I haven't heard from her for twenty years. Oh well. Sometimes just keeping your mouth shut would be a good idea.

My good friend Henry Trujillo, the one who was born on my ranch, offered to take the job of caretaker until someone else came along. He loved it up there. I shared the emotional ownership with him and his entire family. I knew his father Elautario quite well. He was a retired prospector: he loved to look for gold, he dreamed of discovering gold. Henry had caught his fever and did the same, constantly taking dirt samples and going home where they cleaned the dirt and looked for the precious ore they were after. They saw some gold but it was in such small quantity that it was unmarketable. Elautario was a big man; he had been sheriff of Mora for a while. Most of his life he had been a logger, and Henry grew up logging with his dad in the forests around Mora.

One of those first summers that Henry was the caretaker, we logged a small patch of timber just east of the house and we split the money. I learned a lot. Logging was the hardest work I had ever done. Anyone who works in the forest all day at that altitude wielding a twenty-five pound chain saw is in good shape. The cool thing about Henry was that the moment I arrived in the spring, he left. He went back to his own house where he lived with his wife Elsie, which left the cabin available for visitors.

For a few years there was a steady stream of visitors. Lorraine met a young lady named Cameron at her accountant's office and they became friends. Her husband Allen had been a professional bass player and toured with several big bands throughout the seventies and eighties. Allen started to jam with Rio, Chuck and me in rehearsal rooms around L.A. He was equally good on keyboards and with Chuck on bass, Allen added the synthesizer sound to our trio.

One summer he and Cameron visited us and were staying in the cabin. I usually got up early and on one of those mornings in the early light I saw two large elk down by the lake in front of the houses. I woke everyone up and we were all stood in the yard watching these two large animals. These were precisely the animals Henry and I had been chasing through the forest for ten years. I had never seen a six pointer in my life but had heard stories about them. With the binoculars I counted one with six points and the other with seven. This was a rare moment, the two large males just standing there oblivious to the spectators.

Something snapped in me and I went for the Mauser, the gun Georgia's father had taken off a dead German soldier and brought back from Germany. By now the elk had sensed the coming sunlight and perhaps the gawking spectators, and started drifting into the tree line about four hundred yards from us. I headed down along the creek in the same direction they were headed. I crossed over the stream and found a spot where I could see through the trees all the way to where the elk should be headed. I lay down and rested the Mauser on a log. It was originally a sniper rifle and had a long distance site mechanism on it. I raised the measuring indicator, set it for three hundred yards and waited. I saw the first one step into my line of vision but he was moving too fast. The second one stopped right in the zone and turned to look back. I pulled the trigger and the bull elk jumped straight up into the air and landed flat on his side. Unbelievable. I stood up and rushed toward the animal; I was trembling all over. He was still alive and tried to gore me with his large set of horns. I shot him again in the throat, which would kill him and also help to drain the blood. I had a little knowledge of what I was doing. I cut his back feet tendons and returned to the house, grabbed a beer and calmed down.

I called Henry and told him what had happened. My second call was to Ernesto, a friend of Henry's and mine who hunted and cut wood with us all the time. We had discussed a code in the event something like this happened: "I killed the pig and need help to clean it." They arrived soon after and we spent the rest of the day cleaning and bringing the meat up to the house in the 4-wheelers. We shared the five or six hundred pounds of meat three ways. Funny story: when Henry was dressing out some of his share of the meat at his house, he found an old arrow shaft imbedded in the hindquarter. It must have been there for a while because the flesh had grown around it. Ernest and Henry said that it was the largest rack of horns that they had ever seen and they had been hunting all their lives. It measured six by seven points. The thickness of the antler suggested the massive size of the animal. The measurements of the rack put it in the Crockett Boone category, which is a trophy classification. I still have that head hanging in my garage today. I never killed another animal again. I'm not even sure why I killed that one. Hunting is very addicting; there is something primal about the experience. The movie "The Deer Hunter" has some good moments that depict the frenzy and excitement of the hunt.

Some generals or something from Albuquerque had owned the next property up from us for as long as I could remember. Well, they sold it to a group of investors led by a tax consultant named Mark Mattes out of Pojouque, New Mexico. They were dividing the large parcel into several pieces and were selling the one that adjoined our place, so all of a sudden one day there were for sale signs next to our property. Well, here came civilization! We freaked out and called the number on the sign. It was complicated because Mattes, who was the principal negotiator, didn't want to sell us the good part, only a small piece. We wanted all of it, all the way to the next fence line, which would have been the Pando's property. We negotiated for the better part of a year; Lorraine did most of the legwork.

Another piece of property came up for sale down along the river. Mattes wanted it and to raise money, he agreed to sell us the whole 240 some acres which made our ranch a total of about 276 acres. We paid an average of five hundred dollars an acre; by today's prices, it was a pretty good deal. There were a couple of small seasonal lakes, plenty of timber, and old logging trails that led all over the place.

We put an ad in the Taos paper for a caretaker and got a response from a Taos Indian. Steve, his wife and nephew that he was raising, came for the initial visit. We got along. His wife had been in a horse accident and her neck was in a brace. There was a rig attached to the brace that kept her head from moving while her neck tried to heal. It was quite a sight. They needed a place to rest while her injury healed.

Steve had some history in Taos. He was a cocky type of guy that had social troubles and he felt it was a good time to get out of Taos for a while. They moved in and became our caretakers. Steve was an artist; he painted Indian designs on anything he could get his hands on. He would scour the dumps and junkyards looking for gears, mostly the kind from transmissions. They were circles, of course, and had teeth around them. He painted them like mandalas. I had always wanted to learn to paint. I found an old cow skull and tried my hand at painting it. It came out good. Steve wanted to paint a cow head too, so we went to the local slaughterhouse and bought four fresh skulls dripping with flesh and brains. The maggots had started to clean them out but hadn't finished. I filled a 55-gallon barrel with water and built a fire under it. After about three hours the water was near boiling. We boiled the skulls until they were almost clean. Once they dried we picked off the small pieces of meat and sanded them until they were ready for paint. With a coat of white paint they looked like they had weathered naturally. We then painted them with all kinds of cool designs and we sold a few of them in the local arts fair in Mora. We called ourselves the Skuller Brothers.

The first year the new land was officially our's, we fenced the one mile along the road. Chuck, Rio, Steve and I worked for the better part of two weeks doing it. I was a busy camper in those days. The year before that I had skinned two dozen straight logs and dragged them down to the yard. Leroy and Trini and the gang went from building the garage/studio to building a barn, which turned out to be the biggest barn anyone had ever seen. The crew complained about the immensity of the project but when it was completed we all stood back in awe. I had gone to the Albuquerque train station and bought a used cargo container. Before I took it up to the ranch I had Jackie Roper, a friend who had a welding shop, build a lockbox arrangement around the handle. You would have to blast your way into this container! After the foundation for the back wall was built I pushed, shoved and cajoled the twenty-foot container into place along the back side, and then we built the rest of the barn around it. This was to be the tack room. It was impenetrable: just the thing for a remote ranch. When I left in the winter to go to work I locked everything of value in there: not only saddles but guns, chainsaws, televisions, anything of value. One of the questions most asked was, how did we get the cargo container into the barn? Well, of course, the answer was that we built the barn around it! By the time Steve came, I was digging holes in front of the barn and cementing iron posts into the ground, getting ready to weld a proper corral complete with stalls for six horses. It turned out wonderfully.

I had given Lorraine the first young foal from Misty; she was pregnant when I bought her from Leroy Tafoya. She was born at the time of Haley's Comet and we named her Haley. Before Haley, Lorraine had purchased a string of mean horses. She always went for the wild stallion look, which took her to horses that were very difficult to control and took a lot of work. She was only at the ranch for days at a time and the horses went green on her; this meant that when she did show up, the horses hadn't been used for some time.

At one point she had a roan buckskin; roan meant it had a dark stripe down its back. He was beautiful but a complete handful. We had all saddled up ready for a serious ride. She was by the wood shed when she put her foot into the stirrup. As she pulled up onto him he moved suddenly to the side. Lorraine got her leg over the saddle before he started to buck; he bucked her from one end of the yard to the other. It was a serious moment; she was hanging on for dear life and she finally flipped off. We eventually got Buck under control and Leroy rode him for a while up the road. Lorraine transferred onto him after a mile or so and the rest of the trip was uneventful, but you don't forget something like that. I convinced her to sell the horse and that's when I gave her Misty's foal, who by then was ready to ride. We took her to Jake Regensburg for training. The day he brought her back Lorraine got on down by the highway and rode her up to the ranch. After the 5-mile ride she was in love. Haley had the same smooth walk as her mother, Misty. It was kind of like a Tennessee walker: a fifth gait that was like a fast walk but smooth. My horse Misty always pulled into the lead of a herd of horses. With or without riders, she wanted to be first. I spent so many enjoyable miles on her back.

Black Boy was a big thoroughbred that didn't do well when Jake tried to race him at the track. Jake sold him to me because he had turned into a first class pack horse. Black Boy loved Misty to death and even though he was castrated, tried to mount her forever. She let him; she was his. He loved to pack behind Misty; his nose was right up her ass as they walked. I had the perfect team and I rode those horses all over the Pecos Wilderness.

Once I rode them all the way to Santa Fe. Now, that was an adventure! Leroy, his son Travis who was about 10 years old at the time, Jackie Roper and I set out on the four day ride. We had taken my two horse trailers to Santa Fe and got permission to leave them at Bishop's Lodge, a famous old time hotel. One of the trail heads that reached Santa Fe came right down to the Lodge. They rented horses and took trips up that same trail. We set out in what looked like great weather. It started to rain once we reached the summit at around twelve thousand feet, and it rained most of the entire four days. We were prepared for rain but four days of it got real old. Black Boy was loaded down with five cases of beer and cokes. We drank and sang "Blue Skies" all the way to Santa Fe.

The fishing is fantastic in the middle of the Pecos Wilderness. Sometimes the trails are hard to see from non-use. They are littered with dead trees and there are many such obstructions to go around, which causes the trail to meander and made it hard to follow. Leroy was the leader; he was the best at reading trail and we only got lost a couple of times. We pretty much rode all day from sun-up to sunset and we saw some very pristine country: Trail riders Wall, Lost Horse Meadow, Outlaw Meadow and several small lakes, each loaded with fish. We ate a lot of fish on that trip. We stopped at each good fishing site we came to, and by dinner we had some fish to eat.

It was getting to be dusk and the clouds were heavy as we approached the big mountain behind Santa Fe. It started to rain again, we took a wrong turn in the dark and ended up traveling east. At a certain point we could see a narrow canyon below with lights from houses, but it was not Santa Fe. It was around eight thirty and dark and it was hailing. We found a spot with a lot of wood and started a giant fire. We put up the tent and got a little dry. The thunder was cracking all around us lighting up the dark sky. Travis was crying; I didn't blame him, I wanted to cry too. We were all fatigued beyond belief. We ate something and crawled into the tent. In the morning we discovered we were sleeping on top of a large pile of elk dung. They had also found this sheltered spot and had spent many nights there.

It's cold in the mornings at that altitude. Leroy got up and made breakfast. The smoke rose up straight from the fire. There was no wind and the air smelled great. The water from the night's rain still sat on the leaves and they sparkled as the sun caught them. We saddled up and backtracked ourselves, and found where we had taken the wrong turn. We got to a sign that said Santa Fe Ski Basin, three miles. That was the deal! Our spirits were lifted and the horses could smell grass. Misty seemed to pick up the pace and by the time we were coming to Bishop's Lodge they were practically running. The trail ran along a stream bed. As we galloped along the trail, the horses snagged leaves from the trees with their mouths and munched. Misty finally looked like a racehorse: she had lost a lot of weight. She was normally a rather heavy horse but now you could see her flanks and she looked great. The trail came down on the small highway and we had to ride along it for a quarter of a mile to our trailers. I'll never forget that when we passed some people who were hiking along the small road, one of them looked up at me and said, "You guys look like shit." I laughed and thought he was probably right: I felt like shit. But as it turns out it was the great ride of my life, of all our lives. We bragged about it whenever we could. We had done a famous thing!

Travis had ridden Pretty, an older mare that I bought from one of the Pacheco boys as they came down the road after a trip to the lakes. One of their horses had gotten untied and headed home and stepped into the cattle guard at the forest gate and broke its leg. The whole family had to witness shooting of the horse and cutting its leg off so they could remove it from the cattle guard and pass by. Pretty's son was also in the group and the two horses had trouble when they got separated. It's a situation that I've seen before: the mother and her offspring are inseparable. Pacheco had enough of that situation and wanted to separate them once and for all. I think I gave him a hundred and fifty for Pretty. She was an Appaloosa and she did just fine for her age; she made it to Santa Fe with the best of them. I decided to breed Misty again to a stud Jake had over at his house, a beautiful paint horse, large and handsome. My caretaker, Steve was a very good horseman and lamented the fact his father had never given him a horse. I offered him the chance of breeding Pretty; he had to pay the stud charges. He accepted and we took the two mares over to Jake's place.

A mare ready to breed is similar to a female human. She ovulates at a certain time, and that is when she is fertile and ready to become pregnant. A female horse starts blinking her vagina when she is coming into that fertile time. The stud sees the horses arrive and gets agitated, pacing back and forth. The girls sense his desire and that turns them on even more. We left the two horses there for several weeks. Jake called me when they came into heat, and I went over to his house to watch him breed Misty and Pretty. He used a head stall and tied her into a corner of a special stall built just for breeding. He hobbled one hind leg to her front leg so she can't kick the stud as he approaches from the rear. His penis is hard and slapping against his stomach with anticipation. The stud grunts and foams at the nostrils as he mounts her. Most of the time they find their way inside the mare. She is so wet that there is fluid running down her legs and it is quite easy for the stud to penetrate. On occasion I saw Jake reach in and grab the fourteen-inch penis and actually place it into the mare's vagina. Once they start mating, it goes on for several days. At the end of this period the female horse no longer accepts the male's advances and it is over. Jake did both Misty and Pretty in much the same way. We left them there for another month to see if they showed signs of impregnation. They both looked pregnant and we went and got them with the trailer. The gestation period for a horse is ten or eleven months. I went back to work in L.A. and Steve and his small family wintered at the ranch.

Lorraine and I had made an offer on an antique building in downtown Las Vegas. It was on the historic list but was badly in need of renovation. It is a somewhat famous building because it can be seen as the tourists pass by on the old highway. The reason for its fame is that during the filming of "Red Dawn", the film crew had painted a huge picture of a cowgirl on the side. It was a commercial for Calumet, whatever that was, and it was frequently photographed.

After we owned it, Lorraine called me at the ranch one day and told me someone had contacted her about using the building in a big time commercial that was shooting in the area. If I wanted to, I could open up and stand by while they shot. We would get a thousand dollars. Not a bad haul for an afternoon's work! Funny thing about it was I knew the Key Grip; his name was Tom Ramsey. He was a wild man that I used to work with from time to time. He had keyed "Easy Rider" in 1969 for Vilmos and had been right there in old Las Vegas in the sixties, where it had been shot. We laughed about the circumstances surrounding this meeting and we ate lunch together. They packed up and left for the next location, and I closed the building and headed back up into the mountains. Ramsey had been the Key on the 1988 Robert Redford pic that shot up in the Truchas, New Mexico area on the other side of the mountains from us called "The Milagro Beanfield War." He called me and came up to the ranch for a weekend. We rode the horses, smoked some pot, drank some beer around the campfire and gazed at the stars.

Once, years before, we were shooting a commercial in Pasadena, California in one of those old Victorian mansions. The owners only allowed the production to use one of the bathrooms in the house, and it wasn't enough. A honey wagon is film jargon for mobile toilets, and the production hadn't brought a honey wagon for this small shoot. Anyway, Tom got really pissed off about the situation with the toilet and he took a shit right on the backyard walkway. Everyone had to pass it and definitely saw it. He retired a while back and I mean to call him soon. He was a San Fernando Valley cowboy; he always wore cowboy boots. I liked him a lot.

Hanania and I did another Jaglom film called "Venice/Venice" and had two parts to it; one part was shot in California and had some locations in Venice Beach; the other shot in Italy. I did the one in California. The Jaglom style of filmmaking was still alive and he even acted in this one. There was one scene when he and the lady are in a canoe on one of the Venice canals, the Venice in California. There was some serious dialogue going on and some young gang wannabes started heckling the two actors from the shore line. Jaglom got so mad he stood up and started screaming at them. Well, the canoe tilted hard to the side and dumped him into the canal. That water was pretty rank; in those days it was a little dirty around there. The whole crew burst out laughing as Henry stood there in the water up to his chest as the water drained off his pork pie hat. He got mad a second time at us for laughing. Finally he gave up and just laughed with us. We dried him off and continued shooting. Man, he had deserved that! Anyway, his little films are not without merit; they are kind of like Woody Allen meets Peter Bogdanovich, but without the big budget. I think his films appeal to actor types and the fans of acting more that they appeal to movie lovers.

After we finished "Venice, Venice," I called up Steve Burum looking for work. He had been at UCLA when I was there and was now a successful Director of Photography. His credits included "The Outsiders" and "Rumble Fish," both directed by Francis Ford Coppola; plus "Body Double," "The Untouchables," "The War of the Roses," and "Carlito's Way." He was big time. He finally called me out of the blue and I did a commercial with him. I forget the product but it was for Lucasfilm Ltd. We had a great time; he was very easy to work for. I didn't hear from him for a while after that.

Meanwhile, Hanania's old friend Arthur Seidelman was directing a teen-oriented chase film "Rescue Me" that was to shoot in Aurora, California. This was up above Sacramento not far from where Gregg and I had shot "A Cry in the Wild." Go figure … after the three films on the Mississippi River, and now the second one in the same mountains of California. It was strange, to say the least. During a phone conversation with Rio, I mentioned to him about the film going to Aurora and asked if he was interested in working on the film with me. It was non-union and I could get him on. I had a large crew for a change, and he accepted.

I was using John Minardi as my Best Boy. He had come out to California soon after we worked on "Mystery Train" and looked me up. He was a good worker and I enjoyed working with him. He eventually got into the union and now works and lives in California. A friend of John's named Gregg Fausak was an extra hammer. Another friend of Minardi's, Nelson, was on dolly. Nelson proved to be a great guy and Dolly Grip. All the crew was great. Rio drove down to Encino from Santa Barbara and we drove up to the location together in my Cadillac. I had this mint 1978 4-door Caddy Seville, white with a sunroof. It was a fast car. Rio took a turn driving and got a ticket for speeding coming down off the grapevine into the central valley area. It's only five or six hours to drive up there and when we arrived, we found our little motel that they were putting the crew up in and checked in. It was just a truck stop along the freeway, but it was home to us for the next six weeks.

The film starred Michael Dudikoff, Stephen Dorff and Ami Dolenz, the daughter of Mickey Dolenz from the group, The Monkees. God, time was marching on. They were like a virus during the time of The Doors: commercial rock and roll, T.V. series and throbbing hearts, famous amongst the very young. She was actually very cute. Ami's character gets kidnapped during a botched robbery by two crazy characters that bungle everything. Stephen Dorff plays her high school classmate / admirer who sets off in pursuit of them trying to save her, and along the way enlists Michael Dudikoff's character. There are plenty of car chases, shootouts, and general mayhem. This was a busy film for the Grips: plenty of car mounts and rough terrain with dolly shots aplenty.

The very first shot of the film was a real doozie. There was a scene inside a bank where Dorff runs in to try to get the ransom money. The small town was up in the mountains and there wasn't a level street in the place. Hanania wanted to follow the guy into the bank and then out again in one long shot. I didn't have enough apple boxes and cribbing to get even close to the height needed to jack up the track enough to enter the bank. It was four feet higher than the original starting place of the shot. I was carrying curved track and we used it to turn from the sidewalk and enter the door of the bank. What to do? One of the local hires on the teamsters' crew had become a friend, and I asked him if there was a dairy in the town. He said yes. I asked him to call and see if we could borrow eighty milk crates. When he said, "Yea, they have them," I sent a couple of guys with him and they returned with enough boxes to do the shot and then some.

By the time I had the rig assembled there were a hundred people from the town watching. The first time Nelson pushed Hanania down the street and into the bank, there was a thunderous applause. They had a great chance to see what Grips do on the first day of the shoot. From then on we had a gallery of people who followed us around the area, eager to see Hollywood at work. About two weeks into the shoot Steve Burum called with another commercial. I had to tell him I was at work on a feature in northern California. This film was really way too complex for the Grips for me to leave, even for four days. He never called me again; what a shame. He went on to shoot some big stuff and Hanania returned to Israel a year later. Who knows what course my life would have taken if I had accepted that job with Steve and left Hanania for a week? Oh well.

There were a lot of dolly track and traveling shots in the mountains. There were some snowy days up near the summit, so cold you had to wear a parka. The next day you could be down lower and it was hot. There was poison oak everywhere, and we were given special instructions in case we got exposed to it: vinegar in a cold tub of water. We were careful, to say the least, and no one got it. We carried the dolly down into the American River Gorge and built track.

The good news was there was a little club next door that had a live band and our crew partied there a lot. Nelson would grab the drums when they weren't being used. He was very good and always drew a crowd. Toward the end of the shoot there was a big shoot-out in an old turn of the century hotel. It took the better part of a week to shoot all the sequences. There were squibs placed behind the velvet wallpaper and doors rigged to explode. Squibs are little explosive pellets that can be exploded from a remote position. The special effects guy, working the triggering device, has to watch the action and when the actor fires his gun trigger, he has to fire the squib.

The town was called Grass Valley, a cool little town with hippie stuff and plenty of bars with entertainment. The production had rented the entire second floor of the old hotel. I arranged to sleep in one of the rooms overnight, and Nelson did the same. We went out that night after the rest had packed up and left and raised a lot of hell. We visited every bar in the town and ended up wandering around drunk in the wee hours of the next morn. We headed back to the hotel and grabbed a couple of hours of sleep before the production started arriving.

When you are young enough, you can work fourteen hours and party afterwards, grab a couple hours of sleep and head back to work night after night. Rio seemed to be having a good adventure. Minardi was a little hard on Rio, being the boss's son and all, but Minardi was hard on everyone, even himself. Rio learned a lot and became friends with Fausak, who was also a surfer. They ended going on a surfing trip to Costa Rico together. After we wrapped the northern California part we came back to L.A. where we continued to shoot for a few more weeks. One location took us to Pear Blossom, which is on Highway 14 heading to Palmdale.

Chuck Crivier, Rio's friend and our bass player, decided to pay us a visit. He liked what he saw. He wanted to grip. He wanted to push dolly. I said cool, and gave him the numbers of Chapman and Fischer, the two dolly companies, and he took some lessons. He was a worker.

Hanania had another low budget film, this one the lowest yet. It was for a guy named Doumani. He had inherited a lot of oil money from his family and wanted to make films. I hired Rio to Best Boy for it. He had never done it before and had to rise to the occasion. Chuck was getting real good on the dolly, working in the valley somewhere at a non-union place that turned out cheap little films. I hired him to push dolly for Hanania and they hit it off great. Chuck had satisfied one of the most picky camera operators around. Hanania loved him. Chuck's personality was great and he got along with everyone; he was a very confident young man. On the other hand, Rio was putting much effort into figuring out what a Best Boy did. He was a little behind and that was getting in the Grip crew's way. It was only his second experience on a crew. I could not treat him like a baby. I had to give him orders and I had to correct him when he fucked up. It's hard to teach someone who doesn't want to learn. Rio has had a hard time taking any teaching from me since he was a little boy. It wasn't any different here.

I had some time in between jobs and I wrote a treatment for a T.V. show called "Shrink." based on Marilyn Ruman's practice. It was kind of good and she wanted to have it re-written and take control of it. Problems started over who initiated the project, who owned it, and a host of other issues. They were also trying to cut me out of "The Woman at Otowi Crossing". When I say they, I mean Marilyn and none other than my wife, Lorraine. I couldn't believe Lorraine didn't back me up on some things she knew to be true. I realized she wasn't loyal to me. From there we descended slowly into a spiral of arguing, and eventually I fell out of love with her.

Hanania got another Jaglom film called "Lucky Ducks". They had short shooting schedules, like six days or so. We shot it with little fanfare. It was a caper type story with small time gangsters etc.

SIT-COM LAND

Gregg Heschong called and asked if I would Key a show he had at Paramount. I needed some union hours and I agreed. Called "Big Wave Dave's," it was a pilot with an order for nine shows. Andy Ackerman was directing. I didn't really want to do T.V. but I needed the hours and the money. Besides, Lorraine kept nagging that she was providing the bulk of the income. If nothing else, T.V. is lucrative and steady at times. This show was nine or so weeks with a couple of hiatuses thrown in, during which I was carried with pay. The best thing about that show was the cast of actors they had assembled. It starred David Morse, one of my favorite actors. I had worked with him before on "St. Elsewhere." He played Big Wave Dave, a guy who relocates to Hawaii on an impulse with three of his best friends who tag along. They open a surfboard shop and go through the typical sitcom humor. It also had Adam Arkin and Jane Kaczmarek, two fine young actors. Jack Lord played the old Kahuna character on the beach that they befriend. It was a fun show with beach bunnies running around with skimpy bathing suits, etc. We finished the nine shows and wrapped in the spring of 1993.

I headed for the ranch alone. Lorraine wanted to stay in L.A. to work on her career. This was getting to be old; there I was by myself again, heading for the ranch. I put Buster and Coco, the female we had gotten to keep Buster company, into their traveling cages. Lorraine insisted I feed them formula and I brought a load with me; she took better care of those dogs than she did of me. Steve's family had gotten a puppy that became quite a little badass. Buster didn't take well to sharing his yard with another male, and they snarled and fought. Steve's dog wasn't fully-grown but as the summer progressed, he got bolder and started inflicting damage on Buster with his young razor sharp teeth. I had to take Buster to the vet a couple of times.

I started going to Las Vegas to work on the Calumet building. Leroy was helping with the major construction. First I shaped up an area on the ground floor that had been rented before but needed a new bathroom. It rented out soon after, and that provided the income to pay the mortgage. That was cool. I then turned my attention to the upstairs area. We were pretty far along turning the front half into a first class apartment/office. I ordered some fancy windows in Santa Fe that Leroy framed into the front of the building. The front looked out onto one of the main business blocks, and the windows looked great from the street. Scott Oram came out for a while and he was a great help. The summer seemed to fly by.

Lorraine came out at the end of the summer. We drove back together and we started to talk about what was wrong with us. She was so driven by her desire to succeed as a Director that her personal life wasn't that important. She admitted to me that she wasn't happy unless she was working. On the other hand, I wasn't happy unless I wasn't working: I truly wanted to be at the ranch. Between Marilyn and her agents, Lorraine had an agenda that didn't include the ranch anymore. I had become her caretaker, construction chief, and dog and horse sitter.

THE GEORGE CARLIN SHOW 1993

Back in L.A., I tried to find work but it was a little slow, which aggravated the situation with Lorraine even more. Gregg had taken over a show at Warner Brothers called "Family Matters." He called me but I passed on more television; I was still waiting for Burum to call, I guess. Finally Gregg took on a second show at Warner Brothers, just two stages from "Family Matters." It was "The George Carlin Show," a pilot with twelve episodes: just what I needed to pick up the slack in the career. I readily took him up on the offer and there I was in the fall of 1993. George Carlin was a sweetheart and his brother Patty was just as sweet. They were a blast to be around. Carlin played a New York cabbie that couldn't keep his nose out of other people's business. His sardonic wit provided a perfect platform for the writers. He was also a writer on the show, and they expounded on every political and social subject they wanted to.

One of the sets was a facade of several two-story New York apartment buildings. It had to have a day look and a night look. Gregg, again, came up with a great idea; a giant silk that was mounted on a pulley system that extended out from the scaffolding to the building. Above it were coops and other soft lights. The silk diffused the lights and that provided the general daytime lighting for the entire set. The silk could be pulled back out of the way for the night look. Gregg was so inventive.

Another principal set was the cab Carlin drove. They made the choice not to have a process situation, where the background was added afterwards in post-production; instead it was just in limbo, against a black backing. Gregg and I came up with a large revolving drum affair that suspended over the windshield. We had the art department paint buildings on either end of the drum with the tops of the buildings being in the middle. The reflection in the front window of the cab was a skyline of buildings that rolled by, creating the effect the car was moving. A Grip turned the drum slowly or faster, depending on the scene. It was the only sense of movement except for an occasional light that was panned across the car to simulate headlights from another car or a streetlight. It was a huge success. We still talk about it more than ten years later.

Christmas and New Year's came and went, and Lorraine and I were still growing apart. At 4:30 a.m. on the morning of January 17th, 1994 Lorraine and I and a lot of other people were jolted awake from the biggest earthquake I had ever felt. All we could hear was glass breaking and furniture being hurled around the room. Lorraine jumped on top of me and hung on for dear life. I thought it was the end for us. I had lived in L.A. all my life and had never felt anything that strong. The electric had gone out and we were in the dark. There was broken glass all over the floor as I got out of bed. Of course, I didn't have any slippers and had to walk across the broken glass in the dark to the closet and my shoes. I couldn't find a flashlight right away but when I did, we looked around and saw the inside of our house was littered with our possessions. Another aftershock hit just a few minutes later and this time we ran outside to the front of the house where all the other neighbors were standing in their bathrobes. There were to be 10,000 aftershocks. It was a 6.7 magnitude quake and it lasted 15 seconds. Now, that doesn't seem like a long time but believe me, it seemed like an eternity. This was the first major earthquake to strike directly under an urban area in the United States since the Long Beach earthquake of 1933. I wasn't born then, thank god. I had felt a lot of quakes growing up in L.A. but never anything like this. This magnified my sleeping problem that first grabbed my attention in County Jail a hundred times. I certainly did sleep with a flashlight by my bed from then on.

Our house had increased in value from the 78 thousand dollars we paid for it. It was appraised at around 240 thousand, just before the quake, so that we could borrow money to pay for the property we bought next to the ranch. After the quake, people were selling like mad and the property prices dropped to around 160 thousand. I made a promise to myself that I wouldn't live in the valley close to a known fault, ever again. I spent my spare time fixing all the brick work in the back yard that had cracked and fallen over. I just did a patch job. Let me give you some advice: don't build with brick in the valley!

This brought the problem between Lorraine and me to a head. I wanted to live at the ranch and commute to work. I'd stay in a motel, if need be; my jobs were all over the country. On the other hand, Lorraine's jobs at that time were only in L.A., and she wanted to stay in L.A. and buy a bigger house. Once when I was complaining about not having a wife that took care of me and led a simple life, she sympathized with my comment and added she needed a wife also. She wasn't happy when she was not working. I wasn't happy when I was working. That pretty much sums it up. I went to the ranch early that year by myself.

Hanania had gone to Israel with Shuli. They were thinking of moving back to the homeland for good at that time. Hanania's mother lived in Jerusalem, she was not in good health, and his heart was being pulled back to his roots.

I got back to the ranch and almost right away, my dog Buster and Steve's dog were going at it. He was bigger and surer about his claim on the turf. His teeth were young and sharp; Busters were old and brown with rot. It was no match. I asked Steve if he would tie his dog up, and he and his wife refused. We had a confrontation about it and I gave him an ultimatum that either he ties his dog up, or they had to find a new place to live. Well, he lit into me about how I wasn't paying him enough, I was a terrible person, this and that.

Richard Fresques sided with him and agreed that I was taking advantage of Steve.

Richard pulled a fast one on the Pacheco property just in front of my house that I had rented for 10 years. He went to Jacob, one of the three Pacheco brothers that inherited the land from Fermin, their father. I got along with both of Jacob's brothers quite well. Jacob officially ended up with the property I am talking about. He was racist and a La Raza supporter in the early days. It was no secret he was part of the anti-white sentiment in the area. Richard talked Jacob into renting him the land and when I arrived that spring, Richard was standing by the ditch. He waved and said "Hi neighbor" while pointing to the land I had been renting. Jacob had switched renters without even talking to me! I went down to Jacob's house and asked him if it was true. He said Richard made him a deal to plant one of his fields in return for the land I had been renting. I asked him why he didn't give me a chance to help plant his fields, and asked wasn't that a little radical of him to not even give me notice? He said, "It was just more practical." I was pissed but what could I do? I turned and walked out.

Richard was starting to become a problem for all the neighbors and me. He had grown into an amplified version of his father. They called his father the fox; he was cagey and could cheat you if you let him. Richard's nickname in high school was Cheetah, like the Tarzan monkey. I always thought it was referring to the thieving nature of a chimp, but I found out later it referred to his large ears.

Anyway, Steve and I stood toe to toe and had a very heated verbal exchange. He brought up things that had happened in the past, one by one. He had a list of everything that had happened. He was truly an unhappy camper and he said he would move out at the end of the month. Richard backed up to the ditch on his new land and helped Steve move out. I was so tired of caretaker problems. They left and I was by myself at the ranch for the first time in a while. It felt good. I liked being by myself. Not many people like being alone; most people run from the feeling. That's why there are cities. People are scared and want to live near hospitals and police and running water. I feel sometimes that I was born in the wrong generation. I probably would have been a good frontiersman or explorer. Lorraine came for a short visit that year, and then I was alone most of the time. My good friend Henry visited me once a day sometimes. I let him gather firewood and we still continued to hunt together every winter.

Now we had a nice mountain we could call our own. The land we bought headed up behind the original piece and was a mountaintop. It had cliffs of rock that I could see from the house. If you climbed straight up from the house you would find them. Once you reached the top of the mountain behind the house, the property settled down and was semi-flat on top as you headed west. In the middle of the land and on the top was a depression that filled up with water in the winter. It was called the dry lake because it dried up in summer. Most of the time it had water and was a drinking spot for all the animals in the area. Years later when I was single and in charge, Henry and I agreed that he should clear and cut wood around the northern part of the dry lake, which he did. He called me in L.A. to tell me he had found what appeared to be Indian dwellings along the rock outcrop just above the dry lake: amazing! He said he counted seven separate dwellings. I told him great, and don't touch a thing until I get there.

After Steve left I got bored with painting skulls and the whole cleaning process, etc. I decided to try my hand with my newfound painting talents, imitating the art of Southwestern rug weavers and using canvas as my palette. The rugs were beautiful and I always wondered how they came upon the designs. I had a beautiful old rug that I had bought in a Taos plaza store. I laid it out on paper to the best of my ability, transferred the design to canvas and started painting. It was an experiment that grew into an obsession. Painting is like being totally in control. No other art is like that. There are always critics, editors, contributors, crew, and committees: you are never alone. In the painting process, there are no people around.

During "The George Carlin Show," the father-in-law of one of my extra hammers passed away. His wife found a huge jar of morphine pills when she cleaned up his house. She wanted to sell them and I bought the whole jar for a hundred bucks. Lorraine and I were breaking up. Steve was leaving and I was in no mood to start interviewing new caretakers. I had no job offers, and I decided to spend the winter at the ranch and care for the place myself. I had all the best CDs of the day and a great sound system in the studio. The long winter nights, the morphine, and the studio with my music, provided the space for me to grow into a painter/rock guitarist. In a way I was preparing myself for something.

Babe was involved in a terrible accident at Sony Studios. One of his best friends fell to his death right in front of his eyes. Babe had become the swamper at that studio. That's a guy that sits in a little office and is on call to the electricians who need a Grip for some reason or another. I was told he brought a 6-pack of beer to work in the morning and it was gone by noon. Typical. Babe could drink with the best of them. I am afraid he had turned into an alcoholic. Anyway, one day he was working on a gang that was hanging scaffolding on Stage 27, where he was running a hoist. The hoist is called a mule by Grips; it is used to carry heavy equipment into the air and deposit it on the scaffolding or into the perms. Perms are the large wooden beams that are at the top of a stage, and they are what all the scaffolding hangs from. The hoist has a motor that turns a drum that a rope is coiled on. A pulley is placed hanging off one of the perms and the rope feeds up through it and back down to the floor. The rope is tied to the equipment and it is hauled off the floor. The person running the hoist is in charge of the movement.

Years later I pieced some of this together from what Babe told me when he came to the ranch in 1995. On Stage 27, the highest stage at Sony and the highest stage in all of Hollywood, the perms are 80 feet up. The only access to the perms was a ladder that went straight up the wall. That damn ladder made it sometimes acceptable to ride the hoist hook-up to the perms. Babe's friend Pat was going to use the ladder. Babe told me he challenged Pat to ride the rope up to the perms. Pat put his foot in the hook at the bottom of the rope and Babe started the motor with a foot switch. As the rope and Pat lifted higher and higher, he started to spin. When he reached the perms, he couldn't reach the wood to pull himself up. Babe couldn't see what was happening, it was too far away. Pat slipped off the hook and fell the 80 feet back to the floor and bounced a couple of times and died, right there in front of Babe.

Babe panicked and ran away. No one saw him for days. There were investigations all over the place. The police were involved, insurance companies, studio people. Babe finally settled down and faced the situation. He felt responsible for the accident. He wasn't legally liable, thank god, but he knew he had been involved in the decision that caused Pat to ride the hook. He went through a lot of therapy and counseling but he just started drinking more and more. He blamed himself. It's understandable; he felt guilty for egging Pat on. The Grips are rough and tumble kind of guys. They are the kind of guys that would have been up in the rigging on a pirate ship, or in the front lines of the Crusades. It was robust fun Babe was having. He meant no harm, but the circumstances turned deadly and that was that. No one wanted to hire Babe after that. He went on disability.

There is a scene in "Feast of Friends" where we are on a large sailing ship heading out for a sunset cruise. All The Doors and Dorothy, Lynn, and Babe are on board. Jim is asleep cupped in the main sail. Babe stands there with his full beard blowing in the wind. The sun sets. The music I had cut to the scene swells up, it's from the "The Planets" by Gustav Holst, the Neptune track. In my mind for a moment, Babe and Jim looked like pirates. It was a historic moment. "Feast of Friends" is only available on bootleg prints. There are some very precious moments in that version of the footage I had shot. I cut that sequence by myself before Frank was hired, and it was one of my favorite scenes in the world. It was so peaceful. We were truly in the center of a Rock and Roll storm and it was nice to feel the calm.

By the end of 1994, the year of the earthquake, Lorraine and I were spiraling out of control. We got into a terrible fight. She would yell and scream and then when it was my turn to reply, she would run away and slam the bedroom door between us. It had a lock on it, so when we went to the ranch someone could watch the place but not be able to enter our office/bedroom. Well. the door slammed in my face and I kicked it open, busting it into pieces.

Another time she and I were fighting and she started to run away and I restrained her against the wall. I wasn't trying to hurt her, just trying to stop her from running from the argument. I wasn't thinking clearly or I would never have touched her. I guess every guy says that when he flies off the handle with a woman but it was true, at least that was what I experienced. I trained as a boxer and a wrestler in college. I was in a gang that liked to look for fights. Women know they are playing with fire when they yell and strike their mates. It seems a little bit strange that women and men are so fucking different. I would say something meaning one thing, but what Lorraine heard was completely different from what I meant. No matter what we were yelling at each other about, there was just no communication

I was working at Culver Studios pushing the dolly for Jack Anderson. His usual Dolly Grip left unexpectedly and I was filling in. Jack had been on "Mad About You" for several seasons and knew everyone on a very personal level. He even shot a short film one year for one of the female stars on the show. In those days the camera crews only worked on the block and shoot days, and were carried for a third day. It was just part of the deal; sometimes they actually ended up working on that carry day but not too often. This allowed them to do two shows in a week: a Monday-Tuesday show and a Thursday-Friday show. Jack's second show was "NewsRadio" at the Sunset Gower Studios on Sunset and Gower in downtown Hollywood. Gregg Heschong was the Director of Photography. I also pushed dolly on that show for him. It was like old home week: Gregg, Jack and myself.

Ray Manzarek called me up to tell me he had a Christmas present for me, and could I come over and pick it up. He was living on Rodeo Drive in Beverly Hills, just south of Wilshire. Their son Pablo was growing up; he had his own band and a recording studio upstairs. It must have been great to be born in Ray's house and like music. Dorothy looked great. She had become quite the gardener and the landscaping was beautiful. Ray presented me with a couple of framed awards for the videos The Doors had released. "Dance on Fire" and "Live at the Hollywood Bowl" both sold a million or more copies and these plaques were witness to that. He also handed me an envelope. When I opened it, I found a check for 10,000 dollars. It said "for photography." I was totally surprised. It was very generous of The Doors. They didn't owe me anything. I knew what I had sacrificed by selling my rights to my photography to them. It was to save the ranch; I didn't think of the consequences. I asked Ray what it was for and he simply said, "Because you are a good guy." Ray told me he was busy writing a book.

I came home from work one night and my key didn't slide into the lock like it was supposed to. Once it was in, it didn't open the door. Lorraine had changed the locks! I was officially thrown out of my own house. It was winter of 1994. I had gotten sick and was slowly recovering in a motel on Sepulveda Boulevard. Somehow Lorraine found me and called my room; she was worried about me. I asked her how she had found me, and she said she had called every motel in Culver City. I told her I was okay. It was better we didn't see each other for a while. I am sure Marilyn Ruman, my nemesis, was advising her.

Anyway, we tried therapy; I was ready. Marilyn gave Lorraine the name of a lady who didn't want to see us together; she wanted to talk to Lorraine first. Later, I finally went to a meeting. The lady was a German lady with short-cropped hair. If she wasn't a lesbian, she was a heartbeat away from it. She was very strong. While I was at the ranch, I had called Lorraine at 8 o'clock every evening. It was simple that way: I knew when to call and she knew when to expect a call. Well, I walked into the office and the first thing out of the lady's mouth was how I was trying to control Lorraine with the 8 o'clock phone calls. I looked at Lorraine who looked away from me. I looked back at the psychologist and asked her, 'Are you kidding?' She answered that no, she was not kidding. I stood up and announced that I felt they were out of line with that thought and were ganging up on me. I wasn't going to get a fair trial in that room!

I was in pretty bad shape at this time. A divorce is not easy for anyone. I couldn't let go of the anger and hurt and it was making it hard to concentrate. Jack Anderson noticed it as we made our moves. I just wasn't all there. I wanted to try meditation so I called Bob Angers. He was really into Tibetan meditation and he went on retreats, and I figured he could guide me to a place to learn. He sent me to the Dharma Dhatu on Third Street near La Cienega. The first chance I had, I went to an evening beginners briefing. I was taught the basic breathing exercise and the position to sit in, and was placed into a large class. The class consisted of lecture, discussion and actual practice, the actual meditation. They teach you that you have to practice a lot to get it right. I got it a couple of times, but I am way too fidgety to sit still for the amount of time it takes to be really good it.

The winter finally ended with me living behind Hanania's in his guesthouse. We shot some stupid film by the Arab guy Doumani. Once that was all over I headed to the ranch where I stayed for almost two years.

A lady from Chicago, Patricia Butler, had been calling me for about a year. She was writing a book about Pam Courson, Jim's wife. We had long conversations that went on for hours. It was winter and the nights were long. After I would come back from painting all night in the studio, the phone would ring. We became very, very good friends. I was going through a divorce and she was single and the long conversations turned sexual. I am not sure if she used the phone sex to interview me or if she was truly having orgasms as she claimed. Whatever, it helped to pass the time. I had a lot of time on my hands during the long winter nights. She also become acquainted with Babe at this time and witnessed his troubles with the accident. When her book was finished she sent me a copy and autographed it, "To Paul, one of the best friends I never met. Thanks for everything. Love Patricia."

Patricia had interviewed Paul Rothchild, The Doors record producer, and fallen in love with him. Paul was dying from lung cancer and she was devastated when he finally died. Patricia Butler is a unique individual; at least, by my definition. She comes from a broken home in the Midwest. She is a studious person that had been in Paris and witnessed the madness that happens at Pere Lachaise, the cemetery where Jim is buried. She didn't know who The Doors were. She was so moved by the fans and their devotion that she came back from her trip to Paris and decided to write a book inspired by the frenzy she had witnessed: people rioting, smoking pot, shooting up. Tear gas. Arrests were made. What the fuck were they so worked up about? In researching the subject of The Doors, she became interested in Jim's girlfriend, Pam. She wrote the book about Pam's relationship with Jim and called it "Angels Dance and Angels Die." Patricia made Pam famous. She uncovered a story about Max Fink and Jim's dealings with a homosexual that was trying to blackmail Jim. Evidently on Max's deathbed, he related to his wife the story about how they dealt with it. I pleaded with her not to use it; it was so negative. Babe and I were very close to Jim and if he was bisexual, we would have known. She ended up discussing the incident, but she didn't sensationalize it too much. I still don't like the fact she wrote about it. She did the most thorough research any human could do, and the book turned out fantastic. But alas, it is just a second hand account.

In the winter of 1994 Lorraine and I tried to work out the terms of the divorce. Of course, she felt that she had contributed the bulk of the money in all our endeavors and she wanted to be compensated. Well, I had done the work on everything and I wanted to be compensated. She had an appraiser come up to the ranch and measure everything. This was my second time going through this; the ranch was going up for sale again. I talked to my lawyer from my first divorce and he asked me about Lorraine's assets. He found out she was a Director and said that they had very large retirement funds that could be considered communal property. I would never have thought about that, asking for a portion of Lorraine's retirement fund. I am just not that kind of person. But, faced with the possible loss of the ranch I so loved for the second time, I brought up her pension plan in our next phone conversation. I simply told her that I had a lawyer now and that he had advised me of her pension program. She went quiet. Finally she said something like, "How could you fucking do that to me? You #$@*%&#$@*%& bastard." She called back the next night with an offer that I could keep the entire ranch but nothing else, in return for me not using the pension fund thing. I accepted; that was all I wanted, the ranch. She felt like she had gotten the shaft somehow. She wanted the ranch in her mind, but didn't want to spend any time there. That wasn't going to happen. She and her lawyers filed the papers in April of '95.

May 1st I got a call at the ranch from my sister. My father had died. He hadn't been sick or anything like that, his heart just gave out. He had been seeing a doctor for problems with peeing and stomach bloat, but there was no indication of heart problems. My mother says that he started acting very strange, like he was dizzy or something. He went to the bathroom and shit for a very long time. When he came out he sat down in front of her and raised his arms and shrugged his shoulders, as if to say, 'I don't know.' That was that. He went down and she called the ambulance. He was pronounced dead on the spot. I called Henry and asked him to look after the ranch while I went to my father's funeral. He came up the next day and I headed for Palm Springs, where my parents were living. Lorraine came out of respect; we sat beside each other during the eulogies.

Before the ceremony the presiding priest talked to the family: my mother, my sister and her husband Richard, Lorraine, and me. He asked each person to say a little something in private in memory of my father. When it came to me, I started remembering how bad he had treated me as a youngster. I grew up really pissed off. I remember getting in between my mother and him as their arguments escalated. I got old enough to actually push him back once. I started crying. For the first time in a long time I cried. I spoke out involuntarily about how he had treated me and that I had trouble forgiving him. I still loved him because he was my father, but I hated him deep down. My mother told me later that day that when I was very young, he had hit me in front of people at his store. I had completely blocked it out. I knew I didn't like him but didn't know exactly why. It was like a light went off in my head. There it was, the source of all my anger, just like in "Rebel Without a Cause." James Dean calls his dad out. He hates him, and he says so. He was talking for a lot of us in that movie. A peace came over me. It was over: the mystery about my anger.

Lorraine and I tried to get together for a day or so and it didn't work out, and I went back to the ranch. My father and mother had been to the ranch a few years earlier. My dad fell in love with the iris plants in Walker Flats, and he had asked for his ashes to be spread in that meadow. His ashes were put into a brass box and I took them with me. A funny thing happened at the airport. I approached the luggage scanner and I put everything on the conveyor belt. The light went off and I was questioned about the small, very heavy box. They thought it was a bomb and wanted me to open it. It was sealed very well and I couldn't open it. I told the supervisor that approached that it was my father's ashes; he felt sorry for me and let me pass.

It was the middle of May and I was in back in Mora. The brass box was on the mantle of the fireplace. Everything was in bloom and the flowers covered the ground. It was glorious in the springtime. Springtime in the Rockies is not just a song or an idle statement; it's real and it's a fantastic thing to behold. I was alone but now I was the owner of my own destiny. How rare to be free. How lonely. How grand. I went to town around late June to stock up on supplies, mainly beer. On the way back as I was pulling into Mora, there just opposite Joe's Service Station sat a beautiful German-looking blonde girl in her twenties. I thought I was dreaming. I had been a while alone up on the mountain and I was starting to think about women a lot. I parked and went right up to her and struck up a conversation. She was working in the German guy's furniture store behind us. She seemed a little sad; she told me was going through a breakup with a guy that she had come from the east with. They had bought a trailer in Guadalapita and it wasn't working out between them.

She wanted out and I wanted in. I offered her a place to stay up at the ranch. I gave her directions and she said she would visit. She did, and the next thing she was moving in! Karen was from Germany all right. She had a heavy accent. She also had the most beautiful body I had ever seen. She was a recovering speed freak. She had done the coke speed thing in Germany. She had cuts on her arms from razor blade cuts she had self-inflicted; they had healed long ago but the scars were still visible. She was into Buddha and liked to meditate. Boy, was that cool. I showed her my meditation area upstairs and she used it every day. I had the most lovely wooden carved Buddha up there, and it was always warm and sunny.

Bob Angers and his family had called ahead and planned to visit around the Fourth of July. Rio was coming and I called Chuck and Christine and told them that the head of the Fox Grip Department was coming for a visit. Why didn't he come at the same time and get acquainted? It couldn't hurt. My son and his friend Dave Moore were visiting at the same time. We were having a great time riding the 4-wheelers, the horses and lighting up fireworks around the campfire. I went to town and when I came back Rio approached me with the news that Babe had showed up.

I was renting out the cabin for a while to a guy named Gene. He had just gotten a divorce from a lady in the next canyon over, had suffered a heart attack and he needed a place to stay. That was the only time anybody ever paid me to stay at the place! Just before I got back, Babe was acting drunk as usual and was waving a pistol around. It was Tim McIntire's pistol; Babe had saved it from the vultures that looted Tim's place when he died. Babe was remembering how I had asked him to leave and was bitter: he had a bone to pick with me. Everyone was worried about what was going to happen but the minute I saw Babe we hugged; it was all good. We had seen a lot of water pass under our bridge. It didn't stop us from still loving one another.

We had a great Fourth of July that year. Bob and his son Robyn had brought a load of fireworks and we set them off below the ditch in the field. It was magnificent. Bob liked Chuck; everyone likes Chuck. Chuck had developed an interest in Buddha, and that went well with Bob. Soon after, Chuck and Rio went to visit Bob at Fox and he gave them the tour. They had it made. Rio decided not to wait for the opportunity and went back to Santa Barbara to surf and park cars. Chuck stuck it out and became a regular fixture at Fox. He got his thirty days and joined the local grip union.

Babe stuck around when everyone left for the summer. He had nowhere to go and needed a rest. He was hanging out on the porch of the cabin with Gene a lot. He loved that porch. After about a week or so I was surprised when Gene told me he was leaving. He said that Babe told him about being a drunk and liking to beat people up. Gene had just had a heart operation and didn't need any extra stress. The thought of spending the winter up there with Babe was unbearable. Gene found a trailer for rent down at Ricky Lucero's and Babe moved into the cabin.

Babe was living from one disability check to the next. Considering there was no rent or utilities to pay, it wasn't bad. He had what he called 'episodes,' periods when he became very depressed and cried a lot. He wanted to end his life several times. Tim's gun was always present on the kitchen table. I held his body several times while he wept and I told him about all his friends that cared for him. No one thought he was responsible for the accident. He told me he just couldn't forgive himself for coaxing Pat onto the rope; I told him that Pat didn't have to listen to him; it was his choice to step onto the hook. It didn't help. Babe continued to drink from morning until afternoon when he passed out. Sometimes I drank with him just to be near him and add comfort. I knew it was a difficult situation and I knew that I wasn't prepared to deal with it; I could only provide a safe place for him to try to heal. Karen, the blonde German girl, had gone through therapy for suicidal thoughts. On occasion she sat with Babe for hours trying to help with her soothing voice.

Papa Bear started to visit and spend time up with us at the ranch. Babe had a big old Cadillac that he took to Vegas to shop, etc. He met James Papa Bear down there and rekindled their relationship. James had an old house in Las Vegas, New Mexico and was making jewelry. Babe talked his disability people into paying for a retraining program. They agreed and James became his instructor. Babe moved down to Las Vegas into a small shack in the back of James' house, next to the jewelry factory. I visited him as often as I could. He seemed to be getting better. Maybe having more people around him helped to keep his mind off his private thoughts.

Karen continued working down at the furniture store in Mora. Her boss was chasing her around for sex and he wanted to marry her. I introduced her to Michael Gregory, my lawyer, and she retained him to do her divorce.

Lorraine called and asked how things were going. When I told her I had a girlfriend up there and wasn't so lonely anymore, she flipped out! She asked if I was sharing my bed with her, and was the quilt her mother gave us for Christmas still on the bed? I said yes. The terms of the divorce were the furnishings of the houses were to be divided equally. She had all our stuff in the Encino house. The next thing I knew, she told me she was on her way, coming for her stuff with a truck driven by Rio's friend Dave Moore. When they arrived Dave apologized for what was happening, but he needed the money that Lorraine had offered him. I understood. I even helped him take the stuff out of the house: anything to get rid of the maniac Lorraine once and for all. She took my bedding, the furniture including the kitchen table, and anything else she wanted!

Karen and I sat out on the porch while Lorraine rampaged through the house. The house was a mess when they were done, like when someone moves. There was shit scattered everywhere. It looked so bare. I had to go to my camping gear for some blankets, etc. I made a kitchen table out of scraps and we ate dinner as Lorraine and Dave headed down the highway back to L. A.

Karen had brought a small dog up to the ranch. She called her Dala, I think after the Dalai Lama. Dala had fallen in love with Lacy, my main dog, and fit right into the small pack of dogs. About a month later I went to get my pot stash that I kept in the bedroom in a small plastic bag and I could not find it. When Karen came home that evening she said she had taken it to work in case she wanted to smoke some during her shift. I asked her, what about if I had wanted to smoke some? She promised it wouldn't happen again.

With Babe living in the cabin, I felt comfortable leaving the ranch and I took Karen to Santa Fe. We stayed overnight at Tony Schramm's castle up on Cerro Gordo. His eyes fell out of his head when he saw Karen. She was quite lovely to look at. She later told me he hit on her that same day. Schramm told us he had a girlfriend, and he called her Annie Oakley because she kept a shotgun by her front door. They were pretty hot and heavy. You could see a woman's touch at work in his house. It was clean for starters, and more cozy.

Karen and I went back up to the ranch. Her ex-husband approached me down in Las Vegas; he had a hunch I was the one she was living with. He wasn't angry, thank god. I asked him about her and he told me of her troubled past. He said she didn't want to have sex with him: big problem. He thought she might be gay. I found out later she did have a few women lovers. I was feeling uncomfortable living with her after she had helped herself to my pot stash. I told her it wasn't working for me, but she could stay in a small trailer that I had for spillover guests. She moved into the trailer.

It started to get a little chilly; fall was approaching. One of Karen's girlfriends from Albuquerque came up and was sleeping in the trailer with her. Finally she left and I lost track of her for a while.

Babe had moved down to Bear's house in Las Vegas, I was once again alone and finally there was peace and quiet. But, it wasn't long before I was getting horny again. I had seen a Santa Fe paper with singles ads. I got one and started calling the advertisers that seemed right for me; this started a whole new thing. Santa Fe was always known for its swinging singles and now gay communities, but there were a lot of single women flocking to the new age city and it appears a lot of them were very lonely. You had to call a number and leave a message and if the lady liked your message, she called you back.

Lorraine had taken all the money. I was broke and living off unemployment. If you had to be living off unemployment, the ranch was the place to do it! On every other Thursday I would get a check for around seven hundred dollars.

When I called the numbers in the Santa Fe singles ads, sometimes they would return my initial message with a call that lasted for hours. Other times the ladies would hear my story about the ranch and horses, my lifestyle and my age, and it would go nowhere. A few times it really paid off. First, I had to prepare the ranch. I fed everyone, meaning the animals. I turned on strategic lights and left the radio playing in the kitchen. I had a brand new white Suzuki Sidekick 4-wheel drive with the money Ray Manzarek had given me, so at least I had transportation.

I headed down the road midday and would arrive in Santa Fe three hours later. I arrived at a condo complex at the prescribed time for a date I had made. The lady at the door was not the lady described on the phone: she was heavy, unattractive, and very Jewish.

All my life I've been polite to women, even the time in high school when we were all in our favorite bar and this old lady sitting next to me came on to me. I mean, she was fifty or sixty, she was old, and she was drunk. She whispered in my ear and started to stroke my cock. I was drunk too, and started to dig it. We went out behind the bar and crawled into my friend's Woody. I pushed the surfboards to the side, made a spot and fucked that old lady until she moaned. When you're young fucking is like, so easy: the pumping, the breathing, the sweating.

Anyway, this Jewish princess offered me some wine and I accepted. The next thing I knew, I was telling her the truth about how she was not my type. She moved over near to me and told me she understood, but first she unzipped my pants and the next thing I knew, she was sucking me like she hasn't seen a man in a long time. It was all good. I needed that, anyway. I said goodbye and went to my favorite bar hangout where I drank for a while.

Another time the girl was a massage therapist. What could be wrong with that? She was beautiful: young, blonde and very strong looking. She had breasts like Karen: bold and straight out there. Her plan was to go on a picnic to her favorite swimming spot at a small lake twenty minutes north of Santa Fe. When we got there she directed me to inflate a couple of rafts. We took off our clothing; she was so hot in a bikini. Oh my god, this was too good to be true! We swam out and around a point to a small cove. It was deserted. Here we go! I started to turn into the beach but she kept on going, like Stone dog used to do: he just swam and swam and swam. As it turned out, I got extremely tired. I was a mountain man and hadn't really kept my swimming skills together. I had to turn back, past the cove and to our starting place where the car was parked. She showed up about twenty minutes later and we ate lunch and visited with some kids. Maybe later it would happen. When we got back to Santa Fe we had dinner, laughed a lot, and drank some more wine. She was a member of a dance club that one of my neighbors in Mora went to. Please, she asked, don't tell him I have an ad in the paper. His name was Dan Cassidy.

I had run into him once before at a place he was working at in Santa Fe when he was tending bar. I was with Lorraine, Marilyn Ruman, Audi Aragon and his girlfriend, and a woman writer who lived in Santa Fe. Lorraine had optioned one of her books. We all met for dinner in one of the upscale restaurants, and that's where Cassidy was tending bar. We sat in the back of the place next to a door that could be opened onto the parking area. It was winter and cold outside. The waiter came and opened the door and he put a chair there to keep it open. Everyone at our table was cold so I asked the waiter to please close the door. He didn't want to. I told him the women were cold; he came back with some serious attitude. When it came time for the bill to be paid, everyone gave me their share and I was to pay the bill, which was about a hundred dollars or so. When I paid it, I gave him a one dollar tip. We bundled up and were in the parking lot talking and getting ready to leave when the waiter came running out to find me. He said I must have made a mistake and showed me the bill; I told him there was no mistake. He got in my face and I was about to have the pleasure of kicking his ass when Audi stepped in and tried to calm us down. Dan Cassidy came out to see what all the excitement was about. Everyone has had a waiter that was so rude, and this time I actually did something about it. It felt so good!

Anyway, I told the massage therapist I wouldn't tell Dan. We went back to her small apartment and when I asked for a massage sample, she told me she never gives a massage to someone she is dating. I ended up sleeping on the floor next to her bed; she would not let me sleep with her, no matter how hard I tried. Sometimes you just have to accept life as it is, no matter how horny you may be. We had a good swim though, and I still think about that day.

At Thanksgiving I got a call from a friend of Tony Schramm's. She wanted me to come and meet Schramm's Annie Oakley. Tony had told her about me and she loved horses, blah, blah, blah. It turned out Karen had looked Schramm up and they had left for a road trip to Colorado. It seemed cool; we were just switching girls. I hoped he was happy with Karen. He was half German and he loved blondes with large breasts. Hell, I think everyone loves them. I got to the Thanksgiving party and it is just the host, her boyfriend and Wendy, Schramm's ex. Well she was just giddy about meeting me. She was interested in the ranch, the horses, and talked about my painting hobby. She ended up in my lap with her arms around my neck. I was a little surprised by the aggressive but cute attention she was paying to me. We ended up going to a movie later on, just Wendy and me. We necked through the whole thing; I don't even remember seeing the movie. I took her back to her pickup truck and followed her to her place in Tesuque. She lived at the end of a dirt road that led into the forest. Wendy and her ex-husband had bought a shack with drug smuggling money. He was a black dude from Belize. They had two beautiful children. She was a Polish chick and mixed with black, the children were golden with traces of blonde kinky hair.

Wendy was sleeping on the floor. They had two very large dogs, Mastiffs. A dog doesn't get much bigger than a Mastiff! She was breeding them and selling pups. The dogs were in the house when we arrived. I was a little bit scared. The male was cool about me, and the female was licking me all over. She put them in their cages and we all fell asleep. She had a small amount of wood outside and kept her stove going all night long. I was feeling very sexy. We were all in the same room and once the kids fell asleep, she quietly sucked my anxiety away and we slept.

In the morning we were paid a visit by her neighbor, who she had been seeing. He confronted her about having me there, and she sort of broke up with him right in front of me. She used all kinds of excuses why she was dropping him. She told him he never took her dancing, he never helped her with anything; all he did was fuck her when she hiked over to his house. I stayed out of it. She hadn't really broken up with Schramm either, and that came back to haunt me. I visited her a lot at first. I brought her wood and repaired this and that.

She had an organic outhouse attached to the house on the porch. It was one of those that you fed peat and the shit decomposed into useable manure. Yuk. It was overflowing and needed to be cleaned out. They were using an alternative old outhouse that someone had built. The only trouble was that it was right above the small stream in front of the house, the same stream that they got their drinking water from. The three of them were so helpless.

After she had broke up with the black guy, the children's father, she hooked up with an Indian dude that made Beaded belts. He made belts with beautiful designs created by stringing beads together on a loom. She picked it up from him and was doing quite well in a small way. She made a few belts a week, sold them in Santa Fe, and fed her two children and paid her bills. They were living below the poverty line. The trouble with the Indian was that he started beating her; at least that is what she told me. He had also trained her in the Greek method of sex: anal. I got along with her kids quite well; I get along with all kids, for that matter. We used to take the dogs for long walks up the road in front of her cabin that led to the forest. I think I was adopting a small family of waifs. Wendy had a beautiful face but a used-up body: no breasts with a large back side and thighs. She was in her late thirties. On the other hand, the fact didn't escape me that I was twenty years older. She kept saying that our age didn't matter. She was a borderline nymphomaniac, just what a recently divorced mountain man needed.

From time to time the kids went for visits with their dad, who still lived in Santa Fe. When that happened she flew up to the ranch in her truck, and she got used to Mora. She told me she was a "live at the end of the road kind of girl." Well, my ranch was at the end of the road, so to speak. Mine was the last dwelling before you reached the National Forest. Her father had ended up owning her cabin somehow, and I suggested she make a deal with him to refinance, improve the place, and rent it out. She wanted to move to the ranch and I needed the company and the sex. She pulled it off. Her father signed it over; she refinanced and added a bathroom and running water. I plastered the walls that needed it, and it was no trouble to rent it out.

Wendy moved to the ranch and the kids went down the hill to Mora everyday to school. She took care of her kids like a devoted mother should. I must give her that; she would have killed for those kids. We were having a blast. I taught them all how to ride horses. It was like they had been waiting for that all their lives.

The colt that came from Pretty the time Steve and I bred the two horses, had grown up and was a feisty little guy. I got Jake Regensburg to come up and castrate him soon after Steve moved away. He and his wife separated and Steve ended up in Florida acting as a stuntman / extra on a low budget film. He called me to ask about his horse, told me he was broke and asked if I wanted to buy the pony. I played hard to get, but secretly I wanted the colt so bad. Misty hadn't gotten pregnant when they were bred.

I still remember the day I got up early to check on the horses. Pretty was so big she had trouble getting through the gate. At the far end of the little field above the house there were three horses. Misty had a newborn standing next to her. I walked fast toward them. The colt saw me coming and ran up to me like he knew me. He stopped and examined me from head to toe. His little legs were still wobbly and he could barely stand. When I got closer to Misty and Pretty I saw that Pretty was all bloody and wet around her vagina and Misty was clean. It was Pretty's foal! Misty had just pushed her way around and ended up with him by her side. She was like that. She pushed Pretty around like she did all the horses. She was the queen. I led the two mares and the colt back to the barn and got Pretty and him into a stall I had prepared, lined with fresh hay. When Steve finally sold him to me, I named him Karma for obvious reasons. Karma was white with red Appaloosa spots on his rear and very handsome.

By the time Wendy arrived, Karma was old enough for training. Manuel Valencia's brother Orlando Gold had become a good friend of mine, and I had him break Karma down in Las Vegas. It was a short amount of training and he came back to the ranch needing to be used a lot. We rode him to the lakes. Rio liked Karma; they were a good pair. The fall turned into winter. The Crivier boys visited, Chuck and Christine and his brother Chris and his girlfriend. Wendy and the children were fitting in good with my friends.

Wendy took an interest in my paintings. She had set up a small bead factory in the studio and she even incorporated some of my designs into her beadwork. I had been waiting to have an exhibit in old town Las Vegas. My turn finally came around in December. The night of the show a blizzard came blowing down the east face of the Rockies and came to a rest in Las Vegas, where it dropped a small amount of snow. There were maybe twenty people that showed up, mostly local people that could walk or travel a short distance, being there was a blizzard and all. The paintings looked good. One older lady said she had been waiting for paintings like mine for a long time. Wendy helped with my show. She and the kids served punch spiked with vodka, Moon juice, and cookies, bless their hearts. Nothing sold, but some people made the trip up to the ranch to see more.

My divorce to Lorraine was final in late December. It was a long cold winter and we fired up the potbelly stove in the studio. Wendy beaded and I painted and practiced my lead guitar. We had the most pleasant winter in memory. When spring came I showed the three of them all my secret places that I hiked to every day. They got used to the horses.

Up the road going toward Walker Flats is a piece of property that was the Pando place. Ray Villa from Las Vegas had bought it. I was friends with him and his family. Someone gave him a horse, and they put her in the Pando field by herself. She was white with tiny speckles of black with huge dark mournful eyes. She was so lonely. When we passed by, she used to run up to the fence and travel along with us until she couldn't go any further. She stopped by the fence and stared after us. I felt so sorry for her. This was during the period when Babe was in the cabin. I asked Ray Villa if I could put her in with my horses for the winter. He said she was 'un-ride-able' and asked if I wanted her as a gift. I said sure, and Babe and I went up on the four-wheelers and brought her down to our place. She moved in at the bottom of the pecking order. She was so timid; you never know what an animal has experienced. Maybe something desperate had happened to her; you just don't know. It is like that with dogs and cats as well: any domesticated animal has a history.

When Wendy and the kids arrived, the white horse was a part of my herd. Wendy's little girl Ursula grew to be friends with this horse and we started gentling her up. She went ballistic when I tried to put a bit in her mouth. She freaked us out. Was she crazy? I thought we'd try a hackamore bridle, it doesn't use a bit and some horses don't need a bit. A bit is simply a method of hurting the mouth of a horse just enough to make them do what you want them to do, such as steering and stopping, etc. She was a completely different horse without a bit, totally calm. When I put the saddle on her and stepped up onto her back, she was totally passive. That was the trick. I put Ursula on her back and she was so gentle, it was Ursula's horse from then on. Wendy's little boy Isaiah rode Pretty, Wendy rode Black Boy and of course, I was on Misty. It was a hot summer; we had a great time. It felt good to have kids at the ranch.

I built a large kennel-type enclosure made of heavy wire just above the main house where Wendy kept her two monster dogs. They took considerable work to maintain. The big male was spooky; I think his eyes were weak and he just couldn't see well. We let them loose for walks and stuff, but most of the time they were locked up. The lady that ran the second-hand store near the building I had been working on with Lorraine came up from Las Vegas with her husband to visit. Wendy's dogs were locked up, and the lady was admiring them. As she bent over to make like a kiss toward the big male, he lunged toward the fence and pushed it far enough so that he could take a bite at her and bit her lip pretty bad. It took me some time to stop the bleeding and calm her down. From that time on we all knew how dangerous he was, it was just a matter of time until Wendy made the decision to put him down. He had some mental problems that, coupled with his blindness, made him very unpredictable. We drove him to the vet when the kids went for a visit with their dad. The vet came out to the truck and put a needle into his rump and that was that. He got weak and looked like he was falling asleep. We carried him around back to an area where the corpses were and went home. I had never done that, put a dog to sleep.

Wendy didn't like Henry for some reason: maybe jealousy or something. Around the Fourth of July 1996, I got a call from Gregg Heschong asking me if I wanted to do a sitcom for him. I told him I was getting pretty broke and needed to work, and I accepted. I told Wendy about the job offer and asked her if she was okay with me leaving her alone for three weeks at a stretch. She said it wasn't a problem. I put up plenty of wood, packed some things and left around the middle of July. Around this time Lorraine called and asked if I would like to try getting back together again. Now that everything had been divided, there weren't any questions about ownership, etc. I told her I was engaged to Wendy. She remarked that I probably didn't trust her anymore. Duh!!!!

NEWSRADIO 1995-1999 (SITCOM SECURITY)

The show was "NewsRadio." A Grip named Bear, Glenn Davis, had been doing the show. He and Gregg were doing both "Family Matters" and "NewsRadio." Something had happened and the producers of "NewsRadio" asked Gregg to get a full time Grip for their show. Glenn wasn't happy about it; he was making two full-time checks for the week, splitting his time between the two shows.

I found a small apartment not far from Sunset Gower Studios, where the show was shooting. I literally had no money. I used cardboard boxes for my furniture. I bought a mattress and a lamp and a chair, and that was it. Wendy had given me her old telephone answering machine and a few odd kitchen things from the stash at the ranch.

I had to get a new crew. I still had all my equipment in storage. As it turned out on the small independent lot of Sunset Gower, I could get some of my equipment on the show. I was pulling down some good money. I had met a young Grip named David French while we were working on something else. I called him and offered him the job of Best Boy. He had never been Best Boy before, but he was smart and picked it up fast. He hired a couple of guys he liked, Bill Yriarte and Alex Salazar. We started off the season fairly strong. It was a fun show; we invented stuff all the time. Gregg is always fun to work for. We did three shows and then there was a hiatus: the show literally goes down for a week. The Keys and sometimes the Best Boys were carried: that means they got paid for the week they don't work. It doesn't get any better than that! I flew home to Mora every hiatus I got. I landed in Albuquerque and took the shuttle to Santa Fe. Wendy would pick me up, we would do a massive shopping for food, and then head up to the ranch.

Once Wendy arranged for her kids to be with their dad for a week and flew out to L.A. to visit. She used the time and my car to drive around to some high-end western stores to take orders for her belts. She got a couple of accounts while she was there and she visited the set a couple of times. The week she visited there were a couple of large breasted bimbos on the show; I know this because it came up later on in a discussion with Wendy.

Wendy went back to the ranch and the season progressed. She was becoming increasingly unhappy about being alone all the time and let it be known. I understood, but I also knew I had to keep doing this work again to get back on my feet. It was my shot at some income. I told her it was cool if she wanted to find somewhere else to live; I wasn't attached to the situation that much. It had been fun but it was time to move on. I didn't see myself raising two half-black kids in Mora all my life, anyway.

When I was in L.A. I sometimes got a sexy massage by a lady I knew. She left a message on my phone machine about a friend of hers coming to town, and she wanted to arrange a session with two masseuses. I am sure that Wendy accessed her old phone answering machine and listened to that message, because she started accusing me of having a girlfriend in L.A.

One day I got a call from Richard Fresques about the ditch or something; he needed money from all the members to hire a backhoe. I told him to ask Wendy for the money, then I called her and told her to give him the money, and told her I would pay her back. Well, I guess they hit it off! He had two small kids, was single and living next door. They bonded. I got a call from Henry a few months later that Wendy was gone: the ranch was empty of people. He checked it out and called me later and asked me to guess where Wendy had gone: Richard's place. Henry said he would be the caretaker until I returned in the spring.

Wendy left me with a three hundred dollar phone bill among the other problems that occurred. I was glad to be rid of her; Richard did me a favor. I wasn't happy to learn later from Richard's sister that he was sleeping with Wendy in my house, or that she didn't wait until I arrived to move out. Henry was glad to see her leave: he didn't have to put up with her shit anymore.

Wendy and I talked once or twice out of necessity, and she told me that she knew I wasn't happy about her small tits or something like that ... and what about the big-titted ladies on the show? Jesus, she was crazy ... like, the actresses on the show were going to pay any attention to me! She also told me she had found a price tag in my drawer at the ranch for a bra marked 36C. It was probably left over from when Karen lived there. In some grand case Wendy was concocting, it was evidence of my deception. This thing about her tits, what was that about? God, the insecurities! It's probably why she was more comfortable with men of color.

"NewsRadio" wow, never a dull moment! Paul Simms, the creator / Executive Producer was hot off writing for the David Letterman and then the "Larry Sanders" shows. Like its name suggests, "NewsRadio" takes place at a news radio show station in New York. All the characters are employed around the station and its offices. The cast was very special. Simms was a crazy kind of guy and the scripts were constantly late. The writers he had gathered around him were a real set of crazies also: barefoot and cigar smoking. Simms always wore a dark trench coat. They worked on the script like musicians trying to play the right notes. Sometimes the scripts, the sets, and even the actors weren't ready, but somehow it all pulled together by the live audience shoot. It was real showbiz in that respect, like live theatre.

The writers huddled by the monitors as the scenes were shot, re-writing as we went. They listened to the laughter of the audience. They could tell when a scene wasn't working. When the audience went home, the work began. We went until 2 or 3 a.m. several times: new words that punched up the jokes, new blocking of the cameras and sometimes, new lighting. It was a lot of work but I enjoyed it. The Grips shared a room with the Electricians. Joey Alvarado was the Gaffer and easy to get along with. His original Best Boy got in trouble with the production about union this and that. Joey replaced him with a guy named Matt.

Matt had some serious social problems that Joey didn't see, or maybe ignored. There was constant fighting when it came to dealing with Matt for anything, and David French reached his limit several times. We threatened to build a wall through the room to block Matt out. It all came to a head when Lonnie, the medic on the show, tried to sack out in the Grip/Electricians room one night. He was sick and on some medication. He rode a motorcycle and didn't feel he should try his commute home to Pasadena. It was just Lonnie and Matt, and Matt refused to let him sleep on the couch. They got into it and had an argument. The next day Matt told the production office that Lonnie was on drugs and trying to sleep in the Grip/Electricians room. Well, all they needed to hear was the word 'drugs' and Lonnie was called into the office.

When he came back down to the stage he was enraged and he wanted to find Matt. I was calming him down when Matt walked by. Lonnie tore away from me and rushed up to Matt. Lonnie was about six-foot and about two hundred and twenty pounds. Matt was a skinny guy, maybe five-foot six or so, and maybe a hundred fifty pounds wet. I watched the encounter unfold. Lonnie accused him of costing him his job by saying he was on drugs. He told him that he, Matt, was the biggest druggie on the stage, which was probably right. Matt always carried a stash of pot and a pipe. Lonnie couldn't control himself; he lifted Matt into the air and started to shake him like a rag doll.

He was screaming, "You can't do something like that to me." But in fact, he had. Lonnie came to his senses and let him go and Matt dropped to the floor. Well, the police came, the Producers came, and it turned into a big deal. Matt had called the police and wanted to press charges. The production people and the police interviewed everyone. Lonnie was fired.

I had written some songs at the ranch. I had enough material that Rio and Chuck joined me on the weekend in rented studios to rehearse the songs and whip them into good enough shape to record them. We had a blast. It is so fun to play live with your best friends. It is so much like good sex. Everyone says the same thing. I became friends with Kent Zbornak, the Line Producer. Living so close, sometimes I would go to the stage on the weekends and find Kent repairing the floor or painting an area of the stage. He was totally hands-on and I had to admire him for that.

One day I casually asked him if I could play some music on the stage over the weekends. He said yes, and I got keys to the outside doors. No more rehearsal spaces. The sound in a large space is so cool. We had the greatest time on the large stage with no one to bother us. We could play as loud as we wanted. We rehearsed for a year and I started looking for a small inexpensive studio near me to record us. I called the group Pilgrim, like the people that wander the earth looking for salvation in any form. It turned out David French played the guitar and had put together bands with his brother Michael, who played drums, since they were kids in Orange County. David hired his brother Michael on occasions when we needed an extra body. Michael was an ex-professional dancer who played drums. He was in the process of starting classes at a recording engineering school in the valley. David and he wanted to build a small recording studio at David's house.

I had heard stories about "Saturday Night Live" with Belushi and the gang, and this cast seemed similar. Phil Hartman had been on SNL and brought some of the zany vibes with him. After a show night it was customary to get drunk in the prop room. A wild lady nymphomaniac showed up and gave everybody a blowjob in one of the dressing rooms. The after-show parties continued to the old Columbia bar on the corner, now called Pinot's. It got pretty wild in there once the fans started figuring out where to go. There was a mix of fans and actors. Anything could happen, and usually it did: fights, sex, and debauchery were the menu for that place. Some of the cast members were married and some weren't. This made for a mix that could potentially cause trouble, and sometimes it did.

CHUCK, RIO AND PAUL, "PLGRM"   PHOTO BY
KRISTINE CRIVIER

BABE AND PAUL

We were all cruising along quite nicely on the show. Gregg really wanted to direct and he was given a few shows. His shows went well and he was slowly building a directing reel.

There was a really cool Christmas party at Paul Simms' super bachelor pad up in the hills. I decided to give him a present and I bought him the latest live recordings of Led Zeppelin. He was very appreciative.

Joe Rogan was a big pool player and I used to bump into him at the local pool halls in Hollywood. Sometimes the "NewsRadio" parties were held at the Hollywood Athletic Club, which is mostly a glorified pool hall. It was close to where I lived. The large room, which had a running track around it, has since been turned into a live music venue.

I developed a casual speaking friendship with Khandi Alexander. She asked me about my meditation practice and I gave her a copy of "Autobiography of A Yogi." It is a real closer for anyone that is interested in the art of meditation. Years later I ran into her at the Bob Hope Health Center on La Brea. She instantly recognized me and gave me a very long hug. Yes, she had finished the book and remembered me giving it to her. She was working on "CSI Miami" and had a wonderful career going on. I wished her all the luck in the world. She is a genuine good person. She reminded me of Carol Wayne: that same playful Marilyn Monroe vibe backed up with a very intellectual knowledge of life.

We usually had very nice dinners on show night that were catered affairs. For some reason one of the shows got canceled, the food arrived and it just sat there. I decided to pack it up and deliver it to the homeless. It was very rewarding to give food to hungry people. I got the idea to make it a weekly ritual of gathering up extra food and taking it to a homeless shelter I had found not far from the studio. Kent, our Production Manager, heard about it and told me I had to stop. Our producers were concerned about the liability issue. I went to the shelter and talked to the boss and I asked him to sign a waiver to release our show from any liability, which he did. He also gave me a receipt for four hundred dollars for the donation of the food I brought. I took the waiver to Kent. It worked, and I was in business! When they saw the receipt for the food, they really appreciated the situation. This meant they could deduct some of the food bill for the production from their taxes as a donation. It was a cool experience, and others on the crew got into it and helped gather up the leftovers and pack it into my car. There is so much waste in Hollywood. I always have felt guilty about wasting food. My mother would always say, "Think of the starving people in China". That sure has changed.

One of the stand-ins was talking one day of wanting to go into the producing end of film. She was a very cute lady that was a friend of Linda Cooper, the set decorator. We talked a lot. I told her that if it were me that wanted to make a small movie, I would do a behind-the-scenes of the cast of "NewsRadio." She liked the idea and wrote up a proposal that the production approved. She scraped together people and equipment and she did interviews of cast members. I actually held the mike boom on the interview with Phil Hartman. His interview was interesting: Phil got very reflective about his life and his children and his wife, etc. He wasn't his usual funny self, but we didn't think too much of it until later.

Later I was at the ranch later during the summer hiatus when I got a phone call from Patricia Butler in Chicago, who was two hours ahead of us in California, to inform me that Phil Hartman was dead. I said thanks and immediately called Gregg and told him the news. He didn't believe me, but it was true. Phil's wife and the mother of his children had shot him and then herself in their Encino home. She had been fighting with mental illness and drug addiction for some time. Maybe she caught him cheating. Who knows? Anyway, she killed him. He was dead. The cast reassembled the next spring and "NewsRadio" continued, but it was never the same again.

I was dating a cute little Chinese girl that year. She met Phil at the wrap party but didn't recognize him. After his death and the stories were all over the T.V., she finally figured out who she had met. It was so tragic, an apparent murder-suicide. The police arrived after a 911 call that shots had been fired at the family's home in Encino. The police found their two kids, a boy nine years of age and a girl six years old. As they were removing the children from the house they heard a single shot. They went to a bedroom in the house where the shot came from and found the bodies of the couple. Brynn Hartman had killed her husband, and then shot herself as the officers were in the house. Phil joined the list of people from "Saturday Night Live" that died untimely deaths.

"PLGRM" recorded ten songs in a little studio on Hollywood Boulevard. It was on the third floor of an old building and we had to carry equipment up in an elevator and down the hall. It was a fifteen dollar an hour place but the engineer was cool. I essentially produced it; it was a pretty good demo for the songs. Meanwhile, Michael French had finished a small recording situation at David's house and we recorded two more songs, completing what became the Pilgrim album. Michael mixed all the songs and I had them mastered in Hollywood. There are some great songs on the album, even if I say so myself.

After the young lady finished the shooting of her behind-the-scenes of "NewsRadio," she showed it to Kent Zbornak who offered to help her put it together. Following the tragedy of Phil's death, the footage vanished from the post facility. This turned into a big deal: the police were called, reports were filled out and eventually the footage showed up. She was able to get several screenings of her Phil Hartman interview on various TV shows such as "Entertainment Tonight," "Extra," etc. The soul searching that Phil had done in the interview I mentioned earlier, was especially poignant after his untimely death. She made a few dollars in the process. It wasn't bad for her first venture into producing. She promised to take me to dinner for my idea that sparked her into making this footage in the first place.

Phil's character was replaced with Jon Lovitz but it just wasn't the same. At the end of the fourth season we were filming the cast in a tank of water; it was the 'Sinking Ship' episode. Gregg had been negotiating his deal for the next season to direct more episodes. Tom Cherones, one of the Executive Producers who also directed many of the episodes, had come from "Seinfeld" along with a lot of the crew. The "Seinfeld" show came to an end. Wayne Kennan, the "Seinfeld" cameraman, started to visit. I don't know what happened exactly, but we weren't asked back for the next season and Wayne took over the show. It didn't really matter because in one more season, they pulled the plug on "NewsRadio." Almost immediately Gregg was offered the new Ted Danson show at Paramount. It was called "Becker" and Andy Ackerman, who also did some "NewsRadio" shows, was one of the executives as well as the principal Director. We got lucky. If we had stayed on "NewsRadio," we wouldn't have been available for this show. "Becker" went for six years.

One of the camera crew on "NewsRadio" had recently been to Thailand and was raving about his trip. He showed me pictures and brochures. I was single, a Buddhist, horny, and ready to see Southeast Asia … and I made plans! Gregg's wife Liz, the one he met in Quincy, visited the set often.

She brought her dad Jim Porter to visit and watch the show. He started a conversation in which he told me he had been to Bangkok, Thailand. In fact, he had just gone in on a condo in Phuket, Thailand. He said he would be there over Christmas and gave me his address. I had a destination.

Thai Town was not far from where I was living in Hollywood and I started to hang out there a lot: dinner, massage (which was only twenty bucks an hour then), and general sightseeing. Around this time I turned on to the Asian dating clubs around town. They were mostly Japanese, Chinese and Filipinas. I went to dances and parties, meeting women. It cost a few bucks but I met a lot of ladies. Jim Porter was back in L.A. then and accompanied me on a few excursions to Monterey Park and Alhambra where most of the girls lived and the parties were held. Although Chinese ladies are very beautiful to look at, they are too material for my tastes. If the ladies that I met are any indication, the Chinese will take over the world. Just you watch. I wanted a simple country girl from Thailand that could love my life at the ranch. I chose Thai because my research indicated that 97% of the Thai population was Buddhist. I wanted to be with a person that lived in the Buddhist tradition. Compassion. Simplicity. Do not desire what you cannot have.

I put an ad in the local Thai newspaper, The Siam Media. I told the lady on the phone to translate my ad. It said the usual with a mention of my love for Buddha. Well, that was the ticket; my phone was ringing off the hook. I met as many of the ladies that called as I could. Some were very shy and we just had tea; others came to my place and fucked my brains out. One lady called from Seattle. "How did you get my number?" I asked her. She said a friend in L.A. had called her with the number. She said she would like to visit. I asked her to send a picture first, which she did. Wow! She was in black undies with lace, like a porno. Her letter was intimate and sexy. She told me she liked oral sex the most. I reached for the phone! I sent her a ticket and she flew down. She left after a couple of days of heavy sex. We promised to stay in touch but didn't. There were a lot of interesting dates that I met for lunch or dinner. Some of the girls were too old and some were too young.

The apartment I was living in had some earthquake damage from 1994. Nothing serious, but the landlord didn't get along with the neighbor and the neighbor turned him in for some broken walls in the mutual adjoining area. Inspectors arrived and they red-tagged the place, which meant we had to get out. There was about a month left at work and I wasn't about to move. First the gas went off, and then the electricity. I didn't leave; I bought a zillion candles and took showers at the studio.

I met my Chinese girlfriend Michelle in a massage parlor. She was in a marriage of convenience with some American man she had met in Monterey Park, but she still dated me. She had the most incredible breasts of any small Asian I had met so far. Her nipples were large and almost always erect. I think I loved her. She was young and making her way in America. Her English was very broken but I got used to it and we conversed. One night she was visiting me in the red-tagged apartment, and we were in bed and going at it. She didn't always let me penetrate her but this night I was in and we were sweating. My neighbors, who also were living in their apartment, were sneaking around in the dark hallway. They knocked on the bathroom window and Michelle jumped like a scared deer. She grabbed her clothes and hid in the closet. I talked to my neighbors for a moment about something and they left. Michelle was dressed and ready to leave. She kissed me and I walked her to her car. That was to have been a wonderful sex experience. Oh well. When people are in this country illegally and they are married, they tend to be a little spooky. It was dark and all, and we had to be quiet. We weren't supposed to be in the building in the first place.

One of the Chinese ladies I met had been trying to set me up in a marriage with her young rich friend. They had offered me ten thousand dollars to marry her. I told them I was into it. It never happened, but almost did a couple of times, then went away for good.

Back in Mora, Henry was ready to leave as I pulled into the yard of the ranch. We did the customary hug and I gave him some money and he left. I was spending a nice quiet summer. I had gone through a rather hectic scene with the ad and all the Thai ladies that called. It was fun; don't get me wrong. I was chilling at the ranch. Leroy's son Shane had grown up and was now driving his bike, hitchhiking, or borrowing a car and coming up to the ranch. I was glad to have his company. He was a great kid. He slept by the T.V. and we rode the horses and worked. I paid him some money by the hour worked and it was his summer job. He learned how to round up the horses, bring them to the corral and saddle them. Wow. He could work a chainsaw like a grown man. He was a big kid for his age, and handsome like his father. I called him Shaq, like the L.A. Laker.

The Plaza Hotel in Las Vegas had been a favorite hangout of ours forever. Babe was thrown out of there more than once when he moved to Vegas. It was a calm by day, wild by night kind of place. I was having a beer there one afternoon and was sitting next to a very pretty red haired lady. She was a little plump, not my type. She looked sad and I struck up a conversation. Her name was Martha; she had been visiting her cowboy boyfriend in the area and he had just dumped her. She was an artist and a teacher, and she was staying in the hotel. She showed me some photographs of her paintings. I told her I was also dabbled in painting. I invited her up to the ranch. She accepted and said she would come visit the next day.

We went up to her room. I had never been in one of the hotel's rooms and I liked it. It was furnished in turn of the century fashion with a big steam heater coil under the window. She said that the night before she had trouble sleeping. Someone in the bar had told her about the ghost in the hotel. People have actually seen the ghost on more than one occasion. The place had quite a reputation in the old days with all sorts of famous people and events that took place within its walls. I left her there. She was a little tipsy. Did I mention she was heavy, red haired and giggled at everything?

Martha came up the next day. She fell in love with Dala first, the little black bundle of love that Karen had left, and then she moved on to Lacy. I showed her the place and told her she could stay for a while if she liked. She accepted and promised to paint a picture of the ranch for me, which she did. She stayed for a long time, actually. She even told someone in town she was Mrs. Ferrara. She said she would like to spend the winter in the cabin. I told Henry and he said, "Cool." He wouldn't have to sleep up there, just come up once in a while and look in on Martha. It worked out pretty good; it was a mild winter and not too much snow. She liked the area and wrote a lot of resumes that she sent to the local schools looking for work. One of Henry's friends was asking her out. I don't know how far he got, but it kept his attention for some time.

That summer my sister called and asked if she and my mom could visit. "Are you kidding? Sure." My sister had never been to the ranch and my mother hadn't visited for some time. They flew from Palm Springs to Denver, then landed at the small airport just south of Santa Fe in a commuter jet where I picked them up. We went up to Walker Flats where my father's ashes were and had a picnic. My mother got real misty about it. The lilacs were in bloom and the aspen trees had luscious green leaves; the white trunks of the aspens are very lovely. I took some great photos of my mom in the exact place I had deposited the ashes when the first snow had started to fall. I remember opening the brass box and dumping the ashes out. A wind had suddenly appeared and blew the ashes right into my face. I gasped. My father's ashes went into my nose. We had a great picnic.

My mother went for a walk on her previous visit when Buster, the dog Lorraine and I shared, still lived there. She tells the story about how she got lost, and he grabbed her hand with his mouth and led her back to the house. He had mystical qualities, that dog. He also went a little mad toward the end of his life. His pedigree had caught up with him. I will never seek out a pedigreed dog again: they are too mental.

My sister was in the bathroom and her back went out. She was screaming that she was on the floor and couldn't reach the lock on the door. Luckily, I had put the hinges on with the pins facing out. I popped the hinges and there she was, on the floor with one arm draped over the toilet. She was in real agony and we got her to her bed. I had some powerful pain pills; I always try to keep some around. You never know when your back can go out and mine has given me trouble all my life. I doped her up and in a couple of days she felt she could travel. She wanted to get back to her doctor in Palm Springs. I drove them to the Santa Fe airport and helped carry my sister onto the tarmac and into the commuter jet. They flew off and I returned back to the ranch. While my mother and sister were at the ranch I slept on the couch in Martha's cabin, but one thing led to another and I ended up in Martha's bed. She was so prudish, but she actually slurped when engaging in sex. Go figure.

When my family left it was good to be back in my own bed. One of the Thai ladies had called the old number and was given the ranch number. She called and asked when I was coming back, and said she had never forgotten me. I barely remembered which lady she was but I had a pretty good idea. I was impressed with her finding me and following up, and I told her I would call her when I returned to L.A.

I returned to work the next season. Chuck and Christine were living in Woodland Hills and had an extra bedroom that they offered me until I found a place to live. I accepted and stayed there for a few months.

Mone, a friend or should I say a lover of mine, called me at Chuck's house when she heard I was back in town and told me to come over right away.

Mone was a little Thai lady and she had a massage business she ran in her apartment. I saw her ad in the paper for Thai massage and started seeing her. I had developed a relationship with Mone before Wendy lived at the ranch. We used to get together late at night and drink beer and smoke pot. She was writing a book about her life. We talked constantly about authors and painters. She was an educated young lady with quite a story to tell. She was raised in Thailand by her mother and stepfather along with her four sisters. The stepfather had raped her since she was a little girl. She tried to protect her sisters by supplying him with what he wanted. She finally ran away and was abducted off the streets and sold into sexual slavery. She was held in a whorehouse against her will for two years. She was having sex thirty times a day. Girls died in front of her. She was beaten and starved and she finally escaped. The scars of that experience are still with her today. She drinks like a fish and loves to get high; I'm sure it is to forget. I comforted her many nights and mornings as she softly cried in my arms. I could not refuse her offer and left right away and went to see her. She gave me a long sensual bath and made love to me like a lover should. There was never any talk of payment. I think she really had a love for me.

I finally called Sandy, the Thai lady that had called me at the ranch, and I asked her if she was ready to spend the night with me. She said yes, so I rented a motel on Sunset and we spent the weekend together. She was so sweet, the right age and very down to earth. On Sunday I took her back to her home and went back to Chuck's.

I found an apartment and moved back to Hollywood. The apartment was in one of Joseph Kennedy's old buildings; Joseph was the father of John F. Kennedy and his brothers. He was fond of falling in love with movie stars and building a place for them to live in. It was just up the street from Paramount where I was working. The place was old world Mediterranean with tile roof and patio complete with water fountain. It is rumored that John F. Kennedy met Marilyn Monroe in the apartment next to mine for their romantic affairs. I loved it at first but the unit I rented turned out to be noisy.

I set up my paints and was actually turning out some paintings in there. Sandy called and was crying a little bit, and told me the Chinese lady she shared a house with was being mean to her. She said she was going to Thailand in two weeks and asked if she could stay at my house until then. I said okay and picked her up; she had very little. She was sleeping on the floor sharing a small bedroom with her friend Tippewon. I think I am a sucker for a woman that needs help. When she came to stay with me she started cleaning and cooking, and it was great having her around. I figured it was just temporary until she went to Thailand; what did I know? When she was gone her daughter called me and I explained that I wasn't ready to live with her mother. I had been married for twenty something years and was enjoying my freedom. She said she understood. She talked to her mother in Thailand and told her what I had said.

While Sandy was gone, Mone came for a late night visit. I still loved her. I have a thing for hookers; I can't really explain it. They have this tremendous ability to view sex like a male. It's just physical; it's not about love all the time. This may go back to my very first full bore sexual encounter with Vera, the black prostitute, that me and my high school buddies used to visit in downtown L.A. She was the first lady to ever stick her finger in my ass, which of course brought my orgasm crashing through my member like lightning. For whatever reasons, I have never forgotten Vera, still today.

Sandy came back from Thailand and she asked if she could stay with me a little longer until she could find a place, and I said sure. She was sobbing one night. I knew a little about her life and how hard it had been. She had three children and raised them as a single mother. She had worked in every sweatshop from Paris to L.A. and she seemed so lonely. Like all foreigners do, she came to America in search of a better life, to make some money. The money gets sent back to their homeland and feeds a large family in many cases. It's hard; it's a hard life they lead. We don't know how good we have it, being born in America. Anyway, she was crying and I was holding her and I asked her if there was any way I could help her. I was not thinking clearly. She said the same thing all the ladies had said: could I help her get a green card by marrying her? I told her I would do it, but I would not commit to a husband/wife relationship and she would have to sign a pre-nuptial agreement. She asked what that was, and I tried to explain to her. We found a Thai man that runs a translation service in Hollywood. He explained what it meant and helped us with our paperwork. She signed it and I married her in a small chapel on Wilshire Boulevard, and she started her immigration stuff.

Spring came and I was heading to the ranch. Sandy helped me put my stuff into storage and she accompanied me to New Mexico the first year. She loved the country. She was from the country. She fit right in; all my friends out there loved her right away. I taught her how to ride a horse. We found a Viet Nam community in Albuquerque that sold Asian groceries and she cooked Thai food for everyone. She is one of the best cooks in the world; she could have a restaurant if she wanted. The locals flipped out and Shane and his buddies showed up a lot expecting, Pad Thai, a delicious noodle dish. I was getting used to her. I had told her that I had planned a trip to Phuket, Thailand to visit Jim Porter, Liz's father, and I told her I wasn't ready to settle down before we got married. She said okay, and just said that I should take a lot of condoms with me.

At the end of the summer we headed back to L.A. and we stayed at Bill and Linda Yriarte's house in Mission Hills. Bill had married the Filipina lady he met at one of our Asian party safaris. Sandy and I drove into Hollywood every day, apartment hunting. We found a cool apartment on Bronson between Hollywood and Sunset, close to all the bus lines that Sandy needed to get to work. She was a seamstress. Her jobs jumped around a little but always close to Hollywood.

I went back to work at Paramount. It was 1998 and "Becker" was in full swing. It didn't have great ratings all the time, but the critics liked it. It was a smart show. David Hackel, the writer/creator, was an informed and opinionated person who wrote plenty of stuff meant to question the life we lead. Becker, played by Ted Danson, used to walk into the diner at the head of every show and rant about the condition of human beings and how we had to live in the midst of chaos every day. Terry Farrell played the lady who ran his habitual haunt, the diner. He was too cheap to eat anywhere else. She would calm him down as he stormed into the place looking for coffee, then the week's story would unfold.

Ted's character smoked like an addicted smoker does. He tried to quit. The anti-smoking people wanted him to quit. I wanted him to quit. Hackel kept him smoking right up to the end. Ted Danson was not a smoker; he was smoking some organic brand of cigarettes for the actual filming of the shows. They truly stunk. Ted actually started to smoke cigars. He had a little bit of high blood pressure and worked on his diet. Our craft services guy Billy, the one who took care of the food on the show, prepared him special food all the time. He ate very clean food, only whites of eggs type of stuff. He took Niacin, which made him flush sometimes. His face got beet red but his blood pressure lowered. Ted was the first person I knew to drive one of those weird hybrid cars that Honda made. He had several other cars but delighted to be part of the solution. He was part of a group that was trying to clean up the oceans.

Hackel was a writer on "The Love Boat" and had written an episode of "Frasier." He was co-executive producer and writer on "Wings." That is called a hyphenate in the biz: when you are a successful writer on a series, they give you another credit as in co-executive producer to spice up your salary. These days there are so many producers on a show it's crazy. There could be ten or twelve listed on the credits of any given show.

Andy Ackerman was an editor in the old days. He had worked on "WKRP in Cincinnati" and "Cheers" as an editor when someone gave him a shot at directing. He had a natural talent for working with the actors. He had the smarts of an editor and knew exactly what shots he needed to cut a scene together, and he has become one of the premier directors in sitcomland. He was the steady director on "Becker" for several years straight. We had great writing, great directing, and great acting. "Becker" was poised to be the next "Cheers" for Ted Danson, who had struggled on T.V. sitcoms ever since his hit show "Cheers" had finished. When the "Becker" season came to an end, Sandy and I were living in the Bronson apartment that we kept when we both went to the ranch that summer.

I had an idea to raise living Christmas trees. Sandy and I started digging up small Christmas trees, three to six inches high, and put them into pots. It was early spring and there was still snow under some of the trees. I had bought a hundred black nursery type plastic pots in Oxnard, California. We went in the 4-wheelers every morning and dug baby trees. It was so much fun and who knows, it could have developed into a cottage business.

We had a great summer; it was full of joy. It was fun showing the tricks of the mountain to Sandy, especially to a person from the jungles of Thailand. I put Sandy on Pretty and she experienced horses. She had tended the family water buffalo as a child on the farm in Thailand, but there is nothing like riding a horse. Their interaction with man is their sole mission in life; it gives them purpose. The rest of the time they just eat. It's quite a relationship we have with the horse. Some horses look forward to being ridden; we can thank the Spanish for that. They were the first to bring horses to the Americas. Imagine that: there were no horses here at one time. They escaped or were abandoned by the Spanish and easily adapted to the grass of the western United States and flourished as wild herds. Later they were rounded up by the Indians and the settlers and tamed. I don't think the America we know would exist without the introduction of the horse. At the end of the summer we headed back to L.A. Sandy found some work and I went back to "Becker."

THAILAND

I bought a ticket for Thailand that fall and held Sandy to our agreement, which was that I was going to visit Jim in Phuket. Jim gave me some simple directions. He said when I arrived in Bangkok, buy a ticket to Phuket at the airport and then spend a few days in Bangkok. He said to head to the Hotel Nana, check in and then step outside, and I would get the picture. I landed, bought the ticket to Phuket, changed some currency and found a cab outside the airport. I told the cab driver Hotel Nana; he knew right where it was and we arrived in twenty minutes. They were booked solid and they sent me across the street to another hotel. As I walked across the street there were twenty or thirty girls that said "Hello." Oh my god!

The second hotel was full but called ahead for me and confirmed some vacancy at the Hotel Nana Thai at the end of the street. I got a tuk-tuk and made the short trip to the Nana Thai. A tuk-tuk is a three-wheeled motorcycle that has a passenger seat in the back. It is a favorite type of transportation in Bangkok; I wouldn't mind having one myself. Anyway, I checked in and took a shower. It was hot in November. My room was in the back and the window looked out over a large canal. The water in the canal was dirty but interesting to look at. I changed clothes, headed out the door and walked the couple of blocks back to the Hotel Nana and the Nana district, as it is called. There is a lot of activity there. There were maybe twenty girls sitting around at a small outdoor bar in front of the Nana Hotel. The tables were filled with males, mostly tourists. The girls' wait on you and for a thousand baht will go to your hotel room and have sex with you. My favorite beer in the world is Singha and it is very cheap in Thailand. I threw down a few cold ones and tried to relax.

The flight from LAX had been around 18 hours and another hour or so in between connections. I was whipped and I caught a buzz from the 6.0% alcohol that Singha contains. A beautiful young girl approached and cleaned my table. She was maybe twenty years old, thin and pretty, and she started a conversation. I paid the papa-san two hundred baht, which is around 5 dollars, for the permission to leave with her, and we jumped in the back of a tuk-tuk and headed for my hotel. She took a shower and came from the bathroom wrapped in a towel. They all take showers first. They are shy for the most part, but as soon as the cuddling starts, off comes the towel and they get aggressive and uninhibited. It is a pleasant quality. The Thai girls I met were simple and uncomplicated. It was just what I needed after twenty some years of marriage, complications and divorces. I think I had three girls the first night; I was like a kid in a candy shop! The girls charged around twenty dollars American money for what is called a short time, which meant just an hour or so.

Baht is the Thai currency. At that time, one American dollar bought forty baht. A good hotel was a thousand baht a night. Everything was so cheap. This was going to be fun! Across the street from the small outside bar was a complex of buildings two stories high. They formed a circle around various bars and stalls selling food etc. Inside the building were strip bars, one after another. In those days the girls danced totally nude and there were thirty girls dancing in every club. The disco music was pounding and the seats were full of tourists, ex-patriots, and locals. The girls had small numbers on their bodies. A mama-san came around after every song and asked if you were all right. The girls in the clubs were a step up from the girls outside. The fee you paid to take one of these girls was a little more but worth it, and the clubs became my favorite place to pick potential love partners. You could watch them, make eye contact with them, and sometimes after their short shift of songs they would put on their bikini and walk up to you and talk. If you had made eye contact or smiled, it was enough of an introduction for them to follow through with a visit. You could always tell the mama-san what number was written on the girl you wanted and she brought her over.

I spent two days and three nights in the Nana Plaza area and then got my flight to Phuket. It was a short flight and I arrived within a couple of hours at Jim's door. He had guests staying with him but suggested I look directly down the street for a room. The street was named Ban Benjamas and it was lined with small hotel/ bars, mostly two stories high. They were whorehouses for the whalers and shippers of old that had been bought by ex-patriots from all over the world, fixed up, and now the rooms were for rent. The new owners were mostly European with a scattering of Middle Easterners who had either married Thai persons, or had a connection to buy land in Thailand. I found a great room upstairs facing the street. It was clean and neat. The lady that ran the place was an Englishwoman who always had some cute Thai girls around her. She made Thanksgiving dinner for all the guests.

If you walked two short blocks straight down the street, you ran into the Indian Ocean. It's called the Andaman Sea around there. The sides of the street were lined with little streets called sois that led off and housed bar after bar. Each bar had maybe twenty girls. It was paradise and the beach was perfect: you could get a massage for four dollars and a cold Singha delivered to your towel. The vendors walked up and down selling fresh fruit and food, as well as goods from Thailand. They sliced open fresh pineapples, coconuts and pomelos and practically put them into your mouth. The water was warm, calm, clear and that tropical greenish blue. The coconut trees pushed down to the sand and offered a little shade from the tropical sun.

The sun is hot at that latitude and people walk around with third degree burns all over the place. The best time to go to the beach is the early morning up until around noon, and later around evening time. In between, you sit in a cool bar surrounded by the many lovelies that inhabit the resort. When you get sleepy you pick out a nice girl to go home with, have some sex and take a nap. She leaves and you get up and get ready for the evening, and it starts all over. In the evening, the ladies double in number. So many girls, so little time. The area is famous for its fresh seafood. For a fish eater like me, this is heaven.

I met Jim Porter and a few of his friends for breakfast and sometimes dinner. Jim and I are the same age; we were all in our late fifties. One night I hooked up with two girls at a disco toward the end of the night. I had just bought some over-the-counter Viagra and was feeling lucky. The three of us walked back to my room and had the greatest time. One went home and the other slept with me. In the morning we met Jim and some other people across the street for coffee. The second girl that was with us reappeared on her motorcycle and joined us. I was with those two girls for a couple of days.

I suggested we go to the next beach south of us called Kata. It was cleaner water and less crowded. About eight of us piled into a songtel, a small pickup that has been rigged in the back with benches along the sides and a cover on top. Six or ten people can fit in them. It is a favorite form of transportation and there are plenty of them. It was worth it. I had to buy one of the girls a bathing suit. Paradise is all you can say when you think about it! This is the same Phuket that was hit with the tsunami, in December 2005, which rocked the Indian Ocean. Jim is there now and tells me everything is getting rebuilt and business is trying to get back to normal, but I have a feeling it will be a while before the emotional scars heal.

The two weeks flew by and it was hard to pull myself away, but I did and I arrived back in L.A. ready to work. The jet lag and the time change can cause sleep problems for about two or three weeks. All in all, it's worth it. I decided I wanted to be with a Thai lady who believed in Buddha. Most of Asia has forgotten about Buddha except for Tibet and Southeast Asia. Even Burma, now called Bhutan, has suppressed Buddhism. Thailand is the most peaceful nation on the earth. There are twenty seven thousand temples in that country. Thai seemed like the likely choice for a female mate. Wasn't I living with a Thai lady? In fact, married to her? Every wife I have had has shown up with a suitcase at my door. I must be easy; I have never proposed.

Another season of "Becker" was coming to a spring close. We had been picked up for the next season and everything was good. Gregg and our crew did a couple of sitcom pilots as usual. Pilots are a way of presenting an idea to the T.V. audience. It tries to spark some interest and if it does, it becomes a series of shows and if that is successful, it can run for years and years.

David French bought a new house and we built a studio in the back of his place, where there was a large workspace. The old owner used to build stuff out there. Funny thing, while David was crawling around in the attic one day he discovered some old guns that were worth a lot of money. The old guy that lived there had stashed them there without telling his wife or anyone.

Things changed and Michael French had switched over to digital. Everything was computerized. David and his brother formed a company called the French Brothers. The name came from my suggestion. It was based on the Dust Brothers, the ones from Silver Lake that made the Beastie Boys' early hits.

I was still writing a lot of song lyrics. I brought some material over to the French studios and off we went. I wrote a whole new album that contained eleven songs. It became PLGRM 11. Michael had the ability to take my ideas, understand them and mold them into something. I give him a lot of credit for what happened with those songs. We both loved Radiohead, early Moby and Coldplay. I bought a knock-off Radiohead "Kid A" in Phuket, Thailand and listened on my Walkman. I wrote a lot of lyrics there. Writing is such a solitary thing. The distance from everything you know can cause you to concentrate on what you have within you. I cannot escape my roots and the songs were based on my blues upbringing. Now it was called Tek Blues.

TEK BLU

LOVE IS BLIND
BUT CAN LEARN TO SEE
END THE HATRED
AND SET US ALL FREE
WE JUST WANT TO MAKE LOVE TO YOU
MAKE LOVE TO YOU
I DON'T WANT YOU TO BE MY SLAVE
I DON'T WANT YOU TO BE UNDERPAID
IN FACT I DON'T WANT ANYTHING FROM YOU
I WANT TO KNOW ABOUT YOUR NEEDS
FEEL YOUR BREATH ON MY SKIN
UNDERSTAND YOUR BELIEFS
FIND YOUR SOFT SPOT

MAKE YOU COME OVER HERE
IT BREAKS MY HEART
THE PROBLEM IS SO LARGE
IN THE QUIET THE TEARS FALL LIKE RAIN
LOVE IS BLIND
BUT CAN LEARN TO SEE
END THE HATRED
AND SET US ALL FREE

These songs progressed in the studio for the better part of two years. When we went back to the ranch again, I took the tracks with me and worked up the lead guitar parts etc. Sandy had a learner's permit and was learning to drive. I had helped her with a series of driving lessons in L.A. and now she was driving the old '81 Cherokee at the ranch. She drove it all over the property and sometimes down to town.

One day Sandy saw our neighbor Richard cutting trees in the back of our property just over the fence. We didn't think anything much until later that summer when a real estate guy from Las Vegas drove into our yard and asked about the property just behind us. He said he heard it was being logged. He was representing the owner, Richard's cousin, and the cousin wanted to sell. He asked me to show him where it was. I was interested. I showed him the place. Richard did not have his cousin's permission to log the and the real estate agent took some pictures and left. This developed into several phone conversations with Richard's cousin who lived in California. He was an elderly gentleman and he wanted my help. He wanted to have Richard arrested. His big problem was that he didn't have clear title to the place, but he was working to get his papers in order. Meantime, he wanted Richard to stop cutting his trees. He hired a lawyer and was pursuing his paperwork and the prosecution of Richard for cutting his trees. Henry thought that Richard might try to cut our trees next, and he suggested that we block our property off.

When Lorraine and I bought the land behind us, I had improved an old horse trail that connected the back of Richard's dad's land and the road up from Vallecitos to the main road up to Walker Flats. It was now a road we could use to access our new property. When I finished fixing the horse trail into a narrow road, it started to rain. Richard must have been watching the progress. Even though it had just rained and the fresh fill dirt was wet, he drove through. I saw it the next morning and freaked out. There were deep ruts in the road where I had built it up and the ruts were twelve to fourteen inches deep. I called Richard's house and his mother picked up the phone. She assured me that Richard would fix the damage. I waited but he didn't fix it. I had to bring the equipment back in and fix it with a new round of roadwork and grading.

The second day after I fixed the road Richard had ruined, I was sitting by the house enjoying an evening fire and drinking a beer. I heard a truck off in the distance: it stopped and then started, and then stopped and then started again. Someone was pulling through the small gate and entering the road we are talking about. I grabbed a pistol and took off on the 4-wheeler. I arrived in time to head off the truck that was approaching me with its headlights off. I turned off the 4-wheeler's engine and sat in the middle of the road as it approached. I could see three heads in the truck through the windshield; I thought it would turn into a big deal. Richard pulled to a stop, and I walked up to the truck and talked to him through the driver's side window. It was his two kids sitting on their knees next to him. I yelled at him for driving through when it was wet and ruining it. He said he would fix it. I told him not to drive in a truck through my property and to get his truck the fuck off my property. I told him I had a gun. He backed up the whole quarter of a mile and left the way he had come in.

The next day I went down to the Sheriff's office and told him about the confrontation, just trying to cover my ass. He said Richard had already made a complaint, and claimed I had pulled a gun on him. I told the Sheriff that I never pulled a gun on him; the Sheriff knew Richard and believed me. The situation calmed down. Richard went back to riding his horse or an ATV on the new road, which was ok with me.

After Wendy had gone down to Richard's there was a big search for Richard's mother. She was in her eighties and had disappeared, and the situation seemed desperate. When we heard about it, Shane and I went out in the pitch-black night with flashlights and looked for her. During this time Richard took advantage of the new road I had built to search for his mom and that time I looked the other way.

The next morning the search was still going on. A large military helicopter, a Huey, was hovering overhead. They landed in the large field below our house, and Shane and I thought they had found something. It was a huge thing to happen in our neck of the woods, and we hiked down to check it out. When we approached the huge helicopter we saw Tony Martinez. He ran the local bar after his father passed away and was the Sheriff at this time. He was a good friend of mine from my early days in Mora. We hugged and he told me that they were still searching, and they had landed in the field to take a leak. We all laughed and they took off.

The next day, Richard's mom Agatha was found down in the canyon where she used to live at the Grace's. Oddly enough she was found by her older son Timmy. He had come in from the south on his 4-wheeler and just happened on her by the river behind the Grace's barn. She was badly dehydrated but alive and a little delirious. She said she was trying to find her house so she could eat lunch. It turns out that she wasn't getting the best care in Richard's house. Wendy and Richard were living off his parents' welfare checks. Richard's sister Idene told me she had visited her parents at Richard's house and it wasn't a pretty sight. Wendy didn't get along with any of Richard's family and it was constant trouble.

Richard's parents were eventually taken from that house and put in a care facility in Taos. Henry assured me that what Richard claimed was his right to cross our property on the road was bullshit. It had never been a road; at best, it had been a horse and cart road but it hadn't been used since Timmy blocked it off down by Vallecitos in the late fifties.

After we saw Richard stealing his cousin's timber, we placed a large iron post in the middle of the lane where it connected with our property. I wrote on it: "No vehicles beyond this point". Well, that started something! Richard claimed that the trail I had opened up was an old county road and he reported the post to the county commissioner's office, which sent me a letter. I told them there was no proof that the trail was part of the county's road network. They said they would get back to me. I had to leave to get back to "Becker" and Henry took over the caretaking. Henry called me when he discovered the post had been yanked out and dragged down to Richard's. I told him to get the Sheriff and make a report. The Sheriff came up and Henry showed him the trail Richard left dragging the post down to his house. The Sheriff paid a visit to Richard. I'm not sure what happened at their meeting, but the Sheriff told Henry that he had been in the area all his life and had never seen this trail/road before.

Later that winter Henry confronted Richard when he was driving a large army GI truck across our property. Richard had left the gate open that led to the Walker Flats road. Henry found it open and waited; he knew who it was. Sure enough, Richard came down the Walker Flats road and started to enter our property where he had left the gate open. Henry called him on his trespassing, and Richard told him to get out of the way or he would run him over. Henry stood his ground. Henry tried to approach Richard in his GI. Richard told him not to come any closer or he would shoot him with the gun that rested in his lap. Henry said go ahead, and in Spanish told him he didn't have the balls to shoot him. Henry finally left the scene and after he left, Richard opened the gate and went through, back to his property. Henry checked and Richard had closed all the gates. Both Henry and Richard reported this down in Mora at the Sheriff's Department and there was a small investigation.

The Sheriff told Henry to block the road with berms. Henry called me and I said it was okay with me to block it. I called Ernie Olivas, my friend in Mora that had worked on my roads and in fact on the road we're talking about. He contacted Henry and they made an appointment to block the road. I told Henry to make the part that I had widened back into a narrow trail, which he did. That did it. It stopped all large vehicle travel, and Richard went back to his 4-wheelers and horses when he needed to cross our property.

Sandy was getting better at driving the Jeep. One day she came into the yard after her morning practice drive and was walking toward me with her back to the car. Sometimes the Jeep had a problem with staying in park. The door was still open and it started rolling backwards very slowly. Sandy ran toward the car and jumped in. The door knocked her over; she was holding on to the steering wheel, and the Jeep was dragging her. The Jeep slowly came to a rest as it ran into a large pile of wood. Sandy was roughed up a little. It was the Jeep's fault but she got a good lesson about cars that day.

Another time I was pulling the trailer with this great 4-wheel drive Ford diesel tractor that I had. The hitch on the trailer wouldn't stay put, so usually

I had Shane or someone stand on it as I moved very slowly. I asked Sandy if she would stand on it for me. She braced her hands against the back of the tractor. I hit a dip in the road and as the trailer jumped across it, it threw Sandy flying through the air. Thank god she wasn't hurt but she still talks about it today.

Every morning I took a walk with the dogs, regardless of the weather. I would go out the back and along the road we were fighting about, and then up to the dry lake. Sandy started to join the dogs and me. It was a wonderful event that took place every morning. I had built some benches in strategic spots scattered around the property. We could stop and catch our breath while gazing at spectacular views of the valleys that lay below.

Every day we saw where Richard would pass through and throw rocks into the holes left by the berm making. He cut trees and tried to fill them up. He even brought heavy equipment onto our place and was starting to knock down the berms. Henry saw this activity and fixed them with the tractor every time Richard messed with them. It was a running battle. Richard was like an insurgent striking in the dark. It was hard to catch him doing it.

On our walks we usually got to the dry lake and crept up slowly hoping to see some elk or deer. On many occasions we saw wild animals on our walks, it was one of the highlights of our day whenever it happened. There is something about a wild animal sighting that is so exhilarating. We explored the Indian ruins every day. We would sit down inside the walls and rest in the sun. It was a perfect spot, a south-facing ridge with an unobstructed view of the lake.

During November the elk would go into rutting season. The females would start being fertile and allow the males to mount them. The males would fight with each other over the small herds or harems of females that usually only followed one male. This was so exhausting and caused so much heat inside their bodies that they used the water in the shallow lake to cool off. They rolled and covered themselves with water and mud. This must have presented quite a target to the ancient hunters that were hidden in their rock hideouts, the same little dwellings we sat in from time to time. The bull elk has a call that signals his search for a female. The female answers with a different sound to bring him near. It is at this time of year that the Game Department sells hunting licenses. The hunters have elk calls made just for imitating the call of the females. In most hunts the females are off-limits.

You can only kill a male elk with two or more spikes on their horns. At this time of year if you sit quietly in the forest around there you can hear the elks signaling each other. It takes a certain knack to blow the small device just right. I had one hunting license issued to me every year by the landowners hunting association, which I usually gave to Henry. If one person had a permit, several people could accompany him. If you didn't have a permit you were not supposed to carry a rifle, but we always did. If someone in the group happened to see an elk and shoot it, Henry would put the permit on it.

One year Henry and our two friends Ernesto and Chemo built a small log cabin tucked away at one end of the small lake on our property. There was a small stove inside and a place to watch the lake. Chemo has hours of footage he shot on his video camera of elk playing and rolling in the water and generally hanging around. We put salt out for them and sometimes Henry put hay. It was our private sanctuary. The elk seemed to travel like gypsies from one pasture to another, slowly working their way down from the high country as the winter progressed. In the dead of winter there were elk in our garden next to the house. The herds moved through in the night, sometimes standing just outside the hay that was stacked in the barn. The horses stood with them. Horses, elks, deer, and for that matter cows, all seem to get along and can stand next to each other grazing like one big happy family. They only had a few formidable enemies and that was a rogue bear or a lion. There were lions in the area but I never saw one. Michael Grace had bear dogs and from time to time would kill one or conduct guided hunts during lion or bear season. He also did elk hunts in the high country, but that was another matter.

I was alone on my morning walk with the dogs and cutting through the center of the property. You have to keep your eyes pretty much on the ground where you are walking, or the terrain can trip you. I looked up and I saw what looked like a large dog approaching from the opposite direction. It was a large brown bear, maybe two hundred and fifty pounds, a young one. He has his eyes on the ground in front of him and he didn't see me. I think the dogs, the bear and I all saw each other at once. I froze in my tracks. I had no gun. The dogs, led by Lacy, charged at the bear. The bear sized up the situation and headed for the nearest small tree and started to claw his way up. The bear made a decision about the dogs that were approaching and the size of the tree he was climbing, and descended quickly and ran for it. The dogs chased him for a while and then stopped and barked as the bear ran off in the distance. Lacy, what a dog, she was truly my bear dog! She saved my life, I think. I called myself 'Walks with Bears' after that.

As with any show in Hollywood that runs for years and years, there are adjustments that occur from time to time. They are not always good nor are they always bad. There had been rumors of syndication deals, and renegotiating of contracts that were based on Becker's popularity as well as the impending syndication. Syndication is when a show has shot at least one hundred episodes and is sold for viewing on smaller stations worldwide. There was an unequal pay difference between the actors that was based on their original hiring. It probably was negotiated by their agents and had to do with where they were in their careers. Ted Danson was a bankable actor. He made about two hundred fifty thousand an episode. Terry Farrell, on the other hand, made twenty or so thousand. They formed an actors' walkout and were supported by Ted. It didn't last long but now the producers knew who was going to be trouble, or was already. Terry Farrell was eventually replaced. She says she quit; the production says she was not asked back. She was supposed to be a love interest for Becker but it was an asexual relationship that never seemed to move beyond flirting. When the ratings started sagging around the fourth year, they simply didn't ask her back and replaced her with Nancy Travis.

Hackel tried desperately to build a relationship between Nancy's character and Ted's character. It was still a flawed relationship that was more like Tracy and Hepburn. They fought, they made up, and they fought more. They had feelings for one another. Ted's character was so based on being the loner, the survivor of a bitter divorce, the pessimist, that he was almost set up not to have happiness or even sex, for that matter. I do think it was one of the downfalls of the show; his character seemed one-dimensional. Hackel, the creator and writer, seemed unwilling to let his character grow.

Ratings. Ratings are what everything is based on and ours seemed to slowly be falling from the top ten toward the fifties. The people that buy the advertising from the networks pay for the time their commercials air based on ratings or how many people are watching. A network and in this case their partner Paramount, were breaking even on the show. Most shows are like that unless they are a runaway success like "Seinfeld" or "Friends." Becker wasn't making any money and its future was riding on selling the syndication rights.

The news about syndication marketing was that it wasn't looking that good. Around 2002 there were some serious rumors about possible cancellation. They changed writers, hoping that something would pick the show up. There were defections among the writers and arguments about content. Ultimately Hackel won and hired new writers but it didn't get any better. 2003 was to be the last season. It was gloomy around there but the actors managed to stay upbeat. I have never worked with a friendlier group of actors.

There were a lot of musicians in the cast. Alex Désert was one of the lead singers in a group called the Hepcats. Shawnee Smith had a band she fronted that did punk attitude rock. Hattie Winston was a cabaret singer. They were fun to be around.

At the end of the season there was this drama going on about whether the show was going to come back. We were ending production in late March and they announced the return sometime in May. They were at just around one hundred episodes. The show was not selling as planned in syndication. The critics and the fans had rallied around. Paramount didn't have that many hits. "Frasier" was their one big hit but It was approaching its final year and then what did they have?

Kelsey Grammer was a former cast mate of Ted Danson on "Cheers." He made a guest appearance on "Becker" as did other well-known stars, but nothing seemed to pick up the ratings. At the last moment an order was given for 13 more episodes. There was a wonderful wrap party for the year at Barfly, a nightclub on the Sunset Strip. It was named after the film I had worked on about Charles Bukowski. That film starred Mickey Rourke, whose girlfriend at the time was Terry Farrell, the actress who had been on "Becker."

David French seemed very interested in my past experiences with The Doors. Everyone was curious and asked me over and over what Jim was really like. It was just something I couldn't avoid. He asked me about HWY, the film I had shot with Jim. He was most interested in the song Jim used that Georgia and I had recorded, "Bald Mountain." We started digging into what had happened to HWY in the last thirty years. Turns out, it is a huge cult classic in Europe. When Jim carried his films to Paris before he died, he must have let them out of his sight for a while because you can buy bootlegs of not only "HWY" but also "Feast of Friends," the other film I made. There are websites dedicated to The Doors and Jim Morrison in particular, all over the world.

He asked me about that song and where we recorded it. He asked if there were other songs. I explained about the songs the three surviving Doors recorded with us and told him I had a lot of tapes at the ranch somewhere. He told me to bring them back to L.A. I found them all the next summer; there were thirty some songs. When I got back to L.A., I found a facility that specialized in restoring old analog tape recordings. I had them baked, as they called it, and then transferred to digital. The French brothers really got into them and wanted to put out an album of Paul and Georgia songs. At this time one of the artists that they were working with, Kyle Vincent, heard the stuff and wanted to be a part of the project. He had done some restoration projects in the past and could hear the beauty of what we had. David had them all digitally re-mastered and the selection process began. Finally there were about seventeen songs that made the cut. The artwork was something that I took control of and helped to completion. "The Paul and Georgia Album," as it was finally called, contained "Bald Mountain" of course, and there was a notice of its inclusion on the album cover and Jim's name in bold print. The recordings, some done at big time studios such as Elektra, sounded fantastic. I was hoping that the interest in these old songs would generate some interest in my new songs.

Henry called me that winter and told me he had been served with papers, and that we were being sued by Richard Fresques. Soon after that phone call I got a call at six o'clock a.m. Sunday morning. There was a package for me. I kind of knew what it was, and I was right: I was being served. Richard claimed he was crossing our property and fell into one of the holes we had dug, and we were trying to kill him. I called my insurance people that did the ranch, Farm Bureau. They said they would take care of the claim and not to worry. I wanted to go to Thailand again for my Christmas time hiatus. Sandy couldn't get the time off from work; besides, her paperwork at the INS didn't allow her to leave the country.

I asked Bill Yriarte, my extra hammer on "NewsRadio" and then "Becker," if he wanted to join me and he agreed. His wife wasn't that happy with his decision and Sandy was less happy this time, as well. She was feeling married and I guess I was too. I just couldn't let the remaining time in my life slip by without enjoying what I had longed for, for so long. I guess your age creeps up on you. I was 62 and not getting any younger! I had already purchased my tickets. When he agreed to go, I helped him arrange for his tickets, etc.

He had a slightly later flight and the plan was for him to hook up with me at the Nana Hotel. I arrived a day ahead of him and everything went as planned.

Bill called me in my hotel room and informed me he was in a hotel not far from me. I told him to meet me in the outdoor bar in front of the Nana Hotel. I went down and sat at a table and soon he approached walking up the soi. A soi is a small street. I yelled his name; he saw me and came over. We embraced and I ordered him a beer. There were maybe twenty girls sitting around at various tables. Two came over by us and one asked what Bill would like to drink. Singha, he replied; I had trained him in the fine art of Thai beer back in L.A. We drank a toast to the success of our meeting. The flight from L.A. was about eighteen hours. It was grueling, to say the least. It's the only bad thing about traveling to Thailand.

We sucked up a couple of beers and two girls joined us. They were very young and cute. This was Bill's first glimpse of the female population and it was a good one. He didn't quite know what to make of their aggressive attitude. I told Bill to take the cute one to his hotel and allow her to take a shower. They both knew what I meant and left. I stayed drinking. In about an hour they returned and Bill had a huge smile on his face. He got it right away. He chose another and then another. By the time night fell, we were in full party mode. I showed him all the go go bars across the street and he connected with a woman that looked surprisingly like Linda, the lady he was married to. I didn't see him the rest of the night.

Tan was a tall, thin Thai girl and was sitting a few tables away from me. She wore dark glasses but I could see she was crying. I approached her and asked if she was okay. She told me she was waiting for her guy to come back. I think it was a generic story. All the Thai girls are waiting for that one guy who will marry them and take them to the States or Australia … anywhere but Bangkok. The only way to make it in Bangkok is to hustle tourists. I calmed her down and we talked. She was in a sad mood. The man she referred to told her he would be back. She was turning tricks and waiting. She was really sweet and quite easy on the eyes. I asked her if she was hungry; she said yes and we walked across the soi and bought some Muslim style chicken, which we both enjoyed. She was settling down and asked if I had a room nearby. I told her it was right across the street, and she asked if she could freshen up. I took her to my room and one thing led to another. We visited for two days until my flight for Phuket left early in the morning. Bill and I had tickets on the same flight, and we said our goodbyes at the same time leaving the two girls standing in the alley behind the hotel. The taxi pulled off and that was that.

We drove the 45 minutes to the Bangkok airport and boarded a small plane headed to Phuket. Jim Porter wasn't going to be there this time, but it didn't matter. I had made reservations at the same English lady's place I had stayed at the year before. Bill's birthday is one day away from mine in November, and we celebrated our birthdays with our good fortune to be alive and in Phuket. The first thing we did was grab our towels and head for the beach. We plunged right into the warm Indian Ocean, just what we needed after being in Bangkok. Bangkok is not on the ocean and it has a severe pollution problem. It is congested with autos and motorcycles trying to get from point A to point B. The fumes, mixed with the intense heat, are a little overwhelming. The ocean felt good; it was why we came.

We got out of the water and walked up to our towels. We lay down and right away there were cold beers, fresh pineapple and pomelos being offered to us. We ate the fruit and drank the beers and went back in the water. The massage girls were twenty feet from us. It costs two hundred bhat for a one-hour massage on the beach, which is around four or five dollars. We both got one and a half hour massages, then back into the water, then another beer. This was living! There were bar girls all over the beach in small groups spending the day, waiting for the evening when their shifts started. They all worked in the open-air bars that lined Ban Benjamas and the surrounding sois. It made the scenery even more breathtaking.

Phuket and its famous Patong Beach are picture perfect. The sand is white, the coconut palms bend over toward the ocean, and there is a gentle ocean breeze to keep things a bit cool. It was toasty in November when we were there, between 85 and 90 degrees most of the days. It was wise to go inside around noon. We usually took a nap and toward the evening we met up again.

There was this great little kitchen on a small soi that I ate at almost every night. I took Bill and we ate the steamed whole fish that was fresh caught that day. It was delicious. They served a chili sauce that you spread on the fish and it was beyond belief. We were to be in Phuket for seven days and we took some tours, one to the Phuket town in the center of the mountainous jungle. It was old and was the center of the fishing and importing business in the south of Thailand. Bill bought silk shirts and sarongs for everyone he knew. They were pretty cheap and quite beautiful and hard to resist. Down below the small city was a bustling harbor. We took a tuk-tuk for a visit to the harbor. When we returned to Patong later in the day, we started to amble around to the various bars. There were so many girls that it was overwhelming. You have to use good judgment or you could go bonkers!

Bill met one girl that he got along with and he pretty much spent all his time with her. She was 19 or 20 and had a very cute personality as well as being easy on the eye. I lost track of Bill for a day and a half. I saw her when I walked by the bar where we had met her, and I asked if she had seen Bill. She told me he had gotten sick and he was at her house. She led me there through holes in fences, down a small alley through another fence, and across a field. There, behind all the business of tourism, were the workers' quarters: row upon row of cement two-story buildings. We entered her room and there was Bill lying on the floor, pale and weak. He had been throwing up and had diarrhea for two days and was too weak to move. He told me he was getting better. The sweet young girl had given him some Thai soup and herbs and brought him back from what I think was dysentery. He said he remembered eating some shellfish. That could have been the cause but nevertheless, he was a few pounds lighter when I saw him.

The time passes fast when you're having fun. It is one experience to be alone in a place like that and another experience to be with a friend. It magnifies the encounters, the experiences, the fun. I like it. Bill is a good traveling pal. He had been to the ranch a few times and we hung out good. He is one of the most generous people I have ever met; he would give you the shirt off his back. When he saw the conditions those people live in, his heart went out. He tipped heavy, like me. He even arranged to send money to a couple of bank accounts of girls he became fond of. I think I later talked him out of that. I told him they all had the same story: the bank account; I will wait for you; I love you; please help me. Porter calls it the 'sick buffalo' story. Somewhere, every Thai girl has a hardship that needs help. Their father's buffalo is sick and they need money to send home for the buffalo. They relate the story and it's hard to resist.

We were there for Thanksgiving and Sheila cooked a turkey dinner. Where she actually got the turkey, I don't know. She was an ex-patriot from

England and had married a man who worked in the Middle East oil fields. A lot of the people there had ties to the oil fields of the Middle East. She had been divorced for some time and like I said before, she always had cute girls with her. If she was a madam, she never let me know. I would rather think she was bi and those were her girlfriends. Her son had a bar in the Nana Plaza and when we went back to Bangkok, we looked him up. I recommend Sheila's guesthouse and restaurant on Soi Sansabai, Patong Beach. She was quite sweet and always made sure we had what we needed. It was only eight hundred bhat a day, which was around twenty bucks or so. Cute girls were always cleaning your room and tending to your every need. They even learned to cook scrambled eggs and bacon in the morning: no easy feat for Thai girls that never ate scrambled eggs with melted cheese and bacon, let alone had never seen a bread toaster before in their life. Even butter was a new experience for them. Thailand doesn't have a dairy business to speak of, and the Thai people were raised on coconut milk and soybean milk. Good coffee is hard to find, so most places serve instant coffee. Yuk. There are some places like the German hotels and the more expensive big hotels that serve good coffee but at Sheila's it was instant.

Cows, as we know them in America, do not exist in Thailand. There are no big open spaces for grazing like in the U.S. All of Asia is like that, so beef is a rare commodity. In the small villages a buffalo or a cow would be slaughtered occasionally and the meat would be sold house to house, but it was rare. Now there is a McDonald's on every large street. Where is all that beef coming from? My guess is Australia.

After what seemed like the most glorious beachside vacation two horny guys could have, we headed back to Bangkok where our two favorite girls from before were waiting. We spent a couple of nights in the Nana area and then back to the Bangkok airport for the flight back to L.A. By the time you do two weeks in Thailand, you are so burnt out that when you finally get into your seat on the plane, you are ready for some zzzz's.

We got back to L.A. and went through the usual jet lag experience where you sleep a lot. But still, we went back to work on "Becker" the next day. I had very little for my sweet little wife. I was beginning to love her; she had so many qualities I loved. She was meticulous. She cleaned the apartment like it was a surgical operating area. She cooked with an intensity that was scary. She had a desire to learn and she asked me questions about everything. She enjoyed the American movies I took her to. She asked me questions about them and I did the best I could to explain. It's surprising how much she got from her limited understanding of English and the pictures. I guess pictures have a way of conveying the story line, which is probably why even silent movies were successful. They extended the "Becker" season and it continued until the spring.

Sandy decided to go to the ranch for only two weeks and take the train back to L.A. Her job was going good and she didn't want to lose it. Previously she had left her job and stayed with me at the ranch for several months. She then had to find a new job when we went back, and that was getting old.

Henry told me the guy from our insurance had been in contact with him and was waiting to come to the ranch. He came up when I got there. He was a bit skeptical in the beginning: after all, we had sabotaged the road that Richard had claimed he got hurt on. It was up to us to try to convince him that Richard had no right to be on the road and that he had, in fact, been trespassing. The trial was practically a year and a half away, so we had plenty of time to research.

Our lawyer's name was Ron Childress. He came from Albuquerque and was retained by my insurance company. He seemed to enjoy making the trip up into the high country. Henry and I walked him all over the place and he took new pictures. We had already taken a set of photos of everything and every incident that had occurred, going back to the illegal logging and the placing of the post to block access to our property. He saw the piles of petrified wood I had gathered and remarked that his young son just loved petrified wood, so I gave him some. We gave him a list of people he needed to talk to, the first being Henry's father. He was the most knowledgeable, since his father's father had pioneered the land. At one time they had owned damn near everything up to the forest. Gradually the Trujillos sold off pieces until they didn't own anything anymore.

Ron warmed up to us after awhile, and we felt great by the time he left with his list of people to interview. When the time came he was to contact Henry, and Henry would set up a group of people to interview. Henry was listed along with me as the defendants. It appeared the insurance was going to pay for the whole deal. Henry and I breathed a sigh of relief. Henry didn't have any extra money, and I didn't want to spend my small savings.

Henry and his son Dennis wanted to buy a small piece of land from me. We went back and forth until we came up with a plan. I went down to the county and pulled a land division permit. Originally they only wanted to buy an acre, but I didn't want to go to all the trouble for one acre and I talked them into 10 acres. It was a quiet little corner sandwiched in between Pando's and our property. There was another small seasonal pond there that was very pretty. It was a little overgrown but it had a grove of beautiful aspen trees around the lake. The elk and other game also liked to play there. Henry's plan was to get it surveyed in the fall, but it turned out that it was quite expensive to get a surveyor up there. We tried the best we could to count the feet off and build a small description of the land. I guess Henry or Dennis had told some people about the impending deal because it became known and other people started to ask about buying land, but I was not interested.

The seasons had gotten increasingly drier for about the last eight years and every year there were many more fires. You may remember the Los Alamos fire during the spring of 2000. The fire was so devastating and the area so large, that the smoke plume could be seen from outer space. The wind brought the smoke directly over Mora for some time. In the late spring of each year there were two factors that came into play: dry lightning storms and heavy wind coming out of the southwest. The lightning often struck in the wilderness areas, sometimes fifty times in one night. They didn't all start fires but some did, and those often went undetected for days until the size of the fire was already large.

In the case of the Los Alamos fire, it was a controlled burn. That is when the Forest Service decides to let an area burn just to clear it of dead trees and undergrowth. Well, what a time to start a fire, during the spring windy season. Duh! Anyway, Henry was helping me clear and thin as much timber as we could around the house. We got an invitation by a logging company that was in the area to come and give an estimate on our timber. We made arrangements for the estimator to visit; we figured about thirty acres behind the house could be harvested. We wouldn't make a ton of money, but the thinning was the only prevention against a fire that could sweep down on us from the southwest direction. They started logging that fall and continued through the winter. There was not much snow that year, which was good for the loggers and their machinery. They made and improved roads all over the place; that was a perk for putting up with the logging and the after-mess.

When they logged down close to the road that Richard and we were arguing about, I told them to leave the debris on the road; it further discouraged anyone trying to pass through the land.

Henry informed me that his son had backed out of the land deal, and his wife was scared about spending their savings on the land. I told them it was cool; I didn't want to sell the land anyway. Our lawyer wanted to break the lawsuit into two parts: the road issues, and the accident Richard says he had on our property. He legally maneuvered to have a first trial by the judge to determine the question of the road. The second trial would be about the so-called injury Richard claimed was due to Henry's and my maliciousness.

THE TRIAL

First, the determination of the road question: at this point, the insurance company that was representing the claim didn't want to pay for the trial to determine the status of the road. Ron suggested I retain Michael Gregory, my lawyer of twenty-five years, to join our team. He had more knowledge of the locals and their ways. I might add that he was also a close friend of Timmy Fresques, Richard's brother. Timmy had blocked the road in the first place in the late fifties, at the request of his father. Timmy was now the grounds keeper/landscaper at the Pendaries Golf Course in a small town tucked back into the mountains halfway up from Las Vegas to Mora. Michael Gregory was a principal participant in the development of the area and his son was the main real estate person in Pendaries. Michael could get to Timmy where an insurance lawyer from Albuquerque could not; they made a formidable team.

We had satellite photos of the area showing the logging roads and the county roads, and sometimes the photos were good enough to see trails. The photos showed the small groupings of the houses and barns of the various ranches. It was a good way to see the area and get an idea of the layout. It was easy to lose track of the layout or even become lost when walking through the forest. The trial was in early spring and there was snow on the ground. It was supposed to have taken place in Mora but was moved to Las Vegas due to the heavy snows the night before.

Richard's lawyer was an obnoxious Spanish man from Albuquerque, an ambulance chaser. Everyone knew Richard was lying except him. His witnesses were all so lame, some said they had hunted bear there in the sixties and had used the road. One said his dad had taken him hunting in the old truck there in the fifties. Wendy, my old girlfriend and now Richard's wife, detailed what she knew of Richard's and my relationship. She talked about my getting mad when Richard assumed the land below me and waved "Hello Neighbor". She brought up things from the past that was supposed to present me as a mad, vengeful person. Upon cross-examination of Wendy, Childress asked her if she was seeing Richard while she was living in my house. Of course, the answer was yes. That did a lot to discredit her testimony, whatever it might have been.

Now it was our turn to call our witnesses. A lot of my old friends stood up for me and I will never forget them. Michael Grace testified that it had always been a horse trail; it was too narrow for anything else. He lived on the next property over and used the trail a lot. Ricky Lucero, my old friend from the high country, testified that he only used it with horses and had never seen a vehicle on it. To cap it all off Timmy, Richard's brother who he didn't get along with at all, testified that he had sealed the small trail off from vehicles at the request of their father in the fifties. That was the definitive testimony. Richard had a reputation that preceded him. The trial ended and I went back to "Becker." We felt we had won. We still worried; Richard and his lawyer were capable of anything. We had to wait almost one year for the judge's verdict.

Jacob Pacheco was the son of Fermin Pacheco. He had inherited the land directly in front of me; he was my neighbor in front of my house. Jacob hired my loggers to dig out his pond and put in a road down to a future cabin site. A long time ago the two properties, his and mine, were owned by the Trujillo's. The house I was living in was right next to the acequia, which later turned out to be the boundary between Jacob's land and mine. When he finally fenced his place, he positioned the entrance just below my property line. When the bulldozer pushed the road to his cabin site, he did it right below the ditch, which was about thirty feet from my bedroom window. I freaked out. I asked the bulldozer operator if he was on the right path. He said Jacob had laid it out, and he was only following directions.

Jacob's kids were all getting older and his boys were high school age. They started to have all night parties down by the lake. When the guests came and went, they used the new road next to my house. Their cars had amps and extreme equipment that was so loud the dogs crawled under the bed. No one could sleep. They had such a big graduation party that it got out of hand. Someone killed one of my neighbor Benji Vigil's cows, and they cut it up and barbecued it. Someone else broke into the small cabin up the road from us. The law came down on them, but the parties continued on a regular basis.

It wasn't the same anymore. When I had come, it was the most solitary place in the world. Pristine. We had the mountain to ourselves. Now civilization was creeping up the road. I was alone most of the time. I started to feel that maybe my time there was over. I was angry all the time. I was fighting with Richard behind me, and the punks and their disrespect in front of me.

About this time Ray Villa, the neighbor directly up from me who had given me the white horse, visited and told me he had heard I wanted to sell some land. Someone had told him about the land Henry and his son were trying to buy. He said he wanted to buy some more land and would I sell him some. I asked him how much and he said the whole thing. I laughed. He made me an offer of four hundred thousand dollars. It was a good price, not huge but not small. I told him what was going on with the case with Richard, and that I didn't think it would be a good time to sell the ranch. I needed to settle the question of the road that cut through the property; he understood. I also informed him I was intending to thin the timber behind the house. This stuff was going to take a little time. I told Ray that he had the first option to buy, and we left it at that.

The next spring as the snow began to melt Henry started to irrigate the fields. He loved to irrigate. Every time he turned the water from our ditch into the field someone came along during the night, and shut it off. It had to be Richard; he was the only one using the water after us. They went back and forth. Henry finally resorted to taking all the water and running it down the mountain. He claimed that Richard and his family had no water rights on the property Richard was irrigating. They had been stealing the water for years. He said "If he wants to fuck with me, I will return the favor."

The Fresques people came at night to steal the water. Henry said he heard the voices of what sounded like several people, echoing from the backfield. In the morning Henry would go to the backfield and change the work the night raiders had done, so the water again flowed down onto our place. This went on for a while until one night Henry had taken his shower and was watching T.V. and getting ready for bed. Evidently the Fresques night raiders had come a little further than usual, and were looking down on the cabin where Henry was now laying in bed. The T.V. was a little loud. In the morning he saw where there were bullet holes around the bathroom window. Henry claimed he didn't hear anything. One bullet passed through the glass and imbedded into the wood on the wall. The night this happened, Henry could have been standing in the exact spot the bullet passed through. He could have been killed. He called the Sheriff the next morning and there was a short investigation. I think the deputy went down to Richard's house and asked him if he had shot at Henry last night. Of course Richard denied it, and explained the legal difficulties he was having with Henry and me. There were no charges pressed. Henry freaked out. His wife told him he could no longer stay up there alone. I lost my caretaker.

That was enough to send me over the edge. I could no longer deal with the problems that kept arising. It had become a liability instead of a paradise. What about all my animals? When it all boiled down to what mattered about the ranch, it became clear that my animals were a big part of it: my horses, dogs and cat. I couldn't take them with me if I left. I had some serious questions to figure out.

Jacob Pacheco, the neighbor who had just put a road next to my house, was doing some fencing and came across the ditch to visit. He came into my house and sat down. He had heard that I was considering selling the place and he wanted to announce his interest in purchasing it. I told Jacob I had a tentative deal with Ray. Jacob offered me more money and he returned a few days later with an offer that was twenty thousand dollars more. In addition, he wanted me to carry the paper, something I hadn't considered before. By carrying the paper on the loan, I could make a nice additional chunk of change in the transaction. I decided that if someone has to make that extra money, it might as well be me instead of the bank! I thanked him for his offer. I had no intention of selling to him after how he had treated me as a neighbor.

I told Ray Villa that I had a better offer and he said he would match it. I told him I was looking for a new caretaker for the upcoming winter since Henry had quit. Ray told me if he was to buy it, he didn't want anyone but himself to be caretaker of the place. We signed an agreement that allowed him to occupy and eventually buy the place upon the completion of the legal battle and the logging.

One of the main conditions of the sale was that Ray and his wife, who was a lovely person, would care for my animals until they expired. They had been at the ranch all their lives and the thought of taking them to a new place was unacceptable. Henry had brought one of his daughter's German shepherd pups up to the ranch. We named her Queenie because she was the most dominant female ever. As she grew older she became very aggressive. She was a good dog for a walk: very alert, didn't run off and stayed with you. All five of the dogs were female. The other dogs stopped walking with me when Queenie went; they were intimidated. Queenie didn't like any other dog getting close to me. Oh well, it gave the other dogs a rest.

Queenie had the habit of chasing Black Boy. He was the only male horse and easy to pick on. Black Boy kicked her a couple of times in the head. You'd think Queenie would have learned. The cat that had adopted the ranch ten years earlier was called Kitty. As a puppy, Queenie tried to chase her. Kitty had conquered a lot of dogs; Wendy's big mastiffs wanted to eat her and she knew how to fight. She would evade them for a while and then turn on a dime and rake their tender noses with her razor sharp claws. That really is the cat's only weapon against a larger animal. It seemed to send a message for most dogs but Queenie never did give up. Her nose was constantly scratched and bleeding.

Leaving the ranch and my loved ones was by far the hardest thing I had ever done. It was worse than a divorce. My knees and feet were giving me a lot of trouble and I couldn't walk like I used to. My back was still the same problem from time to time. Riding the horses became very painful. I felt like a fighter who had passed his prime; I was taking too many punches. I had built a one-of-a-kind ranch in the middle of nowhere perched on the side of the most beautiful mountains in New Mexico. I had 'been there' and certainly had 'done that.' I was proud of my memories, my friendships, and the way I had conducted myself. I could always come back and visit Mora. Some of the best friends I ever had live in Mora and I will never forget any of them: my compadre, Amber's father Leroy and his whole family; Henry and his wife Elsie; Johnny Bonny; the Graces; Michael and Maria: the list is long. I shall return forever to Mora, if not in body, in spirit. My father's ashes are scattered in a purple iris patch in Walker Flats. My mother, who is in her mid-90's now, has asked for her ashes to be placed near his. So far I have never thought of a better place for my ashes, as well. It's funny how the Ferrara's found their way to New Mexico and then up a long dusty dirt road to Walker Flats, but they did.

Sandy and I planned to go to Thailand together for once, and I bought tickets for late November of 2002. We were still living on Bronson in the large one bedroom apartment. The apartment was on the third floor and had an east facing wall that was made of glass and a large balcony that received the morning sun. We made a small garden of pots; Sandy had a green thumb and no matter what she planted, it flourished. The view from the balcony allowed me to see a person placing a for-sale sign on a condo complex across the street. I walked over and we talked. I took a look and it seemed like a good thing. It needed a lot of work but the price was right. David French's brother-in-law, who is in real estate finance, helped me. I put a down payment on it and it was ours.

Sandy had a small house just south of Bangkok in a province called Samut Prakan. Her son and his fiancé were living in it, and Sandy had a room upstairs she called her own. Sandy's house and the rest of the community had been built on a converted rice field. With time, the houses sunk and filled with water when it rained. They filled up the ground level floors with cement. This lowered the ceiling and when I visited in 2002, my head was banging into the rafters and I had to walk bent over. Whatever. The Thai people are traditionally short, and this didn't affect anyone but me.

I borrowed David French's video camera for the trip. I was to see Thailand from inside the culture, no longer as just an American tourist. Sandy had two brothers that were Marines and stationed in Sattahibe. I paid for a van they rented from a fellow Marine and we drove up to Sandy's dad's house. Sandy's family were rice farmers. Sandy's birthplace in Lop Buri, was in the middle of the central rice fields of Thailand. Her brothers were cool. I couldn't talk to them much but we all enjoyed Thai beer, which leveled the playing field. Sandy's father was in his early eighties and her sister, who recently had returned to her father's house when her husband had died, was living there with her small niece. There was a little trouble in the family due to the recent change of the will. The will left the house to the sister; it usually goes to the whole family, mainly the son.

The visit started off pretty good with plenty of beer I purchased in Lop Buri. The house was in a very small village in the middle of the country. It was a traditional pole construction. The floor of the house was elevated on large beams so that underneath there was an area about 10 feet high that could be used for storage of rice and the tending of the buffalos that every rice farmer had owned in the old days. The elevated style of the house was also useful during the flooding that happened periodically during the rainy season. The rainy season in Thailand is like nothing else you ever saw. The drops of water are huge and the clouds that drift up in the summer from the Indian Ocean once a day deliver a monsoon type rain. The rainy season lasts for three to four months. The water table is rather shallow and the main source of drinking water is the rain. Every roof is equipped with a system of collecting the rain and storing it in large ceramic pots: by large, I mean maybe four feet high and at least four feet across. The yards in the country are lined with these large containers. Sandy's father had maybe eight or ten and they were all full.

On the way to her father's house we stopped at a sacred temple, Sarat Buri, where the footprint of Buddha is encased in a shrine. This is very far off the beaten path and only a tourist that is looking for the sacred spots in Thailand would be there. Mostly it is Thai pilgrims that have made the journey with a scattering of foreigners. The respect and worship that the Thai people show for Buddha is awesome. They are forever conscious of their faith and it is the thing that draws me to them. Even the girls that prostitute themselves on a daily basis light incense and say a prayer on the way to work. The population of Thailand is made up of 95% Buddhists. There is a lot of worshipping going on. The people reflect this ethic in their demeanor. They are the most respectful and courteous people I have ever met.

I tried to photograph the temple and the footprint the best I could. Her brothers got into the photography like trained grips, helping me carry and organizing the flow of traffic in front of the lens. They were great; I liked Sandy's family so much. They made me feel at home. Most of the arguing over the transfer of ownership of the house was done in Thai but I could hear the voices slowly getting louder as the two days progressed.

There wasn't enough room at Sandy's father's house for everyone to sleep so late at night, drunk and singing, we walked to her brother's father-in-law's house a mile away. We slept there in another traditional platform house on the edge of the fields, with crickets and frogs singing to us all night long. We were awakened rather early by the crowing of the family rooster; he was very vocal! The houses are not sectioned off with walls and hallways like a regular house, but are big and open. People sleep along the walls a little distance from one another on the beds that are on the floor and are draped with mosquito netting. Oh yea, did I mention mosquitoes? It was hot and the first idea is to dress lightly at night. Shorts and tank top felt comfortable until the next morning when the bites became noticeable. Wow. I learned quickly about getting eaten at night. Never again, I don't care how hot it is!

Sandy's father was great; he had been a doctor in the military for years and was a well-respected man in his village. Up until recently, he was giving shots and taking care of his villagers for pennies. Sandy's mother died at an early age and her father stayed a widower all this time. Sandy's sister Somled had raised all the kids. Her husband had died and she was raising her granddaughter, Ploy. It was good that Sandy's sister had moved back to his house, as her father needed someone around.

At the end of the visit we left in the van and stopped at another famous Buddhist site on the way back to Samut Prakan and Sandy's house. Wong Pachan Mountain is another place Siddartha had visited. It was a great experience for me to see her humble beginnings: the heart of Thailand, the rice producing regions in the center of the country.

We had some time left on our two-week vacation. I bought two tickets to Chiang Mai, a city in the far north that grew up around a famous Buddhist shrine. A long time ago in the fourteenth century, a wandering Thai monk had returned from India with a small piece of bone said to be from the corpse of Siddartha. Ashes and bones are revered in Thailand; the same is true in India where Buddha was born and died. The Monk brought the small piece of bone to the prince of a small province in northern Thailand, and the prince decided to build a temple around the bone. There was much debate about the exact spot the temple was to be located. The story goes that they placed the bone on the back of a sacred white elephant. The elephant was turned loose and the villagers followed the animal for three days, waiting for a sign. The elephant eventually made his way up the only small mountain in the area and lay down. It was settled. It was the sign the people were waiting for. The Prince built the temple on the small mountain, and the town of Chiang Mai next to it began to grow into a city.

The city of Chiang Mai is built along a river. It is at a higher elevation than the south of Thailand and more temperate. The center of town is lined with market stalls selling the crafts of northern Thailand, which are the most artistic in all the country. The weavings of the north are famous. In the cool evenings we walked through the marketplace and I bought several hand woven silk weavings.

We took a tour to the hill tribe region up near the border with Burma. The people that inhabited the area were a mixture of Chinese, Burmese, and Thai. One tribe called the Long Necks is famous for the women wearing a series of rings around their necks. It seems to stretch their necks but I think it is an illusion. The village was reached on foot, and the trail was shared with elephants and the people that tended them. This truly was the most exotic thing I had ever experienced, right up there with the time I got lost in Bangkok on my first visit to Thailand.

That time, I was drunk and the taxi driver took me to an out-of-the-way brothel, the kind where there are thirty ladies sitting behind a wall of glass and no one spoke a word of English. The smell of opium was in the air. The women all looked at me as I sat at a table and had a beer. I was just drunk enough to rationally choose the youngest one to go upstairs with. Even in my drunken state, I think I put on two condoms. I never ventured out into the suburbs alone again, it was too scary ... but something about the scary makes the sex so vivid and wild! It's hard to explain. The anxiety and fearfulness seem to heighten the experience. That is another story.

We bought several hand made items in the Long Neck village, mostly weavings of silk that they wove on ancient looms made of bamboo and wood. One of the stars of the village was a young woman named Mana. She sang songs and accompanied herself on a guitar that her brother had carved from the trunk of a tree. She sang a few songs popular in America in English; the tourists ate it up and she made a small bundle of bhat for her efforts. I photographed her with the video camera singing her songs.

We visited a couple of other famous sites, like the caves where the Buddhist monks hid during one of the invasions by the Burmese. The caves were natural formations with shafts of light from holes above that illuminated shrine after shrine built into the walls of the dark, cool underground grotto. Before our visit to Thailand came to an end, Sandy had a contractor named Poon come to look at raising her house up and rebuilding the first floor.

He gave her a price and she agreed to send him the money from the United States. He had done several houses in the area and his work was great.

This trip was different, I saw Thailand with new eyes. Her small community in Samut Prakan was a friendly place and I made many friends. Sandy had a younger son named Boonyarit who lived with his father. He was ten years old and very handsome. When we arrived, he came to stay with us and Sandy and he spent valuable time together. They made up for a lot of time they were apart, and it was good for both of them. He didn't have a bicycle and I promptly bought him one. Every kid in the world should have a bicycle. If I had the means, I would head the 'Bicycle For Every Kid' foundation.

Boonyarit and I got along great. None of her family or neighbors spoke English, so Sandy did a lot of interpreting the best she could. We had great dinners with the neighbors joining us every night, great quantities of Thai beer were had by all. The food was purchased fresh every day and everyone helped cook. Every night was a feast. At night it was a little bit warm upstairs in our bedroom but with the help of a fan and open windows, we managed to sleep. What a great trip! Sandy's other son Bancha and his girlfriend Bun were planning to get married the next year, and we all looked forward to the remodeled house and the wedding upon our return the following year.

THE TRIAL

The trial in New Mexico was set for March 18. We did "Becker" while facing constant threats of the network pulling the plug, meaning the end of production. I had David French take over the job of keying the show and I left for the trial. For some reason my feet got extremely sore. The doctors thought I had gout. I couldn't put my shoes on and I had to wear slippers for the whole trip. It probably was the stress.

Our lawyer Ron picked me up when I got to Albuquerque and we proceeded to Mora. He checked in at the Las Vegas Plaza Hotel, and I stayed with Henry and Elsie up in Mora. The night before the trial was to begin in the Mora courthouse it snowed about 14 inches, which pretty much shut everything down. We made our way to the courthouse and found out the trial had been moved to Las Vegas. That meant all the witnesses, as well as Henry and I, had to make the thirty mile trip south to Las Vegas.

The judge that presided over our case was Eugenio S. Mathis, and he just happened to be Henry's father's lawyer from the old days. Henry had helped him get elected several times. Ray Villa, the man who was buying the land from me, was also a friend of his. Ray was going to inherit whatever decision the judge made about the road. Ray wanted the land to remain private, of course, and he wanted to block any access to the land he could.

The lawyers had prepared their cases based on the depositions everybody gave and the raw evidence. They presented aerial photos of the land. It clearly showed the logging roads for the most part, but the road we're talking about was not visible. This was good for us. At the last minute I found an old letter from the lawyer that was doing the title work on old man Fresques' property, the same property that Richard had inherited. The lawyer just happened to be my current lawyer, Michael Gregory, my second counsel. Richard's dad Floyd had written on his survey map that the road in question, the road that Richard claimed was a county road, was a stock access for the property owners that bounded the area. Along with various testimonies from my neighbors and others, this proved beyond a doubt that the trail was not a road. We had to wait for the judge's ruling, but we left after two days of trial feeling very confident.

Ray Villa and his wife Rosemary attended every day of the trial; they were among the only people in the audience. I was sure his relationship with the judge and his visibility at the trial would count. We waited month after month for the ruling. Nine months later we got it. It was about the same time the insurance company settled with Richard for his bogus accident he claimed happened due to the closing of the road. The judge ruled in our favor. He politely said that Richard had not sufficiently proved his case and it was over. When the insurance settled with Richard about his medical claims, they made him sign a document that stated he could never open the case about the road again. I think that meant it was settled for all time. I hope so, for Ray and Rosemary's sakes.

I was upset that the insurance company gave Richard any money at all. He was lying: it was insurance fraud. At one time the lawyers suggested that we get someone to follow him around and photograph him doing work and riding his horses, etc. It never happened. They paid him around thirty thousand dollars. I am sure his lawyer took plenty, and Richard had to pay his medical bills out of it also. Ron, my insurance lawyer, was free but Michael Gregory cost me around ten thousand dollars. That was just about exactly what I had made selling the timber behind the house. Oh well, at least the property got thinned.

Sandy and I went back to New Mexico early the following summer to finish the paperwork with the people handling the sale of the land. The transaction took several days to complete, and Sandy and I slept in the small trailer I had parked in Henry's yard. It was fun, like camping out. We finished the transaction in Vegas and left with a cashier's check and an agreement to carry the papers on the rest of the money Ray owed. Ray has the right to pay it off early. He hasn't missed a payment yet. I trust those people. Based on New Mexico law, the language in the paperwork states that after two consecutive missed payments, I can initiate foreclosure proceedings and become the owner of my ranch again. I doubt it will ever happen, but anything is possible. I bought a few items I needed like a new car, computer, and a Canon GL digital camera.

The sale of the land in New Mexico was complete around the first week of June 2003. In late August of the same year we went back to "Becker" for its final season. It was a short order for thirteen episodes. We had a great final wrap party at Barfly again. It had been a good show and for the most part, working on it had been a pleasure. We all said our goodbyes and shed a few tears. Ted, Alex, Shawnee and Hattie were all so personable and polite to the crew, we truly had a family thing going on. I shook David Hackel's hand and told him thanks for the experience. He thanked me and wished me well. He had bought an avocado farm somewhere near Ojai and was going to spend some time there and think. It should be a good thing for him. Who knows, maybe he will come up with another great idea. Ideas come and go, as we all know.

It was Christmas of 2003. Sandy arranged with her boss to take four weeks off and we headed for Thailand. Sandy's son was getting married upon our arrival. I took my Canon digital camera and was able to record the entire ceremony. After the wedding we went to Sandy's father's farm where I was determined to interview him on camera. He had led an interesting life. He was a doctor in several wars and had stories beginning with the Indochina war, where the action between the French and the Cambodians spilled over into

Thailand. The Thai men fought alongside their neighbors to stop the French from taking more of Southeast Asia. Sandy interviewed him off camera and got him to open up about many things.

When Sandy was 11 years old her grandmother lived with them and as she was dying, scolded Sandy's mother for being hard on Sandy. She told Sandy's mother she would take her with her upon her death. Three days after Sandy's grandmother died, Sandy's mother went to sleep and never woke up. She was dead while she was still in her thirties. I don't think anyone knows for sure what she died of.

Sandy's father Boonjan went on to talk about the Japanese that were all over Southeast Asia during the second World War. They were trying to find a route over land to get supplies to the coast of Burma. This was the famous time of the "Bridge on the River Kwai". He remembered details that only he knew. This was what I was after: first hand accounts of life in Thailand. I would like to interview all the old-timers and record forever the events of their lives. He got out his journal he had kept for all those years; it was tattered and brown with age. As he thumbed through the pages, he read the history of his children and their children. It was magnificent.

The neighbor had several pigs, and the stench from their shit was so overwhelming I couldn't breath. We had planned to stay for several days but we cut our visit short and headed back to Sandy's house. We had some time on our hands and I bought us a trip to Koh Samui, an island in the Gulf of Thailand. We stayed right on the beach for a week and we had a great time. We had massages every day on the beach for around four dollars, and ate fresh seafood every night for dinner.

We returned to L.A. and Sandy went back to work. I didn't have any work planned. 2004 turned out to be a dry year for Gregg and our crew. We did some pilots but nothing seemed to click.

I was approaching retirement age and I was ready. Looking back at your life is an interesting experience. The minutes seemed so long and the years flew by. Time does pass by fast when you are having fun, and my life has been fun! Of course there were bad times, but they were so outweighed by the good times that they seem insignificant in comparison. I have always let the flow carry me. Sometimes I have been ahead of the flow and other times trying to catch up. Like the wind, the flow can take an interesting path at times. The one thing that seems to be obvious is that the inter-connectedness of people is so complete a system that it's invisible.

I recently saw "Crash." It is a very unusual film. It manages to give the viewer a sense of this inter-connectedness I talk about. I won't tell you what happens in the film, only that it leaves you with a spiritual feeling, an overview. It's like you are hovering above and able to see the movement of people and things, yet you are right down in the slime. The horror and the resurrection. What goes around comes around, and all that. Wow. It is the thing that made me gravitate toward the cinema in the first place. I can't speak enough about "Crash". Let me know what you think.

I have essentially retired from gripping and the film business, but I feel my true contributions are hopefully yet to come. I am making music and painting. I have a website so all the kind people around the world that have come forward and made contact with me can have a place to talk to me, see my current photography and paintings, listen to my music, and view an occasional piece of cinema that I produce. I'm retired but not done. The glow of creation is still there. I am not sure what it is that drives me, but I seem to need to express myself. Oh well, as long as I don't hurt anyone, why not?

I feel attracted to the stories of the small people and the forgotten souls that inhabit this earth. There is a guy who lives under the freeway on-ramp at Hollywood Boulevard. I see him every day when I take my morning walk. I want to make a movie about him, but I am a little scared to approach him. I have said "How you doing?" to him, and he replied" Fine." Fine is an interesting choice of words for a hobo to use. Maybe he is not a hobo or homeless, as we call them now. Who knows? I think about that guy as much as I think about who Brad Pitt is fucking. It all seems important and meaningless at the same time.

I also want to help children who are struggling without parents, without food, you know what I mean. Maybe I want to help Father Joe in Bangkok with his orphanages. Maybe they need someone to clean up or repair the buildings or something. I want to pay back for the life I have had. It wasn't a fancy life but a good one. So much stuff happens when a person is a child. It follows them forever. Every kid needs a bike, some food, and some love.

Not too long after I sold the ranch I had a dream that featured Black Boy, my famous packhorse. He was jet black, as his name suggests. I was in the corral working with him and cleaning his feet. It was warm and the sun felt good on my back. He was in a pleasant mood. He was always gentle to be around for his size. He was from thoroughbred stock and looked like a large racehorse but he didn't run well; that is why Jake had sold him to me. He sure did pack well though. The three of us covered a lot of trail. You could fire a gun from his back and put fresh meat on him and he never put up a resistance or freaked out. Two days after my dream, Ray Villa, the guy that bought the ranch, called and told me he had found Black Boy dead in the corral. There were no signs of foul play and he couldn't figure out what had happened. It hit me hard. I mourned for days and days. I am still not over the loss.

Not long after that he found Lacy, my best dog, the one that saved me from the bear, in a sleeping position behind the small cabin. She was dead also. I knew they were all getting old. We are all getting old. These losses helped to finalize the end of the era of the ranch. The animals were the soul of the ranch.

I think of the ranch always; the ranch and New Mexico are always in my dreams. In the end you are nothing but a body that is falling apart and a mind full of your memories and dreams. If you are lucky like me, you will have a lot of memories and dreams to fill the void of getting old, incapable of living like you did when you were young.

CDBaby.com is a website where we are selling "The Paul and Georgia Album." The reviews that are posted there are great. There has been a radio show in Portugal designed by Rui Silva that was dedicated to the album and its significance to The Doors legacy.

The new Doors manager, Jeff Jampol, took over when Danny Sugerman passed away. He seems like a bright, super Doors fan. He contacted me and we went to lunch one day. He tried to make me feel important, like an "I was there" kind of thing.

Somehow I feel that if The Doors hadn't been so pig-headed about managing themselves, they might still be The Doors today like the Stones are still the Stones today. They needed a good manager, one who could hang with them, who could keep it together and try to protect Jim from himself. Siddons never stepped up and became Jim's friend. He never really had a handle on what was happening. He went to Paris when Jim died, but he never saw the corpse. The myth that grew from that inconclusive report was perhaps a double-edged sword. It provided for endless speculation: was Jim alive? It kept The Doors in the press for years. They tried to continue as a trio but it failed.

The other edge of the sword was that there was no closure, not like James Dean where there was a corpse and you could mourn. The mourning of Jim Morrison was confused. However, he has joined the ranks of James Dean and lives forever as a myth of staggering proportions. I meet people from strange lands that know who both of them are.

Jeff Jampol has contacted me and informed me that he thinks he is finally going to get my films "Feast of Friends" and "HWY" packaged on a DVD. This is great news!

There is talk of a Doors documentary. Jampol told me that Dick Wolf, the creator of the "Law & Order" franchise, is producing it with his documentary partner directing, his name is Jankowski. I just hope it is not another sensational trip like the Oliver Stone film. "Law & Order" is very dark and predictable. Jampol is making an attempt to involve me in some way. I would be proud to stand next to these projects in anyway I can.

I did an interview, set up by Mr. Jampol, with a writer from Rolling Stone. He wanted to know about the two films, "HWY" and "Feast of Friends." He had heard that Jim carried the films under his arm when he arrived in Paris. Bless Jim's soul, he was so proud of our little films. When he died he supposedly had left them in a brown paper bag at a friend's house in Paris. That brown bag had writings as well as the two films in it. Its contents were recently auctioned off somewhere. This is probably the answer to the mystery about the bootleg copies throughout Europe of both films. Today you can buy a bootleg copy on eBay.

There are websites devoted to "HWY" and constant chatter from internet travelers about Jim's famous film. I hope that someday it can be seen in all its splendor, digitally enhanced and given the full treatment that modern equipment has to offer. It's coming and I hope I live to see it. It has already been forty some odd years and nothing. I never made a penny off that film. Now I have my fingers crossed.

When I talked to Jampol, he made reference to wanting to put out "HWY" as it should have been. That scared me. The Doors have wanted to use the footage forever. Frank and I are in sync that the film has to remain as Jim left it. It was the only film that he completed, besides film school. You wouldn't change one of his poems because you didn't like it, would you? They only want to make some money with Jim's image. Only a Jim Morrison fan understands.

When I packed up the ranch I found some Super-8 footage of the making of "HWY" that I cut to 'Bald Mountain.' It is a nice little music video featuring Babe, Frank, Jim and me. I threw in some shots of Georgia and Rio for good measure. It will be available for viewing soon.

A Doors collector named Jerry recently sent me a letter telling me he just purchased an old issue of a Teenset magazine from 1968 that used my photos for the cover and story inside. It would be nice to remember all the magazines that used my photos. I plan to archive them on the website, like a museum.

Jim and I didn't just take photos; we had experiences surrounding the times we spent together. I managed to get it together enough to shoot film, but most of the time we were caught up in the experience.

I heard recently that the dark and dangerous legacy of The Doors was still a current topic and ready to be exploited any time. Well, dark and dangerous: there is a certain amount of research that goes on. Jim and the rest of us were doing research. There were no barriers between Jim and me. We had lived as close friends and that included the good and the bad. We were stripped bare of the normal concerns that photographer and subject experience. I was able to penetrate; this was really my most valuable asset as a photographer. It was something I must have learned in acting class. I had the ability to direct my subjects in a way that put them at ease. Ask any photographer. It's not easy to gain the trust of your model but once you do, you gain access to the kingdom.

I am still practicing the art of portrait photography with my step-granddaughter, my friends and their families and anyone else that will sit still for my camera. Once I start shooting, it is like time has stood still and nothing has changed. It is the same feeling I experienced when I started: the collaboration becomes complete and the contact has been made. The rest is mechanical: pushing the button at the right moment. At the right moment!

So much of life is about timing. If I hadn't met Dawson I wouldn't have been in the band and met the girl that helped to put me in jail. If I hadn't been on parole from jail, I wouldn't have gotten a job at Urie's commercial house. At Urie's I met Bailey, and he introduced me to Ron Joy. At Gamma I met Pamela Courson and reconnected with The Doors.

Staying in the moment. The right place at the right time.

FINAL THOUGHTS AND CORRESPONDENCE

I was watching KCET one night. It was a beautiful documentary of a Brazillan Tribe deep in the Amazon. My wife sat down and asked, "Is this the olden days"? My wife is Thai and had never seen anything like this. I said "No it is right now". They were mostly naked. I mean naked. My wife stared at the screen. They were caught up in ritual and the passing on of legacy. There was such jubilance. I think that was what Jim was trying to explore. A place where the Shaman has the most power after the King. In this particular tribe the people of the village turned against the Shaman. He made a mistake about something and the people killed him. The Lizard King went into a foreign country. He Shamanized. He made the mistakes but made his point, and the people tried to kill him. They wanted him in jail. He wasn't welcome anymore.

Jim bent over on one foot shaking the Mariachis, keeping time, he seemed to lose his balance but no, he would shift to the other foot without missing a beat. He took huge drags on the cigarette dangling from his lips. He was trancing. Now-a-days trance music is very popular. They are electronic Shamans. Hypnotizing us with repetition. I am so deep into this metaphor I can hear "The End" The Doors song with the long instrumentals, Jim trancing, the audience in rapture.

The phone rings and I am snapped back to reality. A familiar voice and interesting timing, for at that moment I am thinking of them. Ray Manzarek says "Hello man, how are you? " Wow" I say. Funny I was just writing about them. We do some small talk...Ray says "I am going to be 67, who would have thought." I told him I was only a few months after him. Ray says " So I got this email from my agent. Some Hollywood people want to buy the rights to Jim"s script "The Hitchhiker". "Can you talk to them and find out what's on their mind?" He asks me who owns the script for "The Hitchhiker". I tell him probably the Coursons. Ray " Well you co-wrote it, right?" "Not really co-wrote it", I say.. " but I was pretty close to the project." Ray knows about my fascination with the "Hitchhiker" script. He says, "Well, you know more than anyone else, will you talk to them?" I answer O.K. He says he will forward the e-mail from his agent to me and let me take it from there. I ask about Dorothy. "She is fine, we're raising some chickens and we're about to go shopping for some fruit trees at the nursery." We say goodbye.

The email comes through as we hang up the phone. Ah...technology. Now the whole idea of a Shaman is that once he loses control, spirits and knowledge channel through him. He can heal the sick, predict the future, but he loses control. Usually he eats something or smokes something that is hallucinatory...and during this intense drug state he does his magic, his stuff. So out of control at times that it doesn't resemble human activity. Maybe animal or ghost but not human like we know it. Jim did drugs and alcohol and danced wildly to the musical drum beats, whatever it took. He wanted to reach that trance state where he became the Shaman. I am convinced he was not in control at times, leaping and writhing about the stage. Some of his poetry came from his mouth for the first time in this state. If you knew him in his natural state, as I did, sober, quiet, almost shy at times, you would know what I'm talking about.

So Jim writes the short script "The Hitchhiker" in order to have a map or picture to follow so we can shoot a screen test. Now, after all these years, someone from Nashville or Hollywood or somewhere wants to make a feature film based on that short ten page script.

Up to this point this book has been a memoir. Now I am going to report what has happened recently. I'm going to publish the jist if not the real thing of all the e-mail and phone conversations that took place from Ray's phone call until now. You will see how complex all this crap can be.

Paul Ferrara

♦♦♦♦♦♦♦♦♦♦♦♦♦♦♦♦♦♦♦♦♦♦♦♦♦♦♦♦♦♦♦♦♦♦♦♦♦♦

Begin forwarded message: To Paul
From: T.K.
Date: Tue Jan 24, 2006
To: Ray Manzarek
Subject: FW: "The Hitchhiker" motion picture rights

Hi Ray...Hope this finds you well. It's been awhile since I've seen you. This got forwarded to me...Looks legit, so I thought I'd pass it on to you for you to decide.

Best Regards T.K.

Hello,

We are producer/screenwriters working with Tony Romano of Romano/Shane Productions (I, Robot; Catch Me if You Can). We are interested in contacting Ray Manzarek regarding the acquisition and development of the unfinished screenplay "The Hitchhiker" by Jim Morrison.

The piece is featured in the book "The American Night: The Writings of Jim Morrison" published by Vintage. We are currently attempting to track down the film rights. Any help that you could provide us with would be greatly appreciated. Thanks so much.

Sincerely,

....

Finally someone gets it. For years I have known that "The Hitchhiker" script is the key to many things including Jim's film "HWY". Now someone else is interested. Well, I called them. We have a nice talk. They are young film makers working out of Nashville, Tennessee. of all places. The brother I talk to says he read the script in Jim's book ten years ago and never forgot it. He now has some connections and wants to complete the script and make a feature film. He says he wants me to co-write with them. Sounds good to me. I tell him I will pass this on to Ray.

....

Paul to Ray:
Ray, I talked to the Buckholts brothers and they seemed cool. I sent them an excerpt from my book that described the circumstances surrounding

the creation of the Hitchhiker script and the subsequent filming of the hitchhiking scenes that evolved into the film "HWY". They want you to do the music.

Ray to Paul:

"Sounds pretty good. They may be on to something. Could you send me the pages from your book again?"

....

I send the pages from my book to Ray and the Buckholts boys like I said I would.

....

Ray wrote:

"Now in regards to these two guys, they did not do "I Robot!" Evidently they are 28 years old and this may be a fishing expedition. Do not send them anything until you talk to Jeff Jampol. He suggests we keep this project in-house. I agree. " I think, unfortunately, that they just want to run with the name Jim Morrison. Hey look, we have the rights to Jim Morrison! Shit, we can do that ourselves."

I send them a copy of HWY.

....

From: John Buckholts Jan 30

Paul, " Very interesting. Reminded Paul (my twin brother) and I of our film school days...the drugs, booze and improvisation with the camera. I think we owe it to Jim to build on his original premise and create a well-crafted, thought-provoking script. We see this as a film noir piece set in the abandonment and isolation of the desert. Does that make sense to you? A surreal experience that speaks about American society (not just in the 60's) and one's loss of soul because of it. Because I am curious...what were your thoughts on Stone's' film "The Doors"? I myself am not a huge fan of it... but I do respect his body of work. "Platoon" is the definitive Vietnam War film. "Natural Born Killers" blew me away (visually and with the soundtrack) but really lost itself by becoming a victim of the very idea it was trying to parody. Stone glorified the violence and became one with the media that he ridiculed.

We are excited about working on this project with you.

From Ray Manzarek   Feb. 2

Well, call Jeff anyway and see what he has to say. I agree on HWY, great shots of Jim in desert and in car. Sunday is my birthday! 67! Who would believe it, huh? Made it this far. Of course, it's really all because of Dorothy. My girl.

From Paul Ferrara to Ray   Feb. 2

Jeff and I had lunch a while back maybe six or so months ago and he said he wanted to put me together with someone about the coming documentary. I felt he was picking my brains. He never called back. The in-house as you call it has left the HWY project alone for so long, I have given up hope. I don't know if Jeff sees the true value of Jim's project. Meanwhile, there is Frank Lisciandro who keeps telling me he is close to a deal on "HWY" and for me not to talk to anyone. I discovered some 8mm footage of us making HWY that I have cut into a music video for "Bald Mountain", the song Georgia and I recorded and Jim used in the soundtrack. I was thinking of releasing it as a give away inside my autobiography that is almost done, "Flash of Eden". Between the Hitchhiker script and the film HWY there is a story and a DVD that is possible that can be true to Jim and maybe improve upon his idea. I just looked at HWY several times as I was burning a disc for you. There are some incredibly bad choices in the editing. I don't know who was in charge, Frank or Jim. The titles suck and for the most part the soundtrack sucks. { except of course for "Bald Mountain".} The actual hitchhiking and the Shelby Mustang footage is pretty good and Jim looks great. You know, he was sober in those days and it shows.

From the Buckholts twins:

I'm waiting to hear from Jeff Jampol on the Morrison/Courson estate's response to our idea. I have a feeling that Jeff may be hard to deal with. That being said, hopefully we can get Ray onboard and get this project going... John..

Paul to Buckkholts twins

Ray wrote me that he and Jeff think you are only fishing. They told me they couldn't find your credits and don't know who you are. You have opened a can of worms. They think they can shop Jim's script themselves. If you have some concrete financing plans now would be the time to tell them about it. This is just a heads up and I really didn't tell you this. They are very covetous of all the material.

From: Buckholts:

We understand the concern in regards to our limited credentials... we'd like to sit down and meet with you and Jeff. We're not involving ourselves in this endeavor to waste anyone's time. bla, bla, bla,... The three of us (Paul Ferrara/John and Paul Buckholts) would make up the creative team fronting the development of the script. Romano/Shane would secure the deficit financing, distribution, etc. We would be more than happy to include Ray Manzarek in any capacity he sees fit (including Executive Producer, Creative Consultant, Composer, etc.)

We hope this helps. It would be very disheartening (to say the least) if they decide to move forward on this without our inclusion. That being said, we have enough irons in the fire to keep us from losing any sleep over it...PS - Please feel free to share our thoughts on this with Ray...we need him in our corner. Let's make this happen...If not for any other reason ---for Jim.

Paul to Ray:

Ray, I very politely explained the situation to the Buckholts brothers. I tried to express your concerns and leave it alone. Somehow they have included me and you in their plans. It's flattering but I am not holding my breath.

....

I call Jeff Jampol and we schedule a lunch/ meeting. It goes well. He is a powerful person that dominates a meeting. I tried to explain what my vision for the project consisted of. He wants me to work for them to put both "Feast of Friends" and "HWY" into a condition ready for a release.

Thirty-six years after Jim handed me the ten-page script for "The Hitchhiker" my slumber has been awakened. I divorced myself from the past and had moved on. The sadness and disappointment I endured when my two films were put on hold and locked up in an estate controlled by two old fogies, who probably never met Jim, took its toll for awhile and then I became satisfied that I had done what I had done and was happy and proud to have done it. The films lived on in spite of a Doors management that has never even explored what it is that remains in their vaults. They let people sift through the boxes and take pieces that fit their need. There is footage that has no sound. It may be there and then again it may not. Who knows? They don't seem interested enough to spend the money to have the footage reassembled.

After my meeting with Jeff Jampol he sent me an e-mail that outlined his ideas about what we had talked about:

....

Hi, Paul: Feb 16 2006

Thanks for the great hang today. As we discussed, I wanted to outline for you the scenario I see working as we move forward together:

After discussion between Ray, Robby and I, and after my meeting with you, what I'd like to do is undertake to get the Hitchhiker, HWY and Feast of Friends completed, put into the best shape possible, and ready for release, hewing as closely to Jim Morrison's vision as we can. Robby, Ray and I feel that as one of the original Doors' inner circle, or "Rabbi," as I like to put it, you are in the best position to creatively supervise these projects, under my direction-and of course, I take my direction from The Doors themselves. However, as I told you during our meeting, I am a manager- not a creative director, writer or editor. I leave the creative process to The Doors and you, and I will guide this project from a management and marketing point-of-view.

The way I'd like to move forward is with you as the producer of the project, and as such, to share in a piece of the profits.

As we also discussed at our meeting, I will have to discuss this with the Morrison and Courson families, as well as Densmore, and obtain each of their blessings before we can commit in stone, but I don't foresee any major problems there. In the meantime , if you feel comfortable, let's start moving forward.

Welcome (back) aboard, thanks for being there for us, and I am very grateful to have a chance to work side-by-side with you!

Thanks Jeff

....

Feb 17 from Jeff Jampol: I just got the okay from Densmore.

John and Paul Buckholts wrote:

Paul,

We are not willing to stand idly by as Jeff Jampol blocks our planned adaptation of Jim's The Hitchhiker. Jampol's short-sightedness and lack of respect has only fueled our resolve. His hijacking of Morrison's name and legacy is sickening. We would like to contact both estates and explain our interest in the unfinished screenplay and our idea for a feature film based on the screenplay by Jim Morrison.

That being said, after speaking with Jeff Jampol, it seems that he is not interested in our proposal. We do not trust Jampol and are not certain that his actions and words spoken at your last meeting weren't meant to just appease you. We wanted to contact you first and allow you the chance to consider our idea and make sure that we leave out all of the politics and dirty dealings. Basically we are asking for your approval out of respect. It we reach an agreement and the project moves forward, you have our word that it will not be done without your inclusion.

Sincerely, J and P

....

They write again after talking to Jeff J: They are not sure where I stand and they are not sure why I forwarded our message to Jampol. They say that it is typical Hollywood bullshit. Regardless, if I am not on board with them...then they are out...period. What have I gotten myself into? Thanks, Ray. Now I know why you wanted me to talk to these guys. I have suffered enough about these projects.

....

From Paul to J and P,

I thought you were ok with me forwarding our correspondence. I am in the middle. I will work with whoever is in charge of the project. I have a lot at stake emotionally with the project. I will wait to see who gains access to Hitchhiker. If you get the rights to Hitchhiker I will be on board with you. I promise.

From Buckholts boys:

Then we shall do our best. We didn't mean to sound condescending...it wasn't directed towards you...more toward our frustration with the process.

We'll keep you posted. Regardless, we'd like to sit down and talk with you. We'll be in LA. Let's have a drink.

From Jeff Jampol to Buckholts:

I think you may have been confused a bit. I represent the Morrison and Courson families as well as The Doors Music Co.

When you tell Paul Ferrara you "want to speak directly to the estates, " you ARE, in fact, speaking to the families when you are dealing with me.

Having said that, and after direct discussion with the Morrisons and the Coursons, they appreciate your interest and thank you for your inquiries, but the families do not wish to move forward with you - or your project - at this time.

I have copied the families and other relevant parties on this email.

From Jeff J. to Paul... on March 4,

The estates are going to be fine with our arrangement. I spoke with them, and while they still have to give me formal approval, I am confident they are supporters.

....

After watching what happened to the Buckholts twins I realized that I was dealing with a Jeff Jampol that was a little bit unprofessional and perhaps greedy when it comes to exploiting The Doors and the Estates. I was proceeding slowly and not getting my hopes up too much. Jeff publishes an item on The Doors website, "The Lizard Lounge" in response to a fan's request to have Feast of Friends officially released. "Ray, Robby, John, Paul Ferrara and I are working on this already. I'll let you know when we have something to report. And yes, HWY, too."

....

I get an email from a guy calling himself Jay Becker. He wants to warn me about Jeff Jampol. I will quote only a small part of the email that was quite long. "Jeff Jampol is quite possibly worse than Sugerman ever was in terms of business practices, decisions and stepping on people to get to the top. Jampol is selling out The Doors legacy and going over the heads of the three surviving Doors to release half hearted, lifeless, tasteless rap/remix versions of Doors classics. I know you're a very private person and a close friend to Jim Morrison. You are one of the very few that were loyal to his memory and Doors fans around the world will be forever thankful. We cannot wait for your new book. But please, please, please...Do not allow Dutkowski (the

Doors webmaster) or Jampol to get too close! Thank you for your time. I do not expect a reply. This is the last time you will hear from me.

JB

....

Oh my god, are my fears actually correct? Am I really swimming with the sharks once again? I was so looking forward to finishing my old projects that I was overlooking a lot of gut feelings. I called around and investigated some of this JB's accusation . I heard conflicting reports about Jampol. I didn't know who this JB was. I forwarded the email from JB to Jampol and wanted to get his take on what the guy was saying.

....

Email from Jeff Jampol To Dave Dutkowski and Paul Ferrara Mar. 23....

I'm already working with Paul. He's a great guy, and we are friends.

He, Ray and I are in the midst of launching a new project, so he already is a "member of the team"!

I wouldn't worry about those guys sending that anonymous email. They're just disgruntled fans...as you know. Just keep doing what you're doing. You ARE The Doors archivist, Paul Is a member of our team, Ray and I are the best of friends and are working closely together....and I never met or saw Danny in a Rehab.

This is all most likely stemming from Paul Edge, who loves to try and divide our camp because Ray and I turned down his remixes. Don't sweat it.....comes with the territory."

....

I decide to proceed but to leave a paper trail of my ideas and discussions if possible. I call Ray and tell him some of my ideas about HWY and how best to combine it with Jim's "Hitchhiker" script. I told him about my thoughts regarding the presentation of "The Hitchhiker", filming a reading of the script in Royce Hall, UCLA. He liked the idea. A while later, I have another meeting with Jampol and verbally lay out the plan to film the reading of the script. He also liked the idea. I thought about that reading and the filming a lot...there was something wrong and I didn't quite know what. I read the script several times and finally found the answer: there was very little dialogue. What were the actors going to read? I hated the idea of the actors describing the scenes, the pictures. I called Ray and told him about my concerns. He saw my point. It came to me in my sleep. Pictures of the script a storyboard of all the scenes, drawings depicting the actual visuals that Jim had written. I loved the idea too much. I called Ray with the new idea. He got it. I had gone on-line and found the local artists that did story boards and began choosing the style and artists; it had to be just right. I then communicated this change of plans to Jeff.

....

To Jeff May 10...

Jeff...after much deliberation and having studied the "Hitchhiker" again and again, I came to the conclusion that it is very light on dialogue and heavy on images. Therefore I think the stage reading is not going to work. I came up with a plan to have the pictures Jim described made into a beautiful story board, like the "Ah Ha" video from the eighties music video "Take On Me". Then we photograph it and have a good vocal reading of the script over it. This way, Jim's pictures are presented and no one is making up stuff.

I went on-line and found several story board artists that, on the average, charge between three and four hundred dollars a frame. We need several thousand dollars worth of pictures. But they will live forever in your vaults and once the DVD comes out, possibly could be used for advertising. See the web site below.....

I think both projects are do-able in no more than six months depending on the post process. I could start June 1st. I think a reasonable figure for my direction of these two DVD projects is 25 thousand. A profit share as you mentioned could be negotiated. It should be a play or pay situation as it is subject to decisions beyond our control. No written contract. I should also be given credit as director on any materials I produce, no matter when or where they are used.

I had mentioned that I was leaving for a couple of weeks to New Mexico. I will check my emails from time to time. Kick it around with the others and hopefully we can have a deal where I feel comfortable, and my efforts are not in vain. I have talked to Ray and he loves the idea of the story board film. Am sending him a copy of this proposal. He also requested a copy of the Hitchhiker script. I thought you could send him the same one you sent me as it is in good shape..

Paul...

....

7-20-06

TREATMENT FOR FINISHING F.O.F

AND HWY

There is overwhelming evidence from the fans that completed, good quality versions of "Feast of Friends" and "HWY" are desired.

These two projects were incomplete, yet they made it into the bootleg market and have proliferated.

The idea we have is to finish the two film projects and still maintain the integrity of the original concepts.

THE HITCHHIKER / HWY

I quote from Jerry Hopkins book "The Lizard King":

"By late February 1970, Jim had started meeting with James Aubrey, the one-time programming chief at CBS TV, then between jobs but soon to be president of MGM. After their first meeting, Aubrey turned to an assistant and said, "Jim Morrison's going to be the biggest motion picture star of the next ten years. He's going to be the James Dean of the seventies."

"This resulted in a contract and an agreement to have Jim work with Michael McClure in turning Michael's unpublished novel, 'The Adept', into a screenplay." "Aubrey and Bill Belasco, a former agent whose company, St. Regis Films, was the joint venture partner in the project with Jim's company, HiWay Productions." "Belasco told me, Jim was co-writing the script with McClure. He told me at lunch that if Jim's talent could be harnessed, he could be a filmmaker. Whether that meant director, writer, or producer, or a combination, we didn't know." "As the script was being written, Aubrey moved into the President's office at MGM and Jim began meeting with directors, including Sam Fuller, one of the most influential filmmakers of the post-war period. He was a hard drinker, too, and while Jim had great respect for his talent, ultimately Fuller was found to be unacceptable by MGM."🗙 During all this talk of Jim becoming an actor, he came to me and expressed his fear that he hadn't been in front of the lens as an actor before. He knew I had done some acting and asked my opinion. I said that before we disband the "Feast of Friends" crew, (Babe, my sound recorder, and I), maybe we could shoot a screen test. He thought that was a great idea and we agreed he should write a short script we could use for the test. A few days later he handed me the script for "The Hitchhiker". I read it and was blown away by the depth of the short ten-page piece. I came up with the idea to shoot a brief scene from his script, where he is alone and hitchhiking in the desert. I scouted the locations and we proceeded to shoot the scene. We had film left over and time on our hands so we kept shooting, and Jim became more and more relaxed in front of the lens. We were accomplishing what Jim needed, acting experience.

1. This proposal would begin with the interviews from the James Aubrey - Bill Belasco information. - An interview with Michael McClure about the script he and Jim were writing "The Adept"

2. A storyboard of "The Hitchhiker" script. A storyboard is a hand drawn series of pictures of the scenes described in the script, so that a film can be visualized before the actual filming takes place. This storyboard would be filmed with the narration and dialogue underneath. There are approximately 30 frames to be drawn and photographed.

3. The film Jim made from all the footage that was shot, that he called HWY.

4. My cut of the actual scenes we went to the desert to shoot; i.e., the hitchhiking and the car footage. The soundtrack to this Director's Cut would be "Riders on the Storm". The lyrics from "Riders on the Storm" were conceived during this experience. "Killer on the road", "Give this man a ride, your family will die" and "An actor out on loan " all were ideas embodied in the original "Hitchhiker" script. This DVD should once and for all put to rest the speculation of what Jims film HWY meant and how it came to be.

FEAST OF FRIENDS

The idea here is to extend the original 45-minute version to 1 hour (or more) by adding additional footage that never made it into the film.

I would like to discuss a medley of performances from the Hollywood Bowl footage: moments from the classic songs, tied together with a theme, i.e.:

· Jim dancing
· Ray, Robby and John in various poses
More footage of the band members together and interacting:
    ·   Flying kites

- Hawaii
- Recording
- On the road

This is just a matter of sifting through the footage and finding the pieces that make sense.

SINCERELY

PAUL FERRARA

July 21, 2006

....

I first mail a copy to Ray, he responds a few days later..

....

From Ray ......Aug 1

Paul:

Proposal sounds good to me. Use any Doors song you like on your web site. But be hip and don't use Light My Fire, Break on Through, Riders on the Storm. Everyone wants to use those. Do something a little different.

....

From Jeff.....Aug 2

Yeah, got it sorry I didn't acknowledge that. Looks good, I think I can get everyone on board now. Paul!

....

Well, time started to drift along and no news about the project. The Doors office is working on this 40th Doors Anniversary thing on Sunset Blvd. The Whisky is being recognized and its historic coupling with The Doors as their house band.

My mother is now 95 and living with my sister in Indian Wells, near Palm Springs. She has diabetes, the same as her mother. She has good days and bad. There are signs of dementia that drift through her conversations. She is taking maybe twenty pills a day and has reactions to her medicine that are scary. My sister is on the edge of her seat most of the time. My mother's kidneys are down to 17% ... That means the end is approaching. I visit her about every other weekend. On August 17 the phone rings and my sister tells me they had to ambulance mother to the hospital. She collapsed in the kitchen. Her care-giver, Billie Jo, was with her. Turns out she was badly dehydrated. She was taking pills for her swollen legs that minimized the water in her body. When we got there she was hooked up to a drip system. She had a catheter in her so she could pee. She was wearing diapers and under sedation. It looked like she was responding to the treatment. She was scheduled to move from the hospital to a nursing facility where they could monitor her recuperation. Sandy and I followed the transfer to the new facility and went back to L.A. My sister called the next day. Mother was very agitated. She was tearing the I.V.'s from her arm and was getting out of bed in the night, falling down and hurting herself. I went back to the Springs and moved in with her at the facility she was in. Luckily there was a vacant bed next to her. I basically kept her down and in bed. It wasn't easy, there were hours of conversations about how she wanted to go home. She wanted to run. Escape. She didn't remember what had happened. Those were some long nights. I only napped because just when I started to fall asleep her beeper went off. That meant she was trying to get out of the hospital bed. The beds are high off the ground and the landing was brutal. Her fall also pulled the I.V. out of her arm. Her hand where the needle was taped in place became bruised from re-inserting the I.V. over and over. They had clipped a wire to her gown and when she tried to get up it tore off and set off an alarm. This happened several times a night. Wow, my hat is off to nurses and caregivers. It was very difficult, to say the least. She stabilizes and I come back to L.A.

It seems like everyone is getting on the band wagon. Oliver Stone's people email me with a request to be on camera for an interview that would be extra material in a re-release of the Doors film he made. A documentary of sorts about the times in L.A. and Hollywood, what it was like etc.....I was furious. How dare they want my help to perpetuate that bullshit movie. They wanted me to do it for free.

....

From Paul to Nate Andrews at Silverfish productons

First, I would like to say it is ridiculous to ask for my help in your commercial project without compensation. Are you being paid? With that said, I would like to say that many fans and friends were totally pissed off by the one-dimensional portrayal of Jim and The Doors in Oliver's film. The only thing he got right was the concert footage which I might add, was a mirror of the original documentary footage I shot. I cannot in good faith participate in your project. You wouldn't like what I had to say anyway. "Have I said enough or have I said too much". Nothing personal........ Paul

....

I was getting impatient waiting for Jeff to get around to the real deal of finishing off the Doors film legacy. I started to talk to story board artists on the internet. I found one I liked and went to his apt. and showed him the material and discussed what it was I was doing. He got it right away. He was a Doors fan. Lucky. In one day he emailed me his interpretation of what we had talked about. It was perfect. It looked like a comic book/film thing. I sent it to Ray. He loved it as I did. He said don't change a thing. I sent it to Cory in Jeff's office. He is in charge of the film and photography archive stuff and has a creative side. He liked it, thought it was cool. I asked him to get a copy of it to Jeff. Again no word, weeks go by and no word.

My mother is going to be transferred to another facility because of insurance or something. I want to be there. It's hot in the Springs. 110 degrees, I kid you not. The private ambulance people arrive and shift her onto a gurney. I follow them to Indio a small city just south of Palm Springs. We settle her in and she gets hooked up to a new I.V. She still has the catheter in her and it is causing great discomfort to her. My sister and Billie Jo are visiting her every day. She is just maintaining. Her blood sugar is sometimes 40 and sometimes 500; that is a huge swing. It is taking its toll on her. Her dementia is getting stronger. They give her shots of insulin that are destroying her kidneys ever further. It is an intolerable situation. I don't want her to suffer. She is still trying to escape and falling from her bed in the night. They replace her hospital bed with a bed that is flat on the floor. She cannot fall from this one, only roll to the side, which she does many times. She doesn't want the tubes in her arm and her pussy. She begs me to take her home. Again I tell her that we can't care of her at Marietta's.

My sister wants to take a break. She and her boyfriend go to Vegas and I move into my sister's home and take care of her dogs and spend the days with mother. I hold her hand and bring her treats and walk her outside in the wheelchair. Its air conditioned inside and she is cold. We push outside, she loves it. I park under a shady tree and she smiles at me. She looks at the birds

playing in the water left over from the lawn sprinklers. I take her to my truck
and we listen to music, Beethoven's "Moonlight Sonata". She comments that
she has always loved that song. She falls asleep and I wheel her back in. They
check her blood sugar every four hours. It reads 435, that is high. She gets
some insulin and falls asleep again. I park her in the hallway near the nurses'
station and go get some lunch. In the afternoon we do the same thing again. I
entertain her, hold her hand and tell her how much I love her. She eats a little
dinner in the cafeteria and falls asleep again. I go back to my sister's and feed
the dogs and try to unwind. I am feeling very tired and drained. I get a good
idea of what my sister has been going through for the last couple of years.

The last day I am to be there my mother has a huge drop in blood sugar.
She goes into a deep sleep, almost a coma but not quite. The lights start
flashing. Nurses huddle around her trying to get some sugar paste into her
mouth. My worst fear. A coma. It can last for years. Five minutes pass and
no response. The head nurse is not happy. Suddenly my mother blurts out,
"Boo", everybody jumps back scared. She opens her eyes, smiles, and that
crisis is over. From then on I knew her death is near. I keep the phone with
me at all times. My sister came back and I returned to L.A. According to my
sister this routine sugar swing situation continues on a daily basis. I call every
day. My sister hands the phone to my mother but she sounds incoherent.

I request another meeting with Jeff Jampol. He has bought a house in
Laurel Canyon and is in the process of moving. I meet with him at his new
house. The place is filled with unpacked boxes. We sit outside by the pool.
He wants to know how much my proposed treatment of the films is going
to cost. I tell him I don't know off hand. I thought the producers did the
budget. He hasn't got a clue. If I am ever going to get this thing going I will
have to do it myself. I need to know what condition the Feast footage is
in. No one seems to know. I ask Cory to accompany me to the film storage
vaults. It is freezing cold inside. In my opinion there is a lot of work to be
done. If the sound can be found to sync up with the remaining footage there
is enough stuff to make the Feast film a lot longer. Cory has transferred some
of the visuals to DVD and gives me copies to look at. There are sequences on
the beach flying kites, back stage at Singer Bowl, backstage in Hawaii, more
Seattle Monorail, more studio recording at Elektra, more surrounding the
California concert where the Hells Angels were present, with shots of Babe
with the nagra and January Jansen walking with Jim {the guy who made his

STORY BOARD DRAWING BY   JONATHAN WOODS

leather clothes.} There is enough. If I can find the sound it is a no-brainer.

My mind and my heart are torn apart by the thought of my mother suffering. I want to be there but it is impossible to be there all the time. I try to work on the budget. I do the best I can and send it to Jeff no response. Cory calls and asks if I am available to be in attendance at the Fortieth celebration on Sunset they have planned. I ask him if Jeff has received the budget I sent. He says yes, he got it.

Because no one in the Doors office has any info on the whereabouts of the 35mm print of HWY, I decide to call Frank Lisciandro and ask him if he would like to be involved somehow.

....

From Paul to Frank   Sept. 14

Hello: Frank, Ray and Jeff Jampol have been talking about me working to get Feast and HWY and additional materials together to release next year. Jeff has told me he has the permission to move forward, from the estates. I don't know how much to trust that assumption and am wondering if you have talked to Penny Courson lately. Would you like to be involved or are you content to pursue your own agenda? Or do you have any thought about the Doors being involved with HWY?

I have written a proposal that has been accepted by all three Doors and I think the estates. They now want a budget. It would be produced in house. No studio involved. I know you wanted big money before. This is another approach to get the job done. I am so upset by what I see on uTube that I feel a need to put closure to our old projects at any cost.

Frank to Paul   Sept. 14

Hi.. I read your email with great interest. Thanks for thinking of me. I have not spoken with the Coursons recently so I don't know their current thinking on HWY. The last I knew, they did not want HWY messed with and especially not by The Doors. They still control the copyright. I'll check with them and let you know what they have to say.

I would very much like to be involved in a release of HWY. I don't think the Doors should be involved because Jim didn't want them involved in any aspect of the making of the film, and HWY was and is his film. I would not want The Doors making creative decisions about changing the film, or even making decisions about the context the film should be presented in. It was Jim's indisputable desire to keep his poems and HWY clearly and distinctly separate from his work with the band.

But...I do think the two films could be presented together in a way that establishes their separate identities.

You were the initial spark behind both films and I have always acknowledged and respected your leadership role in moving the films beyond the talking stage into actual projects. I am ready to help you take the films into a public release in any way I can...short of changing HWY. I believe strongly in the integrity of an artist's work.

I really didn't want "big money" for a HWY release; I just wanted the film released by a major distributor so that it would have the widest possible availability. But now can see that it would be ok to have a small but professional release with the highest sound and image quality. If we are of like minds, let's try to find a way to work together on this. If we don't agree, let's at least talk about it.

....

I send Frank a copy of the treatment/proposal.

....

Frank writes:

Sorry about taking so long to get back to you. My dad is in a hospital and not doing well. I'm on my way to Florida tomorrow morning to see what needs to be done. Thanks for sending the proposal. I gave it a quick read and will wait to comment on it until I get back: my brain is too scattered right now to think clearly. I tried to talk to Penny Courson and will try again during the week. It would be good to work together again and close the circle of these projects.

Paul to Frank: Sep 17

I am leaving for Indio tomorrow for five days. My mother is ill and is also not doing well. I guess we are in that period of our life. My mother is 95. Talk to you when we both get back.

Frank Oct. 2:

I am still dealing with my dad's health crisis. I'm home from Florida but I expect to be called back there at any time. I talked to Penny Courson today and she told me that she has not seen your proposal nor has she given The

Doors permission to distribute HWY. Corky has advanced Alzheimer's and he's living at home. I got the impression that at the moment she doesn't want to get involved in anything else. I don't know what Jeff and Ray told you but it seems plain to me that Penny has no intention of involving them in a HWY project Maybe I'm wrong.

Paul to Frank Oct. 2:

I feel like confronting Jeff and Ray with this info. What do you think? Are they jacking me around and fishing for my ideas or what?

Frank to Paul Oct. 3

I don't know about confronting Ray and Jeff. I don't know what Penny Courson might or might not have told them, or what they think she told them. She was definite that she did not see your proposal. But she was less definite about what she intends to do with HWY. She is carrying a big emotional burden right now as well as the continuing legal battle with Ray and Robby- and she doesn't want to deal with anything else.

Paul to Frank Oct. 3

I think you hit it on the head. I will refrain from mentioning your talk with Penny and just see what happens. I am so desperate to finish our project that I may hear what I want also. I think I will push them to finish Feast. I have some ideas on how to expand it with the original material. Have they approached you about this circus thing in Nov. on Sunset Blvd. It is not something I would attend if it were not for a direct request. Sometimes I feel like they are using me, and my history. Our history. Together we present a historic front. We were Jim's friends and helped with his film projects. The fans would welcome our input. If someone else fucks with the films they run the risk of failure. We have a certain amount of power do you agree? What did you think of the proposal? Do you have anything that pertains to the HWY experience to add? I still have the behind the scenes footage. It is 8mm but fun and shows all of us as we were.

Frank to Paul Oct. 7

Sorry about not getting back to you sooner; we are in a couple of simultaneous crisis right now and it's hard to get much done.

Jeff and Cory invited me to the circus on Sunset in Nov., but I had to decline. I really cannot make any plans right now as I might have to go to Florida at a day's notice.

I don't know what The Doors or their management want from us. They call me to talk about projects but then there's not much follow through. Yes, we do present a historic front, and yes, we would draw fans that know our names.

I've read your proposal a couple of times and I think it's strong and well stated. You have a vision for the two films that I don't fully share. I think the films should be presented on a DVD just the way they were finished, just the way Feast was shown at the film festivals in 1969, just the way HWY existed when Jim showed it in Paris. All the other material in your proposal could be part of the bonus extras.

I would be interested in creating a longer version of Feast, especially if I would share creative control. On the DVD there could be 2 versions of Feast, the one we finished back then and the new one containing 20 to 30 minutes of new scenes.

The proposal displays your vision for the films and I don't see how I could add to that creatively.

I usually work with or for other people to earn some money. I use the money to buy time to work on my own projects. Working on HWY and Feast would be a different story, but I would still expect financial compensation for my time, and I would expect to have an equal share of the creative decision making. I don't see how that's possible if I were working to achieve your vision.

Bottom line is that I want the original versions of HWY and Feast released in the highest quality format possible. How you or I or we do that is for us to work out. Let's keep talking.

Cheers

Frank

．．．．．．．．．．．．．．．．．．．．．．．．．．．．．．

My sister needs a few days break from the stress involved, watching her mother die. She is in tears as she talks of our mothers' condition. I offer to house sit and care for mother again. I leave for Indio the next day Monday October 9. I am getting used to the drive. Driving gives you a good chance to catch up with your thoughts. I don't know what to think about The Doors and the project at this point. Either Jeff is lying or dreaming of his importance and power like he did with the Buckholts brothers, trying to control everything, or Penny is lying to Frank or maybe Frank is not telling me the truth. It is so confusing that it is almost a good thing to go and spend time with my mother no matter how hard it is.

I get to the nursing home and it is just before lunch time. My sister is there and when I arrive she goes home to pack. She is going to visit her friend for a few days. My mother looks so weak, but her eyes light up when she sees me. It makes my heart soar. I comb her hair and tell her how great she looks. She says she has no pain. I wheel her into the cafeteria. She won't eat. The food is disgusting and I can't blame her. We go for a walk outside it is maybe 110 degrees and there is a breeze blowing up from a hurricane in Baja that feels very comforting. I push her to the back of my SUV and turn on some music, Beethoven again. My cooler is packed with some fresh sweet grapes and peaches. I feed them to her and she closes her eyes and uses the word "wonderful" to describe the feeling of the grape bursting open and the sweet liquid filling her mouth. She gags a little and gets used to eating slowly. She wants to know what all the stuff is in the back of my truck. I open up my tool box and show her all the neatly arranged tools. She examines them carefully. Although she is mixing her words up and sometimes doesn't know where she is she is remarkably in the moment. She knows what she likes and where she wants to be. We go back inside and she falls asleep. The head nurse approaches and wants to talk to mother. I ask her please not to wake her. She talks to me. She has been going over mothers' recent blood and urine tests and it doesn't look good. She asks if we have considered hospice care. I tell her we have been considering it. Hospice care is when they evaluate her condition and determine how to make the end more comfortable. I don't want her to suffer, but I am selfish and don't want her to leave. That is the main problem, trying to weigh what it is we want and what it is that my mother needs. There are some brutal decisions to make, any way you cut it. She doesn't want dinner; I try to put some food into her mouth but she won't take it. She gets angry and I don't want that so I push her back to the hallway near her room. She falls asleep. It is around seven o'clock and near her scheduled bed time. I say goodbye to the nurses and go to my sister's house. She leaves the next morning and I walk the dogs and prepare some ice and grapes and more peaches for my mother.

The next day is the same; she won't eat but is in a good mood. We spend the day talking and sitting in the shade by my car. At dinner I think maybe if I am not there she will eat, so I wait outside the cafeteria. Another nurse comes up to me and we discuss mother. He says he has been doing this for a long time and he wants to know if I am prepared for the end. He talks of his spiritual beliefs and how people are headed for heaven. He says he thinks my mother has maybe two months left in her life. "She could go anytime" he says. He is only saying what I already know in my heart. That night I go back to my sister's house and drink myself to sleep.

It is Wed. when I arrive to a smiling mother. She sees me coming down the hall and raises her arms to hug me. The warmth I feel for her is amazing, more than I had ever felt before. She says she does not want lunch. I ask her how about a big juicy hamburger from Burger King? "Wow" she says, "I would love it, and some French fries". I leave for a few minutes and get the burger. She eats the entire thing. I realize it must be the food they serve there that she doesn't like. She is very thirsty and keeps asking for cold water. She drinks maybe four or five glasses. Of course this causes her to have to go to the bathroom, which is a big deal. I flag down two nurses assistants and they agree to help. They wheel her into the bathroom and get her onto the toilet. She relieves herself and they put on a fresh diaper. Things are going good. That night at dinner in the cafeteria we sit next to a new lady. She says her name is Marie and I start to sing the Italian folk song "Oh Marie". My mother sings along with me and it is very sweet. We continue to sing the song until we get it right. My mother remembers several verses. Before she falls asleep that night we sing it one more time. She wants to get into bed and with some help I get her down for the night. It was a great day.

Thursday comes with the same routine. Billie Joe calls me and asks if she can bring some home cooking for lunch. My sister is scheduled to arrive as well. Before they get there I push my mother to my truck and we do the grape and peach snack. After we go back inside she wants to sit by the window in the hallway. It is cool inside and the sun from the window warms her. She looks so peaceful sitting there that I run to the car and get my camera. She is sleeping when I get back and I take a couple of shots before she wakes up. She opens her eyes and I take a few more pictures. She smiles and her eyes have a twinkle in them. It is a precious moment. First Billie Jo arrives with a beautiful chicken pie with cheese melted on top and some sugarless cake. My mother loves it and begins to eat all of it. About halfway through my sister arrives and joins us. When she finishes eating there is a moment when my sister says "I love you so much" my mother answers " I love you too". I prompt my mother and we sing "Oh Marie" for the guests. They can't believe their ears. My mother, Catherine Edna Ferrara, is singing in Italian and with perfect pitch. It was priceless. After that she made some funny faces. One was that toothless grin that Gabby Hayes, the western comedian, made famous. We all crack up. My mother starts getting sleepy and begins nodding out. My sister leaves and soon Billie Jo leaves. I sit with my mother while she sleeps. Around seven in the evening I leave and head back to Los Angeles. I sleep well and in the morning Sandy, my beautiful wife, wakes me with the phone in her hand. My sister is sobbing and informs me that mother died in her sleep last night. She says she is on her way to the nursing home and hangs up. I am numb. Did I just dream those great last hours with her or not? I did not dream it I had five photos of her sitting in the sun and smiling at me. It was over. She died on Friday the 13th,which I don't take as an omen but it does seem important because she was born on Friday the 13th.

I will attend The Doors fortieth anniversary at the Whisky on November 8 2006 to commemorate the success of "Light My Fire". As for the welcome Jeff Jampol gave me "Welcome back to the family", it remains to be seen.

My mother's ashes are now in Mora New Mexico next to my fathers. It is now August of 2007 and still no word from Jampol.

SPECIAL THANKS TO:

DAVID and ANN SOPHIE FRENCH... Thanks for your interest in my story. You both were the original spark that led to me writing this book.

IDA MILLER...Without your help I am afraid I would have remained mired in my lack of writing skills. Your undying love of The Doors is inspirational. PHOTO CREDIT for back cover.

RUI SILVA....Thank you for your suggestion of the title for my book. It was right under my nose but I could not see it.

DIGBY DIEHL...Kind words of encouragement and a wonderful foreword.

BABE HILL.....PHOTO CREDIT for front cover.

To those of you that would prefer to see many of the pictures from this book in color please go to my website:
http://paulferrara.net/

Frank Lisciandro http://www.lisciandro.com
David Sygall www.e-shot.com

DISCOGRAPHY
THE PAUL AND GEORGIA ALBUM http://cdbaby.com/cd/paulgeorgia
PAUL FERRARA AND PLGRM http://cdbaby.com/cd/paulferrara2
PLGRM 11 http://cdbaby.com/cd/paulferrara

Made in the USA
Lexington, KY
23 August 2010